Managing
Software Requirements
Second Edition

The Addison-Wesley Object Technology Series

Grady Booch, Ivar Jacobson, and James Rumbaugh, Series Editors
For more information, check out the series Web site [http://www.awprofessional.com/otseries/].

The Component Software Series

Clemens Szyperski, Series Editor
For more information, check out the series Web site [http://www.awprofessional.com/csseries/].

MANAGING SOFTWARE REQUIREMENTS

SECOND EDITION

A USE CASE APPROACH

Dean Leffingwell
Don Widrig

♦♦Addison-Wesley

Boston · San Francisco · New York · Toronto · Montreal
London · Munich · Paris · Madrid
Capetown · Sydney · Tokyo · Singapore · Mexico City

Many of the designations used by manufacturers and sellers to distinguish their products are claimed as trademarks. Where those designations appear in this book, and Addison-Wesley was aware of a trademark claim, the designations have been printed with initial capital letters or in all capitals.

The authors and publisher have taken care in the preparation of this book, but make no expressed or implied warranty of any kind and assume no responsibility for errors or omissions. No liability is assumed for incidental or consequential damages in connection with or arising out of the use of the information or programs contained herein.

The publisher offers discounts on this book when ordered in quantity for bulk purchases and special sales. For more information, please contact:

U.S. Corporate and Government Sales
(800) 382-3419
corpsales@pearsontechgroup.com

For sales outside of the U.S., please contact:

International Sales
(317) 581-3793
international@pearsontechgroup.com

Visit Addison-Wesley on the Web: www.awprofessional.com

Library of Congress Cataloging-in-Publication Data

Leffingwell, Dean
     Managing software requirements : a use case approach / Dean Leffingwell, Don Widrig—2nd ed.
          p.   m.
     Includes bibliographical references and index.
     ISBN 0-321-12247-X (alk. paper)
     1. Computer software—Development—Management.   2. Use cases (Systems engineering)
   I. Widrig, Don.   II. Title.

QA 76.76.D47L45 2003
005.1'068—dc21

                                                                    2003043724

ISBN 0-321-12247-X
Text printed on recycled paper
1 2 3 4 5 6 7 8 9 10—CRW—0706050403
First printing, May 2003

This book is dedicated to Becky, my wife and my best friend.

—Dean

This book is dedicated to my book partner, Dean, who made this effort worthwhile, and to my life partner, Barbara, who makes life worthwhile.

—Don

CONTENTS

Team Skill 4   Managing Scope   **203**

Team Skill 5   Refining the System Definition   **229**

FOREWORD

By Ed Yourdon

THE ROCK PROBLEM

One of my students summarized the issues discussed in this book as the "rock" problem. She works as a software engineer in a research laboratory, and her customers often give her project assignments that she describes as "Bring me a rock." But when you deliver the rock, the customer looks at it for a moment and says, "Yes, *but*, actually, what I really wanted was a *small blue* rock." The delivery of a small blue rock elicits the further request for a *spherical* small blue rock.

Ultimately, it may turn out that the customer was thinking all along of a small blue marble. Or maybe he wasn't sure what he wanted, but a small blue marble would have sufficed.

At each subsequent meeting with the customer, the developer may exclaim, "You want it to do *what*?" The developer is frustrated because she had something entirely different in mind when she worked long and hard to produce a rock with the characteristics she thought the customer said he needed; the customer is equally frustrated because he's convinced that he has expressed it clearly. These developers just don't get it!

To complicate matters, in most real projects, more than two individuals are involved. In addition to the customer and the developer—who may, of course, have very different names and titles—there are likely to be marketing people, testing and quality assurance people, product managers, general managers, and a variety of "stakeholders" whose day-to-day operations will be affected by the development of the new system.

All of these people can become frustrated by the problems of specifying an acceptable "rock," particularly because there often isn't enough time in today's competitive, fast-moving business world to scrap an expensive, two-year "rock project" and do it all over again. We've got to get it right the first time yet also provide for the iterative process in which the customer ultimately discovers what kind of rock he wants.

It's difficult enough to do this when we're dealing with tangible, physical artifacts like rocks. Most business organizations and government agencies today are "information intensive," so even if they're nominally in the business of building and selling rocks, there's a good chance that the rock contains an embedded computer system. Even if it doesn't, there's a good chance that the business needs elaborate systems to keep track of its e-commerce rock sales, its rock customers, its rock competitors and suppliers, and all of the other information that it needs to remain competitive in the rock business. Moreover, for thousands of companies today, those companies whose business is dedicated exclusively to the development and sales of *software products*, their entire business focuses on making their products—intangible and abstract as they are—into tangible rocks that their customers can purchase, evaluate, and apply.

Software systems, by their nature, are intangible, abstract, complex, and—in theory, at least—"soft" and infinitely changeable. So, if the customer begins articulating vague requirements for a "rock system," he often does this on the assumption that he can clarify, change, and fill in the details as time goes on. It would be wonderful if the developers—and everyone else involved in the creation, testing, deployment, and maintenance of the rock system—could accomplish this in zero time, and at zero cost, but it doesn't work that way.

In fact, it often doesn't work at all: More than half of the software systems projects taking place today are substantially over budget and behind schedule, and as much as 25 percent to 33 percent of the projects are canceled before completion, often at a staggering cost.

Preventing these failures and providing a rational approach for building the system the customer does want is the objective of this book. However, this is *not* a book about programming, and it's not written just for the software developer. This is a book about managing requirements for complex software applications. *As such, this book is written for every member of the software team (analysts, developers, tester and QA personnel, project management, product management, documentation folks, and the like) as well as members of the external "customer" team (users and other stakeholders, marketing, and management)*—everyone, really, who has a stake in the definition and delivery of the software system.

You'll discover that it is crucial that the members of both teams, including the nontechnical members of the external team, master the skills required to successfully define and manage the requirements process for your new system—for the simple reason that *they* are the ones who create the requirements in the first place and who ultimately determine the success or failure of the system. The stand-alone, hero programmer is an anachronism of the past: May he rest in peace.

A Simple Metaphor: Building a House

If you were a building contractor, you wouldn't need to be convinced that a series of critical conversations with the homeowner are necessary; otherwise, you might end up building a two-bedroom house when your customer wanted a three-bedroom house. But it's equally important that these "requirements" be discussed and negotiated with the government authorities concerned with building codes and zoning regulations, and you may need to check with the next-door neighbors before you decide to cut down any trees on the property where the house will be built.

The building inspector and the next-door neighbors are among the other *stakeholders* who, along with the person who intends to pay for and inhabit the house, will determine whether the finished house meets their needs. It's also clear that these important stakeholders of your system, such as neighbors and zoning officials, are not users (homeowners), and it seems equally obvious that their perspectives on what makes a quality home may differ from the homeowner's opinion.

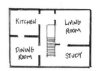

Again, we're discussing software applications in this book, not houses or rocks. The requirements of a house might be described, at least in part, with a set of blueprints and a list of specifications; similarly, a software system can be described with models and diagrams. But just as the blueprints for a house are intended as a communication and negotiation mechanism between laypeople and engineers—and lawyers and inspectors and nosy neighbors—so the technical diagrams associated with a software system can also be created in such a way that "ordinary" people can understand them.

Many of the crucially important requirements don't need any diagrams at all. The prospective house buyer, for example, can write a requirement in ordinary English that says, "My house must have three bedrooms, and it must have a garage large enough to hold two cars and six bicycles." As you'll see in this book, the majority of the crucial requirements for a software system can be written in plain English. In other cases, it would be more helpful to have a picture of what kind of fireplace the homeowner had in mind.

Many of the *team skills* you will need to master in order to address this challenge can also be described in terms of practical, commonsense advice. "Make sure you talk to the building inspector," we might advise our novice house builder, "*before* you dig the foundation for the house, not after you've poured the cement and begun building the walls and the roof." For a software project, we would offer similar advice: "Make sure you ask the right questions of the right people, make sure that you understand how the system is going to be used, and *don't* assume that 100 percent of the requirements are critical, because you're not likely to have time to finish them all before the deadline."

ABOUT THIS BOOK

In this book, Leffingwell and Widrig have taken a pragmatic approach to describing the solution to the rock problem. They have organized the book into eight parts. The Introduction provides some of the context, definitions, and background that you'll need to understand what follows. Chapter 1 reviews the systems development "challenge." The data shows that some software project failures are indeed caused by sloppy programming, but a number of studies demonstrate that poor requirements management may be the single largest cause of project failure. And though I've described the basic concept of requirements management in a loose, informal fashion in this foreword, the authors will define it more carefully in Chapter 2, in order to lay the groundwork for the chapters that follow. Chapter 3 provides an overview of some of the software development models in use today and concludes with a recommendation for an iterative process, one that facilitates additional requirements discovery along the way. Chapter 4 provides a brief introduction to some of the characteristics of modern software teams so they can relate the team skills that will be developed to the team context, wherein the skills must be applied.

The book is structured on the six requisite team skills for effective requirements management.

Each of the next six major parts is intended to help you and your team understand and master one of the *six requisite team skills for effective requirements management.*

- To begin, of course, you will need a proper understanding of the problem that's intended to be solved with a new software system. That is addressed in Team Skill 1, Analyzing the Problem.
- Team Skill 2, Understanding User and Stakeholder Needs, is also crucial.

- Team Skill 3, Defining the System, describes the initial process of defining a system to address those requirements.
- Team Skill 4, Managing Scope, covers that absolutely crucial and often ignored process of managing the customer's expectations and the scope of the project.
- Team Skill 5, Refining the System Definition, illustrates key techniques that you will use in order to elaborate on the system to a level of detail sufficient to drive design and implementation, so the entire extended team knows exactly what kind of system you are building.
- Team Skill 6, Building the Right System, discusses the processes associated with building a system that fulfills the requirements. Team Skill 6 also discusses techniques you can use to validate that the system meets the requirements and, further, to help ensure that the system doesn't do anything malevolent to its users or otherwise exhibit unpleasant behaviors that are not defined by the requirements. And, since requirements for any nontrivial application cannot be frozen in time, the authors describe ways in which the team can actively manage change without destroying the system under construction. Team Skill 6 concludes with a chapter that suggests ways in which the requirements gathering process can improve the quality of the overall project. Special emphasis is given to the iterative nature of modern program development processes and how this yields substantial opportunities for an ongoing quality assessment.

After these descriptions of specific requirements management techniques, the authors briefly review the evolving methods of Extreme Programming and Agile Methods and demonstrate ways of integrating effective requirements management practices into the framework of these software development methods. Finally, in Chapter 31 the authors provide a prescription that you and your team can use to manage requirements in your next project.

I hope that, armed with these newly acquired team skills, you too will be able to build the perfect rock or marble. However, it will never be easy; even with the best techniques and processes, and even with automated tool support for all of this, you'll still find that it's hard work. Moreover, it's still risky; even with these team skills, some projects will fail because we're "pushing the envelope" in many organizations, attempting to build ever more complex systems in ever less time. Nevertheless, the skills defined in this book will go a long way toward reducing the risk and thereby helping you achieve the success you deserve.

PREFACE TO THE SECOND EDITION

By Dean Leffingwell

Much has transpired since the first edition of this text was published in 1999. The "dot.com" bubble economy of the late 1990s (driven in part by the Internet, software, and related technology) has burst, causing significant disruption, economic uncertainty, and chaos in the lives of many. And yet, perhaps order and sanity have been restored to a free market that appeared to have "lost its wits" for a time.

However, innovation in software technology continues unabated, and the industry as a whole is still growing rapidly. The global reach of the Internet continues to change our lives and drive new, varied forms of communication, from the global electronic marketplaces that facilitate the exchange of goods and services to the after-school instant messaging chat-fests that seem to absorb our children's homework time and so much of that expensive Internet bandwidth we rolled out in the last decade.

We are connected to our business associates, friends, and family 24/7. Internet cafes in Australia, in Scotland, and on Alaska-bound cruise ships are open 24 hours a day. We receive e-mails on our PDAs at the grocery store. We can't make breakfast, drive to work, ride an elevator, or enter an office building without interacting with software. Software has become the embodiment of much of the world's intellectual knowledge, and the business of developing and deploying software has emerged as one of the world's most important industries.

Software development practices continue to march forward as well. The Unified Modeling Language (UML), adopted as late as 1997, is now the de facto means to communicate architecture, patterns, and design mechanisms. The Rational Unified Process and similar processes based on the UML are being adopted by many in the industry as the standard way to approach the challenge of software development.

Our personal lives have changed also. After four years at Rational Software, recently acquired by IBM, I have moved on to helping independent software companies achieve their goals. Some teams hope to change the world; some hope to have a significant impact on individual lives by improving health care; still others hope to improve their customers' manufacturing efficiencies or to help businesses grow by translating product data into other languages. However, these teams all have one thing in common: they are challenged by the difficulty of defining software solutions in a way that can be understood by themselves, by their customers, by their marketing teams, by their internal development and testing teams—indeed, by all those who must understand the proposed solution at the right level of detail so that the proper results can be achieved. Fail to do that and they fail to achieve their mission. Because of the importance of their mission on their personal lives as well as those whose products they are intended to help, failure is not an option.

Therefore, while much has changed in the software industry in just a few short years, some things, including the challenge of *Managing Software Requirements,* remain largely the same, and so our work continues in this, the second edition.

ABOUT THE SECOND EDITION

The motivation for the content changes in the second edition is based on different yet convergent factors.

The first set of factors is based on the success of the book in the marketplace, which has generated many positive comments and much encouragement, as well as constructive criticisms. While comments range widely, two consistent themes emerged.

- **The "more use cases" theme.** The first edition (subtitled *A Unified Approach*) reconciled and combined two major viewpoints on requirements techniques. The first, perhaps a more traditional approach, described the way in which requirements specifications are created and detailed to prescribe system behavior using declarative techniques ("the system shall . . ."). The second, the use case approach, described the way in which use cases could be used to define the majority of the functional behavior of the system. We combined these techniques in the first edition in order to create a common, and hopefully more holistic, approach. Based on feedback, we did achieve some success. However, one criticism of the work is that, while we recommended and described the use case method, we did not go far enough in helping the reader develop or apply this technique. Moreover, in presenting both techniques, we confused some readers who wanted to better understand which technique to apply and when.

- **The "it's a big book with many techniques—please be more prescriptive" theme.** The first edition of this book was intended to be a comprehensive work, a one-stop-shopping reference for any technique readers might need to define requirements for a system of any type. We hope this provided value to our readers because we truly believe that there is no "one size fits all" solution to each specific software engineering challenge. And yet, the reviewers' theme remains: "Does it have to be this hard? Can't you be more prescriptive?"

A second set of factors driving this same theme is based on my own experiences in using the book as I work with companies to help them achieve their software development objectives. Some have software applications that require multiple techniques; some can make time for a fairly rigorous introduction to a full requirements management discipline. However, others need to document a specific set of requirements for a specific software application and they need to do so *immediately*. Starting tomorrow. There is no time or interest in a debate about which technique might be more effective or about the nuances of anything. "Just give me one technique, make it simple, and get me started right now," they say.

Fortunately, these two sets of inputs are mostly convergent and the answer to both is fairly clear. **For most teams, in most circumstances, a combination of (1) a well-considered Vision document, (2) an identification and elaboration of the key use cases to be implemented, and (3) a supplementary specification of the nonfunctional requirements is adequate and appropriate for managing software requirements.** In addition, if this is the chosen method, the elaborated use cases can directly become the foundation for system testing.

To this end, this second edition of *Managing Software Requirements* has new content, a new theme, and a new subtitle: *A Use Case Approach*. In this edition, the use case technique is the cornerstone technique, and a more prescriptive approach has been chosen and represented. For example, Chapter 14, A Use Case Primer, has been added to provide a more fundamental basis for understanding and applying use cases. It should serve as a tutorial adequate for an otherwise uninitiated individual to be able to learn and begin to apply the technique. The HOLIS case study has also been updated to reflect a more use-case-centered approach. Chapter 26, From Use Case to Test Case, has been added to illustrate how the use cases can directly drive a comprehensive test strategy as well as serve as direct input to the test cases themselves.

In addition, we've made one substantial enhancement motivated solely by our own purposes. Chapter 17 (which appeared in the first edition as Chapter 18, The Champion), has been renamed Product Management and enhanced with new material designed to help teams understand how to turn a software application into what we call *the whole product solution*. Since getting the requirements "right" cannot by itself ensure commercial success, this chapter provides insight and guidelines for those activities (such as pricing and licensing, positioning and messaging) and other commercial factors that transform a working software application into a *software product people want to buy*.

Also, since modern software development processes are becoming more iterative, we decided to repurpose the first edition's chapter on quality so that this edition's chapter would provide a more comprehensive look at quality within the context of a modern software process. Thus Chapter 29, Assessing Requirements Quality in Iterative Development, speaks directly to iterative techniques for gathering and improving requirements within an overall iterative development framework.

Finally, we also took the opportunity to address a new undercurrent in the industry, a movement toward what are perceived as lighter, less formal methods. In the extreme, *Extreme Programming* (XP), as espoused by Beck and others, could be interpreted to eliminate process entirely. Perhaps more correctly, XP incorporates certain keystone processes, such as direct customer requirements input, directly into programming practices, but it's also fair to note that the concepts of "software process" and the "M" word (methodology) are studiously avoided. Perhaps less extreme and considered by some to be more practical, the introduction of *Agile Methods*, as advocated by Cockburn and others, has also taken root. Though controversial in some circles, these lighter approaches cannot be ignored, and we've addressed these in the requirements context in another new chapter, Chapter 30, Agile Requirements Methods.

Of course, no book can be all things to all people. In order to make this edition as readable as possible, we eliminated a number of topics and chapters from the prior version and shortened others.

We sincerely hope that you will find this revised text more approachable, as well as easier to use and apply, and that it will better help you and your teams to manage your software requirements.

ACKNOWLEDGMENTS

The authors would like to acknowledge and thank John Altinbay, Jim Heumann, and Dan Rawsthorne for their careful and insightful reviews of this second edition. We'd also to thank the many others who contributed to this work, including Al Davis, Ed Yourdon, Grady Booch, Philippe Kruchten, Leslee Probasco, Ian Spence, Jean Bell, Walker Royce, Joe Marasco, Elemer Magaziner, and the following reviewers of the first edition: Ag Marsonia, Frank Armour, Dr. Ralph R. Young, Professor David Rine, and Dan Rawsthorne.

We admit that without their insightful comments, we could not have written a worthy work. In addition, we'd like to thank Kim Arney Mulcahy and the editors and support staff at Addison-Wesley, who tuned our work in process and helped it become a tangible product, like the "rock" described in the Foreword. Lastly, we must again thank our loving families for supporting all the "heads-down weekends" necessary to complete this second edition.

Preface to the First Edition

By Dean Leffingwell, 1999

Context

The knowledge delivered in this book represents the cumulative experience of a number of individuals who have spent their careers defining, developing, and delivering world-class software systems. This book is *not* an academic treatment of requirements management. During the 1980s, Don Widrig and I were executives in a small company producing software solutions for customers. When we developed many of the requirements management practices described in this book, our perspective was of those accountable for both the outcomes of the software systems we developed and the results that had to be delivered to shareholders. As the performance of the delivered software was critical to the success of the business venture itself, we tended to discourage petty biases, personal preferences, and experimentation with unproven techniques.

Over the past decade, the techniques have evolved and have been enhanced by new experiences, extended with the help of additional expertise, in different companies and in different circumstances. But all of the techniques presented are "real-world" proven and have withstood the test of time. Perhaps even more important, they have withstood the technological change that has occurred in the industry during this period. Indeed, most of the principles in this book are independent of changing trends in software technology. We can therefore at least hope that the knowledge expressed herein can deliver some lasting value.

Requirements Lessons from Building Software for Others

At first, I just hated computers. ("What? I stayed here all night and I have to submit this batch job again because I left out a 'space'? Are you crazy? Let me in that room. . . .") My first "real computer" was a minicomputer, which, although incredibly limited in performance by today's standards, was unique in that I could touch it, program it, and make it do what I wanted. It was *mine*.

My early research applied the computer to analyze physiological signals from the human body, primarily EKGs, and the dedicated computer was a wonderful tool for this job. Out of this experience, I began to apply my programming skills and experience with real-time software systems to the needs of the industry.

 Eventually, I incorporated RELA, Inc., and began a long, and perhaps unusually difficult, career as CEO of a contract software development business. My coauthor, Don Widrig, joined me at RELA in the early years as Vice President of Research and Development. He had the primary accountability for the success of the many systems that we developed.

Over the years, the company grew rapidly. Today, the company employs many hundreds of people and has diversified beyond providing just software to providing complete medical devices and systems that encompass software, as well as mechanical, electronic, optical, and fluidics-handling subsystems. However, at the heart of each and every machine, including the latest DNA fingerprinting in-vitro diagnostic clinical laboratory, lies one or more computers, reliably and routinely delivering their steady heartbeats through the rhythm of a real-time multitasking system.

Initially, we would program anything for anybody, from antenna-positioning software to such games as laser tag, automated guided vehicles for amusement parks, educational products, welding robots, and automated machine controls. We even developed a large distributed computer system that automatically detected and counted the presence of commercials on television. (Our motto then was "We make computers to watch commercials so you don't have to!") *Perhaps the only thing the software we developed had in common was that we developed it for others—we were not domain experts in the field, and we couldn't cover our own paychecks if we had to. We were completely dependent on the customer's satisfaction as the final determination of outcome.* In many ways, such an environment was very conducive to effective requirements management. Here's why:

- We knew little about the domain, so we were dependent on customers for the requirements. There was little temptation to make them up; we had to ask, and we had to learn how to ask the right questions the right way, at the right time.

- Our customers often knew little about computers, so they were dependent on us to translate their needs and wishes into technical requirements.
- The fact that money changed hands created a rigorous interface between the developer and the customer.
- Quality was easy to measure: We either got paid or we didn't.

Big Question 1: "Exactly what is this software supposed to do?"

It was in this environment that we discovered the first of two fundamental questions that face software developers on each and every project. This question dominated our behavior for many years and remains today as perhaps *the* toughest question to answer in any software project. And the Big Question is:

So, exactly what is this software supposed to do?

The principles and techniques presented in Team Skill 1, Analyzing the Problem; Team Skill 2, Understanding User and Stakeholder Needs; and Team Skill 3, Defining the System, were developed over more than a decade as a means to discover the answer to this question. Each of these techniques has proved its worth and has demonstrated its effectiveness in many real-world projects. It was also during this period that I first became aware of the work of Donald Gause and Jerry Weinberg, especially their book *Exploring Requirements: Quality Before Design* (1989). Because their book heavily influenced our work, we have borrowed a few key concepts from it for this book, both because the concepts work and because we thought it only fair that you share the Gause and Weinberg experience.

LESSONS FROM BUILDING HIGH-ASSURANCE SYSTEMS

Over time, RELA began to specialize in the development of various types of computer-based medical devices and systems: portable ventilators (breathing machines), infusion pumps, pacemaker programmers, clinical diagnostic systems, blood pumps, patient-monitoring equipment, and a plethora of other diagnostic and therapeutic devices.

It was early during the ventilator development project that the ultimate accountability for what we were doing really hit us: *Whoa, if we screw this up, somebody could die!* Our primary concern was for the patient and for the family of the patient who was tethered to the device, a device on which we were executing some of the earliest, most time-critical, resource-limited software the world had yet seen. (Imagine the challenge of alpha and beta testing. You go first!)

Clearly, this high-stakes endeavor caused us to take software very seriously at a fairly early time in the evolution of the embedded-systems industry. It became clear very quickly that sustainable success would require a combination of

- A pragmatic process for defining and managing the requirements for the software
- A solid methodology for the design and development of software
- The application of various proven, innovative techniques for verifying and validating that the software was safe and effective
- Extraordinary skills and commitment on the part of both the software development and software quality assurance teams

I strongly believed at that time, and I am even more convinced today, that *all of those elements are required to deliver any reasonably reliable software system of any significant scope.* At RELA, Inc., this was to be the only way we could possibly ensure each patient's safety, the very survival of our company, and the economic futures of the employees and their families who depended on the company.

Big Question 2: "How, exactly, will we know when the software does exactly that and nothing else?"

Given our earlier success in the development and application of the various techniques we used to answer Big Question 1, we now moved on to the second fundamental question facing software development teams worldwide. Big Question 2 is

How, exactly, will we know when the software does exactly that and nothing else?

The techniques we used to answer this question form the basis of Team Skill 5, Refining the System Definition, and Team Skill 6, Building the Right System.

So, you can be confident that the techniques presented in this book are road hardened and well proven. Also, even if you are not in the business of developing safety-critical systems, you can rest assured that what follows is useful, practical, and cost-effective advice that you can use to develop software systems of the highest quality.

Although the techniques that we borrowed, modified, developed, and applied at RELA, Inc., to address the two big questions were highly effective, I must also admit to one nagging uncertainty that kept me awake during the most serious crunch times on these projects:

Given the highly manual nature of the requirements process, how long would it be before we made a single, but potentially dangerous, mistake?

And there was also the matter of cost, as manual verification and validation were expensive and error prone. During this period, the discipline of mechanical engineering had advanced from a mechanical drawing arm to 3-D computer-aided design systems. In the same period, our software advances were limited, for all practical purposes, to having increased the level of abstraction in our programming languages: a good thing, for certain, but defect rates, lines-of-code productivity factors, and quality measures were relatively constant. Our experiments with the CASE tools of that period were met with mixed results. Frankly, as a software engineer and entrepreneur, I found the state of the art in "software engineering" to be embarrassing.

Although it was obvious that automation would never eliminate the critical-thinking skills required in software development, I did become convinced that automating some of the manual, record-keeping, and change management aspects of the process would free scarce resources to focus on higher value-added activities. And, of course, we anticipated that development costs would be lower while reliability would be increased!

LESSONS FROM THE REQUIREMENTS MANAGEMENT BUSINESS

So, in 1993, Requisite, Inc., was born, and a number of us committed to a course of action to develop and to market an innovative requirements management tool: RequisitePro. As we were continuously helping customers address their requirements management challenges during this time, much additional material for this book was born. We owe much of this work to those customers, and the customers at RELA, who essentially taught us everything we know on the subject.

This portion of my career was heavily influenced by Dr. Alan Davis, who was Editor in Chief of *IEEE Software* magazine and held the El Pomar Endowed Chair of Software Engineering at the University of Colorado in Colorado Springs. Al joined the company as a director and advisor early on and was instrumental in influencing our technology and the business direction. He is well known for his leadership in the field of requirements engineering. Al was also active in consulting activities and had developed a number of techniques for helping companies improve their requirements process. These techniques were merged with some of the RELA-derived techniques and became the basis of a professional training offering called Requirements College, the basis for parts of this book.

In addition, operating under the insufficiently popular business theory of *"you can never have too much professional help,"* we recruited renowned software author and expert Ed Yourdon to join the board of the company. Ed was also highly influential in guiding the course of the technology and business direction. Both Ed and Al were earlier contributors to this work, and many of the words that appear in this book are theirs. Indeed, we had intended to release the book jointly a few years ago. But times change, and Ed and Al have graciously donated all of their earlier work to us. However, you will often hear them speaking through these words.

EXPERIENCES AT RATIONAL SOFTWARE

Rational Software Corporation purchased Requisite, Inc., in 1997. At Rational, I gained significant additional experience in requirements management as it applies to developing and releasing a full family of application development tools, as well as continuing to help customers address their requirements problems. I also had the unique pleasure of working with some of the industry's foremost software experts and authors, including Grady Booch, Ivar Jacobson, James Rumbaugh, Walker Royce, and Philippe Kruchten. Each of them contributed to my view of the requirements management challenge, and Walker and Philippe were early reviewers of this work.

We also became exposed to the use case technique for requirements capture, and to the concept of using use cases within the design model to provide a common thread to drive architecture, implementation, and testing.

I am also a fan of Rational's promulgation of the *iterative approach* for software development, of which I like to think that we were early practitioners at RELA, as well as the Rational Unified Process, a full lifecycle software development process.

Rational helped me complete this work, and for that I am grateful. Also, Rational graciously provided permission to use certain ideas, text, and diagrams.

SUMMARY

In a sense, few, if any, ideas in this book are original. Instead, it represents harvesting the shared software development experiences of two decades, with a focused, consistent, and measured emphasis on the requirements challenge.

In so doing, the work, we hope, assimilates the experiences and opinions of some of the best minds in the industry on this unique and difficult software challenge. We firmly believe that the result—these *six requisite team skills for effective requirements management*—will help you deliver quality software systems on time and on budget.

INTRODUCTION

It Doesn't Seem Like It Should Be This Hard

Sit down with the customer. Figure out what the customer wants the system to do. Use cool new software languages and tools that didn't even exist two years ago. Craft the application, using the latest languages and tools. Simulate and debug with efficiency and aplomb. Download the new client application remotely. Sit back and wait for awards to come in. Take the entire holiday off. Watch for that bonus check!

Reality Seems Entirely Different

However, for most of us, much of the time, reality seems entirely different. Our lives are dominated by late nights, changing requirements, fickle customers, serious software quality issues, significant project delays, technology that obsolesces before we deploy it for the first time, and missed commitments. In the best cases, our customers are thrilled and we are well rewarded. But even then it comes at a personal cost, and we know we could have done better. In the worst cases, we encounter canceled projects and complete frustration. Bring on the next project! Goodness gracious, we love this business!

Background

In Chapter 1, we summarize some of the ongoing challenges and problems associated with software development and the causes of project successes and failures. The chapter also provides a rationale for investing time and resources in doing a better job of managing application requirements. If you're a veteran software developer, a veteran project manager, or any other kind of software veteran with lots of scars from complex projects gone awry, you may be tempted to skip this discussion and turn directly to Chapter 2.

But if you are new to the industry or spend most of your time outside the software development department of your company—if you're in the marketing department, perhaps, and you're charged with defining a new software product, or if you're in the quality assurance department chartered to acquire an ISO 9000 accreditation for the entire company, or if you're in a "user department" that needs to have information systems developed to support its activities—you should read Chapter 1, as well as the rest of the book!

You are most likely aware that systems development projects tend to be difficult, expensive, risky, and prone to failure, but you may not know *why* this is a common situation in most organizations. Indeed, if you think that no other organization on Earth could be as screwed up as yours, you'll be relieved to discover, from the statistics in Chapter 1, that almost every organization suffers from the same kinds of problems. Knowing why these problems exist and where they tend to be the most severe and expensive is a crucial first step for improvement.

In Chapter 2, we introduce the concepts of requirements management that we'll be discussing throughout the remainder of the book. Even if you think you know what "requirement" means—and after all, who *doesn't?*—we urge you to read this material, for it provides some definitions and foundation-level assumptions that we depend on in subsequent chapters.

In Chapter 3, we present various software lifecycle models, both past and present, and discuss how these models relate to the overall problem of managing requirements during the development process.

Finally, in Chapter 4, we introduce the software team. The software team is part of the case study that will help us understand the challenges of requirements management as we work our way through the six team skills that follow.

Effective requirements management can be accomplished only via an effective software team.

This is not a book about teams, however, and the important topics of building high-performance teams, motivating them, and even managing them within the context of software development are outside the scope of this book. This *is* a book on managing software requirements, and to accomplish this challenge, we need the support of the entire software team. The reason is that, perhaps more than with any other specific software development activity, requirements management is a process that touches every team member, both in the core team and in the extended team of the customer and stakeholders. Indeed, it is a premise of this book that in all but the most trivial projects, *effective requirements management can be applied only via an effective software team.* Further, to achieve success, every member of the team must participate in the process, albeit in different ways, and each team member will need to be knowledgeable about his or her role in requirements management.

Chapter 1

THE REQUIREMENTS PROBLEM

Key Points

- The goal of software development is to develop quality software—on time and on budget—that meets customers' real needs.
- Project success *depends* on effective requirements management.
- Requirements errors are the most common type of systems development error and the most costly to fix.
- A few key skills can significantly reduce requirements errors and thus improve software quality.

THE GOAL OF SOFTWARE DEVELOPMENT

Thousands of software development teams worldwide are engaged right now in developing widely different software applications in widely different industries. But although we work in different industries and speak and write in different languages, we all work with the same technologies, we read the same magazines, we went to the same schools, and fortunately, we have the same clear goal: *to develop quality software—on time and on budget—that meets customers' real needs.*

However, our customers are quite different. . . .

- For some of us, the customer is an external entity, purchase order in hand, whom we must convince to disregard our competitor's claims and to buy *our* shrink-wrapped software product because it's easier to use, has more functionality, and, in the final analysis, is just better.
- For others of us, the customer is a company that has hired us to develop its software, based on expectations that the software developed will be of the highest quality achievable given today's state of the

5

art and will transform the company into a more competitive, more profitable organization in the marketplace.

- For others of us, the customer is sitting down the hall or downstairs or across the country, waiting anxiously for that new application to enter sales orders more efficiently or to use e-commerce for selling the company's goods and services so that the company we *both* work for will ultimately be more profitable and our jobs more rewarding and just more fun.

So, although our customers are varied, we can take some comfort in the fact that the goal is the same.

A LOOK AT THE DATA

We software developers must admit to having a spotty track record when it comes to building nontrivial software systems. Of course, some systems work quite well, and amateurs and veterans alike are often dazzled by what we've been able to accomplish: the Internet, simpler user interfaces, handheld computing devices, smart appliances, real-time process control, online interactive brokerage accounts, and the like. It's also true that there's a wide spectrum of possibilities between perfection and failure. For example, the word processor and the PC operating system we used to write this book collectively caused about two system crashes a day while we were writing this chapter, as well as exhibiting a number of other annoying quirks, idiosyncrasies, and "gotchas." Nevertheless, overall, the word processor and the operating system were "good enough" to support the task of writing this chapter, but they certainly weren't examples of perfect software.

In many cases, the results are far more serious. A study by the Standish Group [1994] reported:

> In the United States, we spend more than $250 billion each year on IT application development of approximately 175,000 projects. The average cost of a development project for a large company is $2,322,000; for a medium company, it is $1,331,000, and for a small company, it is $434,000. . . .
>
> The Standish Group research shows a staggering 31% of projects will be canceled before they ever get completed. Further results indicate 52.7% of projects will cost 189% of their original estimates. . . .
>
> Based on this research, the Standish Group estimates that . . . American companies and government agencies will spend $81 billion for

canceled software projects. These same organizations will pay an additional $59 billion for software projects that will be completed but will exceed their original time estimates.[1]

It is generally wise to take any such data "with a grain of salt," and perhaps things have improved in the industry in the intervening years. However, it's fairly easy for any of us in the industry to relate to such data. We all have a pet project that never went to market or an information system "tar pit" that we built and are still suffering from. So, when there's reasonable empirical evidence that we have a problem and that evidence correlates with our own experience, it's best to admit that we have a problem and to move on to problem solving. After all, that's what we do best. Right? Right?????

THE ROOT CAUSES OF PROJECT SUCCESS AND FAILURE

The first step in resolving any problem is to *understand the root causes*. Fortunately, the Standish Group survey went beyond the assessment phase and asked survey respondents to identify the most significant factors that contributed to projects that were rated "success," "challenged" (late and did not meet expectations), and "impaired" (canceled), respectively.

Here we discover that the emphasis in this book on requirements management is not frivolous or arbitrary; it's a response to accumulating evidence that many of the most common, most serious problems associated with software development are related to requirements. The 1994 Standish Group study noted the three most commonly cited factors that caused projects to be "challenged":

1. Lack of user input: 13 percent of all projects
2. Incomplete requirements and specifications: 12 percent of all projects
3. Changing requirements and specifications: 12 percent of all projects

Thereafter, the data diverges rapidly. Of course, your project could fail because of an unrealistic schedule or time frame (4 percent of the projects cited this), inadequate staffing and resources (6 percent), inadequate technology skills (7 percent), or various other reasons. Nevertheless, to the extent that the Standish figures are representative of the overall industry, it appears that at least a third of development projects run into trouble for reasons that are directly related to requirements gathering, requirements documentation, and requirements management.

---

1. Quotation reprinted with permission of the Standish Group.

Although the majority of projects do seem to experience schedule/budget overruns, if not outright cancellation, the Standish Group found that 9 percent of the projects in large companies were delivered on time and on budget; 16 percent of the projects in small companies enjoyed a similar success. That leads to an obvious question: What were the primary "success factors" for those projects? According to the Standish study, the three most important factors were

1. User involvement: 16 percent of all successful projects
2. Executive management support: 14 percent of all successful projects
3. Clear statement of requirements: 12 percent of all successful projects

Other surveys have even more striking results. For example, the European Software Process Improvement Training Initiative (ESPITI) [1995] conducted a survey to identify the relative importance of various types of software problems in industry. The results of this large-scale survey, based on 3,800 responses, are indicated in Figure 1–1.

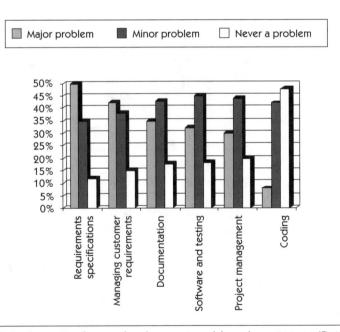

Figure 1–1   Largest software development problems by category. (Data derived from ESPITI [1995].)

The two largest problems, appearing in about half the responses, were

1. Requirements specifications
2. Managing customer requirements

Again, corroborating the Standish survey, coding issues were a "nonproblem," relatively speaking.

It seems clear that requirements deserve their place as a leading root cause of software problems, and our continuing personal experiences support that conclusion. Let's take a look at the economic factors associated with this particular root cause.

The Frequency of Requirements Errors

Both the Standish and the ESPITI studies provide qualitative data indicating that respondents feel that requirements problems *appear* to transcend other issues in terms of the risks and problems they pose to application development. But do requirements problems affect the delivered code?

Table 1–1 summarizes a 1994 study by Capers Jones that provides data regarding the likely number of "potential" defects in a development project and the typical "efficiency" with which a development organization removes those defects through various combinations of testing, inspections, and other strategies.

Table 1–1   Defect Summary

Defect Origins	Defect Potentials	Removal Efficiency	Delivered Defects
Requirements	1.00	77%	0.23
Design	1.25	85%	0.19
Coding	1.75	95%	0.09
Documentation	0.60	80%	0.12
Bad fixes	0.40	70%	0.12
Total	5.00	85%	0.75

Source: Data derived from Jones [1994].

The Defect Potentials column normalizes the defects such that each category contributes to the total potential of 5.00, an arbitrary normalization that does not imply anything about the absolute number of defects. The Delivered Defects column, referring to what the user sees, is normalized in the same way.

Requirements errors top the delivered defects and contribute approximately one-third of the total delivered defects to the defect pile. Thus, this study provides yet another confirmation that requirements errors are the most common category of systems development errors.

The High Cost of Requirements Errors

If requirements errors can be fixed quickly, easily, and economically, we still may not have a huge problem. This last statistic delivers the final blow. Just the opposite tends to be true. Studies performed at companies including GTE, TRW, IBM, and HP have measured and assigned costs to errors occurring at various phases of the project lifecycle. Davis [1993] summarized a number of these studies, as Figure 1–2 illustrates. Although these studies were run independently, they all reached roughly the same conclusion: If a unit cost of *one* is assigned to the effort required to detect and repair an error during the coding

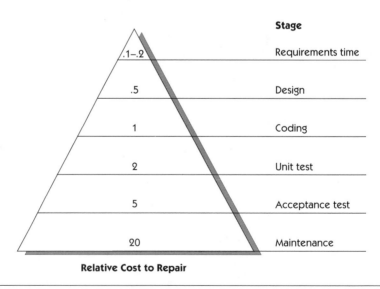

Figure 1–2   Relative cost to repair a defect at different lifecycle phases. (Data derived from Davis [1993].)

stage, then the cost to detect and repair an error during the requirements stage is between *five* to *ten* times less. Furthermore, the cost to detect and repair an error during the maintenance stage is *twenty* times more.

Altogether, the figure illustrates that as much as a 200:1 cost savings results from finding errors in the requirements stage versus finding errors in the maintenance stage of the software lifecycle.

While this may be the exaggerated case, it's easy to see that there is a multiplicative factor at work. The reason is that many of these errors are not detected until well after they have been made.

If you've read this section carefully, you may have noticed that we muddled two issues together in Figure 1–2: the relative costs of various categories of errors *and* the cost of fixing them at different stages in the software lifecycle. For example, the item "requirements time" literally means *all* errors that were detected and fixed during the period officially designated as "requirements definition." But since it's unlikely that substantial technical design or programming activities will have been carried out at this early stage—ignoring, for the moment, the early design or prototyping activities that might be taking place— the mistakes that we detect and fix at this stage *are* requirements errors.

But the errors discovered during the design of a development project could fall into one of two categories: (1) errors that occurred when the development staff created a technical design from a correct set of requirements *or* (2) errors that should have been detected as requirements errors somewhat earlier in the process but that somehow "leaked" into the design phase of the project. It's the latter category of errors that turn out to be particularly expensive, for two reasons.

1. By the time the requirements-oriented error is discovered, the development group will have invested time and effort in building a design from those erroneous requirements. As a result, the design will probably have to be thrown away or reworked.
2. The true nature of the error may be disguised; everyone assumes that they're looking for design errors during the testing or inspection activities that take place during this phase, and considerable time and effort may be wasted until someone says, "Wait a minute! This isn't a design mistake after all; we've got the wrong requirements."

Confirming the details of the requirements error means tracking down the user who provided the requirements details in the first place. However, that person may not be readily available, may have forgotten the requirements instruction to the development team or the rationale for identifying the original requirements, or may have just had a change of mind. Similarly, the development team member who was involved in that stage of the project—often, a person with the title of "business analyst" or "systems analyst"—may have moved on to a different project or may suffer a similar form of short-term amnesia. All of this involves a certain amount of "spinning of wheels" and lost time.

These problems associated with "leakage" of defects from one lifecycle phase to the next are fairly obvious when you think about them, but most organizations haven't investigated them very carefully. One organization that *has* done so is Hughes Aircraft. A study by Snyder and Shumate [1992] follows the leakage phenomenon for a large collection of projects Hughes has conducted over the past 15 years. The study indicates that 74 percent of the requirements-oriented defects were discovered during the requirements analysis phase of the project—that is, the formal phase during which customers and systems analysts discuss, brainstorm, negotiate, and document the project requirements. That's the ideal time and place to discover such errors, and it's likely to be the most inexpensive time and place. However, the study also shows that 4 percent of the requirements defects "leak" into the preliminary, or high-level, design of the project and that 7 percent leak further into detailed design. The leakage continues throughout the lifecycle, and a total of 4 percent of the requirements errors aren't found until maintenance, when the system has been released to the customers and is presumably in full-scale operation.

Thus, depending on when and where a defect is discovered in a software application development project, we're likely to experience the effect of 50–100 times cost. The reason is that in order to repair the defect, we are likely to experience costs in some or all of the following areas:

- Respecification.
- Redesign.
- Recoding.
- Retesting.
- Change orders (telling users and operators to replace a defective version of the system with the corrected version).
- Corrective action (undoing whatever damage may have been done by erroneous operation of the improperly specified system, which could involve sending refund checks to angry customers, rerunning computer jobs, and so on).

- Scrap (including code, design, and test cases that were carried out with the best of intentions but then had to be thrown away when it became clear they were based on incorrect requirements).
- Recall of defective versions of shrink-wrapped software and associated manuals from users. (Since software is now embedded in products ranging from digital wristwatches to microwave ovens to automobiles, the recall could include both tangible products and the software embedded within them.)
- Warranty costs.
- Product liability (if the customer sues for damages caused by the defective software).
- Service costs for a company representative to visit a customer's field location to reinstall the new software.
- Documentation.

SUMMARY

The data presented in this chapter demonstrates two things.

1. Requirements errors are likely to be the most common class of error.

2. Requirements errors are likely to be the most expensive errors to fix.

Requirements errors are likely to consume 25 percent to 40 percent of the total project budget.

Given the frequency of requirements errors and the multiplicative effect of the "cost to fix" factor, it's easy to predict that requirements errors will contribute the majority—often 70 percent or more—of the rework costs. Since rework typically consumes 30 percent to 50 percent of a typical project budget [Boehm and Papaccio 1988], it follows that requirements errors could consume *25 percent to 40 percent* of the total project budget!

Our own experiences support this data, and that is the primary reason we wrote this book. If, with a small investment in a few key skills, we can do a better job in this area, we can save significant amounts of money, increase productivity, save precious time on the project calendar, and ultimately deliver higher-quality results to the customer, not to mention saving some of the wear and tear on the software team.

Chapter 2

INTRODUCTION TO REQUIREMENTS MANAGEMENT

Key Points

- A requirement is a capability that is imposed on the system.
- Requirements management is a process of systematically eliciting, organizing, and documenting requirements for a complex system.
- Our challenge is to understand *users'* problems in *their* culture and *their* language and to build systems that meet *their* needs.
- A feature is a service that the system provides to fulfill one or more stakeholder needs.
- A use case describes a sequence of actions, performed by a system, that yields a result of value to a user.

Based on the data presented in Chapter 1, you can see why we're interested in focusing on requirements management. However, before we can begin explaining the various techniques and strategies, we need to provide some definitions and examples. We'll start by defining what we mean by the term *software requirement*.

DEFINITIONS

What Is a Software Requirement?

Although many definitions of software requirements have been used throughout the years, the one provided by requirements engineering authors Dorfman and Thayer [1990] is quite workable:

1. *A software capability needed by the user to solve a problem to achieve an objective*
2. *A software capability that must be met or possessed by a system or system component to satisfy a contract, standard, specification, or other formally imposed documentation*

This definition may appear to be a little vague, but later we'll develop these concepts further. For now, this definition will do quite well.

What Is Requirements Management?

Requirements define capabilities that the systems must deliver, and conformance (or lack of conformance) to a set of requirements often determines the success (or failure) of projects. It makes sense, therefore, to find out what the requirements are, write them down, organize them, and track them in the event that they change. Stated another way, we'll define requirements management as

> *a systematic approach to eliciting, organizing, and documenting the requirements of the system, and a process that establishes and maintains agreement between the customer and the project team on the changing requirements of the system.*

Let's take a closer look at some key concepts contained in this definition.

- Anyone who has ever been involved with complex software systems—whether from the perspective of a customer or a developer—knows that a crucial skill is the ability to *elicit* the requirements from users and stakeholders.
- Since hundreds, if not thousands, of requirements are likely to be associated with a system, it's important to *organize* them.
- Since most of us can't keep more than a few dozen pieces of information in our heads, *documenting* the requirements is necessary to support effective communication among the various stakeholders. The requirements have to be recorded in an accessible medium: a document, a model, a database, or a list on the whiteboard.

What do these elements have to do with managing requirements? Project size and complexity are major factors here: nobody would bother talking about "managing" requirements in a two-person project that had only 10 requirements to fulfill. But to verify 1,000 requirements—a small purchased software product—or 300,000 requirements—a Boeing 777—it's obvious that we will face problems of organizing, prioritizing, controlling access to, and providing resources for the various requirements. On even a modest-size project, questions will naturally arise.

- Which project team members are responsible for the wind speed requirement (#278), and which ones are allowed to modify it or delete it?

- If requirement #278 is modified, what other requirements will be affected?
- How can we be sure that someone has written the code in a software system to fulfill requirement #278, and which test cases in the overall test suite are intended to verify that the requirements have indeed been fulfilled?

That, along with some other, similar activities, is what requirements management is all about.

This is not something new that we've invented on our own; it's one of those "commonsense" activities that most development organizations claim to do in some fashion or other. It's typically informal and carried out inconsistently from one project to the next, and some of the key activities are likely to be overlooked or short-changed because of the pressures and politics associated with many development projects. So, requirements management could be regarded as a set of organized, standardized, and systematic processes and techniques for dealing with the requirements of a significant, complex project.

We're certainly not the first to suggest the idea of organized, formalized processes; two well-known efforts of this kind are the Software Engineering Institute's Capability Maturity Model (SEI-CMM) and the ISO 9000 quality management standards. (Requirements practices in these processes are described briefly in Appendix F.)

APPLICATION OF REQUIREMENTS MANAGEMENT TECHNIQUES

Types of Software Applications

We suggest that software applications can be categorized as follows:

- Information systems and other applications developed for use within a company (such as the payroll system being used to calculate the take-home pay for our next paycheck). This category is the basis for the information system/information technology industry, or IS/IT.
- Software developed and sold as commercial products (such as the word processor we are using to write this chapter). Companies developing this type of software are often referred to as independent software vendors, or ISVs.

- Software that runs on computers embedded in other devices, machines, or complex systems (such as those contained in the airplane we are writing this in; the cell phones we just used to call our spouses; the automobile we'll use to get to our eventual destination). We'll call this type of software embedded-systems applications, or embedded applications.

The characteristics of the applications we develop for these three different types of systems are extremely diverse. They could consist of 5,000,000 lines of COBOL on a mainframe host environment developed over a period of ten or more years by fifty to a hundred individuals. They could consist of 10,000 lines of Java on a Web server application written in one year by a one- or two-person team. Or they could be 1,000,000 lines of extremely time-critical C code on a complex real-time telephony system.

We'll maintain that the requirements management techniques presented throughout this book can be applied to any of these types of systems. Many of the techniques are independent of application type; others may need to be tuned for the application-specific context before being applied. To enhance your understanding, we'll provide a mix of examples to illustrate the application of the various techniques.

Systems Applications

Requirements management can also be applied to systems development. Most of the techniques in this book will deliver value in managing requirements of arbitrarily complex systems consisting of mechanical subsystems, computer subsystems, and chemical subsystems and their interrelated pieces and parts. Clearly, this is a broad discipline, and we will have to show some discretion to be able to deliver value to the average software team member. Therefore, we'll focus on a requirements management process and specific techniques that can be applied most directly to significant software applications of the IS/IT, ISV, or embedded-systems types.

THE ROAD MAP

Since we are embarking on a journey to develop quality software—on time and on budget—that meets customers' real needs, it may well be helpful to have a map of the territory. This is a difficult challenge in that the variety of people you encounter on this particular journey, and the languages they speak, are quite diverse. Many questions will arise.

- Is this a need or a requirement?
- Is this a nice-to-have or a must-have?
- Is this a statement of the problem or a statement of the solution?
- Is this a goal of the system or a contractual requirement?
- Do we have to program in Java? Says who?
- Who doesn't like the new system, and where was that person when we visited here before?

In order to navigate successfully through the territory, we'll need to understand where we are at any point in time, whom we are meeting, what language they are speaking, and what information we need from them to complete our journey successfully. Let's start in the "land of the problem."

The Problem Domain

Most successful requirements journeys begin with a trip to the land of the problem. This *problem domain* is the home of real users and other stakeholders, people whose needs must be addressed in order for us to build the perfect system. This is the home of the people who need the rock or a new sales order entry system or a configuration management system good enough to blow the competition away. In all probability, these people are not like us. Their technical and economic backgrounds are different from ours, they speak in funny acronyms, they go to different parties and drink different beers, they don't wear T-shirts to work, and they have motivations that seem strange and unfathomable. (What, you never liked *Star Trek?*)

On rare occasions, they are just like us. They are programmers looking for a new tool or system developers who have asked you to develop a portion of the system. In these rare cases, this portion of the journey *might* be easier, but it might also be more difficult.

Problem domain

Typically, this is not the case, and we are in the land of the alien user. These users have *business* or *technical problems* that they need our help to solve. Therefore, it becomes *our* problem to understand *their* problems, in *their* culture and *their* language, and to build systems that meet *their* needs. Since this territory can seem a little foggy, we'll represent it as a cloud. This will be a constant reminder to us to make sure we are seeing all the issues in the problem space clearly.

Within the problem domain, we use a set of *team skills* as our map and compass to *understand the problem to be solved*. While we are here, we need to gain an understanding of the problem and the needs that must be filled to address this problem.

Stakeholder Needs

It is also our responsibility to understand the needs of users and other stakeholders whose lives will be affected by our solution. As we elicit those needs, we'll stack them in a little pile called *stakeholder needs*, which we represent as a pyramid.

Moving Toward the Solution Domain

Fortunately, the journey through the problem domain is not necessarily difficult, and the artifacts collected there are not many. However, with even this little bit of data, we will be well provisioned for the part of the journey that we have perhaps been better prepared for: providing a solution to the problem at hand. In this solution space, we focus on defining a solution to the user's problem; this is the realm of computers, programming, operating systems, networks, and processing nodes. Here, we can apply the skills we have learned much more directly.

Features of the System

First, however, it will be helpful to state what we learned in the problem domain and how we intend to resolve those issues via the solution. This is not a very long list and consists of such items as the following.

- "The car will have power windows."
- "Defect-trending charts will provide a visual means of assessing progress."
- "The program will allow Web-enabled entry of sales orders."
- "An automatic step-and-repeat weld cycle is required."

These are simple descriptions, in the user's language, that we will use as labels to communicate with the user how our system addresses the problem. These labels will become part of our everyday language, and much energy will be spent in defining them, debating them, and prioritizing them. We'll call these descriptions *features* of the system to be built and will define a feature as

> *a service provided by the system that fulfills one or more stakeholder needs.*

Graphically, we'll represent features as a base for the previous needs pyramid.

Software Requirements

Once we have established the feature set and have gained agreement with the customer, we can move on to defining the more specific requirements we will need to impose on the solution. If we build a system that conforms to those requirements, we can be certain that the system we develop will deliver the features we promised. In turn, since the features address one or more stakeholder needs, we will have addressed those needs directly in the solution.

These more specific requirements are the *software requirements*. We'll represent them as a block within our pyramid in a manner similar to the features. We also note that these appear pretty far down on the pyramid, and this implies, correctly, that we have much work to do before we get to that level of specificity later in the book.

SUMMARY

Now let's take a look at the map we've built. In Figure 2–1, you can see that we have made a subtle yet important transition in our thinking in this process. We have moved from the problem domain, represented by the cloud and the

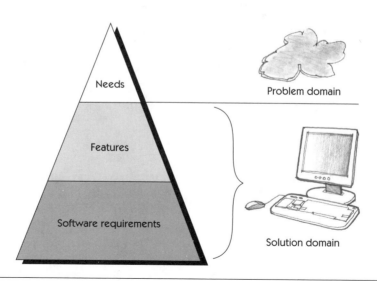

Figure 2–1 Overview of the problem domain and the solution domain

user needs we discovered, to a definition of a system that will constitute the solution domain, represented by the features of the system and the software requirements that will drive its design and implementation. Moreover, we have done so in a logical, stepwise fashion, making sure to understand the problem and the user's needs before we envision or define the solution. This road map, along with its significant distinctions, will continue to be important throughout this book.

Chapter 3

REQUIREMENTS AND THE SOFTWARE LIFECYCLE

Key Points

- The team's development process defines who is doing what, when, and how.
- In the waterfall model, software activities proceeded through a sequence of steps, and requirements were "fixed" early.
- In the spiral model, the first steps were taken to a more risk-driven and incremental approach to development.
- The iterative approach, a hybrid of the waterfall and spiral models, decouples the lifecycle phases from the software activities that take place in each phase.
- The iterative model is a more robust model and provides for successive refinement of the requirements over time.

TRADITIONAL SOFTWARE PROCESS MODELS

Effective requirements management can occur only within the context of a reasonably well-defined software process that defines the full set of activities your team must execute to deliver the final software product. Some software processes are relatively formal, some are informal, but a process is always at work, whether or not it is rigorous or documented.

Your team's software development process defines who (which member of the team) is doing what (which activity is being performed), when (the timing in relation to other activities), and how (the details and steps in the activity) in order for your team to reach its goal. Software processes have been shown to have a significant effect on your team's ability to develop software on time and on budget. In this chapter, we look at a few different software processes and attempt to understand the time-dependent phases and major types of activities in those phases. We then go on to describe a specific, recommended model: the iterative model. Within the context of the iterative model we can begin to understand the key role that requirements play throughout the software lifecycle. Most of the techniques described in this book apply to a variety of software processes, but it is through using an iterative approach that you are likely to achieve the maximum benefits.

The Waterfall Model

Boehm [1988] points out that as early as the 1950s the software industry, recognizing the cost of discovering software defects late in the cycle, adopted a logical, stepwise process model that progressed from a requirement phase to a design phase to a coding phase and so on. This was a major improvement over the earlier, two-phase "code and fix" model, whereby programmers first wrote the code and then fixed it until it couldn't be fixed any more.

In the 1970s, Royce [1970], working at TRW, defined what became known as the "waterfall model" of software development. The waterfall model improved on the strictly stepwise model by:

- Recognizing the need for feedback loops between stages, thereby acknowledging that design affects requirements, that coding the system will cause the design to be revisited, and so on
- Developing a prototype system in parallel with requirements analysis and design activities

In the waterfall model (Figure 3–1), software activities proceed logically through a sequence of steps. Each step bases its work on the activities of the previous step. Design logically follows requirements, coding follows design, and so on. The waterfall model was widely followed in the 1970s and '80s and served successfully as a process model for a variety of medium- to large-scale projects.

Note that, as commonly applied, Figure 3–1 does not reference the prototyping activity that Royce prescribed. This is an unfortunate mistake in history that we'll return to shortly.

The waterfall model has been somewhat successful in reinforcing the role of requirements, which form a first step in software development and serve as the basis for design and coding activities. However, this strength also very quickly became a primary source of weakness, as it tended to emphasize fully elaborated requirements and design documents as a barrier to exit from each

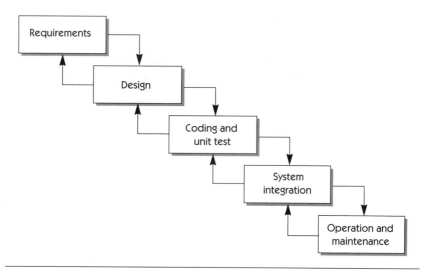

Figure 3–1 Waterfall model of software development

phase. Also, through perhaps its misapplication by overzealous development teams, the waterfall model has come to represent a fixed, rigid approach to development, wherein requirements are "frozen" for the life of the project, change is anathema, and the process of development takes on a life of its own, independent of the changes occurring in the marketplace or in the users' needs.

In this case, over time, the team may become completely disengaged from the real world on which the project was originally based. Disaster invariably results.

As we'll see later, the waterfall model comes under additional pressure when it is aligned to the scope management challenge. Specifically, if the waterfall model is applied to a project that is initiated with too large a scope, the results can be woefully short of the initial expectations. At deadline time, nothing really works, unit test and system integration are forced or abandoned, and significant investments have been made in the specification, design, and coding of system features that are never delivered. The result: nothing deliverable, chaos, poor quality, and software scrap.

Primarily for these reasons, the waterfall model has fallen out of favor. One unfortunate result has been the tendency for teams to leap right into code, with an inadequate understanding of the requirements for the system—one of the main problems the waterfall model attempted to solve!

The Spiral Model

Boehm's pivotal study [1988] recommended a different framework for guiding the software development process. His "spiral model" of software development serves as a role model for those who believe that success follows a more risk-driven and incremental development path (Figure 3–2).

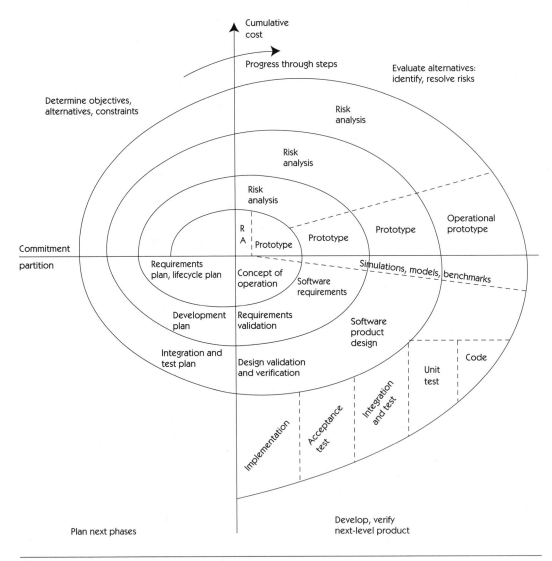

Figure 3–2 The spiral model of development

In the spiral model, development is initially driven by a series of risk-driven prototypes; then a structured waterfall-like process is used to produce the final system. Of course, when misused, the spiral model can exhibit as many problems as the misused waterfall model. Projects sometimes fall into a cut-and-try approach, providing incremental deliverables that must be expanded and maintained with the addition of bubble gum and baling wire. Some refer to this as the process of creating instant legacy code, progress being measured by our newfound ability to create unmaintainable and incomprehensible code two to three times as fast as with earlier methods!

When you look at the spiral model more carefully, however, it provides a sensible road map that helps address some of the requirements challenges noted in this book. Specifically, the spiral model starts with requirements planning and concept validation, followed by one or more prototypes to assist in early confirmation of our understanding of the requirements for the system. The main advantage of this process is the availability of multiple feedback opportunities with the users and customers, which is intended to get the "Yes, Buts" (see Chapter 8) out early. Opponents of this rigorous approach note that, in today's environment, we typically do not have the luxury of time for full concept validation and two or three prototypes, followed by a rigorous waterfall methodology.

THE ITERATIVE APPROACH

In the past decade, many teams have migrated to a new approach, one that combines the best of the waterfall and spiral models and is a hybrid of the two. This new approach also incorporates some additional constructs from the advancing discipline of software process engineering. The iterative approach introduced by Kruchten [1995] has now been well described in a number of texts, including those by Kruchten [1999] and Royce [1998]. This approach has proved effective in a wide variety of project types and can exhibit a number of advantages over the waterfall and spiral models of development.

In the traditional software development process models, time moves forward through a series of sequential activities, with requirements preceding design, design preceding implementation, and so on. This seemed quite sensible. In the iterative approach, however, the lifecycle phases are decoupled from the logical software activities that occur in each phase, allowing us to revisit various activities, such as requirements, design, and implementation, during various iterations of the project. In addition, like the spiral model, each iteration is designed to mitigate whatever risks are present in that stage of development activity.

Lifecycle Phases

The iterative approach consists of four *lifecycle phases*: inception, elaboration, construction, and transition, corresponding to fairly natural "states" of the project at these times (Figure 3–3).

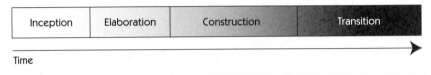

Figure 3–3   Lifecycle phases in the iterative approach

In the *inception* phase, the team is focused on understanding the business case for the project, the scope of the project, and the feasibility of an implementation. Problem analysis is performed, the vision for the solution is created, and preliminary estimates of schedule and budget, as well as project risk factors, are defined.

In the *elaboration* phase, the requirements for the system are refined, an initial, perhaps even executable, architecture is established, and an early feasibility prototype is typically developed and demonstrated.

In the *construction* phase, the focus is on implementation. Most of the coding is done in this phase, and the architecture and design are fully developed.

Beta testing typically happens in the *transition* phase, and the users and maintainers of the system are trained on the application. The tested baseline of the application is transitioned to the user community and deployed for use.

Iterations

Within each phase, the project typically undergoes multiple iterations (Figure 3–4). An *iteration* is a sequence of activities with an established plan and evaluation criteria, resulting in an executable of some type. Each iteration builds on the functionality of the prior iteration; thus, the project is developed in an "iterative and incremental" fashion.

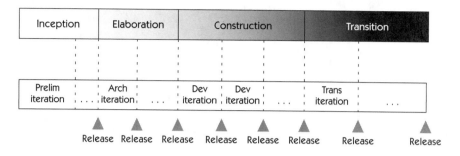

Figure 3–4   Phase iterations, resulting in viable releases

Iterations are selected according to a number of criteria. Early iterations should be designed to evaluate the viability of the chosen architecture against some of the most important and risk-laden use cases.

Disciplines

In the iterative approach, the activities associated with the development of the software are organized into a set of *disciplines*. Each discipline consists of a logically related set of activities, and each defines how the activities must be sequenced to produce a viable work product (or *artifact*). Although the number and kind of disciplines can vary, based on the company or project circumstances, there are typically at least six disciplines, as Figure 3–5 illustrates.

During each iteration, the team spends as much time as appropriate in each discipline. Thus, an iteration can be regarded as a mini-waterfall through the activities of requirements, analysis and design, and so on, but each mini-waterfall is "tuned" to the specific needs of that iteration. The size of the "hump" in Figure 3–5 indicates the relative amount of effort invested in a discipline. For example, in the elaboration phase, significant time is spent on "refining" the requirements and in defining the architecture that will support the functionality. The activities can be sequential (a true mini-waterfall) or may execute concurrently, as is appropriate to the project.

The lifecycle model shown in Figure 3–5 is taken from the Rational Unified Process [Rational Software Corporation 2002]. The process is commonly referred to by its initials (RUP). The RUP provides a comprehensive set of best practices covering the full software lifecycle. For more on the RUP and its integral requirements practices, see Appendix E.

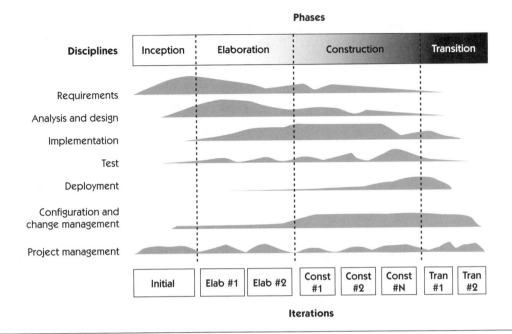

Figure 3–5 Disciplines of the iterative approach

REQUIREMENTS IN THE ITERATIVE MODEL

From the requirements management perspective, the iterative approach provides two major advantages.

1. *Better adaptability to requirements change.* The model recognizes that requirements change and requirements activities are therefore active throughout the lifecycle. Requirements are not frozen, they are understood early at a certain level of detail, and they are refined successively over time. And since they are revisited at every iteration, new requirements can be considered at each iteration.

2. *Better scope management.* If the first iteration is missed by 30 percent, that's an indicator that the project may be badly scoped, and adjustments can be made. Even if scope is not well managed, multiple executable iterations have been developed by the time the deadline is reached, and the last may even be deployable. Even though it lacks some functionality, the release will deliver value to the user if the

features have been picked and prioritized carefully, allowing your customer to meet objectives, at least in part, as you continue with further development iterations. And, if the architecture is robust and addresses the key technical issues, your team will have a solid platform on which to base the additional functionality.

With this software process model in mind, we can move forward to the requirements activities that are pertinent to each phase in the lifecycle. Yet we also recognize that the point in the lifecycle in which an activity occurs is not fixed or predetermined, and indeed, the requirements activities can be revisited as necessary over time as our understanding of the system evolves.

SUMMARY

On the surface, this discussion of software process models may seem to be off-topic in a requirements text. Assuredly, it is not. In the move from a waterfall model to the iterative model, we can finally dispense with the notion that requirements are fully discoverable and can be fully documented *before* development begins and that they can be fixed or *frozen* thereafter. It was an interesting theory, and it appeared to make life for developers more straightforward as they imagined their work could be built on an unchanging foundation. Unfortunately, it simply did not work. Requirements change, and to pretend otherwise is, at best, foolish. We must understand that requirements discovery and requirements management are full lifecycle issues. The more we discover, the more we discover, and the better we understand the system to be built. With this context behind us, we can now move on to discovering that which we need to discover about our impending system. And we'll learn how to manage requirements change in a way that will augment, rather than destroy, the foundation for our development work.

Chapter 4

THE SOFTWARE TEAM

Computer programming is a human activity.

—Gerald Weinberg [1971]

> **Key Points**
>
> - Effective requirements management can be accomplished only by an effective software team.
> - Requirements management touches every team member, albeit in different ways.
> - Effective requirements management requires mastering six team skills.

Individuals choose software development as their career domain for a variety of reasons. Some read *Popular Science* and *Wired* as kids, gravitated to the programming courses available in high school, majored in engineering or computer science in college, and thereby directed their lives down this specific technical path. For others, it was serendipity; finding themselves at a place in space and time when the need for software was apparent, where they could participate in meeting that need, they gradually evolved into making a full-time commitment in the field.

In any case, it was the allure of *technology* that kept the flame burning: We love the bits and bytes, the operating systems, the databases, the development tools, the keyboard shortcuts, the languages. Who else but software developers could have developed the UNIX operating system? We are focused on technology, and that is our driving motivation. Perhaps because of an innate genetic tendency or perhaps because we skipped all the "softer" classes in college—psychology, drama, or, even worse, English!—we are generally focused less on the people side of our business and more on the bits and bytes. We tend not to party well,[1] and some of us have trouble relating to people outside of work, when there is no common technology substrate on which to base a discussion.

One result of this, which was further compounded by the simple single-user nature of the tools we used and the more limited size of the applications we developed, was the tendency toward software development as an individual activity. The programmer defined, designed, wrote, and, typically, tested his or her own work. Perhaps testers were around to help with the heavy lifting at the end, but the focus clearly was on individual activity. The "programmer as hero" was the common paradigm.

SOFTWARE DEVELOPMENT AS A TEAM ACTIVITY

Software development has become a team sport.

—Grady Booch[2]

At some point, the game changed. Why? Humphrey [1989] observed that

> "The history of software develop-ment is one of increasing scale."

the history of software development is one of increasing scale. Initially, a few individuals could hand craft small programs; the work soon grew beyond them. Teams of one or two dozen individuals were then used, but success was mixed. While many organizations have solved these small-system problems, the scale of our work continues to grow. Today, large projects typically require the coordinated work of many teams.

> The requirements management pro-cess touches every team member, albeit in different ways.

Humphrey goes on to observe that complexity continues to outpace one's ability to solve these problems intuitively as they appear. For example, we were involved in a requirements project that simultaneously affected approximately 30 products in a broad product family. The requirements being generated influenced, in real time, the software being written by more than 800 programmers at distributed locations. Success required intense coordination of a "team of teams" all working in a common methodology to address the requirements challenge.

---

1. During an open house, for example, one programmer remained at his desk throughout the party, programming happily, even though his desk was in the middle of the party room. After finishing his work, he simply got up, arranged his desk, and left the building without a word to anyone. What is unusual about this behavior? In our industry? Nothing!
2. A personal conversation with Dean Leffingwell.

What's to be done? Clearly, we have to make the "team thing" work and work well. As Boehm [1981] points out in the COCOMO cost estimation model, the capability of the team has the greatest impact on software production.

Davis [1995] supports this conclusion in his discussion of team productivity: "optimizing the productivity of all individuals does not necessarily result in optimizing the productivity of the team." So, it seems logical that we invest some of our resources in making software *teams* more productive.

> Effective require-ments manage-ment can be accomplished only via an effective software team.

Requisite Team Skills for Effective Requirements Management

In order to help the team, we've organized this book around six team skills that are necessary for a modern software team to successfully address the requirements challenge.

- In Team Skill 1, Analyzing the Problem, we develop a set of techniques the team can use to gain a proper understanding of the problem that a new software system is intended to solve.
- In Team Skill 2, Understanding User and Stakeholder Needs, we introduce a variety of techniques the team can use to elicit requirements from the system users and stakeholders. No one set of techniques will work in all situations; nor will it be necessary for the team to master all of the techniques. But with a little practice and some judicious picking and choosing, the team will gain a much better ability to understand the real needs that the system must address.
- In Team Skill 3, Defining the System, we describe the initial process by which the team converts an understanding of the problem and the users' needs to the initial definition of a system that will address those needs.
- In Team Skill 4, Managing Scope, we arm the team with the ability to do a better job of managing the scope of the project. After all, no matter how well understood the needs are, the team cannot do the impossible, and it will often be necessary to negotiate an acceptable deliverable before success can be achieved.
- In Team Skill 5, Refining the System Definition, we help the team organize the requirements information. Further, we introduce a set of techniques the team can use to elaborate on the system definition, or refine it to a level suitable to drive design and implementation, so that the entire extended team knows exactly what kind of system it is building.

- Finally, in Team Skill 6, Building the Right System, we cover some of the more technical aspects of design assurance, testing, and change management, and we show how traceability can be used to help ensure a quality outcome.

Team Members Have Different Skills

One of the most interesting things about teams is that individual team members have different skills. After all, that's what makes a team a team. Royce [1998] points out that

> *balance and coverage are two of the most important aspects of an excellent team. . . . A football team has a need for diverse skills, very much like a software development team. . . . There has rarely been a great football team that didn't have great coverage, offense, defense, and special teams, coaching and personnel, first string and reserve players, passing and running. Great teams need coverage across key positions with strong individual players. But a team loaded with superstars, all striving to set individual records and competing to be the team leader, can be embarrassed by a balanced team of solid players with a few leaders focused on the team result of winning the game.*

In the software team, we hope that some players have proven their ability to work with the *customers* effectively, that others have software *programming* abilities, and that others have *testing* abilities. Still other team players will need *design and architecture* abilities. Many more skills are required as well. We also expect that the requisite team skills for requirements management will affect various members of the teams in various ways. So, in a sense, we'll hope to further develop every team member's ability to help manage requirements effectively. And we'll try to indicate, where we can, which team members may be best suited to a particular and necessary skill.

The Organization of Software Teams

Software development is exceedingly complex, and the domains in which we apply our skills vary tremendously. It therefore seems unlikely that one specific way to organize a software team will work in all cases or is inherently more efficient than other approaches. Nonetheless, certain common elements occur in many successful teams. Therefore, we think it's important to establish a hypothetical team construct. But rather than invent an ideal team, which would be too easy and too academic, we decided to pattern our hypothetical team on a real software development team.

The team we'll model is based on a real-world software team that has proved effective in two major areas: (1) effective requirements management and (2) delivery on time and on budget. (Of course, we believe that this is an obvious cause-and-effect relationship!) Yet we also admit that many other skills must be present in a team that truly delivers the goods year in and year out. In our case study, the team works for a company called Lumenations, Ltd. that is developing a next-generation "home lighting automation system" for high-end residential use.

THE CASE STUDY

We can meet another objective in this book by developing a case study we can track from requirements start to requirements finish. In this way, we will be able to not only apply the techniques that we are about to discuss to our example but also provide example work products or artifacts (to further illustrate key points and to serve as examples for your own projects). Appendix A of this book provides a sample set of artifacts from the case study.

Background for the Case Study

Lumenations, Ltd. has been a worldwide supplier of commercial lighting systems for use in professional theater and amateur stage productions for more than 40 years. In 2001, its annual revenues peaked at approximately $120 million, and sales are flattening. Lumenations is a public company and the lack of growth in sales—no, worse, the lack of any reasonable prospect for improving growth in sales—is taking its toll on the company and its shareholders. The last annual meeting was quite uncomfortable, as there was little new to report about the company's prospects for growth. The stock climbed briefly to $25 per share last spring on a spate of new orders but has since crept back down to around $15.

The theater equipment industry as a whole is flat with little new development. The industry is mature and already well consolidated. Since Lumenations' stock is in the tank and its capitalization is only modest, acquisition is not an option for the company.

What's needed is a *new* marketplace, one not too remote from what the company does best but in which there is substantial opportunity for growth in revenue and profits. After completing a thorough market research project and spending many dollars on marketing consultants, the company has decided to enter a new market: *lighting automation for high-end residential systems*. This market is apparently growing at 25 percent to 35 percent each year. Even better, the market is immature, and none of the established players has a dominant market position. Lumenations' strong worldwide distribution channel will be a real asset in the marketplace, and the distributors are hungry for new products. Looks like a great opportunity!

The HOLIS Software Development Team

The project we choose will be the development of HOLIS, our code name for an innovative new HOme LIghting automation System to be marketed by Lumenations. The HOLIS team is typical in its size and scope. For the purposes of our case study, we've made it a fairly small team, composed of only 15 team members, but it's large enough to have all the necessary skills fairly well represented by individuals with some degree of specialization in their roles. Also, it's the structure of the team that's most important, and by adding more developers and testers, the structure of the HOLIS team scales well to a size of 30–50 people and commensurately larger software applications than HOLIS will require.

To address the new marketplace, Lumenations has set up a new division, the Home Lighting Automation Division. Since the division and technology are mostly new to Lumenations, the HOLIS team has been assembled mostly from new hires, although a few team members have been transferred from the Commercial Lighting Division.

Figure 4–1 is an organization chart of the development team and the relationships among those team members. We'll revisit this team periodically

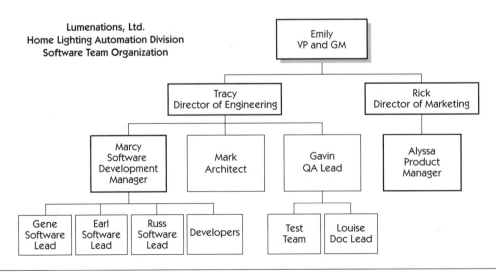

Figure 4–1   The HOLIS software development team

throughout the book and see how it applies its new skills to the requirements challenge for HOLIS.

SUMMARY

It's difficult for anyone to argue rationally *against* the idea of managing and documenting the requirements of a system in order to ensure that we deliver what the customer really wants. However, as we have seen, the data demonstrates that, as an industry, we often do a poor job of doing so. *Lack of user input, incomplete requirements and specifications*, and *changing requirements and specifications* are commonly cited problems in projects that failed to meet their objectives. And we know that a significant number of software projects do fail to meet their objectives.

A common attitude among developers and customers alike is, "Even if we're not really sure of the details of what we want, it's better to get started with implementation now, because we're behind schedule and in a hurry. We can pin down the requirements later." But all too often, this well-intentioned approach degenerates into a chaotic development effort, with no one quite sure what the user really wants or what the current system really does. With today's powerful and easy-to-use prototyping tools, there's a perception that if the developers can build a rough approximation of the user's needs in a prototype, the user can point out the features that need to be added, deleted, or modified. This *can* work, and it is an important aspect of iterative development. But, due in part to the extremely high cost of fixing requirements errors, this process must be within the context of an overall *requirements management strategy*—otherwise, chaos results.

How do we know what the system is supposed to do? How do we keep track of the current status of requirements? How do we determine the impact of a change? Issues like these cause requirements management to emerge as both a necessary and a practical software engineering discipline. We have introduced an encompassing philosophy of requirements management and have provided a set of definitions that support these activities.

Since the history of software development—and the future for at least as far as we can currently envision it—is one of increasing complexity, we also understand that the software development problem is one that must be addressed by well-structured and well-trained software *teams*. In the requirements management discipline in particular, every team member will eventually be involved in managing the requirements for the project. These teams must develop the requisite skills to understand the user needs, to manage the scope of the application, and to build systems that meet these user needs. The team must work, *as a team*, to address the requirements management challenge.

In order to do so, the first step in the requirements management process is to ensure that the developers understand the "problem" the user is trying to solve. We'll cover that topic in the next three chapters as Team Skill 1, Analyzing the Problem.

Team Skill 1

ANALYZING THE PROBLEM

Development teams tend to forge ahead, providing solutions based on an inadequate understanding of the problem to be solved.

The last few years have seen an unprecedented increase in the power of the tools and technologies that software developers use to build today's enterprise applications. New languages have increased the level of abstraction and improved the productivity with which we can address and solve user problems. The application of object-oriented methods has produced designs that are more robust and extensible. Tools for version management, requirements management, design and analysis, defect tracking, and automated testing have helped software developers manage the complexity of thousands of requirements and hundreds of thousands of lines of code.

As the productivity of the software development environment has increased, it should now be easier than ever before to develop systems that satisfy real business needs. However, as we have seen, the data demonstrates that we remain challenged in our ability to truly understand and to satisfy these needs. Perhaps there is a simpler explanation for this difficulty that may represent the "problem behind the problem." *Development teams spend too little time understanding the real business problems, the needs of the users and other stakeholders, and the nature of the environment in which their applications must thrive.* Instead, we developers tend to forge ahead, providing technological solutions based on an inadequate understanding of the problem to be solved.

The resulting systems do not fit the needs of the users and stakeholders as well as could have been reasonably expected. The consequences of this mismatch are inadequate economic rewards for the customers and developers of the system, dissatisfied users, and career challenges. It seems obvious, therefore, that an incremental investment in an analysis of the *problem* will produce handsome rewards downstream. The goals of this team skill are to provide guidelines for problem analysis and to define specific goals for this skill in application development.

In the following chapters, we will explore ways and means of defining just exactly what the problem is. After all, if your team can't define the problem, it's going to be difficult to develop a proper solution.

Chapter 5

THE FIVE STEPS
IN PROBLEM ANALYSIS

Key Points

- Problem analysis is the process of understanding real-world problems and user's needs and proposing solutions to meet those needs.

- The goal of problem analysis is to gain a better understanding of the problem being solved, *before* development begins.

- To identify the root cause, or the problem behind the problem, ask the people directly involved.

- Identifying the actors on the system is a key step in problem analysis.

This chapter focuses on ways in which the development team can understand the real-world needs of the stakeholders and users of a new system or application. As most systems are built to solve a particular problem, we'll use *problem analysis* techniques to make sure we understand what the problem is.

But we should also recognize that not every application is developed to solve a problem; some are built to take advantage of *opportunities* that the market presents, even when the existence of a problem is not clear. For example, unique software applications, such as SimCity and Doom, have proved their worth to those who like computer games and mental challenges or who just enjoy modeling and simulating or playing games on their computers. So, although it's difficult to say what problem SimCity or Doom solved—well, perhaps the problem of "not having enough fun things to do with your computer" or the problem of "too much spare time on one's hands"—it seems clear that the products provide real value to a large number of users.

In a sense, problems and opportunities are just flip sides of the same coin; your problem is my opportunity. It's a matter of perspective. But since most systems do address some identifiable problem, we can simplify the discussion and avoid the problem/opportunity schizophrenia by focusing on the problem side of the coin only. After all, we like to think of ourselves as problem solvers.

We'll define problem analysis as

> *the process of understanding real-world problems and user needs and proposing solutions to meet those needs.*

In so doing, the problem domain must be analyzed and understood, and a variety of solution domains must be explored. Usually, a variety of solutions are possible, and our job is to find the solution that is the optimum fit for the problem being solved.

In order to be able to *do* problem analysis, it would be helpful to define what a problem is. According to Gause and Weinberg [1989],

> *a problem can be defined as the difference between things as perceived and things as desired.*

This seems like a sensible definition, one that at least should eliminate the common problem of developers often thinking that the real problem is that the user doesn't understand what the real problem is! According to the definition, if the user perceives something as a problem, it's a real problem, and it's worthy of addressing.

Sometimes, the simplest solution is a workaround, or revised business process, rather than a new system.

Still, based on this definition, our colleague Elemer Magaziner notes that there are a number of ways to address a problem. For example, changing the user's *desire* or *perception* may be the most cost-effective approach. Doing so may be a matter of setting and managing expectations, providing workarounds or incremental improvements to existing systems, providing alternative solutions that do not require new system development, or providing additional training. Practical experience shows many examples where changing the perception of the difference has led to the highest-quality, fastest, and cheapest solutions available! As problem solvers, it is incumbent on us to explore these alternative solutions before leaping into a new system solution.

However, when these alternative activities fail to reduce the gap sufficiently in perception and desire, we are left with the largest and most expensive challenge: to actively change the distance between perception and reality. This we must accomplish by defining and implementing *new systems* that narrow the difference between *as desired* and *as perceived.*

As with any complex problem-solving exercise, we must start with the goal in mind. The goal of problem analysis is to gain a better understanding, before development begins, of the problem being solved. The specific steps that must be taken in order to achieve the goal are listed below.

> The goal of problem analysis is to gain a better understanding of the problem being solved before development begins.

1. Gain agreement on the problem definition.
2. Understand the root causes—the problem behind the problem.
3. Identify the stakeholders and the users.
4. Define the solution system boundary.
5. Identify the constraints to be imposed on the solution.

Let's work through each of these steps and see if we can develop the team skills we need to move on to providing solutions.

STEP 1: GAIN AGREEMENT ON THE PROBLEM DEFINITION

The first step is to gain agreement on the definition of the problem to be solved. One of the simplest ways to gain this agreement is to *simply write the problem down and see whether everyone agrees.*

As part of this process, it is often helpful to understand some of the benefits of a proposed solution, being careful to make certain that the benefits are described in the terms provided by the customers/users. Having the user describe the benefits provides additional contextual background on the real problem. In seeing the benefits from the customer's point of view, we also gain a better understanding of the stakeholder's view of the problem itself.

The Problem Statement

You may find it helpful to write your problem down in a standardized format (Table 5–1). Filling the table in for your application is a simple technique to help ensure that all stakeholders on your project are working toward the same goal.

Spending the time it takes to gain agreement on the problem being solved may seem like a small and insignificant step, and in most circumstances it is. But

Table 5–1   Problem Statement Format

Element	Description
The problem of . . .	Describe the problem.
Affects . . .	Identify stakeholders affected by the problem.
And results in . . .	Describe the impact of this problem on stakeholders and business activity.
Benefits of a solution . . .	Indicate the proposed solution and list a few key benefits.

sometimes it is not. For example, one of our clients, an equipment manufacturer, was engaged in a major upgrade to its IS/IT system, which provided invoicing and financial reporting between the company and its dealers. The theme for the new program was to "improve dealer communications." As such, the team had embarked on a significant new system development effort.

An exercise in gaining agreement on the problem being solved was enlightening. The development team–defined solution envisioned a powerful new system that provided better financial reporting, improved invoice and statement formats, online parts ordering, and the like. And oh, by the way, the team eventually *hoped* to provide the capability for electronic funds transfer between the company and the dealer.

During the problem statement exercise, company management had the opportunity to provide input. Management's vision was substantially different: the primary goal of the new system was to *provide electronic funds transfer that would improve the cash flow of the company.* After a raucous discussion, it became clear that the first-order problem to be addressed by the new system was electronic funds transfer; other dealer communication features were considered simply "nice to have." Needless to say, there was a substantial reorientation of the objectives of the new system, including a new problem definition that identified electronic funds transfer as the problem being solved. This reorientation also triggered the development of a different system architecture than had been envisioned, complete with the security capability consistent with the risks inherent in electronic banking.

STEP 2: UNDERSTAND THE ROOT CAUSES— THE PROBLEM BEHIND THE PROBLEM

Once you have an understanding of the larger problem, your team can use a variety of techniques to gain an understanding of its causes. One such technique is *root cause analysis*, which is a systematic way of uncovering the root, or underlying, cause of an identified problem or a symptom of a problem.

For example, consider a real-world example: a mail-order catalog company, which we'll call GoodsAreUs, manufactures and sells a variety of inexpensive, miscellaneous items for home and personal use. As the company addresses the problem of insufficient profitability, it uses total quality management (TQM) techniques for problem solving learned in its quality program. Based on this experience, the company quickly focused on its *cost of nonconformance*, which is the cost of all the things that go wrong and produce waste, scrap, and other excess costs. This cost includes rework, scrap, customer dissatisfaction, employee turnover, and other factors that are negative-value activities. As the company quantified its cost of nonquality, it suspected that production waste, or "scrap," was one of the largest contributors. This problem of excess scrap, then, is the next problem the company is trying to solve since it directly affects the larger problem of the cost of nonconformance, which in turn affects *profitability*.

But we are not yet done, for we must still understand the root cause, or the problem behind the problem in scrap, so we can discover a problem that we can directly fix. To do so, it is necessary to determine what factors contribute to the scrap problem. TQM teaches us the use of the *fishbone diagram* (see Figure 5–1) to identify the problems behind the problem. In our specific analysis, the company identified many sources that contributed to scrap. Each source was listed as one of the "bones" on the diagram.

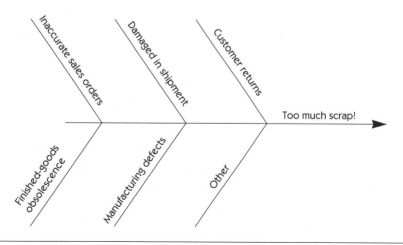

Figure 5–1   Fishbone diagram of root causes

OK, so how do you determine the root causes? Well, it just depends. In many cases, it's a simple matter of asking the people directly involved what they think the root cause is. It's amazing how much people *do* know about the problem behind the problem; it's just that no one—by which we usually mean management—had taken the time to *ask* them before. So, ask them, and then ask them *again*.

If the problem is more serious and simply asking those affected doesn't create a sense of comfort, it may be necessary to perform a detailed investigation of each contributing problem and to quantify its individual impact. This could vary from perhaps simple brainstorming by participants who have knowledge of the space to a small data collection project or, potentially, to a more rigorous experiment. In any case, the goal is to quantify the likely contribution of each root cause.

Addressing the Root Cause

Quality data demonstrates that many root causes are simply not worth fixing.

Of course, the engineer in all of us would like to fix *all* of the root causes on the "bones" of the diagram. This seems like the right thing to do. But is it? Often, it is not; *quality data routinely shows that a number of root causes are simply not worth fixing*, as the cost of the fix exceeds the cost of the problem. How do you know which ones to fix? *You must determine the materiality, or contribution, of each root cause.* The results of this investigation can be plotted as a Pareto chart or a simple histogram that visually exposes the real culprits.

Back to our example. Let's suppose that the data gathering produced the results shown in Figure 5–2. As you can see, the team discovered that a *single* root cause—"inaccurate sales orders"—produced half of all scrap. If, in turn, the existing sales order system was found to be a poor example of legacy code, complete with a user-vicious interface and nonexistent online error handling, there may indeed be opportunity to cut scrap through development of new software.

At this point, and *only at this point, is the team justified in proposing a replacement for the existing sales order entry system.* Finally, we have discovered a root cause problem that we can directly fix. Further, the cost justification for such a system is readily quantified by determining the estimated cost of development and the return on this investment through a reduction in scrap.

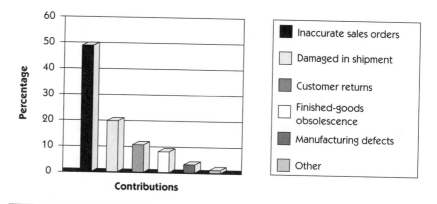

Figure 5–2 Pareto chart of root causes

Lest we lose the forest for the trees, however, let's look at the problem analysis sequence that got us here (Figure 5–3).

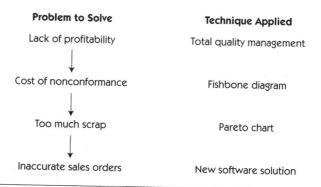

Figure 5–3 Applying different problem analysis techniques as a problem unfolds

A further fishbone analysis could then be used to determine what specific types of errors contribute to the inaccurate sales order problem. This new, more detailed data can then be used to define the features of the software system to address those errors. For our purposes, however, we can conclude our analysis by agreeing that a *replacement of the sales order system* can be at least a partial solution to the problem of too much scrap.

Once we have identified inaccurate sales orders as a root cause of a problem worth solving, we can create a problem statement for the sales order entry problem, as seen in Table 5–2.

Table 5–2   Sales Order Problem Statement

Element	Description
The problem of . . .	Inaccuracies in sales orders.
Affects . . .	Sales order personnel, customers, manufacturing, shipping, and customer service.
And results in . . .	Increased scrap, excessive handling costs, customer dissatisfaction, and decreased profitability.
Benefits of a solution . . .	That creates a new system to address the problem include ■ Increased accuracy of sales orders at point of entry ■ Improved reporting of sales data to management ■ Ultimately, higher profitability

Once written, the problem statement can be circulated to the stakeholders for comment and feedback. When finalized, the problem statement communicates the mission to all members of the project team so that everyone is working toward the same objective.

STEP 3: IDENTIFY THE STAKEHOLDERS AND THE USERS

Understanding the needs of the users and other stakeholders is a key factor in developing an effective solution.

Effectively solving any complex problem typically involves satisfying the needs of a diverse group of stakeholders. Stakeholders will typically have varying perspectives on the problem and various needs that must be addressed by the solution. We'll define a stakeholder as

anyone who could be materially affected by the implementation of a new system or application.

Many stakeholders are users of the system, and their needs are easy to focus on because they will be directly involved with system definition and use. However, some stakeholders are only *indirect* users of the system or are affected only by the business outcomes that the system influences. These stakeholders tend to be found elsewhere within the business, or in "the surrounds" of the particular application environment. In yet other cases, these stakeholders are even further removed from the application environment.

For example, they include the people and organizations involved in the development of the system, the subcontractors, the customer's customer, and outside agencies, such as the U.S. Federal Aviation Administration (FAA) or the Food and Drug Administration (FDA), or other agencies that interact with the system or the development process. Each of these classes of stakeholders may influence the requirements for the system or will in some way be involved with the system outcome.

Nonuser stakeholder needs must also be identified and addressed.

An understanding of who these stakeholders are and their particular needs is an important factor in developing an effective solution. Depending on the domain expertise of the development team, identifying the stakeholders may be a trivial or nontrivial step in problem analysis. Often, this simply involves interviewing decision makers, potential users, and other interested parties. The following questions can be helpful in this process.

- Who are the users of the system?
- Who is the customer (economic buyer) for the system?
- Who else will be affected by the outputs the system produces?
- Who will evaluate and approve the system when it is delivered and deployed?
- Are there any other internal or external users of the system whose needs must be addressed?
- Who will maintain the new system?
- Is there anyone else who cares?

In our example of a replacement sales order system, the primary and most obvious users were the sales order entry clerks. These users are obviously stakeholders in that their productivity, convenience, comfort, job performance, and job satisfaction are affected by the system. What other stakeholders can we identify?

Other stakeholders, such as the sales order entry supervisor, are directly affected by the system but access the system through different user interfaces and reports. Still other folks, such as the chief financial officer of the company, are clearly stakeholders in that the system can be expected to have an effect on the productivity, quality, and profitability of the company. Lest we forget, the IT director and members of the application development team are also stakeholders in that they will be responsible for developing and maintaining the system. They will have to live with the result, as will the users. Table 5–3 summarizes the results of the stakeholder analysis and identifies the users and stakeholders of the new sales order system.

Table 5–3   Users and Stakeholders of the New System

Users	Other Stakeholders
Sales order entry clerks	MIS director and development team
Sales order supervisor	Chief financial officer
Production control	Production manager
Billing clerk	

STEP 4: DEFINE THE SOLUTION SYSTEM BOUNDARY

Once the problem statement is agreed to and the users and stakeholders are identified, we can turn our attention to *defining a system* that can be deployed to address the problem. In so doing, we enter an important transition state wherein we have to keep two things in mind: an understanding of the problem and the considerations of a potential solution.

The next important step is to determine the boundaries of the solution system. The system boundary defines the border between the solution and the real world that surrounds the solution (Figure 5–4). In other words, the system boundary describes an envelope in which the solution system is contained. Information, in the form of inputs and outputs, is passed back and forth from the system to the users living outside the system. All interactions with the system occur via interfaces between the system and the external world.

Figure 5–4   The inputs/system/outputs relationship

We divide the world in two:
1. Our system
2. Things that interact with our system

In other words, if we are going to have to build it or modify it, it's part of our solution and within the boundary; if not, it's external to our system. Thus, we divide the world into two interesting classes of things:

1. Our system
2. Things that interact with our system

Let's identify the "things that interact with our system" generically as "actors on our system." After all, they do have a *role to play* in making our system do its thing. We'll represent an actor with a simple stick figure icon. We'll define an actor as

> *someone or something outside the system that interacts with the system.*

Actor

Once we understand the concept of an actor, we can illustrate a system boundary as shown in Figure 5–5.

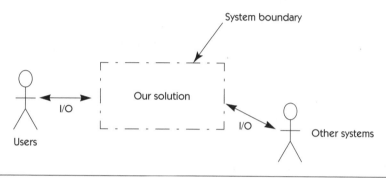

Figure 5–5   System boundary

In many cases, the boundaries of the system are obvious. For example, a single-user, shrink-wrap personal contact manager that runs on a stand-alone Windows 2000 platform has relatively well-defined boundaries. There is only one user and one platform. The interfaces between the user and the application consist of the interface dialogs the user uses to access information in the system and any output reports and communication paths the system uses to document or transmit that information.

In our order entry system example, which is to be integrated into an existing legacy system, the boundaries are not so clear. The analyst must determine whether data is shared with other applications, whether the new application is to be distributed across various hosts or clients, and who the users are. For example, should the production people have online access to sales orders? Is there a quality control or audit function to be provided? Will the system run on the mainframe or on a new client/server front end? Will specialized management reports be provided?

Although it seems fairly obvious, identifying the actors is a key analytical step in problem analysis. How do we find these actors? Here are some helpful questions to ask.

- Who will supply, use, or remove information from the system?
- Who will operate the system?
- Who will perform any system maintenance?
- Where will the system be used?
- Where does the system get its information?
- What other external systems will interact with the system?

With the answers to these questions in hand, the analyst can now create a "system perspective," a block diagram that describes the boundaries of the system, the users, and other interfaces. Figure 5–6 provides a simplified system perspective for the new sales order system.

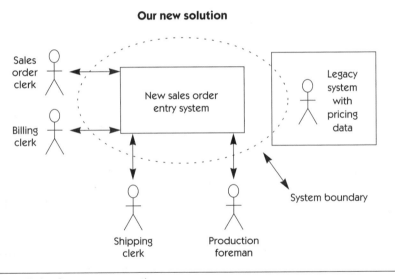

Figure 5–6   System perspective

The dotted line illustrates the system boundary for the proposed solution. The diagram shows that the bulk of the new application will be deployed on the new sales order entry system but a portion of the solution code must be developed and deployed on the existing legacy system. In other words, in order to solve our problem we will have to both develop a new system (new sales order entry system) and modify some elements of the existing system (legacy system).

STEP 5: IDENTIFY THE CONSTRAINTS TO BE IMPOSED ON THE SOLUTION

Before launching a well-intended trillion-dollar effort to revolutionize the state of the art in sales order entry, we must stop and consider the constraints that will be imposed on the solution. We'll define a constraint as

a restriction on the degree of freedom we have in providing a solution.

Each constraint has the potential to severely restrict our ability to deliver a solution as we envision it. Therefore, each constraint must be carefully considered as part of the planning process, and many may even cause us to reconsider the technological approach we initially imagined.

A variety of sources of constraints must be considered. These include schedule, return on investment, budget for labor and equipment, environmental issues, operating systems, databases, hosts and client systems, technical issues, political issues within the organization, purchased software, company policies and procedures, choices of tools and languages, personnel or other resource constraints, and a host of other considerations. These constraints may be given to us before we even begin ("No new hardware"), or we may have to actively elicit them.

As an aid to elicitation, it would be helpful to know what kinds of things we should be looking for. Table 5–4 lists potential sources of system constraints. Asking the questions listed in the table should elicit the majority of the constraints that will affect your solution. It will probably also be helpful to identify the rationale for the constraint, both to make sure that you understand the perspective of the constraint and so that you can recognize when and if the constraint might no longer apply to your solution. The less constrained the solution, the better.

Once identified, some of these constraints will become requirements for the new system ("use the Materials Requirements Planning system provided via our current accounting system vendor"). Other constraints will affect resources, implementation plans, and project plans. It is the problem solver's responsibility to understand the potential sources of constraints for each specific application environment and to determine the impact of each constraint on the potential solution spaces.

Returning to our example, Table 5–5 summarizes the sources and constraints imposed on the new sales order system.

> Constraints are restrictions on the degrees of freedom we have in providing a solution.

Table 5–4   Potential Sources of System Constraints

Source	Sample Considerations
Economics	▪ What financial or budgetary constraints apply? ▪ Are there costs of goods sold or any product pricing considerations? ▪ Are there any licensing issues?
Politics	▪ Do internal or external political issues affect potential solutions? ▪ Are there any interdepartmental problems or issues?
Technology	▪ Are we restricted in our choice of technologies? ▪ Are we constrained to work within existing platforms or technologies? ▪ Are we prohibited from using any new technologies? ▪ Are we expected to use any purchased software packages?
Systems	▪ Is the solution to be built on our existing systems? ▪ Must we maintain compatibility with existing solutions? ▪ What operating systems and environments must be supported?
Environment	▪ Are there environmental or regulatory constraints? ▪ Are there legal constraints? ▪ What are the security requirements? ▪ What other standards might restrict us?
Schedule and resources	▪ Is the schedule defined? ▪ Are we restricted to existing resources? ▪ Can we use outside labor? ▪ Can we expand resources? Temporarily? Permanently?

Table 5–5   Sources of Constraints and Their Rationale for Sales Order Entry System

Source	Constraint	Rationale
Operations	An exact copy of sales order data must remain on the legacy database for up to one year.	The risk of data loss is too great; we will need to run in parallel for three months.
Systems	The applications footprint on the server must be less than 20MB.	We have limited server memory available.
Equipment budget	The system must be developed on the existing server and host; new client hardware for users may be provided.	We need to control costs and maintain the existing systems.
Personnel budget	Staffing resources are fixed; no outsourcing is possible.	The current budget calls for fixed operating costs.
Technology mandate	A new object-oriented methodology should be used.	We believe that this technology will increase productivity and increase the reliability of the software.

SUMMARY

After completing this problem analysis activity, we can be reasonably confident that we have

- A good understanding of the problem to be solved and the root causes of the problem
- Proper identification of the stakeholders whose collective judgment will ultimately determine the success or failure of our system
- An understanding of where the boundaries of the solution are likely to be found
- An understanding of the constraints and the degrees of freedom we have to solve the problem

In other words, we are now better prepared for the journey ahead.

LOOKING AHEAD

With this background, we can now turn our attention to two more specific problem analysis techniques that can be applied in certain application domains. In Chapter 6, we'll look at *business modeling,* a technique we can apply to IS/IT applications. In Chapter 7, we'll look at *systems engineering* for software-intensive systems, which can be applied to applications in the embedded-system domain.

As for the third domain, that of the ISVs, problem analysis techniques are typically focused on such activities as the following:

- Identifying market opportunities and market segments
- Identifying classes of potential users and their particular needs
- Studying the demographics of the potential user base
- Understanding potential demand, pricing, and pricing elasticity
- Understanding sales strategies and distribution channels

Clearly, these are interesting topics to a software product company, but to help us manage the scope of this book, we will not discuss these specific issues further. However, you can rest assured that the team skills we explore in later chapters apply equally well to this class of application, as we will illustrate.

Note: One of the most difficult things about writing this book was attempting to present a variety of techniques to build the team skills sets. No one technique works in all situations; no two situations are the same.

In prior chapters, we focused on a general philosophical approach to problem analysis that appears to work in most systems contexts. However, the problem of selecting a technique to apply becomes even more acute in the following chapters of the book, wherein we define a technique for business modeling and a technique for systems engineering, and then go on to define a variety of techniques in Team Skill 2, Understanding User and Stakeholder Needs, where we present a wide variety of techniques you can use to understand the needs of stakeholders and users with respect to a system you are about to build.

However, we think it's important to point out that the techniques described in this book—from problem analysis to brainstorming—can be used in many different parts of the software process, not just in the part of the process where we have chosen to describe them. For example, the team could use problem analysis to define a sales order entry system problem or to resolve a technical problem within its implementation. Similarly, the team could use brainstorming to determine the potential root causes in a problem analysis exercise or to determine potential new features for a system. We make no attempt to describe every circumstance under which a particular technique will apply; instead, we focus on helping the team develop the skills we describe so that it can add these techniques to its bag of tricks—to be pulled out and used at appropriate points in the project.

Chapter 6

BUSINESS MODELING

Key Points

- Business modeling is a problem analysis technique especially suitable for the IS/IT environment.
- The business model is used to help define systems and their applications.
- A business use-case model, consisting of actors and use cases, is a model of the intended functions of the business.
- A business object model describes the entities that deliver the functionality to realize the business use cases and how these entities interact.

In the context of the IS/IT environment, and in the context of ISV applications that work with disparate systems and other applications, the first problem to be solved has an even broader context than we described in Chapter 5. In this environment business, system, and organizational complexity abounds, and one typically needs to understand some of this complexity before even attempting to define a specific problem worth solving. This environment consists not simply of a user or two and their interface to a computer but rather of organizations, business units, departments, functions, wide area networks, the corporate intranet and extranet, customers, users, human resources, material requirement planning (MRP) systems, inventory, existing applications, and more.

In addition, even when we are focused on a specific application to be implemented, we must continually remind ourselves of the broader context in which the application operates. Perhaps this can be accomplished successfully by asking the right questions, but as with any technique, there's more that can be done in a specific context than in the more generic case.

In these contexts, it would be helpful to have a technique to determine answers to an even broader set of questions such as the following.

- Why build a system at all?
- Where should it be located?
- How can we determine what functionality is optimum to locate on a particular node in the system?
- When should we use manual-processing steps or workarounds?
- When should we consider restructuring the organization itself in order to solve the problem?

Fortunately, there is a technique that's well suited to addressing this particular problem, and that technique is *business modeling*.

THE PURPOSE OF BUSINESS MODELING

Within the context of this book, we can think of the terms *business* and *business modeling* in the broadest possible context. For example, your business may be the business of developing software or manufacturing welding robots, or you may wish to model a not-for-profit business or service organization or an intradepartmental process or internal workflow.

In any case, the purpose of business modeling is threefold:

1. To understand the structure and dynamics of the existing organization
2. To ensure that customers, end users, and developers have a common understanding of the organization
3. To understand how to deploy new systems to facilitate productivity and which existing systems may be affected by that new system

Business modeling gives the team a logical approach to defining where software applications can improve the productivity of the business and helps determine requirements for those applications.

USING SOFTWARE ENGINEERING TECHNIQUES FOR BUSINESS MODELING

Of course, a variety of techniques can be applied to business modeling. However, it's convenient that, as software developers, we have at our disposal a rich set of tools and techniques we already use to model our software. Indeed, we

With the right choice of business modeling technique, some of the work products, such as use cases and object models, will be useful in the solution activity.

already know how to model entities (objects and classes), relationships (dependencies, associations, and so on), complex processes (sequences of activities, state transitions, events, conditionality, and so on), and other constructs that occur naturally in the context of designing our software applications.

If we could apply these same techniques to business modeling, we would be speaking the same language in both contexts. For example, a "thing," such as a payroll withholding stub, described in the business domain might relate to a "thing" that appears again in the software domain—a payroll withholding record, for example. If we can be fortunate enough to use the same (or very similar) techniques for both problem analysis and solution design, the two activities can share these same work products.

Choosing the Right Technique

Historically, we have seen that modeling techniques that were developed and matured in the software domain inspire new ways of visualizing an organization. Since object-oriented visual modeling techniques have become common for new software projects, using similar techniques in the business domain comes naturally. This methodology has been well developed by Jacobson, Ericsson, and Jacobson [1995] and others.

The 1980s and 1990s saw a rapid proliferation of both business modeling techniques and software development methodologies. However, they were all different! At the center of this activity were the various object-oriented (OO) methods and notations developed by various software engineering experts and methodologists.[1] Fortunately, these methodology "wars" are over, and the industry has settled on an industry standard—the Unified Modeling Language (UML)—for modeling software-intensive systems.

The Unified Modeling Language

In late 1997, this graphical language "for visualizing, specifying, constructing, and documenting the artifacts of a software intensive system" was adopted as an industry standard [Booch, Jacobson, and Rumbaugh 1999]. The UML

---

1. Various OO methods included the Booch method by Grady Booch from Rational Software; the Object Modeling Technique by James Rumbaugh, then at GE; Responsibility-Driven Design by Rebecca Wirfs-Brock at Tektronix; Object Oriented Software Engineering by Ivar Jacobson, then at Objectory in Sweden; the Coad-Yourdon method by Peter Coad and Ed Yourdon; and a half dozen more.

provides a set of modeling elements, notations, relationships, and rules for use that could be applied to a software development activity. However, the UML can also be used to model other domains, such as systems modeling and business modeling. A tutorial on the UML is outside the scope of this book. (For this, refer to the three companion books on the UML: Booch, Jacobson, and Rumbaugh [1999], *The Unified Modeling Language User Guide;* Jacobson, Booch, and Rumbaugh [1999], *The Unified Software Development Process;* and Rumbaugh, Jacobson, and Booch [1998], *The Unified Modeling Language Reference Manual.*) Nonetheless, we will use some key concepts from the UML in this section and will build on this foundation in succeeding sections of this book.

Business Modeling Using UML Concepts

One of the goals of business models is to develop a model of the business that can be used to drive application development. Two key modeling constructs that can be used for this purpose are a *business use-case model* and a *business object model.*

A *business use-case model* is a model of the intended functions of the business and is used as an essential input to identify roles and deliverables in the organization. As such, the business use-case model consists of the *actors* (users and systems that interact with the business) and the *use cases* (sequences of events through which the actors interact with the business elements to get their jobs done). Together, the actors and the use cases describe who is involved in the business activities and how these activities take place. Figure 6–1 shows the business use-case model. Note that the oval icon used to represent the business use case has a slash, indicating a business-level use case rather than a system-level use case.[2]

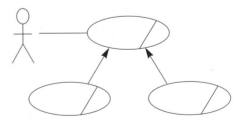

Figure 6–1   Business use-case model

2. The icon is one of many standard UML stereotypes. For further discussion of the modeling icons, see Rational Software Corporation [2002].

A business use-case model, then, consists of business actors and business use cases, with the actors representing roles external to the business (for example, employees and customers) and the business use cases representing processes. Examples of a business use-case model might be

- "Deliver electronic pay stub to employee."
- "Meet with customer to negotiate contract terms."

Examples of business actors are

- "Customer"
- "Employee"
- "Software developer"

The *business object model* describes the entities—departments, paychecks, systems—and how they interact to deliver the functionality necessary to realize the business use cases. Figure 6–2 represents the business object model. The actor-circle icon represents a worker who appears within the business process, such as a payroll clerk or a system administrator. The slashed circle without an actor represents a business entity or something that business workers produce, such as a paycheck or a ball bearing or a source file.[3]

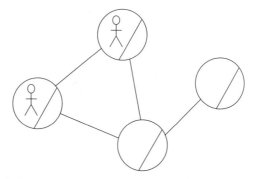

Figure 6–2 Business object model

A business object model may also include business use-case realizations that show how the business use cases are "performed" in terms of interacting business workers and business entities. To reflect groups or departments in

---

3. Ibid.

an organization, business workers and business entities may be grouped into organizational units.

Taken together, the two models provide a comprehensive overview of how the business works and allow the development team to focus on the areas in which systems can be provided that will improve the overall efficiency of the business. The models also help the team understand what changes will have to take place within the business processes themselves in order for the new system to be effectively implemented.

FROM THE BUSINESS MODEL TO THE SYSTEMS MODEL

One advantage of this approach to business modeling is the clear and concise way of showing dependencies between models of the business and models of the system (Figure 6–3). This clarity improves the productivity of the soft-

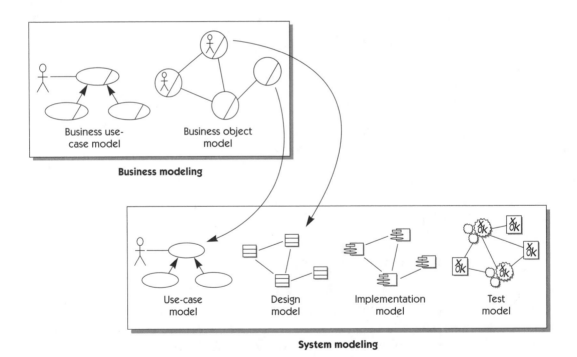

Figure 6–3   Business/system models

ware development process and also helps ensure that the system being developed solves the real business need.

The translation between the two can be summarized briefly as follows.

- Business workers will become actors on the system we are developing.
- Behaviors described for business workers are things that can be automated, so they help us find system use cases and define needed functionality.
- Business entities are things we may want the system to help us maintain, so they help us find entity classes in the analysis model of the system.

In performing the translation, business modeling facilitates the process of moving from an understanding of the business and problems within the business to the potential applications that may be implemented to deliver solutions to the problems identified.

WHEN TO USE BUSINESS MODELING

Business modeling is not something we recommend for every software engineering effort. Business models add the most value when the application environment is complex and multidimensional, and when many people are directly involved in using the system. For example, if you were adding an additional feature to an existing telecommunication switch, you might not consider business modeling. On the other hand, if you were building the order entry system for GoodsAreUs, we could have used business modeling to good advantage to support problem analysis.

SUMMARY

In this chapter, we discussed a specific problem analysis technique, business modeling. In so doing, we defined

- Why you might need to model the business
- How, using the UML, we transpose techniques developed for software engineering and use them for business modeling
- What the two primary artifacts of business modeling are: the business use-case model and the business object model
- How you can define software applications and derive software requirements from models of the business

LOOKING AHEAD

In the next chapter, we'll look at systems engineering of software systems, another problem analysis technique that will help give shape to applications of the embedded-systems type.

Chapter 7

SYSTEMS ENGINEERING OF SOFTWARE-INTENSIVE SYSTEMS

Key Points

- Systems engineering is a problem analysis technique especially suitable for embedded-systems development.

- Systems engineering helps us understand the requirements imposed on software applications that run within the solution system.

- Requirements flowdown is primarily a matter of ensuring that all system requirements are filled by a subsystem or a set of subsystems collaborating.

- Today, the system design must often be optimized for software costs rather than for hardware costs.

In Chapter 6, we looked at business modeling, a problem analysis technique for IS/IT applications. Business modeling helps us determine what application we should build and where we should run that application, within the context of the computing environment of the company and the departments, buildings, and political and physical constructs of the company itself. In other words, this analysis can help us determine *why* and *where* an application should come into existence. In so doing, of course, we make a subtle shift from the *problem space* to an initial look at the *solution space*, wherein the functionality that resolves the problem will exist on one or more applications that meet the user's ultimate need.

In the embedded-systems business, however, the problem domain and the solution domain look entirely different. Instead of departments, people, and processes, the domains consist of connectors and power supplies, racks of equipment, electronic and electrical components, hydraulic and fluidic handling devices, other software systems, mechanical and optics subsystems, and the like. Here, business modeling cannot always provide value. Instead, we must look to a different strategy to help us determine the *why* and *where* questions. Here we find ourselves in the realm of the *systems engineer.*

WHAT IS SYSTEMS ENGINEERING?

According to the International Council on Systems Engineering [INCOSE 2003]:

> *Systems engineering is an interdisciplinary approach and means to enable the realization of successful systems. It focuses on defining customer needs and required functionality early in the development cycle, documenting requirements, then proceeding with design synthesis and system validation while considering the complete problem:*
>
> - *Operations*
> - *Performance*
> - *Test*
> - *Manufacturing*
> - *Cost and Schedule*
> - *Training and Support*
> - *Disposal*
>
> *Systems engineering integrates all the disciplines and specialty groups into a team effort forming a structured development process that proceeds from concept to production to operation. Systems Engineering considers both the business and the technical needs of all customers with the goal of providing a quality product that meets the user needs.*

Phew. That's a long one. Clearly, we won't be providing a comprehensive discussion of systems engineering in this book. However, from the definition provided, we can apply systems engineering as a *problem analysis technique*, one that we can use in certain circumstances to understand the problems our applications are intended to solve. (For more on systems engineering, see Rechtin and Maier [1997].)

In this context, *systems engineering helps us understand the requirements that are going to be imposed on any software applications that run within the solution system.* In other words, we'll apply systems engineering as a problem analysis technique to help us understand the requirements for our software applications, whether they run on an embedded microprocessor or a Linux server within the context of a worldwide telecommunications system.

Pragmatic Principles of Systems Engineering

Systems
engineering
provides
eight pragmatic
principles.

If we choose to view systems engineering as a problem analysis technique, the specific steps, or at least the basic principles of the discipline, should provide us with the process we need to apply to use systems engineering to analyze the problem in our requirements context. The INCOSE Systems Engineering Practices working group [INCOSE 1993] defined a basic set of eight systems engineering principles.

1. Know the problem, know the customer, and know the consumer.
2. Use effectiveness criteria based on needs to make the system decisions.
3. Establish and manage requirements.
4. Identify and assess alternatives so as to converge on a solution.
5. Verify and validate requirements and solution performance.
6. Maintain the integrity of the system.
7. Use an articulated and documented process.
8. Manage against a plan.

This list identifies some pragmatic systems engineering principles. In fact, however, a subset of the systems engineering discipline is based on another process, the successive decomposition of complex systems into simpler ones.

The Composition and Decomposition of Complex Systems

With this process a complex problem, the system (Figure 7–1), is decomposed into smaller problems—subsystems (Figure 7–2). Each subsystem can be reasoned about, successfully designed and manufactured, and then integrated to produce the solution system. The engineering disciplines that support the approach to system decomposition are implied in the attributes of the preceding definition, such as understanding the operational characteristics, manufacturability, testability, and so on.

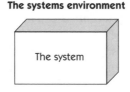

Figure 7–1 A system in its environment

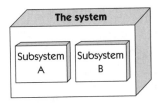

Figure 7-2   A system composed of two subsystems

This decomposition (or successive refinement) process proceeds until the systems engineer achieves the *right* results, as provided by quantitative measures that are specific to that particular systems engineering domain. In most cases, the subsystems defined in the initial composition are themselves further decomposed into subsubsystems, with the result appearing as in Figure 7–3.

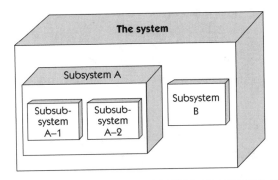

Figure 7-3   A system composed of two subsystems, one of which contains two subsubsystems

In the most complex systems, this process continues until a large number of subsystems are developed. (The F22 fighter aircraft, for example, is said to be composed of 152 such subsystems.)

The systems engineer knows that the job is done and is "right" when the following conditions are met.

- Distribution and partitioning of functionality are optimized to achieve the overall functionality of the system with minimal costs and maximum flexibility.
- Each subsystem can be defined, designed, and built by a small, or at least modest-sized, team.

- Each subsystem can be manufactured within the physical constraints and technologies of the available manufacturing processes.
- Each subsystem can be reliably tested as a subsystem, subject to the availability of suitable fixtures and harnesses that simulate the interfaces to the other system.
- Appropriate deference is given to the physical domain—the size, weight, location, and distribution of the subsystems—that has been optimized in the overall system context.

REQUIREMENTS ALLOCATION IN SYSTEMS ENGINEERING

Requirements
flowdown allo-
cates system
functionality
to subsystems.

Assuming that the systems engineering has resulted in a good job of defining the requirements for the system, the requirements management problem is still not complete. What of these subsystems? What requirements are to be imposed on them? In some cases, the process is one of assigning a system-level requirement to a subsystem. (For example, "Subsystem B will execute the wind speed algorithm and drive the heads-up display.") This *requirements flowdown* process is primarily a matter of making sure that all system requirements are fulfilled by a subsystem somewhere or by a set of subsystems collaborating together.

On Derived Requirements

Sometimes we discover that we have created a completely new requirements class—*derived requirements*—that must be imposed on the subsystem(s). Typically, there are two subclasses of derived requirements.

1. *Subsystem requirements* are those that must be imposed on the subsystems themselves but do not necessarily provide a direct benefit to the end user. (For example, "Subsystem A must execute the algorithm that computes the wind speed of the aircraft.")
2. *Interface requirements* may arise when the subsystems need to communicate with one another to accomplish an overall result. They will need to share data, power, or a useful computing algorithm. In these cases, the creation of subsystems also further engenders the creation of *interfaces* between subsystems (see Figure 7–4).

But are these derived requirements "true" requirements? Do we treat them the same as other requirements? They don't seem to meet the definitions in Chapter 2 (although they may well meet the definitions of design constraints that we'll provide in Chapter 20).

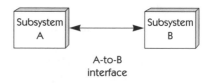

Figure 7–4   Interface between two subsystems

The important thing to recognize is that these requirements, although crucial to the project success, are derived from the systems decomposition process. As such, alternative decompositions would have created alternative derived requirements, so these requirements are not first-class citizens in the sense that they do not reflect requirements that came from the customer. However, from the viewpoint of a subsystem supplier, they *are* first-class citizens because they reflect requirements imposed by the supplier's customer (the system developer).

No magic answer exists. How we treat these requirements is based on the development team's role in the project, the systems decomposition, and other technological factors. The important thing is "to know how we got here" and to treat derived requirements appropriately to the case since they will ultimately affect the ability of the system to do its job, as well as the maintainability and robustness of the system.

A Quiet Revolution

In industry after industry, the intelligence of the device has moved from the hardware components to the software components.

Systems engineering has traditionally been a discipline applied primarily to physical systems, such as aircraft and airframes, brakes and brake pads, power supplies and power-consuming devices, and so on. However, during the last twenty or so years, a quiet revolution has occurred in the systems engineering of complex systems. Gradually, in transportation, telecommunication, industrial equipment, medical equipment, scientific instruments, and many others industries, the systems and devices have become smarter and smarter. To meet this increasing demand for complexity and sophistication, more and more of the delivered functionality has become allocated to software subsystems rather than to hardware components. Software is *softer*, after all, and many algorithms for measuring, metering, assaying, and detecting are much easier, or at least much cheaper in terms of parts cost, to implement in software than they are in hardware. More important, they are much easier to change as they evolve.

So, in industry after industry, the innate intelligence of the device has moved from the hardware components, where they were previously implemented in a combination of electrical and electronic systems, mechanical systems, and even physical chemistry systems, to the software components, where they are implemented in software or firmware on microprocessors or complete mini-computer subsystems.

When Generations Collide: Graying Baby Boomer Meets Generation X-er

For decades, systems engineers were some of the most senior project engineers in the industry. Battle-scarred and field-tested, many of these *senior systems engineers* were specialists in specific disciplines, such as mechanical and electronic engineering, and many were some of the best generalists on the team. They had witnessed the largest disasters and had experienced many triumphs. Older and wiser, they knew the specific application domain—radios, airplanes, HVAC, robotics, materials-handling equipment—incredibly well and were also aware of the differing technical, economic, and political facets of technology implementation.

Suddenly, a new breed of individual invaded their turf. These newcomers—the *programmers*, or on a good day, software engineers—were relatively inexperienced in complex systems and didn't know weight and balance or global systems optimization from their navels, but they could make a microprocessor sing in assembly language. In addition, they seem to have been formed from a different gene pool, or at least a different generation, which added the complexities of culture and generation clash to the systems engineering process. Many interesting situations developed.

For a while, the turf battle was even, and the systems engineers made the ultimate calls for systems partitioning and allocation of functionality. However, in many industries, software technology gradually took over, and systems engineering became dominated, at least in part, by the need to engineer for flexible *software* functionality within the system. There were a number of solid technical reasons for this transition. Over time, a number of facts became obvious.

- Software, not hardware, determines the ultimate functionality of the system and the success of the system in the end user's hands and in the marketplace.
- Software, not hardware, consumes the majority of the costs of research and systems development.

- Software, not hardware, is on the critical path and, therefore, ultimately determines when the system goes to the marketplace.
- Software, not hardware, absorbs most of the changes that occur during development and can even evolve to meet the changing needs of a system deployed in the field.

And perhaps most surprisingly:

- The cost of software development and maintenance, taken in the aggregate and amortized over the full life of the product, has become material to, or in some cases equal to or greater than, the contribution of hardware costs of goods sold to that holy grail of systems manufacturers: *total manufacturing costs.*

Many systems must now be optimized for software, not hardware, capability.

This last one was a killer because it meant the systems engineers had to consider optimizing the system not for hardware or manufacturing costs but for *development, maintenance, evolution, and enhancement of the software contained in the system.* This changed the game significantly, for now, the systems engineering had to be performed with one eye on the computers to be used. Often, this meant:

- Maximizing the system's ability to execute software by providing more than adequate computing resources, even at the expense of cost of goods sold, adding more microprocessors, RAM, ROM, mass storage, bandwidth, or whatever resources the system requires to execute its software
- Providing adequate communication interfaces between subsystems and ensuring that the communications mechanism chosen (Ethernet, Firewire, serial port, or single data line) is extensible, via the addition of software, not hardware

In turn, this change affected the requirements management challenge in two ways.

1. Each of these dimensions creates new requirements that the hardware system must fulfill in order for a successful solution to be built.
2. The bulk of the requirements problem moved to the software application.

Fortunately, at least for the latter point, that is the subject of this book, and we hope to prepare you well for this particular problem.

Avoiding the Stovepipe System Problem

This is all, or at least mostly, well and good. Dealing with systems of complexity requires nontrivial approaches, and a system of subsystems is a means to this end. Surely, the alternatives are worse; we would end up with incredibly complex systems that no one could possibly understand, with indeterminate behavior, and design based on shared functionality, poor partitioning, and threaded code in such a way as could never be unraveled. Systems engineering seems like a good thing.

How does this affect requirements management? When the final tally is made, we may discover that subsystem requirements are far more numerous than external requirements, or those that affect the behavior of the system in the user's environment. In the end, we will invest far more in prioritizing, managing, and identifying the subsystem requirements than those that affect the end user. This doesn't seem like a completely positive thing.

And what happens if we don't do a good job of systems engineering? The system will become brittle and will resist change because the weight of the requirements assets will "bind" us to the implementation. Our subsystem requirements have taken control of our design flexibility, and a change in one will have a ripple effect in other subsystems. These are the "stovepipe" systems of legend, and such systems *resist* change. In their interfaces, the problems may be worse. If the interfaces are not properly specified, the system will be fragile and will not be able to evolve to meet changing needs without the wholesale replacement of interfaces and entire subsystems on both sides.

When Subsystems Are Subcontracts

A further complication often arises. Since subsystems are typically developed by different teams—after all, that's one of the reasons we create subsystems—the subsystem requirements and interfaces tend, in effect, to become *contracts* between the teams. ("My subsystem delivers the results of the wind speed computation in exactly this format. . . .") Indeed, in some cases, the subsystem may be developed by a subcontractor whose pay stub has a different logo from yours. In this case, our requirements challenge has left the system and technical context and has instead become a political "football." ("Darn. The requirements cannot be changed unless the contract is renegotiated.") Soon, the project can be all "bound up in its shorts." A word of warning: *Many large-scale system efforts have met their death at the hands of this problem.*

Addressing the Conundrum

What should we do? Well, doing a good job of systems engineering must be a primary goal when dealing with software applications that have system-level complexities. As you participate in this activity for software-intensive systems, you may want to consider the following recommendations.

- Develop, understand, and maintain the high-level requirements and use cases that span the subsystems and that describe the overall system functionality. These use cases will provide context for how the system is supposed to work and will make sure that you "don't miss the forest for the trees." They will also help ensure that the systems architecture is designed to support the most likely usage scenarios.
- Do the best possible job of partitioning and isolating functionality within subsystems. Use object technology principles—encapsulation and information hiding, interface by contract, messaging rather than data sharing—in your systems engineering work.
- If possible, develop software as a whole, not as several individual pieces, one for each physical subsystem. One of the characteristics of stovepipe systems is that on both sides of the interface (well or poorly defined), the software needs to reconstruct the state of key elements (objects) needed for making decisions on both sides; unlike hardware, the allocation of requirements to both sides does not represent a clear partition.
- When coding the interfaces, use common code on both sides of the interface. Otherwise, there will likely be subtle variations, often blamed on "optimizations," that will make this synchronization of states very difficult. Then, if the boundary between the two physical subsystems later disappears—that is, systems engineering finds out that processors are good enough to support both subsystems A and B—software engineers will have a hard time "merging" the two bodies of software.
- Define interface specifications that can do more than would be necessary to simply meet the known conditions. Invest in a little extra bandwidth, an extra I/O port, or some integrated circuit real estate to provide room for expansion.
- Finally, see whether you can find one of those graybeards to help you with your systems engineering. They've been down this path before, and their experience will serve you wisely. Besides, you might help close another generation gap in the process!

A Story: On Partitioning Large-Scale Software Systems into Subsystems for Distributed Development Teams

In class one day, Bill, an experienced software manager, approached us and stated his problem. We had the following dialogue.

BILL: We are building a large-scale application that runs on a single host system. Our development resources consist of two separate teams of 30 people each; one team lives on the east side of the river in New York City, and the other lives on the west side. The two teams have different managers and different competencies. How can we divide the work and create a system that will run when we are done?

US: Well, Bill, one way to think of this problem is as a systems engineering problem. That is, figure out how you would partition the system into two sensible subsystems. Call them East and West, and allocate requirements to the subsystems as if they were in separate physical systems. Define an interface, complete with the definition of common classes and common services to be used, that allows the two subsystems (applications) to cooperate to accomplish the overall system functionality.

BILL: But won't I have then created an arbitrary system that is not driven by true architectural concerns?

US: True enough, in the technical sense. However, separating concerns along project team logistical lines and specific competencies may be just as important.

BILL: But won't I also create artificial interfaces and a potential stovepipe system?

US: Yes, in a sense, but we'd recommend that you have the interface code for both sides developed by only one team. Otherwise, there will be a lot of redundant work done between the two teams. In so doing, you will indeed create new requirements for the system, including interfaces that would otherwise not have been necessary, or at least not as formalized as you will now make them. And yes, it's important to be aware of the stovepipe problem and to do everything you can to minimize coupling between systems and to minimize the political issues that are likely to result.

THE CASE STUDY: SYSTEMS ENGINEERING FOR HOLIS

So much for a brief introduction to systems engineering. Now let's try to apply what we have learned to HOLIS, our HOme LIghting automation System. At this point, we haven't spent much time trying to understand the requirements for HOLIS. We'll do that in later chapters of the book. So, in a sense, systems engineering is premature. On the other hand, we probably understand enough to make some first-level system design decisions, based on our experience and our understanding of likely requirements. In any case, we haven't committed anything to hardware or software yet, and we can revisit these decisions later. In addition, in the iterative process described in Chapter 3 we were forewarned that we'll visit systems architecture and system requirements interactively, so this is not a bad time to begin.

Preliminary User Needs

Let's assume that a few reasonably well-understood user needs have already been defined for HOLIS.

- HOLIS will need to support "soft" key switches—individually programmable key switches used to activate the lighting features in various rooms.
- Homeowners have requested a means to program HOLIS from a remote center so they can simply call in their needs and not be bothered with "programming" HOLIS at all.
- Other prospective buyers have requested that HOLIS be programmable from their home PCs and that they be provided with the ability to do all the installation, programming, and maintenance themselves.
- Still others have requested that the system provide a simple, push-button, control panel–type interface they can use to change HOLIS programming, vacation settings, and so on, without having to use a PC.
- HOLIS needs to provide an emergency-contact system of some kind.

Problem Analysis

In analyzing the problem, the team discovered that there were actually three different groups of stakeholders, each of whom saw the problem differently. The team decided to develop three problem statements, the first of which seemed to state the obvious problem from the company's perspective (Table 7–1).

Next, the team also decided to see whether it could understand the "problem" from the perspectives of a future customer (end user) and potential distributors/builders (Lumenations' customers). The team developed the problem statements shown in Tables 7–2 and 7–3, respectively.

Table 7–1   Problem Statement for Lumenations

Element	Description
The problem of . . .	Slowing growth in the company's core professional theater marketplaces.
Affects . . .	The company, its employees, and its shareholders.
And results in . . .	Unacceptable business performance and lack of substantive opportunities for growth in revenue and profitability.
Benefits of a solution . . .	Involving new products and a potential new marketplace for the company's products and services include ■ Revitalization of the company and its employees ■ Increased loyalty and retention of the company's distributors ■ Higher revenue growth and profitability ■ Upturn in the company's stock price

Table 7–2   Problem Statement for the Homeowner

Element	Description
The problem of . . .	The lack of product choices, limited functionality, and the high cost of existing home lighting automation systems.
Affects . . .	The homeowners of high-end residential systems.
And results in . . .	Unacceptable performance of the purchased systems or, more often than not, a decision not to automate.
Benefits of a solution . . .	That comprised the "right" lighting automation solution could include ■ Higher homeowner satisfaction and pride of ownership ■ Increased flexibility and usability of the residence ■ Improved safety, comfort, and convenience

Table 7–3   Problem Statement for the Distributor

Element	Description
The problem of . . .	The lack of product choices, limited functionality, and the high cost of existing home lighting automation systems.
Affects . . .	The distributors and builders of high-end residential systems.
And results in . . .	Few opportunities for marketplace differentiation and no new opportunities for higher-margin products.
Benefits of a solution . . .	That comprised the "right" lighting automation solution could include ■ Differentiation ■ Higher revenues and higher profitability ■ Increased market share

HOLIS: The System, Actors, and Stakeholders

From a systems perspective, our first impression of the HOLIS system is simply that of a system inside the homeowner's house. Figure 7–5 is a simple systems diagram showing HOLIS in the context of the homeowner's home.

Step 3 of problem analysis requires that we *identify the stakeholders and users of the system*. Step 4 is to *define the system boundary of the solution system*. Given the additional user needs data we have just been given, we can now improve our understanding of HOLIS's system context by identifying the four actors that will interact with HOLIS (Figure 7–6).

1. The homeowner who uses HOLIS to control the lighting
2. The various lights that HOLIS, in turn, controls
3. Lumenations Services, the manufacturer that has the ability to remotely dial HOLIS and perform the remote programming
4. Emergency Receiver, an undefined actor who will likely receive emergency messages

Of course, the team also discovers that a number of *"nonactor" stakeholders*, both internal and external to the company, care about the requirements for HOLIS, as Table 7–4 shows.

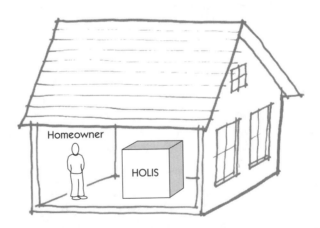

Figure 7–5   System context: HOLIS in its environment

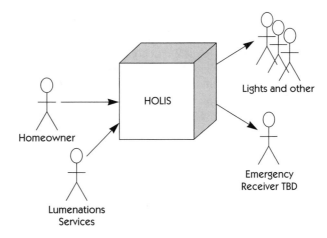

Figure 7–6   HOLIS with actors

Table 7–4   Nonactor Stakeholders for HOLIS

Stakeholder	Comments
External	
Distributors	Lumenations' direct customer
Builders	Lumenations' customer's customer: the general contractor responsible to the homeowner for the end result
Electrical contractors	Responsible for installation and support
Internal	
Development team	Lumenations' team
Marketing/product management	Will be represented by Alyssa, product manager
Lumenations' general management	Funding and outcome accountability

HOLIS Systems Engineering

Now that we understand the external actors for HOLIS, let's do some systems-level thinking to consider how we might partition HOLIS into subsystems.

This process could well be driven by the following kinds of systems engineering thinking.

- It would be good if we could have common software within both the controller device and the homeowner's PC; we'll pick a PC-based implementation for both elements of the system.
- We're not yet certain what flexibility we are going to need in the remote softkey switches, but it's clear that there will be many of them, that some of them will be a fair distance from the main control unit, and that we'll probably need some intelligent communication between those and the control unit.

With this minimalist thinking, we can come up with a new system perspective, one in which HOLIS, the system, is composed of three subsystems: *Control Switch*, the programmable remote switching device; *Central Control Unit*, the central computer control system; and *PC Programmer*, the optional PC system that some homeowners have requested. Now the block diagram appears as in Figure 7–7.

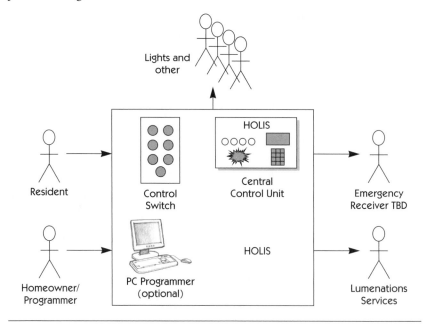

Figure 7–7   HOLIS with subsystems and actors

Note that we have identified a *fifth* actor—the homeowner again—but this time as an actor using the PC to program HOLIS rather than as an actor turning lights on and off. The latter actor is now called *Resident* to differentiate the two roles of the homeowner. The new *Homeowner/Programmer* actor has different needs for the system in that role and therefore is a separate actor to the system. We'll look again later to see the various behaviors that this actor will expect of HOLIS.

The Subsystems of HOLIS

From a systems engineering and requirements perspective, the problem becomes a little more complex. In addition to needing to understand the requirements for HOLIS, the system, we'll now also need to understand the unique requirements for each of HOLIS's three subsystems. We can use our actor paradigm again, at the next level of system decomposition. In so doing, we come up with three new block diagrams: Figures 7–8, 7–9, and 7–10.

In Figure 7–8, when we look at the system perspective from the Control Switch standpoint, we find yet another actor: Central Control Unit (CCU), another subsystem. In other words, from a subsystem perspective, *CCU is an actor on Control Switch*, and later we'll need to understand what kinds of requirements and use cases CCU will impose on Control Switch. This set of requirements is derived from our system decomposition.

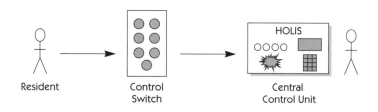

Figure 7–8 Control Switch subsystem with actors

In Figure 7–9, the systems perspective from the viewpoint of the homeowner's PC, we don't seem to learn anything new, at least in terms of actors and subsystems; they've all been identified before. Figure 7–10, however, presents a slightly richer view, and we see that CCU has more actors than anyone else. This seems to make intuitive sense since we have started thinking about CCU as the brains of HOLIS, so it makes sense to think that it has the most stuff to do and the most actors to do it for.

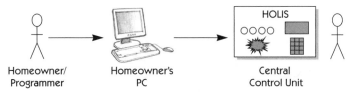

Figure 7–9   PC Programmer subsystem with actors

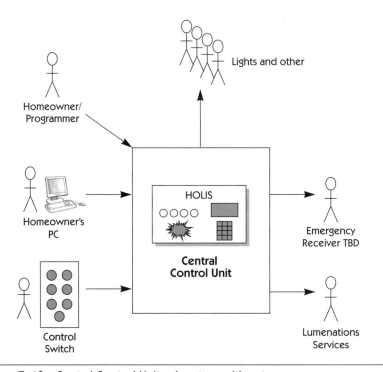

Figure 7–10   Central Control Unit subsystem with actors

To complete the problem analysis, look at Table 7–5, which itemizes the constraints that the team identified, discussed, and agreed to between the HOLIS development team and Lumenations management.

That's enough problem analysis and systems engineering on HOLIS for now. We'll revisit the case study in subsequent chapters.

Table 7–5 Constraints for the HOLIS project

ID #	Description	Rationale
1	Version 1.0 will be released to manufacturing by January 5.	This is the only product launch opportunity this year.
2	The team will adopt UML modeling, OO-based methodologies, and the Unified Software Development Process.	We believe these technologies will provide increased productivity and more robust systems.
3	The software for the Central Control Unit and PC Programmer will be written in Java. Assembly language will be used for the Control Switch.	These choices provide consistency and maintainability; also, the team knows these languages.
4	A prototype system *must* be displayed at the December Home Automation trade show.	We want to take distributors' orders for the first quarter of the fiscal year.
5	The microprocessor subsystem for the Central Control Unit will be copied from the professional division's advanced lighting system project (ALSP).	We can use an existing design and an inventoried part.
6	The only PC Programmer configuration supported will be compatible with Windows 2000 and Windows XP.	This way we can better manage the scope for release 1.0.
7	The team will be allowed to hire two new full-time employees, after a successful inception phase, with whatever skill set is determined to be necessary.	The maximum allowable budget expansion limits us to two new hires.
8	The KCH5444 single-chip microprocessor will be used in the Control Switch.	The company already uses this microprocessor.
9	Purchased software components will be permitted as long as there is no continuing royalty obligation to the company.	We want to avoid any long-term cost of goods sold impact for software.

SUMMARY

In this chapter, we've introduced the application of systems engineering as a problem analysis technique to help us understand the requirements to be imposed on the system we are about to build. We also recognize that the field of systems engineering is broader and deeper than the requirements management discipline that is the topic of this book. Our goal was to provide a simple overview of how this technique can be applied in the context of complex software systems; for even a rudimentary understanding of systems engineering provides a basis for reasoning about complex software applications, most of which may be most effectively considered from the perspective of "a system of systems."

Team Skill 1 Summary

Team Skill 1, Analyzing the Problem, introduced a set of skills your team can apply to *understand the problem to be solved before application development begins*. We introduced a simple, five-step problem analysis technique that can help your team gain a better understanding of the problem to be solved.

1. Gain agreement on the problem definition.
2. Understand the root causes of the problem.
3. Identify the stakeholders and the users whose collective judgment will ultimately determine the success or failure of your system.
4. Determine where the boundaries of the solution are likely to be found.
5. Understand the constraints that will be imposed on your team and on the solution.

Analyzing the problem in this systematic fashion will improve your team's ability to address the challenge ahead—*providing a solution to the problem to be solved*.

We also noted the variety of techniques that can be used in problem analysis. Specifically, we looked at business modeling, which works quite well in complex information systems that support key business infrastructures. The team can use business modeling both to understand the way in which the business evolves and to define where within the system the team can deploy applications most productively. We also recognized that the business model we defined will have parallel constructs in the software application, and we use this commonality to seed the software design phases. Later we will again use the business use cases we discovered to help define requirements for the application itself.

For the class of software applications that we classify as embedded systems, we used the systems engineering process as a problem analysis technique to help us decompose a complex system into subsystems. This process helps us understand where software applications should lie and what overall purpose they serve. In so doing, we also learned that we complicate requirements matters somewhat by defining new subsystems, for which we must, in turn, come to understand the requirements to be imposed.

UNDERSTANDING USER AND STAKEHOLDER NEEDS

The most commonly cited factor on challenged projects was "lack of user input." [Standish Group 1994]

The Standish Group survey [1994] cited "lack of user input" as the most common factor in challenged projects. Although 13 percent of the respondents picked that cause as the primary root cause, an additional 12 percent of the respondents picked "incomplete requirements and specifications." From this data, it's apparent that, for over one-quarter of all challenged projects, a lack of understanding of the users' (and most likely other stakeholders') real requirements was a serious problem that interfered with the success of the project.

Unless we imagine that users worldwide are going to suddenly wake up one day and start doing a better job of both understanding and communicating their requirements, it's obvious that our development teams are going to have to take the initiative. In other words, our teams need to develop the necessary skills to elicit these requirements.

In Team Skill 1, we described the skills that will help you understand the problem being solved. In Team Skill 2, we provide a number of techniques the development team can use to gather and to understand the real needs of prospective users and other stakeholders. In so doing, we'll also start to gain an understanding of the potential requirements for a system that we will develop to address these needs. While we do this, we will be focusing primarily on stakeholder needs, which live at the top of the requirements pyramid.

The techniques we look at range from simple, inexpensive, and straightforward techniques, such as interviewing, to more expensive and quite technical techniques. Although no one technique is perfect in every case, exposure to a variety of techniques will provide the team with a rich set of skills to choose from. For each specific project, the team can then pick from the available techniques and apply the experience and knowledge gained from the elicitation effort on prior projects. In this way, the team will develop a set of skills that are unique and well suited to the environment and that can actively contribute to improved outcomes.

Chapter 8

THE CHALLENGE
OF REQUIREMENTS ELICITATION

Key Points

- Requirements elicitation is complicated by three endemic syndromes.
- The "Yes, But" syndrome stems from human nature and the users' inability to experience the software as they might a physical device.
- Searching for requirements is like searching for "Undiscovered Ruins"; the more you find, the more you know remain.
- The "User and the Developer" syndrome reflects the profound differences between these two, making communication difficult.

In the next few chapters, we will look at a variety of techniques for eliciting requirements from the users and other stakeholders of the system.[1] This process seems so straightforward. Sit down with the future users of the system and other stakeholders and ask them what they need the system to do.

Why, then, is this so difficult? Why do we need so many techniques? Indeed, why do we need this team skill at all? In order to gain a fuller appreciation of this particular problem, let's first take a look at three syndromes that seem to complicate these matters immensely.

---

1. We use the term *user* generically in this context. The techniques apply to eliciting requirements from all stakeholders, both users and nonusers.

BARRIERS TO ELICITATION
The "Yes, But" Syndrome

One of the most frustrating, pervasive, and seemingly downright sinister problems in all of application development is what we have come to call the "Yes, But" syndrome. We have observed it in the users' reactions to every piece of software we have ever developed. *For whatever reason, we always see two immediate, distinct, and separate reactions when the users see the system implementation for the first time.*

1. "Wow, this is so cool; we can really use this, what a neat job, atta boy," and so on.
2. "Yes, but, hmmmmm, now that I see it, what about this . . . ? Wouldn't it be nice if . . . ? Whatever happened to . . . ?"

The roots of the "Yes, But" syndrome appear to lie deep in the nature of software as an intangible intellectual process. To make matters worse, our development teams typically *compound* the problem by rarely providing anything earlier than production code for the users to interact with and to evaluate.

The "Yes, But" syndrome is simply human nature.

The users' reactions are simply human nature, and they occur in various other day-to-day circumstances. The users haven't seen your new system or anything like it before; they didn't understand what you meant when you described it earlier, and now that it's in front of them—now, for the first time after months or years of waiting—they have the opportunity to interact with the system. And guess what: it's not exactly what they expected!

By analogy, let's compare this software process to the development of mechanical devices whose technology and development process predate software by a mere few hundred years or so. Mechanical systems have a reasonably well-defined discipline of proof-of-principle models, sketches, mockups, models, incremental prototyping, pilot production devices, and so on, all of which have tangible aspects and most of which look, feel, and act somewhat like the device under development.

The users can see the early devices, touch them, reason about them, and even interact with them *well* before detailed implementation is complete. Indeed, specific technologies, such as stereo lithography, wherein a rapid prototype is constructed overnight out of a vat of goo, have been developed exclusively for the purpose of providing early and immediate feedback on the conceptual definition of the product. Yet in software, with its enormous complexity, we are expected to get it right the first time!

As frustrating as it is, accepting the "Yes, But" syndrome as reality may lead to real insights that will help team members mitigate this syndrome in future projects.

- The "Yes, But" syndrome is human nature and is an integral part of application development. We should plan for it.
- We can drastically reduce this syndrome by applying techniques that get the "Buts" out early. In so doing, we elicit the "Yes, But" response early, and we then can begin to invest the majority of our development efforts in software that has already passed the "Yes, But" test.

The "Undiscovered Ruins" Syndrome

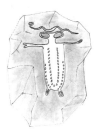

One of our friends was once a tour bus guide in the Four Corners area of the western United States, an area defined by the common borders of Colorado, New Mexico, Utah, and Arizona. The tour bus route included the majestic peaks of the La Plata mountain range and the sprawling ancient Anasazi ruins of Mesa Verde and the surrounding area. Tourists' questions are a constant source of amusement among the tour guide crew and create a certain folklore of the tour business. During one summer season, our friend's favorite silliest-question-ever-posed-by-a-stupid-tourist was, "So, ummm, how many undiscovered ruins are there?"

In many ways, the search for requirements is like a search for undiscovered ruins: *the more you find, the more you know remain.* You never really feel as though you have found them all, and perhaps you never will. Indeed, software development teams everywhere continually struggle to determine when they are done with requirements elicitation, that is, when have they found all the requirements that are material or when have they found at least enough?

In order to help the team address this problem, we'll provide a variety of techniques, both in the Team Skill 2 chapters and in later ones. Of course, as we described in Chapter 5, taking the time in problem analysis to identify all the stakeholders of the system is of tremendous value because many of these nonuser stakeholders are often holders of otherwise undiscovered requirements. However, as with finding all the undiscovered ruins, we must acknowledge that we are on a mission that can never be completed. But we also understand that at some point we will be able to say with confidence, "We have discovered enough for now; we'll find the rest later."

The "User and the Developer" Syndrome

Techniques for requirements elicitation are not new. Application developers have strived for more than 40 years to do a better job. What could possibly account for the fact that understanding user needs remains one of our largest problems? Well, considering the fact that few application developers have any training in *any* elicitation techniques, it's perhaps not all that surprising.

The third syndrome arises from the *communication gap* between the user and the developer. We call this syndrome the "User and the Developer" syndrome. Users and developers are typically from different worlds, may even speak different languages, and have different backgrounds, motivations, and objectives.

Somehow, we must learn to communicate more effectively with these "users from the other tribe." In an article on this subject, Scharer [1981] describes this syndrome and provides some guidelines to help mitigate the problem. Combining her words with our own experiences, Table 8–1 both summarizes the reasons for this problem and suggests some solutions.

Table 8–1   The "User and the Developer" Syndrome

Problem	Solution
Users do not know what they want, or they know what they want but cannot articulate it.	Recognize and appreciate the user as domain expert; try alternative communication and elicitation techniques.
Users think they know what they want until developers give them what they said they wanted.	Provide alternative elicitation techniques earlier: storyboarding, role playing, throwaway prototypes, and so on.
Analysts think they understand user problems better than users do.	Put the analyst in the user's place. Try role playing for an hour or a day.
Everybody believes everybody else is politically motivated.	Yes, its part of human nature, so let's get on with the program.

The hope is that with a better understanding of both the nature of these problems and some approaches to mitigate them, developers will be better prepared for the interesting work ahead.

SUMMARY

Understanding user and stakeholder needs moves us from the technical domain of bits and bytes, where many developers are most comfortable, into the domain of real people and real-world problems. To help bridge this gap, we've described three endemic syndromes that development teams should be aware of. Otherwise, the process of understanding user and stakeholder needs will be neither as straightforward nor as effective as we would like. Just as a variety of techniques can be used for analyzing and designing software solutions, we'll need to apply a variety of techniques to help us gain a better understanding of real user and stakeholder requirements.

In Team Skill 1, we started down that path with problem analysis, a set of questions we can ask about the constraints to be imposed on the system, the business modeling technique we can use for many applications, and the systems engineering technique that we can apply to complex systems. In the following chapters, we'll describe techniques that have proved effective in addressing the three syndromes just discussed. Among the techniques we will discuss are the following:

- Interviews and questionnaires
- Requirements workshops
- Brainstorming sessions and idea reduction
- Storyboards

The choice of a specific technique will vary, based on the type of application, the skill and sophistication of the development team, the skill and sophistication of the customer, the scale of the problem, the criticality of the application, the technology used, and the uniqueness of the application.

Chapter 9

THE FEATURES OF A PRODUCT OR SYSTEM

Key Points

- The development team must play a more active role in eliciting the requirements for the system.
- Product or system *features* are high-level expressions of desired system behavior.
- System features should be limited to 25–99, with fewer than 50 preferred.
- Attributes provide additional information about a feature.

Given some of the problems we've described in the earlier chapters, it seems clear that the development team is rarely, if ever, handed a perfect, or perhaps even reasonable, specification to use as the basis for system development. In the previous chapter, we learned about the reasons for this. One conclusion we can draw is that if we are not going to be given better definitions, we are going to have to go out and *get* them. In other words, in order to achieve success, the development team will have to play a much more active role in eliciting the requirements. As we'll discover, although we can delegate the majority of this responsibility to a senior lead, analyst, or product manager, in the end the entire team will be involved at one or more points in the process.

STAKEHOLDER AND USER NEEDS

It seems obvious that the development team will build a better system only if it understands the true needs of the stakeholder. That knowledge will give the team the information it needs to make better decisions in the definition and implementation of the system. This set of inputs, which we call *stakeholder* or *user needs*, or just user needs for short, provides a crucial piece of the puzzle.

Often, these user needs will be vague and ambiguous. "I need easier ways to understand the status of my inventory" or "I'd like to see a big increase in the productivity of sales order entry," your stakeholder might say. Yet these statements set a most important context for all the activities that follow. Since these needs are so important, we'll spend some significant time and energy trying to understand them. We'll define a stakeholder need as

> *a reflection of the business, personal, or operational problem (or opportunity) that must be addressed in order to justify consideration, purchase, or use of a new system.*

FEATURES

Interestingly, when interviewed about their needs and requirements for a new system, stakeholders typically describe neither of these things, at least not in terms of the definitions we've provided thus far. That is, stakeholders often tell you neither their real need ("If I don't increase productivity in this department, I won't get my bonus this year" or "I want to be able to slow this vehicle down as quickly as possible without skidding") nor the actual requirement for the system ("I must reduce sales order entry transaction processing time by 50 percent" or "The vehicle shall have a computer control system for each wheel"). Instead, they describe what seems to be an abstraction somewhere between ("I need a new GUI-based order entry screen" and "I want a vehicle with ABS").

We call these high-level expressions of desired system behavior the *features* of a product or system. These features are often not well defined and may even be in conflict with one another—"I want increased order processing rates" and "I want to provide a far more user-friendly interface to help our new employees learn the system"—but they are a representation of real needs nevertheless.

What is happening in this discussion? In their minds, the stakeholders have already translated the real need (productivity or safety) into a system behavior that they have reason to believe will solve the real need (Figure 9–1). In so doing, the *what* ("I need") has subtly shifted to the *how* ("what I think the system should do to address this need"). This is not a bad thing since the user often has real expertise in the domain and real insight into the value of a prospective feature. Also, because it is easy to discuss these features in natural language, to document them, and to communicate them to others, they add tremendous richness to the requirements schema.

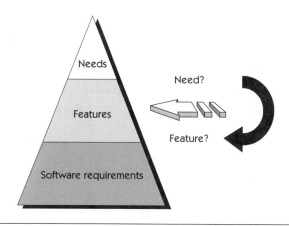

Figure 9–1   Needs and features are closely related

However, there is a caveat to this discussion: if the team leaves the discussion without an understanding of the need behind the feature, then there is a real risk. If the feature does not solve the real need for any reason, then the system may fail to meet the users' objectives even though the implementation delivered the feature they requested. You are right, but you still lose!

In any case, we find this high level of abstraction—these *features*—to be a useful and convenient way to describe the functionality of a new system without getting bogged down in too much detail. Indeed, we will drive most of our requirements activities from this "feature" construct.

We define a feature as

> *a service the system provides to fulfill one or more stakeholder needs.*

With this definition, users' *features* can't be too far removed from their *needs*, and we have a handy way to start to define the system.

Our focus in understanding user needs is on eliciting and organizing the *needs* and *features* of the proposed system. Sometimes we'll get all needs and no features. Sometimes we'll get all features and no needs. Sometimes we won't be able to tell them apart. But so long as we are careful about the distinction in our own minds, we should, all the time, be learning valuable information about what the system must *do*.

Features are easily expressed in natural language and consist of a short phrase; Table 9–1 shows some examples. Rarely, if ever, are features elaborated in more

---

Features are a convenient way to describe functionality without getting bogged down in detail.

Table 9–1   Examples of Features

Application Domain	Example of a Feature
Elevator control system	Manual control of doors during fire emergency
Inventory control system	Provide up-to-date status of all inventoried items
Defect tracking system	Provide trend data to assess product quality
Payroll system	Report deductions-to-date by category
Home lighting automation system (HOLIS)	Vacation settings for extended away periods
Weapon control system	Minimum of two independent confirmations of attack authorization required
Shrink-wrap application	Windows XP compatibility

detail. Features are also very helpful constructs for early product scope management and the related negotiation and trade-off processes. The statement of features does not entail a great deal of investment, and they are easy to describe and list.

Managing Complexity by Picking the Level of Abstraction

A system of arbitrary complexity can be defined in a list of 25–99 features.

The number of features we permit ourselves to consider will effectively pick the level of abstraction of the definition. To manage the complexity of the systems we are envisioning, *we recommend that, for any new system or for an increment to an existing system, capabilities be abstracted to a high enough level so that a maximum of only 25–99 features result, with fewer than 50 preferred.*

In this way, a relatively small and manageable amount of information provides a comprehensive and complete basis for product definition, communication with the stakeholders, scope management, and project management. With 25–99 features suitably categorized and arranged, we should be able to describe and to communicate the gestalt of the system, be it a space shuttle ("reentry and reuse") or a software tool ("automatic defect trending"). In Team Skill 5, Refining the System Definition, these features will be elaborated into detailed requirements specific enough to allow for implementation. We will call those *software requirements* to differentiate them from the higher-level features. We'll deal with that need for additional specificity later. For now, however, we'll keep our thinking at the features level.

Once the set of possible features is enumerated, it's time to start making such decisions as "defer to a later release," "implement immediately," "reject entirely," or "investigate further." This *scoping* process is best done at the level of features rather than at the level of requirements, or you will be swamped in detail. We'll cover scoping in Team Skill 4, Managing Scope.

Attributes of Product Features

In order to help us better manage this information, we introduce the construct of feature *attributes*, or data elements that provide additional information about the feature. Attributes are used to relate the feature or requirements data to other types of project information. We can use attributes to track (name or unique identifier, sponsor, history data, allocated from, traced to, and so on), to prioritize (priority field), and to manage (status) the features proposed for implementation. For example, the attribute *priority* could be used to capture the results of the cumulative voting in a brainstorming session; the attribute *version number* might be used to record the specific software release in which we intend to implement a specific feature.

By attaching various attributes to the features, you can better manage the complexity of the information. Although there is no limit to the types of attributes you might find useful, experience has demonstrated that some common attributes for features apply to most project circumstances (see Table 9–2 on the next page). In the remainder of this book, we'll use these attributes to help us manage the complexity of the feature and requirements data and to manage the relationships, such as dependencies, among the various types of system requirements.

SUMMARY

In this chapter, we've described the concept of a product or system *feature*, which is a simple but critical construct in requirements management. Features are easy to elicit, easy to document, and easy to maintain. They are user friendly, and they can be devoid of technical jargon that could lead to misunderstandings. Moreover, if we force ourselves to write them in such a way that a maximum of 25–50 features can fully encompass a system or incremental release, then we have a simple and elegant way to begin to describe what a system needs to do, as well as how much time and effort may be required to do it.

So, let's move on to developing some team skills that will help us *find* the necessary features of our proposed system. We'll start with interviewing (Chapter 10).

Table 9–2 Attributes of Features

Attribute	Description
Status	Tracks progress during definition of the project baseline and subsequent development. *Example:* Proposed, Approved, Incorporated status states.
Priority/benefit	Assists in managing scope and determining priority. All features are not created equal. Ranking by relative priority or benefit to the end user opens a dialogue between stakeholders and members of the development team. *Example:* Critical, Important, Useful rankings.
Effort	Helps establish realistic schedules, goals, and costs. Estimating the number of team- or person-weeks, lines of code or function points, or just the general level of effort helps set expectations of what can and cannot be accomplished in a given time frame. *Example:* Team months, or Low, Medium, High levels of effort.
Risk	Indicates a measure of the probability that the feature will cause undesirable events, such as cost overruns, schedule delays, or even cancellation. *Example:* High, Medium, Low risk level.
Stability	Reflects a measure of the probability that the feature will change or that the team's understanding of the feature will change. This attribute helps establish development priorities and determine those items for which additional elicitation is the appropriate next action. *Example:* High, Medium, Low stability.
Target release	Records the intended product version in which the feature will first appear. When combined with the Status field, your team can propose, record, and discuss various features without committing them to development. *Example:* Version 2.3.
Assigned to	Indicates who will be responsible for implementing the feature. In many projects, features will be assigned to "feature teams" responsible for further elicitation, writing the software requirements, and perhaps even implementation.
Reason	Helps track the source of the requested feature. For example, the reference might be to a page and line number of a product specification or to a minute marker on a video of an important customer interview.

Chapter 10

INTERVIEWING

Key Points
- Interviewing is a simple and direct technique that can be used in most circumstances.
- Context-free questions can help achieve bias-free interviews.
- It may be appropriate to search for undiscovered requirements by exploring solutions.
- Convergence on some common needs will initiate a "requirements repository" for use during the project.
- A questionnaire is no substitute for an interview.

One of the most important and most straightforward requirements gathering techniques is the *user interview,* a simple, direct technique that can be used in virtually every situation. This chapter describes the interviewing process and provides a generic template for conducting user and stakeholder interviews. However, the interviewing process is not easy, and it forces us to get "up close and personal" to the "User and the Developer" syndrome.

In addition, one of the key goals of interviewing is to make sure that the biases and predispositions of the interviewer do not interfere with a free exchange of information. This is a subtle and pernicious problem. Sociology (oops, another class we missed!) teaches us that it is *extremely difficult* to truly understand others because each of us is biased by our own conceptual filter, one that results from our own environment and cumulative experiences.

In addition, as solution providers, we rarely find ourselves in a situation in which we have no idea what types of potential solutions would address the problem. Indeed, in most cases, we operate within a repetitive domain or context in which certain elements of the solution are obvious, or at least appear to be obvious. We may even be experts. ("We have solved this type of problem before, and we fully expect that our experience will apply in this new case. After all, we are just building houses, and hammers and nails work just fine.") Of course, this is not all bad because having context is part of what we get paid for. The point is that we must not let our context interfere with understanding the real problem to be solved.

CONTEXT-FREE QUESTIONS

A context-free question helps us gain an understanding of the real problem without biasing the user's input.

So, how do we avoid prejudicing the user's responses to our questions? We do so by asking questions about the nature of the user's problem *without* context for a potential solution. To address this problem, Gause and Weinberg [1989] introduced the concept of the "context-free question." Examples of such questions include the following.

- Who is the user?
- Who is the customer?
- Are their needs different?
- Where else can a solution to this problem be found?

These questions force us to listen before attempting to invent or describe a potential solution. Listening gives us a better understanding of the customer's problem and any problems behind the problem. Such problems affect our customer's motivation or behavior and must be addressed before we can deliver a successful solution.

Context-free questions also parallel the questions salespeople are taught to ask as part of a technique called "solutions selling." In solutions selling, the salesperson uses a series of questions focused on first gaining a real understanding of the customer's problem and what solutions, if any, the customer already envisions. The intent of these questions is to allow the salesperson to fully understand the customer's real problem, so that effective solutions can be suggested and weighed on their specific merits. This process can then illustrate the value of the salesperson's wares as an element of a complete solution to the customer's real problem.

SOLUTIONS-CONTEXT QUESTIONS

In our search for undiscovered requirements, it may also be appropriate to move the questions to a point wherein we explore solutions after the context-free questions have been asked and answered. After all, most of us are not typically rewarded for simply understanding the problem but rather for providing solutions appropriate to the problems being solved. This addition of solution context may give the user new insights and perhaps even a different view of the problem. And, of course, our users depend on us to have context; otherwise, they would have to teach us everything they know about the subject.

As an aid to building this skill within the development team, we have combined these techniques into our "generic, almost context-free interview," a structured interview that can be used to elicit user or stakeholder requirements in most software application contexts. Figure 10–1 provides the template for this interview. The interview consists of both context-free and non-context-free sections. It also provides questions designed to make certain that all aspects of requirements, including some of those "gotcha" requirements for reliability, supportability, and so on, are thoroughly explored.

THE MOMENT OF TRUTH: THE INTERVIEW

With a little preparation and the structured interview template, any member of the team can do an adequate job of interviewing a user or customer. (However, it may be best to pick those team members who are most outgoing and are comfortable talking with users and prospects in a relatively unstructured, business setting.) Here are some tips for a successful interview.

- Prepare an appropriate context-free interview, and jot it down in a notebook for reference during the interview. Review the questions just prior to the interview.
- Before the interview, research the background of the stakeholder and the company to be interviewed. Don't bore the person being interviewed with questions you could have answered in advance. On the other hand, it wouldn't hurt to briefly verify the answers with the interviewee.
- Jot down answers in your notebook during the interview. (Don't attempt to capture the data electronically at this time!)
- Refer to the template during the interview to make certain that you're asking the right questions.

Make sure that the script is not overly constraining. Once rapport has been established, the interview is likely to take on a life of its own. The customer

Part I: Establishing the Customer or User Profile

Name:

Company:

Industry:

Job title:

(The above information can typically be entered in advance.)

What are your key responsibilities?

What outputs do you produce?

For whom?

How is success measured?

Which problems interfere with your success?

What, if any, trends make your job easier or more difficult?

Part II: Assessing the Problem

For which *[application type]* problems do you lack good solutions?

What are they? *(Hint: Keep asking, "Anything else?")*

For each problem, ask the following questions.

- Why does this problem exist?
- How do you solve it now?
- How would you like to solve it?

Part III: Understanding the User Environment

Who are the users?

What is their educational background?

What is their computer background?

Are users experienced with this type of application?

Which platforms are in use?

What are your plans for future platforms?

Are additional applications in use that are relevant to this application? If so, let's talk about them a bit.

What are your expectations for usability of the product?

What are your expectations for training time?

What kinds of user help (for example, hard copy and online documentation) do you need?

Part IV: Recap for Understanding

You have told me:

(List customer-described problems in your own words.)

-
-
-

Does this adequately represent the problems you are having with your existing solution?

What, if any, other problems are you experiencing?

Part V: The Analyst's Inputs on the Customer's Problem

(Validate or invalidate assumptions.)

(If not yet addressed) Which, if any, problems are associated with: *(List any needs or additional problems you think should concern the customer or user.)*

-
-
-

For each suggested problem, ask the following questions.

- Is this a real problem?
- What are the reasons for this problem?
- How do you currently solve the problem?
- How would you like to solve the problem?
- How would you rank solving these problems in comparison to others you've mentioned?

Part VI: Assessing Your Solution *(if applicable)*

(Summarize the key capabilities of your proposed solution.)

What if you could:

-
-

How would you rank the importance of these?

(continued on next page)

Figure 10–1   The generic, almost context-free interview

Part VII: Assessing the Opportunity

Who in your organization needs this application?

How many of these types of users would use the application?

How would you value a successful solution?

Part VIII: Assessing the Reliability, Performance, and Support Needs

What are your expectations for reliability?

What are your expectations for performance?

Will you support the product, or will others support it?

Do you have special needs for support?

What about maintenance and service access?

What are the security requirements?

What are the installation and configuration requirements?

Are there special licensing requirements?

How will the software be distributed?

Are there labeling and packaging requirements?

Part IX: Other Requirements

Are there any legal, regulatory, or environmental requirements or other standards that must be supported?

Can you think of any other requirements we should know about?

Part X: Wrap-up

Are there any other questions I should be asking you?

If I need to ask follow-up questions, may I give you a call? Would you be willing to participate in a requirements review?

Part XI: The Analyst's Summary

After the interview, and while the data is still fresh in your mind, summarize the three highest-priority needs or problems identified by this user/ customer.

1.
2.
3.

Figure 10–1   *Continued*

It is OK to wander off course a bit, just as long as the interviewer keeps the goal in mind.

may well launch into a stream-of-consciousness dialogue, describing in detail the horrors of the current situation. *This is exactly the behavior you are striving for.* If this happens to you, do not cut it off prematurely with another question; rather, write down everything as quickly as you can, letting the user exhaust that particular stream of thought. Ask follow-up questions about the information that has just been provided. Then, after this thread has run to its logical end, get back to other questions on the list.

After even a couple of such interviews, the developer/analyst will have gained some knowledge of the problem domain and will have an enhanced understanding of both the problem being solved and the user's insights on the characteristics of a successful solution. In addition, the developer can summarize the key user needs or product features defined in the interview. These "user needs" live near the top of our requirements pyramid and serve as the driving force for all the work that follows.

COMPILING THE NEEDS DATA

Your problem analysis will have identified the key stakeholders and users you will need to interview to gain an understanding of the stakeholder's needs. Typically, it does not take many interviews to get a solid understanding of the larger issues.

The Analyst's Summary: 10 + 10 + 10 ≠ 30

The last section of the interview form, The Analyst's Summary, is used for recording the three most important needs or problems uncovered in the interview. In many cases, after just a few interviews, these highest-priority needs will start to be repeated. This means that you may be starting to get convergence on some common needs. This is to be expected, especially among those users or stakeholders who share a common perspective. So, ten interviews will often create only 10–15 *different* needs. This is the start of your *requirements repository*, a set of assets you will build and use to good advantage over the course of your project. This simple, inexpensive data, even by itself, will help you and your team build a solid foundation with which to initiate your project.

The Case Study

HOLIS
user needs

The HOLIS team decided to have the marketing team (Rick and Alyssa) develop the questions for the interview but wanted everyone on the team to experience the process. That way each team member would have the opportunity to meet customers face-to-face and thereby "see" the problem and a potential solution from the customer's perspective. So, the team divided up the customer and distributor list and had each team member interview two people. The team used The Analyst's Summary to summarize the needs that were provided and weeded out the duplicates. After fifteen interviews, the team had identified about twenty needs to fill in the top of the requirements pyramid.

From the homeowner's perspective:

- Flexible and modifiable lighting control for entire house
- "Futureproof" ("As technology changes, I'd like compatibility with new technologies that might emerge.")
- Attractive, unobtrusive, ergonomic
- Fully independent and programmable or (reconfigurable) switches for each room in the house

- Additional security and peace of mind
- Intuitive operation ("I'd like to be able to explain it to my 'techno-phobic' mother.")
- A reasonable system cost, with low switch costs
- Easy and inexpensive to fix
- Flexible switch configurations (from one to seven "buttons" per switch)
- Out of sight, out of mind
- 100 percent reliability
- Vacation security settings
- Ability to create scenes, such as special housewide lighting settings for a party
- No increase in electrical or fire hazards in the home
- Ability, after a power failure, to restore the lights the way they were
- Programmable by the homeowner, using an existing PC
- Dimmers wherever the homeowner wants them
- Programmable by the homeowner, without using a PC
- Programmable by somebody else, so the homeowner doesn't have to do it
- Ability to turn on some lights manually if the system fails
- Interfaces to the home security system
- Interfaces to other home automation (HVAC, audio/video, and so on)

From the distributor's perspective:

- A competitive product offering
- Some strong product differentiation
- An easy way to train salespeople
- Ability to demonstrate the system in the shop
- High gross margins

A NOTE ON QUESTIONNAIRES

There is *no* substitute for an interview.

- Do it first!
- Do it for every new class of problem!
- Do it for every new project!

We are often asked whether the team can substitute a questionnaire for this interviewing process. In some cases, the need expressed is perhaps a simple desire for efficiency ("I could do 100 questionnaires in the time it takes to do one interview"). In other cases, the need itself may come under suspicion ("Do I really have to talk to these people? Couldn't I just send them a letter?").

No matter what the motivation, the answer is *no*. There is no substitute for the personal contact, rapport building, and free-form interaction of the interview technique. We are confident that after one or two interviews, your worldview will change. Even more important, the vision for the solution will change along with it! Do the interview first. Do it for every new class of problem, and do it for every new project.

Although the questionnaire technique is often used and appears scientific because of the opportunity for statistical analysis of the quantitative results, the technique is not a substitute for interviewing. When it comes to requirements gathering, the questionnaire technique has some fundamental problems.

- Relevant questions cannot be decided in advance.
- The assumptions behind the questions bias the answers.

    Example: Did this class meet your expectations? *Assumption:* You
      had expectations, so this is a meaningful question.

- It is difficult to explore new domains ("What you really should be asking about is . . ."), and there is no interaction to explore domains that need to be explored.
- It is difficult to follow up on unclear user responses.

Indeed, some have concluded that the questionnaire technique suppresses almost everything good about requirements gathering. Therefore, we generally do not recommend it for this purpose.

Questionnaires can be used to validate assumptions and gather statistical preference data.

However, the questionnaire technique can be applied with good effect as a corroborating technique after the initial interviewing and analysis activity. For example, if the application has a large number of existing or potential users and if the goal is to provide statistical input about user or customer preferences among a limited set of choices, a questionnaire can be used effectively to gather a significant amount of focused data in a short period of time. In short, the questionnaire technique, like all elicitation techniques, is suited to a subset of the requirements challenges that an organization may face.

SUMMARY

When all is said and done, one of the easiest ways to find out what a system needs to do is to *ask the prospective stakeholders!* If we approach this requirements gathering activity in a structured way—we know who the stakeholders are likely to be and what questions we need to ask of them—we are likely to discover *real* requirements (though they may well be specified variously as needs, features, or technical specifications). In other words, if we ask the right stakeholders the right questions in the right way, we'll build that solid understanding we need. In the next chapter, we'll elaborate on some additional techniques we can use to augment this fundamental process.

Chapter 11

REQUIREMENTS WORKSHOPS

Key Points

- The requirements workshop may be the most powerful technique for eliciting requirements.
- It gathers all key stakeholders together for a short but intensely focused period.
- The use of an outside facilitator experienced in requirements management can help ensure the success of the workshop.
- Brainstorming is the most important part of the workshop.

ACCELERATING THE DECISION PROCESS

In the prior chapter, we introduced interviewing as a primary requirements gathering technique. In this and following chapters, we'll introduce additional techniques that can be used to elicit and organize requirements. In general, the more elicitation and requirements gathering techniques the team has in their toolkit, the more effective the team will be. However, occasionally the team does not have the luxury of time to either master or apply a variety of techniques. They have to pick one technique and go.

If we were to be given only one requirements elicitation technique—one that we had to apply in every circumstance, no matter the project context, no matter what the time frame—we would pick the requirements workshop, which we will describe in this chapter. The requirements workshop may well be the most powerful technique in this book and one of the few that, when mastered, can really help change project outcomes, even when it's the only elicitation technique applied.

The requirements workshop is designed to encourage consensus on the requirements of the application and to gain rapid agreement on a course of action, all in a very short time. With this technique, key stakeholders of the project gather together for a short, intensive period, typically no more than one or two days. The workshop is facilitated by a team member or, better yet, by an experienced outside facilitator and focuses on the creation or review of the high-level features to be delivered by the new application.

A properly run requirements workshop has many benefits.

- It assists in building an effective team, committed to one common purpose: the success of this project.
- All stakeholders get their say; no one is left out.
- It forges an agreement between the stakeholders and the development team as to what the application must do.
- It can expose and resolve political issues that are interfering with project success.
- The output, a preliminary system definition at the features level, is available immediately.

Many organizations have had great success with the workshop technique. Together, we have participated in hundreds of such workshops, and rarely, if ever, has the workshop been unsuccessful in meeting its desired goals. The workshop provides a unique opportunity for stakeholders from various parts of the organization to work together toward the common goal of project success.

In this chapter, you will learn how to plan and run a successful requirements workshop.

PREPARING FOR THE WORKSHOP

Proper preparation for the workshop is critical to success.

Selling the Concept

Proper preparation is the key to a successful workshop.

First, it may be necessary to sell the concept inside the organization by communicating the benefits of the workshop approach to prospective members of the team. This is typically not a difficult process, but it's not unusual to encounter resistance: "Not another meeting!" "We can't possibly get all these critical people together for one day." "You'll never get [name your favorite stakeholder] to attend." Don't be discouraged; if you hold it, they will come.

Ensuring the Participation of the Right Stakeholders

Second, preparation also involves identifying stakeholders who can contribute to the process and whose needs must be met in order to ensure a successful outcome. These stakeholders will have already been identified if the team followed the problem analysis steps, but now is the time for one last review to make sure that all critical stakeholders have been identified.

Attending to Logistics

Third, a conscientious approach to logistics is necessary and will pay dividends in that a poorly organized workshop is unlikely to achieve the desired result. Logistics involve everything from structuring the proper invitation to travel arrangements to the lighting in the workshop meeting room. A literal belief in Murphy's Law—"Whatever can go wrong will go wrong"—should be your guideline. If you approach logistics with a high degree of professionalism, it will be obvious to the attendees that this is indeed an important event, and they will act accordingly. You'll also have a more successful workshop.

Providing Warm-Up Materials

Fourth, send materials out in advance of the workshop to prepare the attendees and also to increase productivity at the workshop session. These materials set each attendee's frame of mind. We call this "getting their minds right." One of the messages we need to deliver is that *this is not yet another meeting. This may be our one chance to get it right.*

We recommend that you provide two types of warm-up materials.

Warm-up materials should spur both in-context and out-of-the-box thinking.

1. *Project-specific information.* This might include drafts of requirements documents, bulleted lists of suggested features, copies of interviews with prospective users, analyst's reports on trends in the industry, letters from customers, bug reports from the existing system, new management directives, new marketing data, and so on. Although it's important not to bury the prospective attendees in data, it's also important to make sure they have the right data.

2. *Out-of-the-box thinking preparation.* Part of "getting their minds right" is encouraging attendees to think "out of the box." "Forget for a minute what you know and what can't be done due to politics. Forget that we tried to get management buy-in last time and failed. Forget that we haven't yet solidified our development process. Simply bring your insights on the features of this new project, and be prepared to think 'out of the box.'"

The workshop leader can assist in this process by providing thought-provoking and stimulating articles about the process of creativity, rules for brainstorming, requirements management, managing scope, and so on. In this atmosphere, creative solutions will more likely result.

Tip: Do not send the data out too far in advance. You do not want the attendees to read it and forget it, and you don't want the long planning cycle to decrease their sense of urgency. Send the data out anywhere from two days to one week in advance. In all likelihood, the attendees will read it on the plane or at the last minute anyway. That's OK; it will help them be in the right frame of mind for the session.

To help you with your out-of-the-box thinking and to help set the context for the workshop activity, we've provided a memo template in Figure 11–1. Parenthetically, we'll also "read between the lines" a little bit to provide insights on some of the challenges you may already face in your project and on how the workshop is intended to address them.

Choosing the Facilitator

If possible, have a facilitator who is not a team member run the workshop.

To ensure success, we recommend that the workshop be run by someone outside the organization, a nonstakeholder, someone who is unaffected by any particular outcome and has no role in the company other than to see a successful workshop outcome. Ideally, the facilitator will also have experience with the unique challenges and charged atmosphere of the requirements management process. However, if this is simply not practical in your environment, the workshop could be facilitated by a team member *if* that person:

- Has received some training in the process
- Has demonstrated solid consensus-building or team-building skills
- Is personable and well respected by both the internal and external team members
- Is strong enough to chair what could be a challenging meeting

If the workshop is to be facilitated by a team member, that person must *not* contribute to the ideas and issues at the meeting. Otherwise, the workshop is in danger of losing the objectivity that is necessary to get at the real facts, and it may not foster a trusting environment in which a consensus can emerge.

In any case, the facilitator plays a pivotal role in making the workshop a success. After all, you have all the key stakeholders gathered together, perhaps

Memo:

To: **Stakeholders in the _____ project**

Subject: **Upcoming requirements workshop**

From:

I am the product [project] manager for the _____ project. The project was [or will be] initiated on _____ and will be completed on its deadline of _____.

(We know it, we mean it, and we intend to complete it on time.)

As with most projects, it has been difficult to gain consensus on the new features of this application and to define an initial baseline release that meets the needs of our diverse group of stakeholders.

(It's harder than heck to gain agreement on anything with this group, so we're going to try something a little different. Here's what that is. . . .)

In order to facilitate this process, we will be holding a requirements workshop on _____.

The goal of the workshop is to finalize the new features for the next baseline release of the product. In order to do so, it's important that all stakeholders' inputs be heard. The workshop will be facilitated by _____, who is an experienced requirements management facilitator.

(Since, as stakeholders, we may also be biased, we will have someone from outside the team help us make sure that the workshop is managed in a fair and unbiased way.)

Results of the workshop will be available immediately and will be distributed to the development and marketing teams the next day. You are cordially invited to attend the workshop and to provide the input that is representative of the needs of your [team, department, customer]. If you are unable to attend, we strongly recommend that you send a team member who is empowered to make the decisions representative of your needs.

(We are going to initiate development the very next day; if you want your input to be heard on this project, be there, or send someone who can speak for you. In other words, speak now or forever hold your peace.)

Included with this memo is a brief description of the currently anticipated features of the product, as well as some reading material about the workshop and brainstorming process. The workshop will last until 5:30 P.M., and we will convene promptly at 8:30 A.M.

(This project, and this workshop, is going to be professionally run; to demonstrate this, we have provided some advanced reading material to help you be better prepared. We need you to be there, to contribute, and to help us get this project off to a proper beginning.)

We look forward to seeing you there.

Sincerely,

[Project Leader]

Figure 11–1   Sample memo for kick-starting a requirements workshop

for the first and last time on the project, and you cannot afford a misfire. Some of the responsibilities of the facilitator include the following.

- Establish a professional and objective tone for the meeting.
- Start and stop the meeting on time.
- Establish and enforce the "rules" for the meeting.
- Introduce the goals and agenda for the meeting.
- Manage the meeting and keep the team "on track."
- Facilitate a process of decision and consensus making, but avoid participating in the content.
- Manage any facilities and logistics issues to ensure that the focus remains on the agenda.
- Make certain that all stakeholders participate and have their input heard.
- Control disruptive or unproductive behavior.

SETTING THE AGENDA

The agenda for the workshop will be based on the needs of the particular project and the content that needs to be developed at the workshop. No one agenda fits all. However, most structured requirements workshops can follow a fairly standard format. Table 11–1 provides a typical agenda.

Table 11–1   Sample Agenda for the Requirements Workshop

Time	Agenda Item	Description
8:00–8:30	Introduction	Review agenda, facilities, and rules
8:30–10:00	Context	Present project status, market needs, results of user interviews, and so on
10:00–12:00	Brainstorming	Brainstorm features of the application
12:00–1:00	Lunch	Work through lunch to avoid loss of momentum
1:00–2:00	Brainstorming	Continue brainstorming
2:00–3:00	Feature definition	Write out two- or three-sentence definitions for features
3:00–4:00	Idea reduction and prioritization	Prioritize features
4:00–5:00	Wrap-up	Summarize and assign action items, address "parking lot" items

RUNNING THE WORKSHOP

Problems and Tricks of the Trade

You can see that the facilitator has a crucial role to play. To make matters even more exciting, these workshops are often characterized by a highly charged atmosphere. In other words, there are reasons why it is difficult to get consensus on these projects; nearly *all* these reasons will be present at the workshop.

Indeed, the setting may even be politically charged, confrontational, or both. This is yet another reason for having a facilitator; let the facilitator take the heat and manage the meeting so as to not exacerbate any problems—past, present, or future—among stakeholders.

Many facilitators carry a "bag of tricks" with them to help manage this highly charged atmosphere. At RELA, we evolved a set of highly useful "workshop tickets." Although they seem pretty odd, and even juvenile at first, you can trust us that they have proved their worth in a variety of settings. The more difficult the workshop, the more valuable they become! They also tend to spur "out-of-the-box" thinking. What's more, they are fun and they contribute to a positive tone for the session. Figure 11–2 provides a sample set of workshop tickets. Feel free to adapt them and use them, along with "instructions" for use.

Table 11–2 describes some of the problems that can occur in the workshop setting and also provides suggestions on how you can use the workshop tickets to address the problems. The facilitator must also introduce these rules at the beginning of the meeting and, ideally, reach a consensus that it's OK to use these silly tickets for this one day.

Brainstorming and Idea Reduction

The most important part of the workshop is the brainstorming process. This technique is ideally suited for the workshop setting: it fosters a creative and positive atmosphere and gets input from all stakeholders. We'll cover brainstorming in the next chapter.

Production and Follow-Up

After the workshop, the facilitator distributes the minutes from the meeting and records any other outputs. Then the facilitator's job is over, and responsibility for success is again in the hands of the development team.

Rule: Each participant initially receives one free coupon for being late. Thereafter, participant donates $1 to the penalty box.

Objective: Keep the momentum going.

Rule: Each participant initially receives one free coupon for a "ding" or "knock" on a person or department. Thereafter, participant donates $1 to the penalty box.

Objective: Have a little fun and make people aware of the political issues in the project.

Rule: Participant initials both coupons. Participant gives coupon to any participant who provides a great idea. Goal is to spend your coupons.

Objective: Give incentive and reward creative thinking.

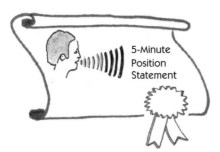

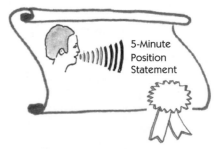

Rule: Participant spends coupon at any time. Facilitator gives podium to participant and sets timer. Everyone listens. No interruptions!

Objective: Allow for a structured process of ad hoc input. Assure everyone gets their say.

Figure 11–2 Workshop tickets

Table 11–2 Problems and Solutions in the Requirements Workshop Setting

Problem	Solution
Time management: ■ It's difficult to get restarted after breaks and lunch. ■ Key stakeholders may return late.	The facilitator keeps a kitchen timer for the meeting and times all breaks. Attendees who are late must contribute a "Late from Break" ticket while they have one or pay $1 to the penalty box.
Grandstanding, domineering positions	The facilitator enforces use of the "5-Minute Position Statement" ticket to regulate input. He or she also creates a "parking lot" list for later discussion of ideas that deserve discussion but are not relevant to the agenda item.
Lack of input from stakeholders	The facilitator encourages attendees to use their "5-Minute-Position Statement" tickets and their "That's a Great Idea!" coupons. Make it clear that no one should leave the workshop without having used the tickets or received a "That's a Great Idea!" coupon from others. (Suggestion: Make a simple reward for the use of each one.)
Negative comments, petty behaviors, and turf wars	Use "1 Free Cheap Shot" tickets until the participants don't have any more; thereafter, have them make charitable contributions to the box (the group decides how much).
Flagging energy after lunch	Do whatever you can do to keep things moving. Serve a light lunch, provide mid-afternoon snack breaks, move the furniture, rearrange the participants' seating, change the lighting or temperature.

Thereafter, it's the project leader's job to follow up on any open action items that were recorded at the meeting and to organize the information for distribution to the attendees. Often, the output of the meeting will be a simple list of ideas or suggested product features that can be turned over immediately to the development team for further action. In some cases, additional workshops with other stakeholders will be scheduled, or additional elicitation efforts will be necessary to gain a better understanding of the ideas fostered at the workshop.

SUMMARY

In this chapter, we've introduced the requirements workshop, which can serve as an accelerated requirements gathering technique in a variety of project settings. So far, we've primarily described the mechanics of the workshop, yet it is the creative part of the workshop that delivers the real value, for it is in the creative sessions that new ideas are generated and a clearer vision for the new project emerges. In the next chapter, we'll look more closely at the creative process within the workshop setting.

Chapter 12

BRAINSTORMING
AND IDEA REDUCTION

Key Points

- Brainstorming involves both idea generation and idea reduction.
- The most creative, innovative ideas often result from combining multiple, seemingly unrelated ideas.
- Various voting techniques may be used to prioritize the ideas created.
- Although live brainstorming is preferred, Web-based brainstorming may be a viable alternative in some situations.

When you are in the workshop setting described in Chapter 11 or whenever you find yourself needing new ideas or creative solutions to problems, brainstorming is a very useful technique. It's simple, fun, and an easy way to get all stakeholders to contribute.

In the workshop setting, you probably already have a pretty good idea of the features of the new product. After all, few projects begin with a totally clean slate. However, in addition to reviewing the suggested features for the product, the workshop provides the opportunity to solicit new input and to mutate and combine these new features with those already under consideration. This process will also help in the goal of "finding the undiscovered ruins" and thereby making sure that you have complete input and that all stakeholder needs are addressed. Typically, a portion of the workshop is devoted to brainstorming new ideas and features for the application.

This elicitation technique has a number of benefits.

- It encourages participation by all parties present.
- It allows participants to "piggyback" on one another's ideas.

- It has high bandwidth. Many ideas can be generated in a short period of time.
- The results typically indicate a number of possible solutions to whatever problem is posed.
- It encourages out-of-the-box thinking, that is, thinking unlimited by normal constraints.

Brainstorming has two phases: idea generation and idea reduction. The primary goal during idea generation is to delineate as many ideas as possible, focusing on breadth of ideas, not necessarily depth. The primary goal during idea reduction is to analyze all the ideas generated. Idea reduction includes pruning, organizing, ranking, expanding, grouping, refining, and so on.

Live Brainstorming

Although brainstorming can be approached in many different ways, the simple process we describe has proved effective in a variety of settings. First, all the significant stakeholders gather in one room, and supplies are distributed. The supplies given to each participant can be as simple as a stack of large sticky notes and a thick black marker for writing on the notes. The sheets should be at least 3" × 5" (7 cm × 12 cm) and no larger than 5" × 7" (12 cm × 17 cm). Each participant should have at least 25 sheets for each brainstorming session. Post-its work well. You may also need index cards, pushpins, and a soft wall, such as a large corkboard.

Then the facilitator explains the rules for brainstorming (see Figure 12–1) and states clearly and concisely the objective of the session.

The facilitator also explains the objective of the process. Although it may seem as though the objective is obvious, often it is not. In addition, the way

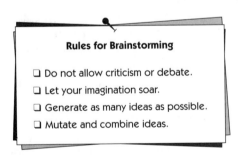

Rules for Brainstorming

❏ Do not allow criticism or debate.
❏ Let your imagination soar.
❏ Generate as many ideas as possible.
❏ Mutate and combine ideas.

Figure 12–1 Rules for brainstorming

the objective is stated will affect the outcome of the session. For example, the following questions are a few ways to state the objective.

- What features would you like to see in the product?
- What services should the product provide?
- What opportunities are we missing in the product or the market?

(Note that the objective also helps you decide when the session is done. When the objectives are met and no one else has anything to add, *quit!*)

After stating the objective of the process, the facilitator asks participants to share their ideas aloud and to write them down, one per sheet. Ideas are spoken out loud to enable others in the room to piggyback on the ideas, that is, to think of related ideas and to mutate and combine ideas. In this process, however, the first rule—no criticism or debate—must be foremost in people's minds. If this rule is not enforced, the process will be squelched, and many bright folks who are sensitive to criticism will not feel comfortable putting forth more ideas, a tragic loss.

Tip: In our experience, the most creative and innovative ideas (those that truly revolutionized the product concept) did not result from any one person's ideas but instead from the combination of multiple, and seemingly unrelated, ideas from various stakeholders. Any process that fosters this is a worthy process indeed.

When a person comes up with an idea, he or she writes it down on the supplied materials. This is important for the following reasons:

- To make sure the idea is captured in that person's own words
- To make sure ideas are not lost
- To enable posting of ideas for later piggybacking
- To prevent delays in the creative process that could be caused by a single scribe trying to capture all ideas on a flip chart or whiteboard in front of the room

As ideas are generated, the facilitator collects them and posts them on a wall in the meeting room. Again, *no* criticism of ideas can be tolerated. It is inappropriate to say, "That's a stupid idea," or even, "We already have that idea on the wall." The sole purpose is to generate ideas. Even a mildly negative remark can have the deleterious effect of suppressing further participation by the "victim." However, remarks such as "Great idea!" are appropriate and will often provide the award of a "That's a Great Idea!" ticket, which can encourage further participation by all stakeholders. Idea generation should proceed until all parties feel it has reached a natural end.

It is common for lulls to occur during idea generation. These are not times to stop the process. Lulls tend to correct themselves as soon as the next idea is generated. Longer lulls might be cause for the facilitator to state the objective again or to ask stimulating questions. Most idea-generation sessions last around an hour, but some last two to three hours. Under no condition should the facilitator end a session that is going strong with a remark like, "I know we're all doing great with this process, but we need to move on." To the participants, this remark says, "Your ideas are not as important as my schedule." The number of ideas generated will be a function of how fertile the subject being discussed is, but it is common to generate 50–100 ideas.

The process tends to have a natural end; at some point, the stakeholders will simply run out of ideas. This is typified by longer and longer gaps between idea submissions. At this point, the facilitator ends the session, and it may well be a great time for a break.

IDEA REDUCTION

When the idea-generation phase ends, it is time to initiate idea reduction. Several steps are involved.

Pruning Ideas

The first step is to "prune" those ideas that are not worthy of further investment by the group. The facilitator starts by visiting each idea briefly and asking for concurrence from the group that the idea is basically valid. There is no reason for any participant to be defensive or to claim authorship for any idea; any participant may support or refute any idea.

Tip: The presence of ideas that can be easily pruned is an indicator of a quality process. The absence of a fair number of wild and crazy ideas indicates that the participants were not thinking far enough "out of the box."

The facilitator asks the participants whether each idea is worthy of further consideration and then removes an invalid idea, but if there is *any* disagreement among the participants, the idea stays on the list. If participants find two sheets with the same idea, group them together on the wall. (This is usually preferable to removing one; its author may feel insulted.)

Grouping Ideas

It may be helpful during this process to start grouping similar ideas. Doing so is most effective when participants from the session volunteer to go to the wall and do the grouping. Related ideas are grouped together in regions of the walls. Name the groups of related ideas. For example, the groups might be labeled as follows:

- New features
- Performance issues
- Enhancements to current features
- User interface and ease-of-use issues

Instead, they may be specifically focused on capabilities of the system and the way they support various types of users. For example, in envisioning a new freight and delivery service, the features might be grouped by:

- Package routing and tracking
- Customer service
- Marketing and sales
- Web-based services
- Billing
- Transportation management

Idea generation can be reinitiated now for any one of these groups if the participants feel that the grouping process has spurred development of new ideas or that some area of key functionality has been left out.

Defining Features

At this point, it is important to take the time to write a short description of what the idea meant to the person who submitted it. This gives the contributor the opportunity to further describe the feature and helps ensure that the participants have a common understanding of the feature. This way, everyone understands what was meant by the idea, thus avoiding a fundamentally flawed prioritization process.

In this process, the facilitator walks through each idea that has not been pruned and asks the submitter to provide a one-sentence description. Table 12–1 gives some examples.

A welding robot feature, such as "automatic reweld," may already be sufficiently described, and no further work is required. It is important not to bog

Table 12–1 Examples of Feature Definitions

Application Context	Brainstormed Feature	Feature Definition
Home lighting automation	"Automatic lighting settings"	Homeowner can create preset time-based schedules for certain lighting events to happen, based on time of day.
Sales order entry system	"Fast"	Response time will be fast enough not to interfere with typical operations.
Defect tracking system	"Automatic notification"	All registered parties will be notified via e-mail when something has changed.

down in this process; it should take no longer than a few minutes per idea. You need capture only the essence of the idea.

Prioritizing Ideas

In some situations, the generation of ideas is the only goal, and the process is then complete. However, in most settings, including the requirements workshop, it will be necessary to prioritize the ideas that remain after pruning. After all, no development team can do "everything that anybody can ever think of." Once the groupings have stabilized and been agreed to, it is time to move on to the next step. Again, a variety of techniques can be used; we'll describe two that we use routinely.

Results of cumulative voting:

Idea 1 $380

Idea 2 $200

Idea 3 $180

Idea 4 $140

Idea 5 . . .

.

.

Idea 27 . . .

Cumulative Voting: The Hundred-Dollar Test This simple test is fun, fair, and easy to do. Each person is given $100 of "idea money" to be spent on "purchasing ideas." (You may even wish to add a kit of "idea bucks" to the workshop ticket inventory.) Each participant is asked to write on a sheet of paper how much of this money to spend on each idea. Then, after the participants have had a chance to vote, the facilitator tabulates the results and provides an order ranking. It may also be helpful to do a quick histogram of the result so participants can see the visual impact of their decisions.

This process is straightforward and usually works just great. However, you should be aware of the following caveats. First, it will work only once. You cannot use the same technique twice on the project, because once the results are known, participants will bias their input the next time around. For example, if you're a participant and your favorite feature is first on the list but your second-favorite feature didn't even get honorable mention, you may put all your money on the second feature. You're confident that other voters will see to it that your favorite feature still makes the cut.

Similarly, you may find it necessary to limit the amount anyone spends on one feature. Otherwise, a tricky participant, knowing full well that "other items" such as "Run faster" and "Easy to use" will make the cut to the top of the list, might put all of their money on "Runs on the Mac platform" and elevate it to a higher priority. On the other hand, you may wish to allow a higher limit, so long as you have the opportunity to understand where the really big votes came from. They may represent high-priority needs from a limited stakeholder community.

"Critical, Important, Useful" Categorization   A colleague taught us another prioritization technique that has also been very effective, especially with a small group of stakeholders or even just one stakeholder (such as when you need your boss's opinion of your priorities). In this technique, each participant is given a number of votes equal to the number of ideas, but each vote must be categorized "critical," "important," or "useful." The trick is that each stakeholder is given only one-third of the votes from each category; therefore, only one-third of the ideas can be considered critical.

- *Critical* means indispensable, suggesting that a stakeholder would not be able to use a system without this feature. Without the feature, the system does not fulfill its primary mission or meet the market need.
- *Important* means that there could be a significant loss of customer utility, perhaps even market share or revenue, or new customer segments served without the feature. If the important items don't get implemented, some users would not like the product and would not buy it.
- *Useful* means nice to have. The feature makes life easier, makes the system more appealing or more fun, or delivers higher utility to some class of users.

Note: With this scheme, all ideas that survived the pruning process get at least a "useful" vote, avoiding insult to those who submitted them.

In a larger group of participants, each item will have a mix of categories, but this is not really a problem. The facilitator has one more trick: Simply multiply "critical" votes times 9, "important" by 3, and "useful" by 1 and add up the score! This will tend to spread the results to heavily favor the "critical" votes, and thus every stakeholder's "critical" need will tend to bubble toward the top of the list.

WEB-BASED BRAINSTORMING

So far, we have discussed a process for brainstorming that works very effectively when all stakeholders can be gathered together at the same time, the participants are relatively proactive and not overly shy, the facilitator is experienced, and stakeholder politics are manageable. Indeed, there is *no* substitute for the developers and outside stakeholders spending this time together. Each will remember the various priorities, concerns, and issues raised by the others, and perspective and mutual respect are often by-products of the process. Therefore, the requirements workshop and live brainstorming are by far our preferred approaches.

But sometimes live brainstorming is not possible. In these situations, an alternative is to use the Internet or an intranet to facilitate the brainstorming process in a collaborative environment. This technique may be particularly suited for developing advanced applications for which research is required or a long-term view is critical, the concept is initially fuzzy, and a wide variety and significant number of user and other stakeholders inputs are involved.

With this technique, the project leader sponsors a list server or discussion group for recording and commenting on product features. The recording of ideas and comments can be done either anonymously or by crediting the author, based on the construct created by the administrator. An advantage of this technique is its persistence; ideas and comments can be circulated over a long period of time, with full recording of all threads for each idea. Perhaps most important, a unique advantage of this process is that ideas can grow and mature with the passage of time.

THE CASE STUDY: THE HOLIS REQUIREMENTS WORKSHOP

Let's get back to our case study. While the interviewing process was under way, the development team met with the marketing department and decided to hold a requirements workshop for the HOLIS project.

The Attendees

After thinking through the issues, the team decided not to bring in an outside facilitator but instead to have Rick, director of marketing, facilitate the workshop. The team also decided to have two development team members participate in the workshop: Alyssa, the product manager, and Marcy, the software development manager. The team felt that both Alyssa and Marcy would speak for the team and also be able to contribute content since they were both new homeowners. Other team members would not participate but would simply attend the workshop in order to observe the process, listen to the customers, and see the results immediately.

The team also decided to include representation from the four "classes" of customers and invited the following participants:

1. Distributors: E.C., CEO of the company's largest distributor, and Raquel, the general manager of the company's exclusive distributor in Europe
2. Rusty, a local custom homebuilder with experience in purchasing and installing competitive systems in the marketplace
3. Betty, a local electrical contractor
4. Prospective homeowners, identified with Betty's help, who were in the process of building or were considering building high-end residences

Table 12–2 provides more detail on the participants.

Table 12–2 Attendees of the HOLIS Requirements Workshop

Name	Role	Title	Comments
Rick	Facilitator	Director of marketing	
Alyssa	Participant	HOLIS product manager	Project champion
Marcy	Participant	Software development manager	Development responsibility for HOLIS
Lucy	Participant		Prospective homeowner
Elmer	Participant		Prospective homeowner
E.C.	Participant	CEO, Automation Equip	Lumenations' largest distributor
Raquel	Participant	GM, EuroControls	Lumenations' European distributor
Betty	Participant	President, Krystel Electric	Local electrical contractor
Rusty	Participant	President, Rosewind Construction	Custom homebuilder
Emily	Observer	VP and GM, Lumenations	
Various members	Observer	Development team	All team members who were available

The Workshop

Prior to the workshop, the team put together a warm-up package consisting of:

- A few recent magazines articles highlighting the trends in home automation
- Copies of selective interviews that had been conducted
- A summarized list of the needs that had been identified to date

Rick brushed up on his facilitation skills, and Alyssa handled the logistics for the workshop.

The Session

The session was held at a hotel near the airport and began promptly at 8 A.M. Rick introduced the agenda for the day and the rules for the workshop, including the workshop tickets. Figure 12–2 provides a perspective on the workshop.

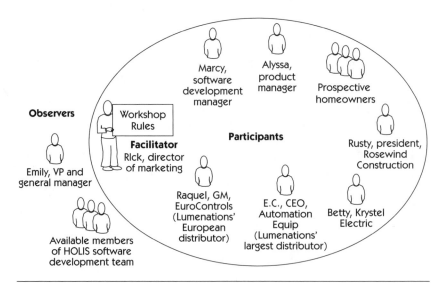

Figure 12–2   HOLIS requirements workshop structure

In general, the workshop went very well, and all participants were able to have their input heard. Rick did a fine job of facilitating, but one awkward period occurred when Rick got into an argument with Alyssa about priorities for a couple of features. (The team members decided that for any future workshop, they would bring in an outside facilitator.) Rick led a brainstorming session on potential features for HOLIS, and the team used cumulative voting to decide on relative priorities. Table 12–3 shows the results.

The Analysis of Results

The results of the process turned out as expected, except for two significant items.

1. "Built-in security" appeared very high on the priority list. This feature had been mentioned in previous interviews but had not made it to the top of anyone's priority list. After a quick offline review, Alyssa noted that built-in security, such as the ability to flash lights, an optional horn, and optional emergency call-out system, was apparently not offered by any competitive system. The distributors commented that although they were surprised by this input, they felt that it *would* be a competitive differentiation and agreed that this should be a high-priority feature. Betty and Rusty agreed. Based on this conclusion, marketing decided to include this functionality and to position it as a unique, competitive differentiator in the marketplace. This became one of the *defining features* for HOLIS.

2. In addition, feature 25, "Internationalized user interface," did not get a lot of votes. (This seemed to make sense to the team because the U.S.-based homeowners could not have cared less about how well the product sold in Europe!) The distributor, however, stated flatly that if the product was not internationalized at version 1.0, it would *not* be introduced in Europe. The team noted this position and agreed to explore the level of effort necessary to achieve internationalization in the 1.0 release.[1]

---

1. This issue demonstrates one of the problems with cumulative voting. Not all stakeholders are created equal. Failure to achieve internationalization, which had not been on the "radar screens" of the team prior to the workshop, would have been a strategic requirements misstep of significant proportions.

Table 12–3   Features from the HOLIS Workshop, Sorted by Priority

ID	Features	Votes
23	Custom lighting scenes	121
16	Automatic timing settings for lights and so on	107
4	Built-in security features: lights, alarms, and bells	105
6	100 percent reliability	90
8	Easy-to-program, non-PC control unit	88
1	Easy-to-program control stations	77
5	Vacation settings	77
13	Any light can be dimmed	74
9	Uses my own PC for programming	73
14	Entertain feature	66
20	Close garage doors	66
19	Automatically turn on closet lights when door opened	55
3	Interface to home security system	52
2	Easy to install	50
18	Turn on lights automatically when someone approaches a door	50
7	Instant lighting on/off	44
11	Can drive drapes, shades, pumps, and motors	44
15	Control lighting and so on via phone	44
10	Interfaces to home automation system	43
22	Gradual mode: slowly increase/decrease illumination	34
26	Master control stations	31
12	Easily expanded when remodeling	25
25	Internationalized user interface	24
21	Interface to audio/video system	23
24	Restore after power fail	23
17	Controls HVAC	22
28	Voice activation	7
27	Web site–like user presentation	4

SUMMARY

As managers, we are constantly amazed by the unique and creative talents, individual skills, and special challenges that our local and extended team members exhibit. Our management goal is to maximize the productivity and achievement of each team member in harmony with the objectives of the project and its mission. The workshop and brainstorming techniques we have described in the last two chapters routinely help us meet this objective, at least within the requirements management context. We encourage you to give them a try, and we are confident you will get the results you deserve.

Chapter 13

STORYBOARDING

Key Points

- The purpose of storyboarding is to elicit early "Yes, But" reactions.
- Storyboards can be passive, active, or interactive.
- Storyboards identify the players, explain what happens to them, and describe how it happens.
- Make the storyboard sketchy, easy to modify, and *not* shippable.
- Storyboard early and often on each project with new or innovative content.

Perhaps no requirements elicitation technique has been subject to as many interpretations as has "storyboarding." Nonetheless, most of these interpretations agree that the purpose of storyboarding is to gain an early reaction from the users on the concepts proposed for the application. In so doing, storyboards offer an effective technique for addressing the "Yes, But" syndrome. With storyboarding, the user's reaction can be observed very early in the lifecycle, well before concepts are committed to code and, in many cases, even before requirements are developed. Human factors experts have told us for years that the power of storyboards should not be underestimated. Indeed, the movie industry has used the technique since the first flickers on the silver screen.

Effective storyboarding applies tools that are both inexpensive and easy to work with. Storyboarding

- Is extremely inexpensive
- Is user friendly, informal, and interactive
- Provides an early review of the user interfaces of the system
- Is easy to create and easy to modify

Storyboards also offer an excellent way to ease the "blank-page" syndrome. When the users do not know what they want or have trouble envisioning any solution to the current problem, even a poor storyboard is likely to elicit a response of "No, that's not what we meant, it's more like the following," and the game is on.

Storyboards can help speed the conceptual development of many different facets of an application. Storyboards can be used to understand data visualization, to define and understand business rules that will be implemented in a new business application, to define algorithms and other mathematical constructs that are to be executed inside an embedded system, or to demonstrate reports and other hard-copy outputs for early review. Indeed, storyboards can and should be used for virtually any type of application in which early user and stakeholder feedback could be a key success factor.

TYPES OF STORYBOARDS

In practice, there are no rules, constraints, or fixed constructs, so a storyboard can be anything the team wants it to be. The team should feel free to use its imagination to think of creative ways to storyboard a specific application.

However, most generally, storyboards can be categorized into three types, depending on the mode of interaction with the user. These are passive, active, or interactive.

- *Passive storyboards* tell a story to the user. They can consist of sketches, pictures, screen shots, PowerPoint presentations, or sample application outputs. In a passive storyboard, the analyst plays the role of the system and simply walks the user through the storyboard, with a "When you do this, this happens" explanation.
- *Active storyboards* try to make the user see "a movie that hasn't actually been produced yet." Active storyboards are animated or automated, perhaps by an automatically sequencing slide presentation, an animation tool, a recorded computer script or simulation, or even a homemade movie. Active storyboards provide an automated description of the way the system behaves in a typical usage or operational scenario.
- *Interactive storyboards* let the user experience the system in as realistic a manner as practical. They require participation by the user. Interactive storyboards can be simulations or mock-ups or can be advanced to the point of throwaway code. An advanced, interactive storyboard built out of throwaway code can be very close to a throwaway prototype.

As Figure 13–1 shows, these three storyboarding techniques offer a continuum of possibilities ranging from sample outputs to live interactive demos. Indeed, the boundary between advanced storyboards and early product prototypes is a fuzzy one.

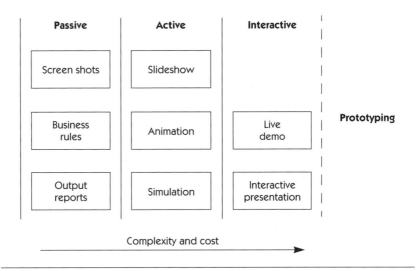

Figure 13–1   Storyboarding continuum

The choice of storyboarding technique will vary, based on the complexity of the system and the risk of the team's misunderstanding of what the system needs to do. An unprecedented or particularly innovative system that has abstract and fuzzy definitions may even require multiple storyboards, moving from passive to interactive as the team's understanding of the system improves.

WHAT STORYBOARDS DO

Disney's *Snow White and the Seven Dwarfs,* the first animated movie ever produced, used storyboards, and they are still routinely used as an integral part of the creative process in movies and cartoons. They represent the raw creative input used to develop the characters and the story line.

In software, storyboards are used most often to work through the details of the human-to-machine interface. In this area, generally one of high volatility, each user is likely to have a different opinion of how the interface should work. Storyboards for user-based systems deal with the three essential elements of any activity:

1. Who the players are
2. What happens to them
3. How it happens

The *who* element defines the players, or the users of the system. In a software system, as we discussed earlier, the *who* are such players as users, other systems, or devices—in other words they are the actors that interact with the solution system we are defining. For users, the interaction is typically described via user input screens or data entry forms, outputs such as data or reports, or other types of input and output devices, such as buttons, switches, displays, and monitors. For devices and systems, interaction will be performed via a software or hardware interface, such as a communication protocol or motor controller drive signal.

The *what* element represents the behavior of the users as they interact with the system as well as the behavior of the system as it interacts with the user. The *how* element provides descriptions of how this interaction happens, showing events, states, and state transitions.

For example, we once created a storyboard for an automated-vehicle amusement park ride.

- The *who* represented the guests who ride on the vehicle.
- The *what* represented the behavior of the vehicle as it provided various events for the guests.
- The *how* provided further descriptions of how this interaction happens—events, state transitions—and described both the guest states (surprised, scared) and the vehicle states (accelerating, braking, unloading).

TOOLS FOR STORYBOARDING

Storyboards can be as varied as the team members' imaginations will allow.

The tools and techniques for storyboarding can be as varied as the team members' and users' imaginations will allow. Passive-storyboarding constructs have been made out of tools as simple as paper and pencil or Post-it notes. More advanced storyboards can be built with presentation managers such as

PowerPoint. Passive, active, and user-interactive storyboards have been built with various packages that allow fast development of user screens and output reports. Interactive storyboards can be built with a variety of specialty software packages for interactive prototyping, and tools such as Macromedia's Director and Cinemation from Vividus Corporation can be used to create more complex animations and simulations.

In a simpler example, at RELA, Inc., one team member also dabbled in cartooning on the side. At the concept stage of a project, he would simply sketch a half-dozen or so simple cartoons that showed the product in its typical use or various aspects of the product's interface. This was a quick and inexpensive way to gain a reaction from the potential users. Also, the cartoon-like nature of the output avoided some of the potential problems of storyboarding, as we'll see later. Unfortunately, no other cartoonists were around when the designer left the company, leaving us to find alternative storyboarding techniques!

In our current efforts, which are focused mostly on ISV applications, we get along reasonably well by using PowerPoint or other common desktop presentation managers, in combination with sample screen shots built by the same tools used to build the graphical user interfaces in the application. Interestingly, the greatest breakthrough in storyboarding technique may well have been the simple addition of the animation capability to PowerPoint. Suddenly, our ability to express dynamics and interactivity increased substantially.

TIPS FOR STORYBOARDING

Storyboards help with "Yes, But" and "Undis-covered Ruins" syndromes.

The storyboarding technique is helpful in gaining early user feedback with simple, inexpensive tools. As such, storyboards are particularly effective at addressing the "Yes, But" syndrome. They also help address the "Undiscovered Ruins" syndrome by eliciting immediate user feedback as to what the system "doesn't appear to do." But, as with any technique, certain caveats apply. Here are some tips to keep in mind as you practice your storyboarding technique.

- Don't invest too much in a storyboard. Customers will be intimidated about making changes if it looks like a real work product or they think they might insult you, a particularly difficult problem in some cultures. It's OK to keep the storyboard clunky and sketchy, even crude. (See the storyboarding story at the end of this chapter.)

- If you don't change anything, you don't learn anything. Make the storyboard easy to modify. You should be able to modify a storyboard in a few hours.
- Don't make the storyboard too functional. If you do, some stakeholders may want you to "ship it." (In one real-world project, we suffered for years supporting an Excel/Visual Basic product that was never intended to be more than a storyboard.) Keep the storyboard sketchy; use tools and techniques that have no danger of making it into the field, especially for storyboards that are coded. (*Hint:* If the application is to be implemented in Java, write the storyboard in Visual Basic.)
- Whenever possible, make the storyboard interactive. The customer's experience of use will generate more feedback and will elicit more new requirements than a passive storyboard will.

SUMMARY

In this chapter, we described another simple and inexpensive technique for requirements elicitation. A storyboard is anything you can build quickly and inexpensively that will elicit a "Yes, But" reaction from the user.

We can say with confidence that there has never been a time when we didn't learn a lot from a storyboard, and there has never been a case in which we left the storyboarding exercise with exactly the same understanding with which we entered it. So here's our advice to the development team.

- Storyboard early.
- Storyboard often.
- Storyboard on every project that has new or innovative content.

By so doing, you will get the "Yes, Buts" out early, which in turn will help you build systems that do a better job of meeting the user's real needs. Moreover, you may well do so more quickly and more economically than you have ever done before. Finally, you might want to read the short, true-life storyboarding story below. It might help you really get the point—it certainly did for us at the time it happened.

A Storyboarding Story

(Some facts have been changed to protect the innocent and the guilty in this very nearly true story.) This story occurred during the development of a complex electromechanical device for a hospital pharmacy. The customer was a Fortune 1,000 manufacturer; the vendor, our company, had been hired to develop this new, complex electromechanical, optical, and fluidics-handling system. The project was in trouble.

One day, the vendor's project manager's boss (we'll just call him "Author") received the following call from the customer's senior management (a senior vice president, "Mr. Big," a powerful individual whom we had never before had the pleasure of meeting).

MR. BIG: Author, how goes our favorite project?

AUTHOR: Not particularly well.

MR. BIG: That's what I hear. Hey, no problem is so big it can't be solved. Just bring your entire team out for a meeting. How's Wednesday?

AUTHOR: *(hastily scrapping every appointment for the entire team for Wednesday)* Wednesday is perfect.

MR. BIG: Great. Come on out and bring your entire team. Hey, don't worry about the travel costs. We'll cover that. Heck, just buy those tickets "one way."

AUTHOR: *(gulp)* Thanks, I think. We'll see you Wednesday.

On the appointed day, we entered a large conference room with the customer's project team all seated at the far end. The team had obviously already been at the meeting for some time. (*Question:* Why did the customer's team feel the need to meet before the real meeting started?) Author, this not being his first such event, walked to the other end of the room and sat down next to Mr. Big (theory being that it's going to be difficult for Mr. Big to scream at him if he is sitting right next to him; also, if he hits Author, there's the chance to win a lawsuit and recover lost project profits!).

After a short discussion, Author noted that among many significant problems troubling the project, the problem of "lack of requirements convergence" is causing delays and cost overruns. Mr. Big said, "Give me an example." Author gave an excellent example. The customer team members immediately started arguing among themselves, perhaps demonstrating that this was indeed a problem. Subcontractor breathed a small sigh of relief. Mr. Big watched the team for a moment and then said, "Very funny. Give me another example." Author's team pulled out five color renderings, each quite professionally done, of the proposed front panel and made the case that "We presented all these design options weeks ago, and we can't get convergence on a design, and we are well into the necessary tooling lead times." Mr. Big said, "This can't be so difficult. Team, pick one." The customer team members then fell out among themselves again. The day passed in this fashion. There was no convergence. There was little hope.

The next morning, Author was asked to meet for an early breakfast with a project team member ("Team Member"). Team Member, also a seamstress by hobby, pulled out a pile of felt, shearing scissors, and colored markers and said, "I'd like to facilitate the user interface portion of the meeting, using these tools."

AUTHOR: Don't be silly; no way that would work. It will look silly and unprofessional.

TEAM MEMBER: I understand, but how effective were you yesterday?

Author, being politically correct, did not speak the first word that came to mind. The second word was "OK."

The next day, the tone in the room was very different. The customer's team was again there early but this time was silent and morose rather than intemperate and excitable. (*Analysis:* They now know they are as helpless as we are. They had been planning to kill *us* but now they know that we are *all* doomed.)

To start the meeting, Team Member put a 3-foot-by-5-foot piece of felt on the wall, generating mild amusement but not disinterest on the part of the customer's team.

Team Member then placed large felt cutouts for the power switch and various therapy-mode buttons on the front panel and said, "How would this design work?"

A member of the customer's team (Customer) looked at the wall and said, "It won't, but why don't you move the emergency stop to the back?"

Team Member said, "Here, why don't you do it?" and gave the scissors to Customer.

Customer took the scissors, and Team Member retired to the back of the room. Customer proceeded to do an interactive design session with felt and scissors. One hour later, Customer looked at the wall and said, "Good enough; build it."

And off we went to do just that with our one-way return tickets home.

Let's see if we can discover the moral to this story with a little reader Q&A.

QUESTION: Why did the fuzzy felt work when the professional renderings did not?

ANSWERS: There are two reasons.

1. Interactability: What could the customer do with five drawings, of which the customer's team liked only a portion of each?
2. Usability: How intimidating can it be to cut out a big piece of felt?

The customer, who had the domain expertise but not necessarily the design expertise, designed an adequate solution to its own problem.

We took the felt home with us and stuck it on the wall, where it stayed for many years as a constant reminder of the lesson we had learned. For the project, the fuzzy felt front panel design, although probably less than optimum, never changed again and was quite adequate for the intended purpose.

But no, the project was not a huge success for the vendor, although the product did eventually go to market and achieved some commercial success. As we said before, that was only one of the problems on this particular project. (The device was operated by software, after all.)

LESSON 1:   Understanding user needs is a soft and fuzzy problem. Use soft and fuzzy tools to address it.

LESSON 2:   Performing research and development is tricky. Think twice before you start a medical device outsourcing business.

Team Skill 2 Summary

In this team skill, we've described three pervasive "syndromes" that increase the challenge of understanding the real needs of users and other stakeholders. The "Yes, But," "Undiscovered Ruins," and "User and the Developer" syndromes are metaphors to help us better understand the challenge ahead and to provide a context for the elicitation techniques we developed.

But since teams are rarely given effective requirements specifications for the systems they are going to build, they have to go out and *get* the information they need to be successful. The term *requirements elicitation* describes this process, in which the team must play a more active role.

To help the team in this mission, we've described a variety of techniques that can be used to address these problems and better understand the real needs of users and other stakeholders:

- Interviewing and questionnaires
- Requirements workshop
- Brainstorming and idea reduction
- Storyboarding

And there are others as well.

Although no technique is perfect in every circumstance, each represents a proactive means of pushing knowledge of user needs forward and thereby converting "fuzzy" requirements to requirements that are "better known." At this stage of development (or at this particular software iteration) that is a significant accomplishment.

Team Skill 3

DEFINING THE SYSTEM

In Team Skill 1, we developed the skills that focus the team on analyzing the problem. In so doing, we came to fully understand the problem being solved before we invested any serious effort in the solution. We were focused fully on the problem domain.

In Team Skill 2, we described a set of techniques the team can use to understand user needs and features proposed for the system. These user needs and features live at the top of our requirements pyramid, representing the most critical information we must understand and driving everything that follows. In so doing, we made a subtle shift in our thinking: we moved *from the problem domain to the solution domain* as we started to focus on *understanding a set of features* we can deploy to address our stakeholders' needs (Figure 1).

The amount of information we must manage increases rapidly as we move lower on the pyramid.

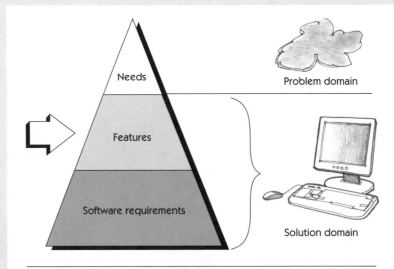

Figure 1 Features in the requirements pyramid

In Team Skill 3, we'll continue to focus on the features we identified earlier. We must also start to provide additional specificity to further define system behavior; thus, the amount of information we must manage increases.

In addition, the team must now also be concerned with a variety of other issues that are unique to the solution space but that were of little concern in the problem domain. For example, if we are developing a software product for sale to the user, we must concern ourselves with packaging, installation, and licensing considerations, each of which may be unique to the solution we are providing. If we are developing a system to address an in-house IS/IT need, we may have to concern ourselves with the requirements for deployment and maintenance, which were of little or no concern to a user not currently using such a system. These considerations may also impose requirements on the system we are about to build, even though they did not arise directly as a stated stakeholder need.

However, we must still remain at a fairly high level of abstraction, for if we sink too far into detail too quickly, we will not be able to "see the forest for the trees." In addition, it's important to pause for a second and to take the time to organize the requirements information before moving into the software requirements section of the pyramid. Thus, we'll describe some basic building blocks in Chapter 14, A Use-Case Primer, and we'll cover organization in Chapter 15, Organizing Requirements Information. We'll explore the importance of creating a shared vision of a project in Chapter 16, The Vision Document. Finally, in Chapter 17, Product Management, we'll describe all the other work necessary to convert the software we've developed into a product or system that someone might actually want to buy or deploy.

Chapter 14

A USE CASE PRIMER

Key Points

- Use cases carry the majority of the requirements for the system.
- The development team, with user involvement, writes the use cases.
- Use cases are built on a common, standard format.
- Use cases later drive test case development.

Earlier in the book we introduced the concepts of the use case and the actors that participate in them. We used them in Chapter 6 to model a business system and in Chapter 7 to help define the system boundaries for our case study. In this chapter, we take a more thorough look at the use-case method, to help you understand the motivation for using use cases and to learn how to apply them in a more rigorous manner.

However, it is not the purpose of the book to teach you everything there is to know about use cases. The purpose of this chapter is to provide a basic grounding in use cases so you can understand how to apply them throughout the requirements-intensive portion of the product development cycle. We'll apply use cases as the primary container for the software requirements we are so intent on managing. We'll use them again in Chapter 25 (to assure that the system design implements the use cases and the requirements we've agreed to) and in Chapter 26 (to provide a pattern to drive our test case development and testing activities).

Use cases are the requirements workhorse.

While it is true that not everything that matters about requirements is a use case and that we are going to have to master some non-use-case methods of communicating certain types of requirements, it is also true that the use case will be the workhorse of our requirements method. So let's get on with the work of applying use cases.

THE BENEFITS OF USE CASES

Why the intense focus on use cases? That's a fair question. The benefits of use cases include the following.

- Compared to traditional requirement methods, use cases are relatively easy to write and easier to read.
- Use cases force developers to think through the design of a system from the perspective of a user.
- Use cases engage the users in the requirements process, helping them understand the system that is being proposed and giving them a way to communicate and document their needs.
- Use cases give context for the requirements of the system. One can understand why a requirement is what it is as well as how the system meets its objectives.
- Use cases provide an ordering mechanism for requirements; one can tell what has to happen before the next thing happens, and so on.
- In most circumstances, developers write the use cases. That means not only that there actually *are* understood requirements but also that the developers know they are responsible for determining them.
- Use cases are a critical tool in the analysis process, helping us understand what the system needs to do and how it might go about doing it.
- Use cases are a critical tool in the design and implementation process, reducing the risk of transitioning from an expression of requirements to a differing implementation (Chapter 25).
- Use cases carry over directly into the testing process, helping to assure that the system actually does what it was intended to do (Chapter 26).
- Use cases serve as inputs to the user documentation, conveniently organized in a step-by-step format.

Use cases simply tell a better requirements story. Use them.

Yes, it's a pretty long list of benefits, yet not an exhaustive one. Simply put, *use cases tell a better requirements story*—a story that can be better understood by the prospective users who use the system, the developers who write and implement the use cases, the testers who use them as a basis for testing, and the documentation team members who develop the user guides and online help. No, you don't have to develop use cases; traditional forms of requirements specifications still work. But isn't your job hard enough already?

USE CASE BASICS

We'll start with a slightly more formal definition than we provided earlier.

A use case describes sequences of actions a system performs that yield an observable result of value to a particular actor.

Use case

Phew—that's a pretty pithy definition. In other words, each use case describes a series of events in which a particular actor, such as Jenny the Model, interacts with a system, such as the Ad Lib Modeling Agency Client Scheduling System, to achieve a result of value to Jenny, such as downloading directions to the next modeling assignment. In the UML, a use case is represented by an oval.

Let's look a little closer at the elements of this definition of a use case.

- *Sequences of actions:* The sequences of actions describe a set of functions performed, an algorithmic procedure, or any other internal process that produces a result. The set is invoked when the actor initiates the use case by providing some input to the system. An action is atomic; that is, it is performed either entirely or not at all. By the way, the atomicity requirement is a strong determinant in selecting the level of granularity of the use case. You should examine the proposed use case, and if the action is not atomic, then the level of granularity should be reduced to a finer level of detail.
- *System performs:* The system works *for* the actor. It exhibits the functionality described in the use case and takes its orders from the actor as to *when* to do what.
- *An observable result of value:* A most important construct. The use case must be "of value" to a user. Therefore, "the resident pushes the light button" is not a valid use case (the system didn't do anything for the user). But "the resident pushes the light button and the system turns the light on" is a meaningful description of a use case, and such a use case is much more likely to motivate the resident to interact with the system!
- *A particular actor:* The particular actor is the individual or device (Linda the resident; the signal from the emergency button) that initiates the action (toggle the light or activate the security alarm).

That is the basic definition. Simple enough, yet nontrivial at the same time. Next, let's move on to see what all these actors have to do with our system.

On Actors

Here's another definition that's important for our discussion.

An actor is someone or something that interacts with the system.

In the UML, an actor is represented by a simple stick figure. For all practical purposes, there are only three types of actors to be considered:

1. *Users:* Users act on the system, and this is the type of actor most people think of when they think of a use case. The homeowner is an actor on the HOLIS control. Authors are actors on the word processing system they employ to do their work.

2. *Other systems or applications:* Most software we write also interacts with other systems or other applications. This is another primary source of actors. The HOLIS Control Switch interfaces and communicates with the HOLIS Central Control Unit. Therefore the HOLIS Control Switch subsystem is an actor on the HOLIS Central Control Unit. The author's word processing application interacts with a Web service to access and insert a selected piece of clip art. When this happens, the author's word processing application is an actor on the Web service.

3. *A device:* Many software applications interface to a variety of input and output devices. The HOLIS control system turns lights on and off. The lights are actors on the HOLIS system. The author's printer is an output device to the operating system. The printer is an actor on the operating system.

Use Case Anatomy

The use case itself is a structure of logical elements that work together to define the use case. Figure 14–1 is a standard template that highlights these elements. Every use case has four mandatory elements.

1. *Name:* Each use case has a name describing what is achieved by the interaction with the actor. The name can be a few words in length and it must be unique for every use case. Names such as "Turn Light On/ Off" (HOLIS) and "Print Document" (word processing system) are good examples because they are short and yet descriptive.

2. *Brief description:* The purpose of the use case should be described in one or two sentences. An example might be, "This use case controls the selected light bank when instructed by the actor Homeowner."

```
┌─────────────────────────────────────────────┐
│            Name of the Use Case               │
│                                               │
│   Description                                 │
│                                               │
│   Actor(s):                                   │
│                                               │
│   Flow of events                              │
│        Basic flow                             │
│                Event 1                        │
│                Event 2                        │
│        .......                                │
│            Alternate flow                     │
│                                               │
│   Pre-conditions                              │
│                                               │
│   Post-conditions                             │
│                                               │
└─────────────────────────────────────────────┘
```

Figure 14–1   Use-case template

3. *Actor(s):* Since a use case has no meaning outside the context of its use by an actor, each actor that participates in the use case must be listed with the use case. This may seem a trivial notion, but as the number of use cases expands and the system complexity grows, knowing what actors use each use case will form a crucial basis of understanding the system.

4. *Flow of events:* The heart of the use case is the event flow, usually a textual description of the interactions between the actor and the system. The flow of events can consist of both the *basic flow*, which is the main path through the use case, and *alternate flows*, which are executed only under certain circumstances. For example, a use case that prints a receipt for a credit card transaction may discover that the printer is out of paper. In that case, an alternate flow of events would describe the behavior of the system in that special circumstance. Or if an application groups all function selections under a single menu tree, each selection is described in an alternate flow.

In addition to the mandatory elements, a use case may have optional elements, as described below.

■ *Pre-conditions:* Pre-conditions are those conditions that must be present in order for a use case to start. They usually represent some system state that must be present before the use case can be used. For example, a pre-condition of the "Print Author's Manuscript Draft" use case is that a document must be open.

- *Post-conditions:* Post-conditions describe the state of the system after a use case has run its course. They often represent persistent data that is saved by the system as a result of executing the use case. For example, a post-condition of the HOLIS "Turn Light On/Off" use case is that the light remains in the set state after the use case is complete.
- *System or subsystem:* In a system of subsystems, it may be necessary to identify whether a use case is a system-level use case (one that causes multiple subsystems to interact) or a subsystem use case. In either case, you need to identify what system or subsystem a use case is identified with.
- *Other stakeholders:* It may also be useful to identify other key stakeholders who may be affected by the use case. For example, a manager may use a report built by the system, and yet the manager may not personally interact with the system in any way and therefore would not appear as an actor on the system.
- *Special requirements:* As we'll see later, the use case may also refer to special requirements, for example, a performance or throughput requirement ("support up to 100 simultaneous users") that applies to the specific use case.

We've provided a more fully elaborated use-case specification template in Appendix C.

That's enough time spent talking about what a use case is. Let's move on to understanding how to apply them.

A Step-by-Step Guide to Building the Use-Case Model

An individual use case describes how a particular actor interacts with the system to achieve a result of value for that specific actor. The set of all use cases together describes the complete behavior of the system. However, we don't determine the behavior of the system by first writing individual use cases and then adding them all up. Instead, we first build a context model of the system and then successively refine this model until the detailed behaviors are understood, *but each of these behaviors (use cases) is refined only within the overall context of the system.* The complete set of use cases, actors, and their interactions constitutes the *use-case model* for the system.

Building the use-case model for the system is an important analysis step, one that will become the basis for understanding, communicating, and refining the behavior of the system over the course of the entire project. Building and refining the use-case model is not a one-time project event. A fundamental premise of iterative development is that "you don't know what you don't know," and this drives a process of continuous refinement wherein each phase of development advances the model to the next level of detail. In addition, as this happens, the model is refactored, new use cases are discovered, they in turn are refined, and the process continues until your model is fully refined.

By then, much of it will already be implemented in code! While there is no one perfect process for developing the model, we have found a simple five-step approach to be effective. However, as we've said earlier, these steps do not all happen at the same point in the project lifecycle, and the iterative nature of development dictates that some steps will be revisited over time.

Step 1: Identify and Describe the Actors

The first step in building the use-case model is to identify all the actors that interact with our system. After all, since a use case provides a result of value to an actor, there can be no use case that doesn't interact with something. As we described in Chapter 7, this is a matter of dividing the world into two classes of interesting things: our system and those things (actors) that interact with our system. Returning to our HOLIS case study, in Chapter 7 we identified six different actors that interacted with the HOLIS Central Control Unit.

To find the actors that interact with your system, think about the following questions.

- Who uses the system?
- Who gets information from this system?
- Who provides information to the system?
- Where in the company is the system used?
- Who supports and maintains the system?
- What other systems use this system?

Step 2: Identify the Use Cases and Write a Brief Description

Once the actors are identified, the next step is to identify the various use cases that the actors need to accomplish their jobs. We can do this by determining the specific goals for each actor in turn.

- What will the actor use the system for?
- Will the actor create, store, change, remove, or read data in the system?

- Will the actor need to inform the system about external events or changes?
- Will the actor need to be informed about certain occurrences in the system?

In our case study, we might discover use cases such as "program vacations settings" and "set clock" since these are important things that a resident (actor) might want to do with the system. If we place these in a simple diagram, it might look like Figure 14–2.

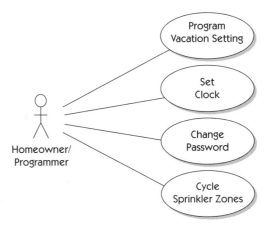

Figure 14–2   Use cases for the Homeowner/Programmer actor

You should consider the *use-case name* carefully. Typically, the name is a few words or a short phrase that starts with an action verb and communicates what the actor achieves with the use case. The use case names by themselves help communicate what the system does and quickly become a part of the project "lingo."

Along with the name, you should provide a brief description that elaborates the intent of the use case. For example, at this point, you might have the following mini-template for an identified use case.

Program Vacation Setting

Actor(s): Homeowner/Programmer

Description: Homeowner/Programmer sets lighting and alarm options for an extended stay away from home.

Step 3: Identify the Actor and Use-Case Relationships

While we've noted that only one actor can initiate a use case, you'll also discover that many use cases involve the participation of multiple actors. When the actors and use cases interact in concert, that's when the system becomes a system. In this step in the process, each use case is analyzed to see what actors interact with it, and each actor's anticipated behavior is reviewed to verify that the actor participates in all the necessary use cases and thereby achieves all the results the actor needs to be successful with the system. In a system of any scope, this can become complex fairly quickly with a large number of use cases and actors, so you'll almost certainly want to represent this part of the model pictorially. That way, a user, analyst, or other reviewer can "see" the overall system behavior at one time and thereby better understand what is being proposed.

Step 4: Outline the Individual Use Cases

The next step is to outline each use case so you can start to gain an understanding of required system behavior at the next level of detail. As you do so, you also start to understand various alternatives and events that can occur as part of the systems operation. Of particular interest at this time is the flow of events, including the basic and alternate flows.

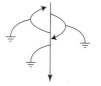

Paths through
a use case

Typically, you will outline the basic flow first. There is only one basic flow (the straight line path on the diagram to the left), the flow that represents the most common path from start to finish through the system. (Some call this the "happy day" flow since there are no problems and no exceptions on this path.)

In addition to the basic flow, you will also typically have a number of alternate flows (the curved paths on the diagram) based on both regular circumstances (the homeowner chooses a factory default vacation program) and exceptional events (the homeowner cancelled the programming effort in order to respond to the doorbell). In order to discover these paths, ask the following questions.

Basic flow:

- What event starts the use case?
- How does the use case end?
- How does the use case repeat some behavior?

Alternate flow:

- Are there optional situations in the use case?
- What odd cases might happen?
- What variants might happen?

- What may go wrong?
- What may not happen?
- What kind of resources can be blocked?

Step 5: Refine the Use Cases

At some point later in the project lifecycle, the time will be right to refine the use cases to the next and last level of detail. At that time, there are a number of additional factors to be considered, and each will play a role in the refinement process.

- *All alternate flows, including exception conditions:* It is fairly straightforward to identify the primary alternate flows of a use case since these are mostly driven by explicit user choices. However, in software development, the "what ifs" become a primary source of concern, and these must be fully explored in alternate flows. "What if the remote server is down?" "What if the resident is programming the system when an intrusion alarm occurs?" All these exceptions must be documented in the use case or the application may not behave as expected.
- *Pre- and post-conditions:* The refinement process will start to identify state information that controls the behavior of the system. This state information is captured in the pre- and post-conditions for the use case. Pre-conditions describe the things that must be true before a use case starts. For example, a pre-condition to programming vacation settings might be that the user has set the calendar clock. If that has not been done, the use case cannot be called on to be executed. Post-conditions describe the persistent states the use case leaves behind. For example, the programmed vacation schedule, which reflects that actual input by the homeowner, must be saved by the system so as to be recalled for later use.

ON USE CASES, STORYBOARDING, AND USER INTERFACE DESIGN
Use Cases and User Interfaces

Remember our formal definition of a use case.

> *A use case describes sequences of events between an actor and a system that yield a result of value to the actor.*

While it's a bit abstract, this definition handles the generic situation quite well. It allows us to express behaviors between systems of systems, between systems and devices, and so on. However, for those development teams implementing systems that directly support human users via Web browsers, client-side graphical user interfaces (GUIs) and the like, development of the use cases may be done in parallel with the design and implementation of a series of user interfaces that users can use to accomplish their larger objectives. Use cases such as "Edit and Approve Machine Translations" and "Establish Material Replenishment Signals to External Suppliers" imply a whole series of interactions (use-case steps) between a user and the system, which are accomplished via a variety of user interfaces that the designers construct for these purposes.

When this is the situation, the world of user interface design and the world of use-case specification tend to lead parallel lives. For example, inside the context of a specific use case, the team must decide

> *what choices the user makes given the screens, dialog boxes, and so on that we have presented to the user, what the system does based on those selections, and what screens, choices, and so on the system presents to the user.*

In other words, each step in a use case is achieved via the presentation of a GUI of some kind, followed by a user selection of some kind, followed by a presentation of a new GUI that moves the user to the next system context, and so on. While it's easy to see how these things relate, teams inevitably come to the following conundrum.

> *How can I express a use case if I haven't designed all the GUIs yet?*

> *How can I possibly design a set of GUIs to implement a use case that is not yet elaborated?*

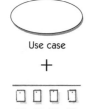

Use case

Fair questions, indeed. Let's see if we've learned any new constructs that can help us address this apparent conundrum.

Use Cases and Storyboarding

In Chapter 13, we described storyboarding as basically any technique a team can use to express system behavior, design, or implementation intent to a prospective user. A storyboard defines

- Who the players are
- What happens to them
- How it happens

If the player is a specific user and the interaction is between that user and the user interface, then storyboarding can help us describe how we are approaching the interaction, and we can use iterative and incremental techniques to converge on the GUI and the use case *at the same time*. In order to address our conundrum, let's apply the use-case technique, the storyboarding concept, and our GUI design tools together with a presentation technique that will allow us to express ourselves to a user or other stakeholder.

A Use Case Storyboard Example

Suppose you want to elaborate a section of a use case that would describe how a user inserts graphic clip art from an online source into a document. Perhaps the sequence of events appears as follows.

Use Case Sequence: Inserting Online Clip Art

(This series of steps within a larger use case allows the user to access an online clip art repository and select and insert a new clip art item.)

1. The user puts the cursor at the desired clip art location and selects the function for inserting clip art.
2. The system displays the clip art source locations.
3. The user selects the "Clips Online" choice.
4. The system launches the browser and automatically navigates to the online library
5. The user navigates to the selected art item.
. . .

You can use Microsoft PowerPoint as your storyboard presentation tool to build one PowerPoint slide for each of the steps in the use case to show the user how you intend the system to work. For example, Figures 14-3 through 14-6 show a series of storyboard slides for the first four steps of the Inserting Online Clip Art use case.

In this fashion, you can develop the use case and the GUIs in parallel while involving the user in the concept review process at the same time.

THE CASE STUDY: THE HOLIS USE CASES

Let's see how we can apply use cases in our case study. In Chapter 7, the HOLIS team applied systems engineering as a problem analysis technique to better understand the systems architecture and design constraints for HOLIS, our state-of-the-art home lighting automation system. During that process the team produced the context diagram for the system (Figure 14–7).

**1. Select function
for inserting clip art**

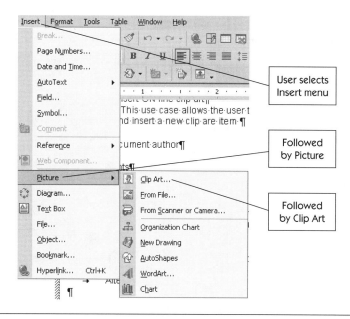

Figure 14–3 Storyboard slide for step 1 of a use case

**2. System displays
clip art source locations**

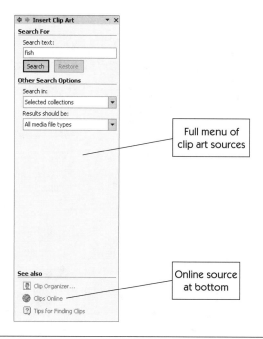

Figure 14–4 Storyboard slide for step 2 of a use case

3. User selects Clips Online choice

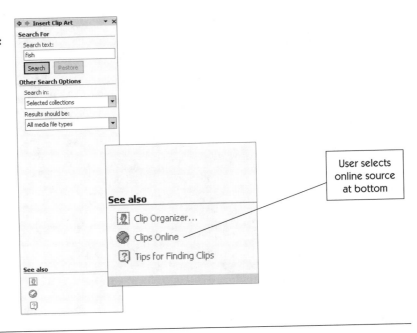

Figure 14–5   Storyboard slide for step 3 of a use case

4. System launches browser and automatically navigates to remote library

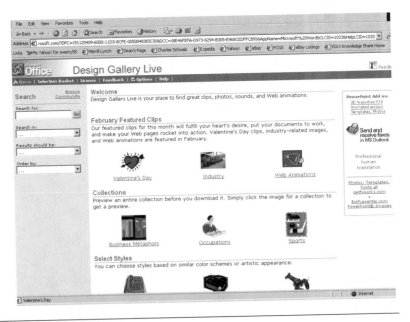

Figure 14–6   Storyboard slide for step 4 of a use case

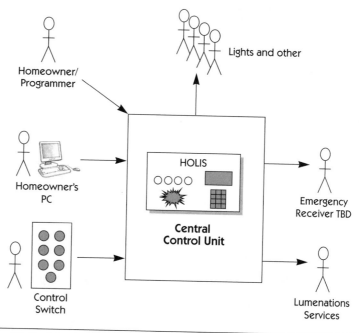

Figure 14–7 HOLIS context diagram

Find the HOLIS Actors

In building the use-case model for the system, the team first revisited the actors, those external users and devices that exist outside the system and interact with the system under development. The process resulted in the discovery of some new actors for the system. Table 14–1 shows the updated list of HOLIS actors (with new names given to a few of the actors identified earlier).

Find the HOLIS Use Cases

The team then held a brainstorming session to identify the primary HOLIS use cases and wrote a brief description for each one. Among others, they identified a simple use case they called "Turn Light On/Off" and described it as follows.

Name: Turn Light On/Off

Actor: Resident

Brief description: The resident initiates a change to the light in the room by pressing the on/off switch in the room-lighting control panel.

Table 14–1   Revised List of HOLIS System Actors

Actor	Description
Homeowner/Programmer	This is the homeowner or other operator who programs the various features, lighting scenes, and so on for HOLIS, using either the optional PC Programmer or the Central Control Unit.
Resident	This is the actor we use to describe how any person interacts with the system on a daily-usage (nonprogramming) basis.
Emergency Receiver	When an emergency signal is activated by a resident, a phone call is made to this actor.
Light Bank	This actor is a set of light banks grouped together for common action.
Wireless Remote Controller	The system also accepts control inputs from IEEE 802.11b (Wi-Fi) standard wireless remote control devices, which also serve as an actor on the system.
Lumenations Services	This actor is a Lumenations, Ltd., service person who accesses the system remotely for remote programming and maintenance service operations.
Motion Sensor	Motion sensor inputs are also actors on the system.

Associate the Actors and Use Cases

After identifying each of the primary use cases for the system, the team built a visual use-case model to illustrate the relationships between the actors and the various use cases with which the actors interact. Figure 14–8 shows a portion of that model.

Outline the Use Cases

Over the course of development, the team proceeded to outline and then further elaborate each of the use cases identified in the use-case model by building a name, description, and initial flow of the events outlined for each use case. That's the appropriate level of detail for the HOLIS project at this time. We'll revisit the "Turn Light On/Off" use case again later in Chapter 21, Refining the Use Cases.

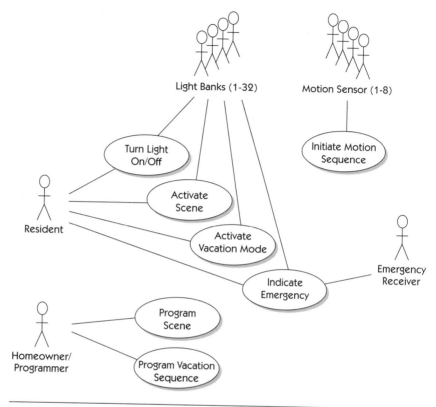

Figure 14–8   A portion of the HOLIS use-case model

SUMMARY

In this chapter, we've elaborated on the concept of the use case, which serves as the workhorse for much of our requirements work. We've described the benefits of the use-case approach, outlined the basic elements of the use case, and defined a step-by-step approach to building the use-case model that serves as the primary requirements information repository for our project. In later chapters, we'll develop these concepts further, including a look at implementation and testing techniques that are use-case-driven.

Chapter 15

ORGANIZING REQUIREMENTS INFORMATION

Key Points

- For nontrivial applications, requirements must be captured and recorded in a document, database, model, or tool.
- Different types of projects require different requirements organization techniques.
- Complex systems require that requirements sets be developed for each subsystem.

Whether expressed as user needs, a list of features, a storyboard, a set of use cases, or another format, requirements *must* be captured and documented. If you were the sole developer for a system on which you will also be the sole user and maintainer, you might consider designing and coding it immediately after identifying your needs. However, few system developments have such simplicity. More likely, developers and users are mutually exclusive, and stakeholders, users, developers, analysts, testers, architects, and other team members are involved. All parties must reach agreement about what system is being built.

Realities of budgets and schedules make it unlikely that all user needs are going to be satisfied in any particular release. Inevitable communication problems inherent in a multiple-person effort demand that requirements be captured in a way that they can be reviewed and approved and to which all parties can agree and refer.

Traditionally large documents, called *requirements specifications*, have been built to capture and communicate this information. The requirements specification for a system or application describes the external behavior of that

165

system. But requirements can rarely be defined in a single monolithic document or in a single use-case model for that matter. There are a number of reasons.

- The system may be very complex, and the volume of documentation demands both organizational and interactive access techniques.
- The system of interest may be a member of a family of related products. No one document can contain all the specifications.
- The system being constructed may be a subsystem of a larger system and may satisfy only a subset of all the requirements identified.
- Marketing and business goals need to be separated from the detailed product requirements.
- Other requirements, perhaps regulatory or legal, may also be imposed on the system, and these requirements may be documented elsewhere.

In any of these cases, you will need to maintain requirements organized into multiple *requirements sets*, each set reflecting the requirements for a particular system, a subsystem, or a number of subsystems together, as in the examples below.

- One set defines the features of the system in general terms, and another defines requirements in more specific terms. Often, the former is called the Vision document (discussed extensively in Chapter 16), whereas the latter set may consist of the system use-case model and associated supplementary requirements (discussed in Chapter 22).
- One "parent" requirements set defines requirements for the overall "system," including hardware, software, people, and procedures, and another defines requirements for just the software subsystem.
- One set defines the full set of requirements for a family of products, and another defines requirements for just one specific application and for one specific release.

The following sections describe what to do in each case. Any or all of these cases can be combined; for example, one set could contain the full set of requirements from which selected subsets are used for specific releases, as well as all business requirements.

ORGANIZING REQUIREMENTS OF COMPLEX HARDWARE AND SOFTWARE SYSTEMS

Although this book focuses primarily on software requirements, it's important to recognize that they are only one subset of the requirements management process in most system development efforts. As we described in Chapter 7, some systems are sufficiently complex that the only reasonable way to visualize and to build them is as *a system of subsystems*, which in turn are visualized as systems of subsystems, and so on, as shown in Figure 15–1. In an extreme case, such as an aircraft carrier, the system may be composed of hundreds of subsystems, each in turn having hardware and software components.

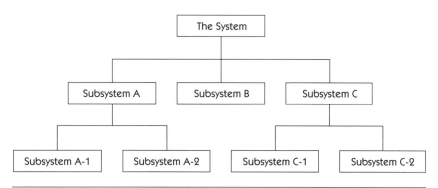

Figure 15–1   A system of subsystems

In these cases, a system-level requirements set is created that describes the system, such as fuel capacity, rate of climb, or altitude ceiling, as well as the system-level use cases that describe functional behavior, without knowledge of or reference to any of its subsystems. As we described in Chapter 7, once the requirements for the system are agreed on, a further systems engineering activity is performed. *Systems engineering* refines a system into subsystems, describing the detailed interfaces among the subsystems and allocating each of the system-level requirements to one or more subsystems. The resulting system architecture describes this partitioning and the interfaces among the systems.

■———
The system design process itself creates new classes of requirements.

Next, requirements are developed for each subsystem. These should describe the external behavior of the subsystem completely, without reference to any of its subsystems. This process causes a new class of requirements, derived requirements, to emerge. This type of requirement no longer describes the external behavior of the *system,* except in the aggregate, but instead describes the exterior behavior of the new *subsystem.* Thus, the process of system design creates new requirements for the subsystems of which the system is composed. In particular, the interfaces among these subsystems become key requirements: essentially, a contract between one subsystem and another, or a *promise* to perform as agreed to.

Once these requirements are agreed on, system design is performed again, if necessary, by breaking down each of the subsystems into its subsystems and developing requirements for each. The result is a hierarchy of requirements sets, as shown in Figure 15–2.

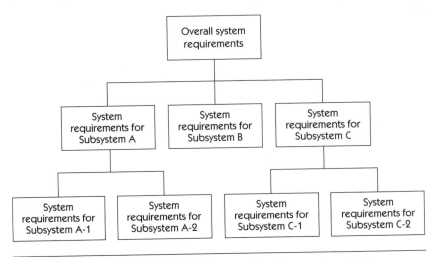

Figure 15–2   Hierarchy of requirements resulting from system design

At every level, requirements from the previous level are allocated to the appropriate lower-level systems. For example, the fuel capacity requirement is allocated to the fuel control subsystem and to the fuel storage subsystem, and new requirements are discovered and defined as appropriate.

As seen in Figure 15–3, the lowest-level systems, that is, those that are not further decomposed, usually correspond to software-only or hardware-only subsystems. Further, any of the requirements in Figure 15–3 may need to undergo an evolutionary process as details become better understood.

ORGANIZING REQUIREMENTS FOR PRODUCT FAMILIES

Many industries build sets of closely related products that have much functionality in common, yet each product contains some unique features. Such product families might be inventory control systems, telephone answering machines, application development tools, burglar alarm systems, and so on.

For example, suppose you are building a set of software products, each with some shared functionality, that may need to share data or otherwise commu-

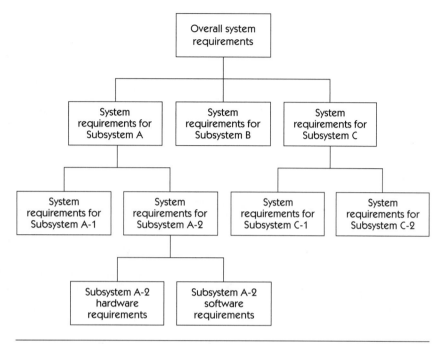

Figure 15–3   Hierarchy of resulting requirements, including software and hardware

nicate with one another when in use. In such a case, you might organize your requirements set with the following approach.

- Develop a product-family Vision document that describes the ways in which the products are intended to work together and the other features that could be shared.
- To better understand the shared-usage model, you might also develop a set of use cases showing how the users will interact with various applications running together.
- Develop a common software requirements set that defines the specific requirements for shared functionality, such as menu structures, common GUIs, and communication protocols.
- For each product in the family, develop a Vision document, supplementary specification, and a use-case model that defines its specific functionality.

The resultant organization is shown in Figure 15–4.

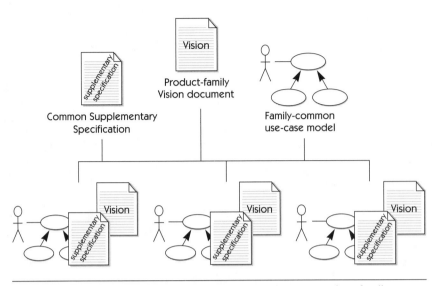

Figure 15–4 Requirements organization for a software product family

ON "FUTURE" REQUIREMENTS

Few development efforts have the luxury of either a stable set of requirements or the ability to build a system that satisfies all desired requirements. During any process of requirements elicitation, requirements will arise that are deemed appropriate for the next release of the product.

It may not be appropriate to include such requirements in the requirements set since we cannot afford to create any confusion about what requirements are and are not to be implemented in a particular release. On the other hand, it's unwise to discard them because they represent value-added work products, and we will want to harvest requirements from them for future releases. More important, the system designers may well have designed the system differently had they known that future requirements of a certain type were desired. So it makes sense to record both types of requirements but to *clearly identify those requirements that are planned for the current release.*

THE CASE STUDY: ORGANIZING THE HOLIS REQUIREMENTS

In Chapter 7, we performed some systems engineering on HOLIS, our home lighting automation system. At this point, we still don't know very much about

HOLIS, but we probably know enough to establish a first cut at the organization for our requirements information. Figure 15–5 shows that the team is using the following elements to describe the requirements for HOLIS.

- The Vision document will contain the short-term and longer-term visions for HOLIS, including the basic system-level requirements and the proposed features.
- The system-level use-case model records the use cases by which the various actors in the system interact with HOLIS.
- After some debate, the team decided to document the hardware requirements—size, weight, power, packaging—for HOLIS's three subsystems in a single hardware requirements specification.
- Since each subsystem of HOLIS is quite software-intensive, the team decided to develop a supplementary specification for each of the three subsystems, as well as a use-case model for how each subsystem interacts with its various actors.

You'll have the opportunity to see these requirements artifacts develop further as we advance the case study in later chapters. A sample of each is included in Appendix A.

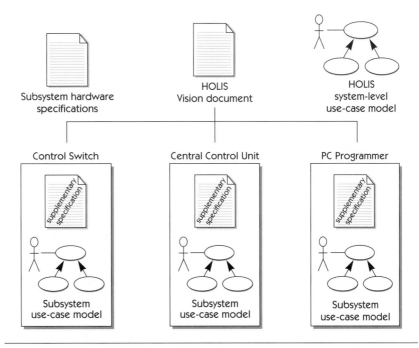

Figure 15–5 Organization of HOLIS requirements information

SUMMARY

In this chapter, we've described a number of ways to organize requirements information for complex systems. The method your team will choose will depend on a variety of factors: the nature and scope of the system under development, the techniques and strategies you use to elicit and capture requirements, and the tooling you deploy in your development and desktop environments. We looked at how the HOLIS team chose to address this problem; now it's time to move forward.

LOOKING AHEAD

In the next few chapters, we will "zoom in" on the process of requirements definition for a single software application so that we can demonstrate more clearly how the requirements management process works at the next level of detail (or at the next iteration in our ongoing software development process).

Chapter 16

THE VISION DOCUMENT

Key Points

- Every software project will benefit from having a Vision document.
- The Vision document describes the application in general terms, including descriptions of the target market, the system users, and the application features.
- The Vision document defines, at a high level of abstraction, both the problem and the solution.
- The Delta Vision document focuses on what has changed.

Vision document
for my project

This chapter focuses on the Vision document, a key component of an effective requirements process. As our colleague Philippe Kruchten, one of the fathers of the Rational Unified Process, once told us, "If, instead of a fully robust process, I were permitted to develop only one document, model, or other artifact in support of a software project, a short, well-crafted Vision document would be my choice."

Why is that? Because the Vision document, even if short or perhaps incomplete, helps assure that everyone working on the project is working toward a single objective. The team has common goals and a common playbook—a shared gestalt, if you will. Otherwise, the team will work toward unknown or conflicting objectives, and chaos will likely result.

Over the years, we have found this document to be of utmost importance, and it has evolved to become a standard best practice for use when defining a software application.

COMPONENTS OF THE VISION DOCUMENT

Scope of the
Vision document

The Vision document captures the needs of the user, the features of the system, and other common requirements for the project. As such, the scope of the Vision document extends over the top two levels of the requirements pyramid, thereby defining at a high level of abstraction both the *problem* and the *solution.*

For a software product, the Vision document also serves as the basis for discussion and agreement among the three primary internal stakeholder communities of the project:

1. The marketing and product management team, which serves as the proxy for the customer and the user and which will ultimately be held accountable for the success of the product after release
2. The project team developing the application
3. The management team, which will be held responsible for the business outcome of the endeavor

The Vision document is uniquely important because it captures the essence of the product from all significant perspectives in a short, abstract, readable, and manageable form. As such, the Vision document is the primary focus in the early phases of the project, and any investment made in the process of gathering Vision document information will pay handsome returns in later phases.

Because virtually all software projects will benefit from having a Vision document, we are going to describe it in some detail. Although our example is oriented toward a software product, it should be a fairly straightforward matter to modify it for your particular system context.

Figure 16–1 provides a briefly annotated outline of a sample Vision document. This outline has been used, with customizations, in hundreds of software products and a wide variety of software applications. A fully annotated version of this document appears in Appendix B.

In summary, the Vision document is a concise description of everything you consider most important about the product or application. Write the Vision document in plain language and at a level of detail that makes it easy for the primary stakeholders of the project to review and understand the document.

1. **Introduction**
   Provide an overview of the entire Vision document.

   1.1. **Purpose of the Vision Document**
        State the purpose of the Vision document: to collect, analyze, and define high-level user needs and features of the product.

   1.2. **Product Overview**
        State the purpose of the application, its version, and new features for delivery.

   1.3. **References**
        Provide a complete list of all documents referenced elsewhere in the Vision document.

2. **User Description**
   Briefly describe the perspective of the users of your system.

   2.1. **User/Market Demographics**
        Summarize the key market demographics that motivate your product decisions.

   2.2. **User Profiles**
        Briefly describe the prospective users of your system.

   2.3. **User Environment**
        Describe the working environment, including elements such as applications and platforms in use, and specific usage models.

   2.4. **Key User Needs**
        List the key problems or needs as perceived by the user.

   2.5. **Alternatives and Competition**
        Identify any alternatives the user perceives as available.

3. **Product Overview**

   3.1. **Product Perspective**
        Provide a block diagram of the product or system and its interfaces to the external environment.

   3.2. **Product Position Statement**
        Provide an overall statement summarizing, at the highest level, the unique position the product intends to fill in the marketplace. Moore [1991] recommends the following format.

For	*(target customer)*
Who	*(statement of the need or opportunity)*
The *(product name)*	is a *(product category)*
That	*(statement of key benefit, that is, compelling reason to buy)*
Unlike	*(primary competitive alternative)*
Our product	*(statement of primary differentiation)*

   3.3. **Summary of Capabilities**
        Summarize the major benefits and features the product will provide.

Customer Benefit	Supporting Features
Benefit 1	Feature
Benefit 2	Feature
Benefit 3	Feature

   3.4. **Assumptions and Dependencies**

   3.5. **Cost and Pricing**
        Describe any elements of continuing product cost as well as anticipated product price points.

(continued on next page)

Figure 16–1   Template for a software product Vision document

4. Feature Attributes

Describe the feature attributes that will be used to evaluate, track, prioritize, and manage the features. The following are some suggestions.

Status	Proposed, Approved, Incorporated
Priority	Cumulative vote results; order ranking; or Critical, Important, Useful
Effort	Low, Medium, High; team-weeks; or person-months
Risk	Low, Medium, High
Stability	Low, Medium, High
Target release	Version number
Assigned to	Name
Reason	Text field

5. Product Features

This section of the document lists the product features.

5.1. Feature 1

5.2. Feature 2

6. Exemplary Use Cases

Describe a few key use cases, perhaps those that are architecturally significant or those that will most readily help the reader understand how the system is intended to be used.

7. Other Product Requirements

7.1. Applicable Standards

List all standards with which the product must comply.

7.2. System Requirements

Define any system requirements necessary to support the application, such as operating systems, network performance, and the like.

7.3. Licensing, Security, and Installation

Describe any licensing, security, or installation requirements that also affect the development effort or that create the need for separate installation software.

7.4. Performance Requirements

Use this section to detail performance requirements.

8. Documentation Requirements

Describe the documentation that must be developed to support successful application deployment.

8.1. User Manual

Describe the purpose and contents of the product user manual.

8.2. Online Help

List requirements for online help, tool tips, and so on.

8.3. Installation Guides, Configuration, and Read Me Files

8.4. Labeling and Packaging

9. Glossary

Figure 16–1 *Continued*

THE DELTA VISION DOCUMENT

The development and management of the Vision document can play a key role in the success or failure of a software project, providing the locus of activity for the many stakeholders, customers, users, product management team members, and marketing staff. Often, even the executive management of the company will be involved in the document's development and review. Keeping the Vision document understandable and manageable is an important team skill that will greatly benefit the overall productivity of the project.

To assist in this process, it is helpful to keep the Vision document as short, concise, and "to the point" as possible. This is not particularly difficult in the first release of the document since nearly every item in the outline will be new to the project or at least must be restated in the context of this particular application.

However, in future releases, you may discover that it is counterproductive to repeat features that have been incorporated in prior releases and other information that has not changed in this particular project context, such as user profiles, markets served, and existing features. We therefore introduce the *Delta Vision document*, which addresses these issues. Let's look at the progression of the Vision document in the lifecycle of a new project.

The Vision Document for Version 1.0

In the case of a new product or application, probably every element of the Vision document must be developed and elaborated. Otherwise, we would simply remove that element from the template we presented, and you wouldn't have to write about it! The Vision document must contain at least the following (see Figure 16–2):

- General and introductory information
- A description of the users of the system and the markets served
- Features intended for release in version 1.0
- Other requirements, such as regulatory and environmental
- Future features that have been elicited but will not be incorporated in the 1.0 release

This document serves as the foundation for the 1.0 release and drives the more detailed software requirements and use cases that will more fully elaborate the system.

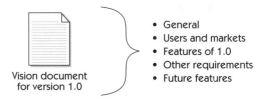

Figure 16–2   Vision document v1.0

The Vision Document for Version 2.0

Vision document
v2.0

As the project evolves, features become better defined. Often, this means that they will be more fully elaborated in the Vision document. New features will be discovered and added to the document. Thus, the document tends to grow, as does its value to the team. As you approach version 2.0, you certainly want to maintain the document that has served you so well. The logical next step in the evolution of the project and this document is to "mine" the future features that were included in v1.0 of the document but not implemented and to schedule them for v2.0. In other words, you want to find and "promote" some future features that will provide value in the 2.0 release. You may also wish to schedule a further requirements workshop or other elicitation process to discover new features that will be scheduled for 2.0 and some new future features that will need to be recorded in the document. Some of these features will already be obvious, based on customer feedback; others will come from the experience of the team. In any case, record these newly discovered features in v2.0 of the Vision document, either as scheduled for incorporation in 2.0 or as new future features.

You will also probably discover that some of the features implemented in version 1.0 did not deliver the intended value, perhaps because the external environment changed during the process and the feature was no longer needed or will be replaced by a new feature or perhaps because the customers simply didn't need the feature as they thought they would. In any case, you may discover that you will need to *remove* some features in the next release. How do you record these "anti-requirements"? Simply use the Vision document to record the fact that the particular feature must be removed or will be obviated in the next release.

As the team works its way through the process, it will discover that the document grows over time. That seems quite natural, as it is defining a system that is growing as well. Unfortunately, you may also discover that the document becomes more difficult to read and understand over time. Why? Because it is now much longer and contains much information that has not changed since the previous release. For example, the product position statement and the target users are likely to be unchanged, as are the 25–50 features implemented in v1.0 that live on in the Vision document in v2.0.

Delta Vision document v2.0

Therefore, we suggest the construction of the Delta Vision document. The Delta Vision document focuses on only two things: *what has changed* and *any other information that must be included for context.* This latter information is included either as a reminder to the team of the vision for the project or because new team members need the context for understanding.

The result is a Delta Vision document that now *focuses primarily on what is new and what is different* about this release. This focus on only that which has changed is a primary learning technique and is extremely beneficial in dealing with complex systems of information. Thus we now have the model shown in Figure 16–3.

- Vision 1.0 is our comprehensive starting point, telling us what we need to know at the start of our project.
- Delta Vision 2.0 defines that which is different in this release.
- Taken together, Vision 1.0 plus Delta Vision 2.0 constitute the whole product definition.

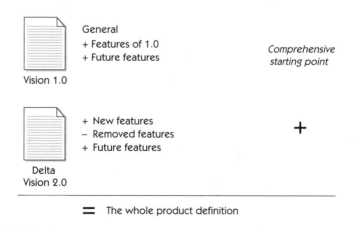

Figure 16–3 The evolving product definition

The two versions must be used together whenever the whole product definition is necessary, as for regulatory or customer requirements, for example, and it is obviously valuable for new members of the team. However, in this case, you will read about features in v1.0 that do not appear in v2.0, as they were removed later, and it is necessary to follow this audit trail whenever you need to resurrect the whole definition.

If and when this becomes awkward, it is straightforward to remerge the contents of Vision 1.0 and Delta Vision 2.0 into a new Vision 2.0 document that represents a comprehensive and complete project picture.

Of course, we needn't be strict about this definition or what each document contains. In other circumstances, we have found it convenient to use the Delta Vision document only for the minor release updates—such as v1.1 and v1.2—and to start with a clean slate and a revised "whole product" statement at each major release—such as v2.0 or 3.0. In any case, application of the Delta Vision document should help you manage the requirements process better by allowing your team to focus on what really matters at each specific time.

The Delta Vision Document in a Legacy System Environment

Rarely, if ever, is it practical to document the complete requirements of a large-scale legacy system.

One of the trickiest problems in requirements management is applying requirements management skills to the evolution of legacy IS/IT systems. Rarely, if ever, are there complete and adequate requirements specifications for the millions of lines of code and hundreds of person years of investment reflected in these systems. Nor is it practical to stop and re-document the past. By the time you have done so, the need may well have passed, and you may therefore fail in your mission by performing "requirements archaeology" when you should be writing code!

So, if you're starting from scratch or with minimal documentation, you must proceed on a best-efforts basis, using whatever resources you can find around you—code, specifications, team members with a knowledge of history—to come to an understanding of what the system does now. Our recommendation in this case is to apply the Delta Vision process and to define your features (and the later use cases) around the *changes* you are going to make to the legacy system. By following this process, you and your team can focus on *what's new* and *what's different* in this next release, and your customer and your team will gain the benefits of a well-managed requirements process. In addition, the requirements record you create will provide a documentation trail for others to follow behind you.

SUMMARY

In this chapter, we've introduced the Vision document, a seminal artifact in an effective requirements process. This document provides an overview of both stakeholder needs and product features, as well as a vision of both the problem space and the solution space. It gives the team a "stake in the ground" around which all can rally or discuss and debate, as the case may dictate. But, in all cases, your team should produce a Vision document and you may be confident that the project will benefit from having done so. Indeed, no effective software team should ever "leave home without one."

Chapter 17

PRODUCT MANAGEMENT

Key Points

- Every project needs an individual champion or a small champion team to advocate for the product.

- In a software products company, the product manager plays the role of the champion.

- The product manager drives the *whole product solution:* the application itself, support, user conveniences, documentation, and the relevant commercial factors.

In Chapter 1, we analyzed challenged projects and discovered a variety of root causes, with requirements management being near the top of the list. In Chapter 16, we defined the Vision document as a seminal document in a complicated software lifecycle; this document directly addresses the requirements challenge and is the one document you can read, at any time, to see what the product, application, or system is and is not going to do. In total, the Vision document represents the essence of the product and must be defended as if the success of the project depended on it, for it *does.*

At some point, the question rightly becomes, "But who develops and maintains this all-important document? Who manages customer expectations? Who negotiates with the development team, the customer, the marketing department, the project manager, and the company executives who have shown such keen interest in this project now that the deadline approaches? Who adjudicates the inevitable conflicts that arise over scope and budget?"

In every successful project we've been involved in—from adventure ride vehicles that put butterflies in the stomach of every guest to life-supporting ventilators that sustain tens of thousands of lives without a single software failure—there was a *champion*. We can look back at these projects and point to one individual (or, in the case of larger projects, a small team of a few folks) who played a "bigger-than-life" role. These champions kept the visions of the products (or systems or applications) in the front of their minds as if doing so were the single most important thing in their lives. They ate, slept, and dreamed about the project vision.

The Role of the Product Champion

The product champion may have a wide variety of titles: product manager, project manager, marketing manager, engineering manager, IT manager, and project lead. But no matter the title, the job is the same. It's a big job. The champion must

- Manage the elicitation process and determine when enough requirements are discovered
- Manage the conflicting inputs from all stakeholders
- Make the trade-offs necessary to find the set of features that delivers the highest value to the greatest number of stakeholders
- Own the product vision
- Advocate for the product
- Negotiate with management, users, and developers
- Defend against feature creep
- Maintain a "healthy tension" between what the customer desires and what the development team can deliver in the release time frame
- Be the representative of the official channel between the customer and the development team
- Manage the expectations of customers, executive management, and the marketing and engineering teams
- Communicate the features of the release to all stakeholders
- Review the use cases and requirements to ensure that they conform to the true vision represented by the features
- Manage the changing priorities and the addition and deletion of features
- And never give up, never surrender

This is the only person to whom the Vision document can really be entrusted, and finding the right champion for this purpose is a key to project success or failure.

THE PRODUCT MANAGER IN A SOFTWARE PRODUCT COMPANY

We once led a workshop for an online service provider confronting requirements challenges. When we got to the part of the tutorial emphasizing the notion of the product champion, the room got very quiet, and the mood changed noticeably. We asked the 25 people present, including developers and senior engineering and marketing managers, how these tough decisions were made in their environment. After a few tense moments, it became clear that no one made these decisions. After discussion among themselves, the best the group could describe was a "group grope," with input waxing and waning like the tides. *No one* had accountability for the tough decisions. *No one* decided when it was good enough.

Eventually, the team looked back at the senior marketing executive for answers, perhaps because that individual had the most input in the process. He looked around for a moment and then said: "*You know what scares me the most about this team? I can ask for any new feature to be added at any time in the process, and no one ever says no. How can we ever expect to ship a product?*"

It's probably clear from this vignette that this company *had not* been able to ship a product for some time. It's also true that history demonstrates that an extremely painful "nonability" affected the group. The company had evolved from a traditional IT background and had moved to providing online services over the years. The notion of an application as a *software product* was new. The team members had no precedents to guide them though the process. They ultimately failed in their quest.

Creating a whole product solution from a set of bits and bytes is not a trivial activity. It requires a reasonably in-depth knowledge of the technology (for example, "Can we really rely on vectoring to a hosted Web-based external Help system?") as well as market factors (for example, "This may not seem like an important feature to you, but our competitors have positioned it as necessary, and we will not be successful without it").

Who makes the tough decisions to help guide teams to commercial success? Who takes the time to understand what supporting services and other user conveniences might be necessary to assure customer success? In most commercial product companies, the product manager is empowered to make these decisions.

Stated more simply, the role of the product manager is

to help software teams build products that customers want to buy.

As Figure 17–1 shows, with two parts requirements management, one part development experience, one part commercial practices, and one part marketing, along with a big dose of common sense, the successful product manager crafts a *whole product plan* that addresses the real market needs. Although there is no one right way to organize and assign a product champion, perhaps we can look to our case study for a suggestion. After all, we did model it on a true-life and effective project team.

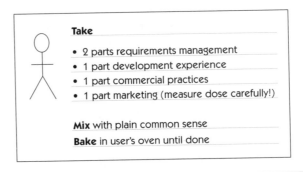

Take

- 2 parts requirements management
- 1 part development experience
- 1 part commercial practices
- 1 part marketing (measure dose carefully!)

Mix with plain common sense
Bake in user's oven until done

Figure 17–1 Product manager's recipe for success

In our HOLIS project, Alyssa takes on the role of product manager (Figure 17–2). Note that, in this case, the product manager reports through marketing rather than through the engineering organization. This is fairly typical for software product companies since, in theory at least, product managers need to be closest to the customer, who will ultimately determine the success or failure of the project.

Perhaps more importantly, product managers often report to marketing because marketing management ultimately shares responsibility for "The Number," that is, the revenue associated with the product line. This is as it should be. Marketing is ultimately accountable for helping the sales team meet its goals and must be correspondingly empowered to make the hard decisions; otherwise, accountability will be lost. However, we have seen a variety of organizational models work, and you can usually recognize a champion or a potential product manager when you see one.

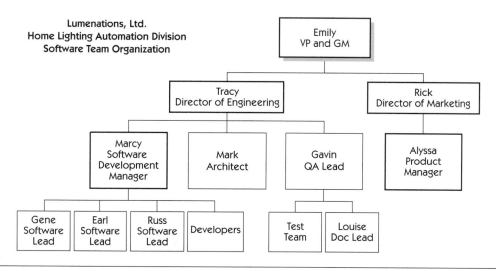

Figure 17–2   Case study: software team organization

PRIMARY ACTIVITIES FOR A PRODUCT MANAGER

What does it take to be a good product manager? On one hand, it requires someone who can focus almost exclusively on the success of the product in the marketplace. That seems simple enough. On the other hand, it requires the skill set of a "jack of all trades," someone who understands software technology and works well with the development team, is comfortable in marketing and customer presales situations, is an excellent communicator, is experienced in the commercial marketplace, understands the competitive environment, and can negotiate with internal and external stakeholders.

Perhaps we can help people in the role of product manager by mapping out some of the primary and supporting *activities* they'll engage in to achieve success, as well as some of the primary work products, or *artifacts*, they'll develop or contribute to. Figure 17–3 defines the set of primary and supporting activities, and the associated artifacts, that the product manager is involved in.

Let's look first at these primary activities.

Driving the Vision

As a former U.S. president once indicated, the "vision thing" is not so easy. It's obvious that you should have a vision, but where does it come from?

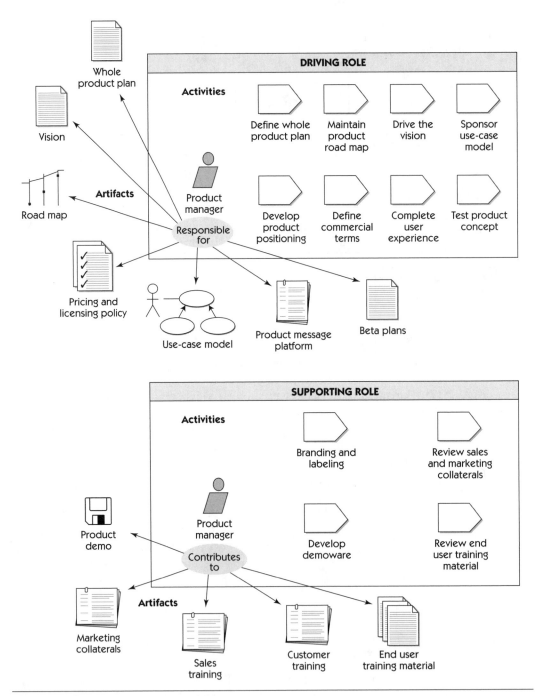

Figure 17–3   Product manager activities

For a product, the answer is that the vision is not so much an input as the output of a process that involves synthesizing user needs, constraints, wild ideas, market trends, competitive factors, and breakthrough technological opportunities into a cohesive whole. Figure 17–4 illustrates these varied sources of input for the process.

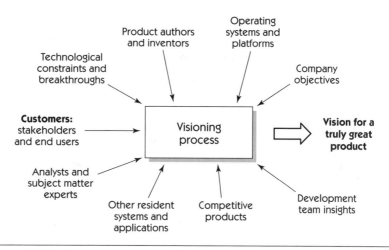

Figure 17–4 Inputs to the product vision

The product manager's role is to facilitate the elicitation and analysis of inputs and to ensure that the proper conclusions are reached. Ideally, the team reaches these conclusions together and truly shares the vision. Even then, however, when push comes to shove and scope must be managed, as is inevitably the case, the product manager must "make the call" based on his or her view of the optimal path through conflicting constraints. If the product manager stays close enough to the customer and close enough to the technology, then the team members know they can trust the product manager to make the call. After all, the product manager's job (and perhaps the team's) depends on it.

Maintaining the Product Road Map

With the vision in hand, the next job is to factor it into a product road map—a graphical view of the various code lines, major release dates, and other milestones for software delivery. Inputs to the process include the product features and relative priorities, resource estimates provided by the engineering team, and knowledge of key external events such as marketing and promotion opportunities, sales training opportunities, and perhaps key dates in the customer's calendar.

The product manager's role is to gain agreement on what should be done and what can be done and to then use this information to synthesize an optimum path to market, based on constraints in the internal and external environment and the allocation of specific features to successive releases. Although the job itself may not be easy, representing the result in a simple graphical model is straightforward. Figure 17–5 illustrates a sample product road map for the HOLIS team's upcoming release cycle.

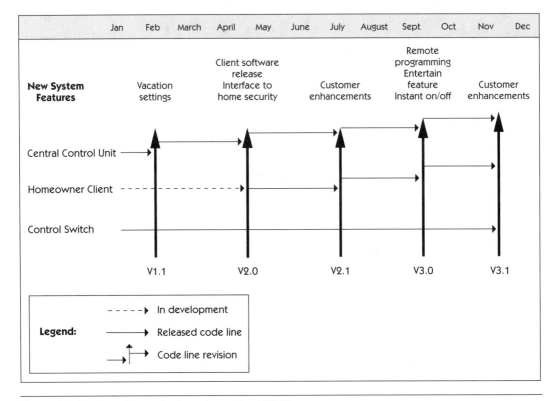

Figure 17–5 Sample product road map for HOLIS

Defining the Whole Product Plan

We've described the role the product manager has in developing and maintaining the vision and the product road map. Although the Vision document itself is comprehensive, it needn't be long. Indeed, controlling the length to a manageable twenty to forty pages is an important skill because so many stakeholders must be able to actually read and understand it. However, the scope of the Vision document, broad as it is, is not broad enough to define the whole product solution we referred to earlier. The whole product solution consists of the product itself plus all the *ancillaries*—in other words, those creature comforts that enable people to use or apply the product successfully.

Here are some questions to help you discover what these might be.

- What specific services will your company provide to help customers succeed with your product?
- What role does your company's customer support team play in assuring customer success?
- Is only one configuration of your product available, or are there multiple possible purchase configurations?
- Are you offering a stand-alone product, or does your customer need to purchase a third-party software application to go along with it?
- Does your product require special hardware, significant bandwidth, secure access, or other computing resources?
- What features need to be provided to support the user in installation, upgrade, maintenance, or support?
- What licensing provisions will be applied for commercial sale and use?
- What price are customers willing to pay for your product, and over what period?

These and similar questions are answered within the scope of the *whole product plan*, which should cover the four dimensions of a successful customer solution:

1. The product itself
2. Accompanying services and support
3. The commercial terms that define the business relationship between you and your customer
4. The documentation you provide to help assure your customers' success

Figure 17–6 provides an annotated template that teams can use to help define the solutions they are proposing for customers.

Introduction	**Services and Support**
Purpose Describe the four dimensions of the proposed whole product solution: product configuration, services and support, commercial terms, and documentation.	*Services* Describe any services (site survey, installation, product training, mentoring, Web services, and so on) that are part of the product solution.
References List additional documents (Vision document, use-case model, architecture document, and so on) that define the solution.	*Customer Support* Define parameters of the customer support plan.
Solution Overview	**Commercial Terms**
Provide a general description of the product, including what problem it is designed to solve and how it will work.	*Licensing* Describe licensing and licensing enforcement mechanisms, if applicable. *Pricing* Describe the proposed pricing model.
Product Configuration	**Documentation**
Components Provide a list of components, bill of materials, and so on.	Describe associated documentation, including user manuals, online help, read me files, installation guides, help guidelines, and release notes (or refer to the Vision document or supplementary specification).
Configurations Describe deployment and configuration options, if applicable.	
Components Supplied by Customer Describe third-party applications or components that must be supplied.	
System Requirements Specify hardware, operating system, and any related application requirements necessary to support the application, or by reference to other documents.	

Figure 17–6   Template for preparing a whole product plan

Sponsoring the Use-Case Model and Supplementary Requirements

As we described in Chapter 16, the vision for a specific product release is typically expressed in terms of a set of product features. Once you have defined that set of features, the next step in the process is to convert them into a set of use cases that describe how each specific user interacts with the system to achieve specific objectives. Taken together, the set of all users and all use cases elaborates the vision in a manner that maps to an implementation in software and ensures that the vision is achievable.

By helping the development team define the use-case model for the product, the product manager can ensure that all prospective users' needs are met in the implementation and reflected in specific use cases. In addition, the product manager can play an active role in assisting with the development, elaboration, and review of the use cases themselves. However, the caveat is that the project team will develop a lot of use cases, and, depending on the level of specificity the team needs to employ, the workload can quickly overwhelm a small product management team. In other words, the product manager will need to manage the level of his or her involvement to make sure that the product management function is looking at the entire forest rather than individual trees.

In addition, the product manager will often lead the team to an understanding of key nonfunctional requirements, many of which will be driven by external marketplace or business partnering arrangements.

Testing the Product Concept

In an effective product development process, the product concepts will be tested at every opportunity with the customer and user community. Although the necessity for this seems obvious, experience has shown that it does not always happen, and the result is often a significant mismatch between the product and the customer's expectations and needs. Table 17–1 illustrates some recommended user "check-in points" and the contribution that a product manager can provide at each point.

Completing the User Experience

In addition to the activities described above, creating a whole product solution also requires that the product manager attend to a myriad of additional artifacts and details that directly affect the user experience. Some of these, such as user documentation, online help systems, and tool tips, are obvious needs. Others, such as embedded copyright notices, startup splash screens, corporate and third-party component logo compliance, and more, may seem trivial at first, but together they create a significant impact on the user experience (and a potentially significant workload on the development team). Table 17–2 provides a checklist of some of these important artifacts and describes the product manager's role in each.

Table 17–1   Check-in Points for Testing the Product Concept

Check-in Point	Product Manager's Role
Concept development	Facilitate requirements workshops; develop storyboards, presentations, and other "soft" models to elicit customer feedback.
Vision	Primary responsibility for development of the Vision document. Circulate to all stakeholders for review. Collect and synthesize input and drive to consensus.
Use-case model development	Facilitate development and view of overall use-case model. Participate directly in development of key use cases. Mentor use-case authors and review all work. Determine key supplementary requirements.
"Alpha" testing (internal usage and early customer access programs)	Define and monitor this testing process. Define scripts and evaluation criteria to assure that all use cases are tested and all feedback is collected.
Beta testing (first formal customer evaluation process)	Work with sales team to identify and engage beta customers. Define and document commercial terms. Manage rollout and customer expectations. Collect feedback and drive back into development cycle.

Table 17–2   Artifacts That Complete the User Experience

Item/Artifact	Product Manager's Role
User documentation	Participate in concept development, design, and content plan.
Manuals, online help	
Other support material: read me files, online help, usage guidelines, release notes, administration and setup notes	
Supporting software	
Installation procedures, auxiliary scripts, embedded tutorials, miscellaneous utilities	
User presentation: corporate logo, product logo, and graphic standards	Locate or define standards, communicate to implementation team, monitor compliance.

Defining Commercial Terms

Another set of decisions that must be made before the product is ready for market is those that define the commercial terms of the relationship between you and your customer. These may well be as critical to your product's success as the product features themselves. Although some of these decisions might be outside the product manager's scope or authority, as the primary product advocate, the product manager must be clear that "the buck stops here" when it comes to driving this set of consensus-building and decision-making activities. Table 17–3 highlights these activities and the product manager's role in each.

Table 17–3   Artifacts That Define the Commercial Terms

Item/Artifact	Product Manager's Role
Licensing	Facilitate or define licensing and licensing enforcement policies. Work with development team to define and implement licensing use cases. Work with legal department to draft license provisions. Work with operations team to define and implement licensing mechanisms.
Pricing policy	Facilitate or define product pricing and discount schedule. Work with sales and operations teams to build and distribute price list data.
Customer support	Facilitate or define support policies, including access mechanisms, support levels, service-level agreements, upgrade policies, and pricing for same.

Positioning and Messaging

If the product manager is a member of (or associate to) the marketing department, he or she may also be responsible for *product positioning*. As the saying goes in retail, the key to success is "location, location, location." In retail, your likelihood of success is in large part based on your ability to attract foot traffic into your store. And people will likely go to your store because it is convenient for them to get there, rather than because of any lead generation or promotion mechanism you deployed to drive them to you.

The same goes for software. But since locations in our industry are *virtual*, rather than physical, the concept of *position* serves as a proxy for location. Your company's responsibility is to create a location in your customers' minds—a position that highlights your product's strengths, minimizes its weaknesses, and ultimately causes customers to select software from your company rather than someone else's. In other words, *positioning* is how you differentiate your products and services from others in the marketplace.

No matter what you and your product and marketing teammates think of your product, *the way potential buyers perceive it will ultimately determine whether or not they will purchase it.*

As an organizing technique for positioning, Moore [1991] recommends the starting point shown in Table 17–4.

Table 17–4 Statement of Purpose for Product Positioning

For	*(target customer)*
Who	*(statement of the need or opportunity)*
The *(product name)*	is a *(product category)*
That	*(statement of key benefit, that is, compelling reason to buy)*
Unlike	*(primary competitive alternative)*
Our product	*(statement of primary differentiation)*

Source: Based on Moore [1991].

If you and your team can agree on this simple statement of purpose, then you will be well on your way to building a solid *message platform.*

Of course, establishing a position does you no good whatsoever unless you can articulate that position succinctly and memorably to the marketplace. That is the role of *messaging.* Messaging puts words behind your position and builds a platform you can use to describe the more detailed aspects of your basic selling proposition to customers and others. The goal of positioning and messaging is *to help create a competitive advantage in the marketplace.*

Your message does not consist of just any old words. Your message contains the *specific words and phrases in the specific sequence* that you and your extended teams will use to deliver your product message to the marketplace, no matter what vehicle you use (for example, print advertising, Web site, sales presentations, and so on). Moreover, in this day of information and communication overload, they are the *only* words you should allow the extended team to use to describe your company's products and services. Each member of your company must learn to *use the same words, in the same way,* when describing your company to outsiders, whether it be trade press, local press, industry analysts, customers, or partners. Otherwise, your customers will become quickly confused, and your message will be lost in the cacophony and constant bombardment of your competitor's more effective promotions.

As you come to agreement on your messaging, it is useful to document your messaging in a *core message platform.* This document summarizes your basic messages, as well as the product or solution features that support it, in a succinct and focused manner. The core message platform then serves as the basic input to all product marketing artifacts, including the Web site, data sheets, demos, and other sales materials.

SUPPORTING ACTIVITIES

Though typically led by others, there is a host of other activities in which the product manager should be involved in order to create an effective whole product solution. These include the following.

Branding and Product Labeling

Although this activity is typically owned by corporate marketing, the product manager plays a key role in defining and contributing to the outcome. Specifically, product management will typically be involved in naming the product and product features and then ensuring that they are applied routinely throughout the documentation and on the startup screens, menus, and other user interface items in the application.

End User Training Materials

Most software applications embody a new method of some kind. Whether it is a process for translating product data to other languages, a new method for doing object-oriented design, or a way to run your manufacturing plant with less inventory, chances are that your software will require user training in both product usage and application method. Competent users are a prerequisite for product success, so the product manager will typically play an advisory role in the development of training and may also be engaged in providing or finding the requisite subject matter expertise.

Product Demo

Nothing kills a prospect's excitement faster than a weakly organized and poorly delivered product demo. A typical engineering walkthrough of product features may well bore your customers to tears. Worse, they may become lost and confused as the demo-jockey jumps from point to point, and perhaps they will even be intimidated by your "easy-to-use" software. If a product demo is done well, however, then there is no better opportunity to show prospects how they can do their jobs better with your product and to *deliver or reinforce your key positioning and messages.* To ensure that the demo effectively positions the solution properly to prospective customers, the product manager must take the reins and provide a specific demo script and supporting data, as well as interfaces and data sets.

Sales and Marketing Collateral

Although sales and marketing collateral are typically owned by product marketing, who other than the product manager could possibly ensure that the features and benefits of the new product are properly articulated? Also, as a representative for some of the more technical team members, product managers may be directly involved in the development and delivery of sales training materials.

THE PRODUCT CHAMPION IN AN IS/IT SHOP

In some ways, from a product championing perspective, the independent software vendor environment is fairly well defined. The customer is external, and we typically have a sophisticated marketing organization we can leverage to elicit the requirements and help determine who is accountable for balancing all the conflicting needs. A customer whose needs are not met is simply *not* a customer. Although that may not be a good thing, at least they aren't hanging around to complain about it.

Such is not the case in an IS/IT shop. There is no marketing department, your customers all work with you, and they will certainly be hanging around after this release to make their feelings known.

Where do you find your champion in such an environment? Perhaps we can again learn from an example.

In one shop, a new enterprise support system was being developed to provide global 24-hour-a-day access to customer records for sales support and license management. The problem analysis exercise identified the following stakeholders:

- Corporate marketing
- Telesales
- Licensing and support
- Business unit marketing
- Business unit financial management

- Order fulfillment
- Collateral fulfillment

Each of these departments was quite vocal in its needs, yet it was clear that not all needs could possibly be met. The question "Who owns the Vision document?" looked like a metaphor for the question "Who would like to make a great career-limiting move by attempting to manage this project?"

Question: What is
  Champion
+ Change control
  board

  equal to?

On analysis, it was clear that none of the leads in the development team had the authority to make such hard decisions, and yet a champion had to be assigned. In this case, the team decided to name Allie, the current project lead, as the product champion and empowered her to elicit and organize the requirements. She *owned* the Vision document. She interviewed the users, established their relative priorities, and collected the data into a feature-oriented format. But a special steering committee, or project change control board (CCB), was also immediately established for the project. The CCB consisted of three senior executives, each with responsibility in a functional area.

Answer:
A fighting chance

Initially, Allie facilitated a decision-making process whereby the CCB established the relative priorities for the initial release. Thereafter, the CCB, *and only the CCB*, had the requisite authority to add or delete features, with recommendations coming from the product champion. In this way, there was only one champion, Allie. The results of elicitation and the vision of the project lived in her head and in the Vision document, but the responsibility for the hard decisions was given to the CCB. The CCB would take the heat for the hard decisions. The champion had "only" to see that the agreed-on features were properly elaborated on and communicated to the development team.

Once Allie was empowered to drive the process and had the CCB, including members of upper management, backing her up and taking most of the heat, the project was successful and was used as an organizational model for new projects. Each new project used different project champions. This provided an opportunity for personal growth and development for these individuals. It became an empowered role within the company. And, of course, we can't forget the CCB. For each new project, the makeup of the CCB was established, based on the themes of each new release and the stakeholders that would be most directly affected.

Although there is no prescription you can follow to create a project champion, it is extremely important for your team to identify one, to promote one, or to empower the one who seems to be leading the process already. Then it is the team's responsibility to assist that champion in every way possible in managing the requirements of the applications. This will help ensure a successful outcome. Besides, if you don't help make that person successful, he or she might ask you to be the project champion on the next project.

SUMMARY

As we have seen, there is far more to building winning software products than simply packaging the application on a CD and adding an installation script. There are a host of additional factors, some technical, some commercial, that must come together to create a whole product solution that addresses the individual user and the user's company business needs. Indeed, many of these related factors may contribute as much or more to commercial success as the features of the application itself.[1] By empowering a product manager (or product champion) to define and drive these additional factors, the software team can help assure that the whole product solution is properly defined, developed, positioned, and finally, delivered to the marketplace.

Although this means a very broad scope of responsibility and a lot of hard work for a product manager, the payoffs are just as substantial. When a product gets this kind of attention and support, success cannot be far behind.

---

1. Real-life example excerpted from a memo from a key customer to the ISV team marketing department: "whoever invented this cockamamie scheme for licensing enforcement should be taken out and publicly flogged and he or she should never be allowed to work in our industry again."

Team Skill 3 Summary

In Team Skill 3, we moved from understanding the needs of the user to starting to define the solution. In so doing, we took our first baby steps out of the problem domain, the land of the user, and into the solution domain, wherein our job is to define a system to solve the problem at hand.

After we learned the use-case technique, we also learned that complex systems require comprehensive strategies for managing requirements information, and we looked at a number of ways to organize requirements information. We recognized that we really have a hierarchy of information, starting with user needs, transitioning through features, then into the more detailed software requirements as expressed in use cases or traditional forms of expression. Also, we noted that the hierarchy reflects the level of abstraction with which we view the problem space and the solution space.

We then zoomed in to look at the application definition process for a stand-alone software application and invested some time in defining a Vision document for such an application. We maintain that the Vision document, with modifications to the particular context of a company's software applications, is a crucial document and that *every* project should have one.

We also recognized that without a champion or a product manager—someone to champion the requirements for our application and to support the needs of the customer and the development team—we would have no way to be certain that the hard decisions are made. Requirements changes, delays, and suboptimum decisions forced by project deadlines are likely to result. So, we decided to appoint one or anoint one: someone to own the Vision document and the features it contains. In turn, the champion and the team will empower a change control board to help with the really tough decisions and to ensure that requirements changes are reasoned about *before* being accepted.

With a requirements management organizational strategy in hand and a champion at the helm, we are now better prepared for the work ahead. But first, we must take a look at the problem of *project scope*, the subject of Team Skill 4.

Team Skill 4

MANAGING SCOPE

So far in this book, we have introduced you to the team skills of analyzing the problem, understanding user and stakeholder needs, and defining the system. These three team skills all focus on a primary root cause of software development problems: the team's forging off into the solution space without having an adequate understanding of the problem to be solved. Although team members will need to practice these skills in order to develop them, doing so does not take great effort. We strongly recommend spending a little more time in these early lifecycle activities; even so, the entire set of activities described so far should consume only a small fraction of the project budget, perhaps only 5 percent or so of the total costs. Although the issues are complex, only a few team members— analysts, the project manager, the technical lead, the product manager/ project champion—need to be heavily involved up to this point.

Hereafter, however, the game changes dramatically as the team size increases significantly. Each of these additional team members must participate in a coordinated team effort, and everyone must communicate effectively with one another. In addition, the investment, or "burn rate," of the project increases dramatically. We create test plans, build design models, refine requirements, elaborate the use cases, develop the code, and create momentum and a larger body of work that must be changed if the definition is not well understood or if the external requirements environment changes.

The requirements pyramid, by its very shape—wider at the bottom— correctly suggests that much more work is ahead of us. The team skill discussed in this section of the book develops a strategy for a most crucial activity: scope management. According to the Standish Group [1994] data, "*53% of the projects will cost 189% of estimates.*" Data from our own experience is even worse: Almost all software projects will be late by a factor of 50% to 100%. Assuming that the other root causes in software development will not be solved overnight, it seems clear that our industry is either incompetent or trying to do too much with too few resources, skills, and tools. We are trying to stuff ten pounds of desired functionality into a five-pound bag. Although the physics of software development are not clear, it should be obvious that this element of our strategy is heading for trouble and that the quality of both our work products and our reputation is about to suffer.

So, *before* we increase the team size, *before* we develop the more detailed specifications, *before* we commit our technology ideas to designs, and *before* we build the test scripts, we must pause and learn how to *manage the scope of the project.* Part psychology, part technology, and part just good project management, mastery of this team skill will dramatically improve the probability of a successful project.

Chapter 18

ESTABLISHING PROJECT SCOPE

Key Points

- Project scope is a combination of product functionality, project resources, and available time.

- Brooks' law states that adding labor to a late software project makes it even later.

- If the effort required to implement the system features is equal to the resources available during the scheduled time, the project has an achievable scope.

- Overscoped projects are typical. In many projects, it will be necessary to reduce the scope by as much as a factor of two.

- The first step in establishing project scope is to establish a high-level requirements baseline.

THE PROBLEM OF PROJECT SCOPE

As with any professional activity, meeting commitments in application development involves making realistic assessments of project resources, time lines, and objectives before the activity begins. For software development, these factors combine to create the "scope" of the project. Project scope is a function of:

- The functionality that must be delivered to meet the user's needs
- The resources available to the project
- The time available in which to achieve the implementation

Figure 18–1 provides a perspective of the "box" we can use to represent project scope.

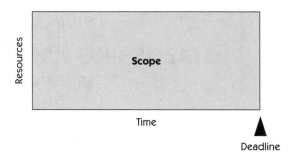

Figure 18–1   Project scope

In Figure 18–1, the area of the box represents the achievable scope of the project. Project scope derives from the following elements.

- *Resources,* consisting primarily of the labor from developers, testers, tech writers, quality assurance personnel, and others.

  As early as the 1970s, Brooks [1975] demonstrated that adding resources to a software project in order to increase the work output is a risky proposition at best. Indeed, Brooks' law states that adding labor to a late software project makes it even later.

  OK, if the time scale is long enough, work output can indeed go up, but it will not go up proportionate to the resources added, and the overall efficiency of the project thereby decreases. Adding resources may even slow a project because the need for training and supporting the new people decreases the productivity of those already on the project. As the competitive marketplace forces us to shorten our time lines, adding resources during a project becomes less and less practical. In addition, as development budgets are stretched and real years become Internet years, adding resources is simply not an option in many environments.

  For the purpose of analyzing scope, let's assume that resources, on the y-axis of Figure 18–1, are constant over the duration of the project.
- *Time,* perhaps a "soft" boundary that is subject to change if the available resources are inadequate to achieve the desired functionality.

  Certainly, history would demonstrate that delivering software late is typically "par for the course." On the other hand, many applications have hard, fixed deadlines. Examples include a new tax program to be delivered in time for tax season, a new-product introduction timed for a trade show, or a contractually fixed customer deadline. In addition, if as a profession we want to ensure our credibility and gain the confidence of our customers, it is important that we not slip the schedule.

So, for purposes of scope analysis, we'll treat time as a fixed factor. The total functionality we can deliver is obviously limited by the available time (fixed) and the available resources (also fixed) we have to apply, so the achievable scope is the area of the box.

In this book, we have used the notion of "features" to represent the value-added functionality we must deliver to the user. *If the effort required to implement the system features is equal to the resources available during the scheduled time, the project has an achievable scope, and we have no problem.* Barring unforeseen circumstances, the software team will deliver on time without sacrificing quality.

However, experience has shown that there is often a poor match between these factors in the scope equation. Indeed, in requirements classes that we teach, we always ask, "*At the start of the project, what amount of scope are you typically given by your management, customers, or stakeholders?*" In response, only a few trainees have ever answered, "under 100 percent." The others have responded with numbers that vary from 125 percent to 500 percent. The median and the average for each session tend toward the same conclusion: approximately 200 percent. This data correlates remarkably well with the Standish Group finding stated earlier, namely, that more than half of all projects will cost close to double their estimates. Perhaps we now understand why.

A Short Story on Project Scope

We once had a student who had recently moved into a new role as product manager for a new software product. Her background included many aspects of product development and product marketing, but she had no direct experience in software development. After hearing the responses to our question about scope, she appeared incredulous. She looked around the room and said, "Do you people really mean to tell me that you routinely sign up for approximately two times the amount of work that can reasonably be accomplished in the available time period?[1] What kind of profession is this? Are you people crazy?" The developers looked at one another sheepishly and by consensus answered, "Yup."

---

1. Many students have commented that it is management that signed them up, often committing them before they volunteered!

What happens when a project proceeds with a 200 percent initial scope?

- If the intended features of the application were completely independent, which is unlikely, only half of them will be working when the deadline passes. The product is limping but provides only half of the intended utility. And it's not a holistic half. The features don't work together, and they don't produce any useful aggregate functionality. An application with drastically reduced scope must be quickly patched together and shipped. Consequences include seriously unhappy customers whose expectations have not been met, marketing commitments that have been missed, and inaccurate manuals and promotional materials that must be quickly reworked. The entire team is frustrated and demotivated.

- If some of the application features do depend on others, at deadline time *nothing* useful will work. The deadline is missed badly. All commitments are missed; a new deadline is scheduled, and a new death march often begins. In the worst case, the entire team is fired, after working overtime for months on end; the final "phase" of this first attempt at the project, the phase called "promotion of the nonparticipants," is declared, and a new manager is added to the project.

What happens to software quality during either of these outcomes? The code, which is rushed to completion near the end, is poorly designed and bug-ridden; testing is reduced to an absolute minimum or skipped entirely; and documentation and help systems are eliminated. Customers take on both the testing and the quality assurance functions. Soon, the customers react to our extraordinary efforts as follows: *"Although we were initially disappointed by how late you were (or how little is working compared to our expectations), now we are really unhappy because we just discovered that what you shipped us is junk."*

THE HARD QUESTION

It may be necessary to reduce scope by as much as a factor of two.

Clearly, in order for the project team to have any hope of success, scope must be managed before and during the development effort. Given the typical scenario, however, the task is daunting: *For if we truly begin the development effort with an expectation of 200 percent scope, it will be necessary to reduce the project scope by as much as a factor of two in order to have any chance of success.*

The team's dilemma in addressing this problem leads to perhaps the toughest question faced by the team: *How does one manage to reduce scope and keep the customers happy?* Well, all is not lost. We'll cover ways to deal with this issue in the following sections.

THE REQUIREMENTS BASELINE

A primary technique in scope management is to establish a high-level requirements baseline for the project (Figure 18–2). We'll define the baseline as

> *the itemized set of features intended to be delivered in a specific version of the application.*

This baseline for the next release must be agreed to by both the customer and the development team. In other words, the baseline must

- Be at least "acceptable" to the customer
- Have a reasonable probability of success, in the team's view

The first step in creating the baseline is simply to list the features that have been defined for the application. Controlling the level of detail in this process is an important key to success. In Team Skill 3, we suggested that any new system, no matter how complex, can be described by a list of 25–50 features. With any more than that, you are viewing the project at a level of detail that is too complex to communicate effectively with the customers and the development team. With fewer than that, the level of detail may be too simplified to provide a sufficient understanding of the application and the associated level of effort necessary for implementation.

If we followed the requirements workshop process (Chapter 11) or any process that creates a similar outcome, we will have at our disposal a list of proposed

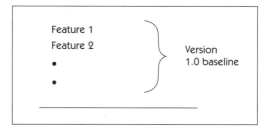

Figure 18–2 Requirements baseline

features. This list provides an itemized high-level description of the capabilities of a new or revised system. This features list is the primary project artifact we will use to manage the scope of the project *before* significant investments are made in requirements refinement, design, code, testing, or other project activities.

For our example, let's consider a shrink-wrapped software product with the following eight features.

Feature 1: External relational database support

Feature 2: Multiuser security

Feature 3: Ability to clone a project

Feature 4: Portability to a new operating system (OS) release

Feature 5: New project wizard

Feature 6: Import of external data by style

Feature 7: Implementation of tool tips

Feature 8: Integration with a version-manager subsystem

SETTING PRIORITIES

As we discussed in Team Skill 2, Understanding User and Stakeholder Needs, establishing the relative priorities for the feature set is integral to scope management. During prioritization, it is important that the customers and users, product managers, or other representatives—not the development team—set the initial priorities. Indeed, this initial prioritization should be done without too much influence from the technical community; otherwise, the level of difficulty in implementing the features will influence customer priorities, and the result of the process will be compromised such that the application may not meet the real customer needs. There will be adequate opportunity for technical input at later phases of the prioritization process. In our project example, let's assume that we vote on the priority of each feature, using a critical-important-useful scale; the results of this exercise are shown in Table 18–1.

ASSESSING EFFORT

Prioritization is only one piece of the scope puzzle. After all, if we could do all the work, the prioritization would be unnecessary. If we can't do all the work, we still haven't figured out how much we can do, and therefore, we do not yet know where to draw the baseline for the project.

Table 18–1 Prioritized Features List

Feature	Priority
Feature 1: External relational database support	Critical
Feature 4: Portability to a new OS release	Critical
Feature 6: Import of external data by style	Critical
Feature 3: Ability to clone a project	Important
Feature 2: Multiuser security	Important
Feature 5: New project wizard	Important
Feature 7: Implementation of tool tips	Useful
Feature 8: Integration with a version-manager subsystem	Useful

The next step is to establish the rough level of effort implied by each feature of the proposed baseline. Doing so is tricky since little useful information is available yet on which to estimate the work; we have no detailed requirements or design output on which to base an estimate. The best we can do is to determine a "rough order of magnitude" of the level of effort for each feature.

Estimating effort at this early time is a learned team skill. The engineering team will be naturally reluctant to provide estimates before feasibility and requirements are fully understood, and yet the first cut at scope management must happen before this next level of detail is known.

Let's assume that the product or project manager is the champion for our project and has the following dialogue with the developers for the project.[2]

PRODUCT MANAGER: *How difficult is this feature to do?*

DEVELOPMENT TEAM: *We don't know. We don't have any requirements or design yet.*

---

2. The team may wish to use "team-weeks" or "team-months" as a gross estimate of the total impact of a feature on the project. This rough heuristic serves as a substitute for a more detailed estimate and is arguably better than the result of this dialogue. Then, using these totals and the total time available for the project, the team can determine where to initially draw the baseline. If it is past the critical-features set, all is well; if not, the project is out of scope, and a new, smaller, project must be defined.

PRODUCT MANAGER: *I respect that, but is it the easiest thing we've ever done?*

DEVELOPMENT TEAM: *No.*

PRODUCT MANAGER: *OK, is it the most difficult feature on the list?*

DEVELOPMENT TEAM: *No.*

PRODUCT MANAGER: *On a scale of low-medium-high, we'll give it a medium. OK?*

DEVELOPMENT TEAM: *OK. Medium it is.*

PRODUCT MANAGER: *OK, on to the next feature.*

Why can we not allow for a process that creates detailed requirements and design information for each feature so that we can create more meaningful estimates? Isn't that the professional way to approach the problem? If the schedule provides time for more detailed estimating at this time, by all means do it!

However, we believe that it is crucial to be able to make some quick decisions about the scope of the activity without a more detailed estimate. Why? Because to do otherwise invests resources in what will later be determined to be "wasted inventory," including requirements specifications for features that will not be implemented, design information for those features, test scripts for requirements that will be scope-managed out of the project later, a false determination of the critical path for the project, and so on. We cannot afford to invest any resources in these scrap-producing activities, or we will fail to optimize the resources invested. In other words, scope management will reduce the number of features that will be developed in the initial release, and since resources are extraordinarily scarce, we cannot afford any additional investment in features that are not going to be implemented in the current baseline. Table 18–2 illustrates the addition of effort information to our feature list.

ADDING THE RISK ELEMENT

Another aspect of managing scope is estimating the "risk" associated with each feature. In this context, we'll consider risk to be the probability that the implementation of a feature will cause an adverse impact on the schedule and/or the budget. Risk gives us a relative measure of the potential impact of including a particular feature within the project baseline. A high-risk feature has the potential to impact the project negatively, even if all other features can be accomplished within the allotted time.

Table 18–2   Prioritized Features List with Effort Estimates

Feature	Priority	Effort
Feature 1: External relational database support	Critical	Medium
Feature 4: Portability to a new OS release	Critical	High
Feature 6: Import of external data by style	Critical	Low
Feature 3: Ability to clone a project	Important	High
Feature 2: Multiuser security	Important	Low
Feature 5: New project wizard	Important	Low
Feature 7: Implementation of tool tips	Useful	Low
Feature 8: Integration with a version-manager subsystem	Useful	High

The development team establishes risk based on any heuristic it is comfortable with, using the same low-medium-high scale used to assess effort. Table 18–3 shows the revised features list for the example.

Table 18–3   Prioritized Features List with Effort and Risk Estimates

Feature	Priority	Effort	Risk
Feature 1: External relational database	Critical	Medium	Low
Feature 4: Portability to a new OS release	Critical	High	Medium
Feature 6: Import of external data by style	Critical	Low	High
Feature 3: Ability to clone a project	Important	High	Medium
Feature 2: Multiuser security	Important	Low	High
Feature 5: New project wizard	Important	Low	Low
Feature 7: Implementation of tool tips	Useful	Low	High
Feature 8: Integration with a version-manager subsystem	Useful	High	Low

Strategies for mitigating risk vary from project to project, and we won't cover that topic here. For the purposes of scope management, it is adequate to simply be aware of the relative risk associated with each feature so that intelligent decisions can be made early in the project. For example, if a feature has a priority of *critical* and a risk of *high*, then an effective mitigation strategy is mandatory. If priority is *important* and the feature hovers around the baseline, the item may be dropped or simply developed "if time is available." There's no harm in the process, so long as no commitment was made to include the item in the release. If the priority of a *high*-risk item is only *useful*, consider skipping that feature entirely.

REDUCING SCOPE

We have made substantial progress. We now have a prioritized features set with associated relative effort and risk. Note that there is often little correlation between priority and effort or between priority and risk. Indeed, many critical items require low effort; many items that are only useful are very difficult. This can help the team further prioritize the features. For example, a feature that is critical priority, medium effort, and low risk may be a candidate for immediate resourcing. Between these extremes, we can determine where to apply our fixed resources so as to maximize the benefit to the customer. Table 18–4 provides a few guidelines for prioritizing the development of critical features based on these attributes.

Table 18–4   Scope Prioritization Techniques

Attributes	Consider
Priority: Critical *Effort:* High *Risk:* High	Alarm! Establish immediate risk-mitigation strategy; resource immediately; focus on feasibility with architecture.
Priority: Critical *Effort:* High *Risk:* Low	A likely critical resource-constrained item; resource immediately.
Priority: Critical *Effort:* Low *Risk:* Low	Resource as a safety factor, or defer until later.

A Reasonable First Estimate

Better yet, if the team uses even a rough, labor-based estimate, it can determine the baseline by simply adding the labor estimates until the time limit has been met; the team will have established the project baseline. Often, however, the team will not have even this data available and yet must make a first cut at project scope. In this case, we still do not know where to draw the baseline, but if it is the team's gut feel that scope is greater than 100 percent, the list will likely have to be cut.

The next step is the trickiest. If we assume, for example, that the features add up to 200 percent scope, the baseline must be chopped in half or more. How do we go about this process?

The first consideration is whether we can do only the critical items on the list. Ask the project manager, "If all else fails, can we be certain of achieving at least the critical items by the deadline?" After all, if we applied the prioritization scheme well, only one-third or so of the items on the list will be critical to the release. Unless some of the critical features represent a highly disproportionate level of effort, the answer should be yes, even if we have 200 percent scope. If the answer is yes, *and in our experience it is almost always yes,* even at this first early cut, we have the beginnings of a plan. If the answer is no, the project is way out of scope (300 percent to 400 percent or more), and a smaller-scope project must be defined and the prioritization process repeated.

Since our estimating process was crude at best, we cannot say for sure how many items beyond the critical ones can be achieved. A further estimating effort, based on more detailed requirements and appraisal of technical feasibility, can be used to refine the baseline further. (Also, this is the time to do the detailed project plan to validate the assumptions that have been made.)

In our experience, however, it is sufficient in many real-world projects to draw the baseline at the critical requirements (perhaps including one or two important items), leaving the development team to make further decisions about the inclusion of other important items, based on project progress. No, it isn't scientific. But yes, it does work.

If expectations are properly set and managed, anything that can be accomplished beyond the baseline will be a bonus. Table 18–5 applies this simple heuristic to the baseline for our sample project.

Features below the baseline are now future features and will be considered in later releases. Such features may be later promoted to a higher priority, based on what is accomplished in the near-term release and based on future customer input.

Table 18–5 Final Prioritized Features List

Feature	Priority	Effort
Feature 1: External relational database support	Critical	Medium
Feature 4: Portability to a new OS release	Critical	High
Feature 6: Import of external data by style	Critical	Low
Feature 3: Ability to clone a project	Important	High
Baseline (features above this line are committed features)		
Feature 2: Multiuser security	Important	Low
Feature 5: New project wizard	Important	Low
Feature 7: Implementation of tool tips	Useful	Low
Feature 8: Integration with a version-manager subsystem	Useful	High

Of course, the features are not always independent. In many cases, one of the features below the baseline is integral to one of the features above the baseline or can be implemented more readily as a result of the accomplishment of another feature. Or perhaps the project team is good or lucky and gets ahead of schedule (now a conceivable notion!) or finds a class library that makes a below-the-baseline feature easy to implement. In these cases, the team should be empowered to reprioritize and reset the baseline so that feature can be included in the release, subject to proper communication processes, of course.

In this fashion, the team should be able to create a project plan, at least at the first order of approximation. However, in all likelihood, many of the desired features did not make the first cut, and there will be expectations to be managed, both inside and outside the company. We'll cover that topic in Chapter 19. But first let's revisit the case study and see what the team came up with for the scope of the HOLIS v1.0 release.

THE CASE STUDY: SCOPE MANAGEMENT FOR HOLIS

After the requirements workshop, the HOLIS team was chartered with the responsibility of assessing the level of effort for each feature and coming up with a first draft of the v1.0 baseline. Rigorous scope management had to be applied because of the constraints on the team, including the "drop-dead" date of having a prototype available at the trade show in December and the (even tougher) date of a release to manufacturing in January.[3] The team estimated the level of effort for each feature via the high-medium-low heuristic and then added the risk assessment for each feature. Table 18–6 shows the full features list, with these estimates added.

For the next step, the team provided rough estimates for each feature and developed a detailed project plan showing certain interdependencies and critical milestones. Also, after negotiation with marketing, which, in turn did some negotiating with Raquel (the international distributor), the team determined that, at release 1.0, it was adequate to internationalize only the CCU user interface, which reduced the scope of this feature immensely. The final internationalization of the optional PC Programmer interface software could wait until v2.0. This caused the team to change feature 25 from "internationalized user interface" to "internationalized CCU user interface" and to add a new feature, "internationalized PC Programmer interface," to the futures list.

Then, based on revised labor estimates, the team proposed the baseline as shown in Table 18–7. This baseline proposal was sent all the way to the executive team, where Emily, the vice president of Lumenations, made the final decision. Before doing so, however, she had the team walk her through the project plan so she could "see the dependencies." (The team was suspicious that she really wanted to see whether it had "done its homework" or if it was just "sandbagging" to get some slack in the schedule.) In the end, the decision was *yes*, but Emily's caveat was, "We accept this proposal for the 1.0 release of HOLIS, but you should be aware that the CEO told my boss, Jason, who told me, that 'thou shall not fail to release the product in January as you have committed.'" Emily commented further, "I'm not sure what he meant by that. I think he meant that if we fail, he's going to have *me* committed, but I don't ever want to find out. Do you?"

Hearing Emily's words very clearly, the team members committed *themselves* to the delivery date and proceeded with the next phase. The next milestone in the project plan was to be an elaboration iteration, which would include a rapid prototype of HOLIS that would be available for demonstration by August 1.

---

3. Although they were given manufacturing lead times, the team members decided that they actually had until the end of February for the final 1.0 software release. This was a crucial additional six weeks that the team was convinced it would need for final modifications, based on feedback from the trade show.

Table 18–6   Prioritized HOLIS Features List with Effort and Risk Estimates

ID	Feature	Votes	Effort	Risk
23	Custom lighting scenes	121	Med	Low
16	Automatic timing settings for lights and so on	107	Low	Low
4	Built-in security features: lights, alarms, and bells	105	Low	High
6	100 percent reliability	90	High	High
8	Easy-to-program, non-PC control unit	88	High	Med
1	Easy-to-program control stations	77	Med	Med
5	Vacation settings	77	Low	Med
13	Any light can be dimmed	74	Low	Low
9	Uses my own PC for programming	73	High	Med
14	Entertain feature	66	Low	Low
20	Close garage doors	66	Low	Low
19	Automatically turn on closet lights when door opened	55	Low	High
3	Interface to home security system	52	High	High
2	Easy to install	50	Med	Med
18	Turn on lights automatically when someone approaches a door	50	Med	Med
7	Instant lighting on/off	44	High	High
11	Can drive drapes, shades, pumps, and motors	44	Low	Low
15	Control lighting and so on via phone	44	High	High
10	Interfaces to home automation system	43	High	High
22	Gradual mode: slowly increase/decrease illumination	34	Med	Low
26	Master control stations	31	High	High
12	Easily expanded when remodeling	25	Med	Med
25	Internationalized user interface	24	Med	High
21	Interface to audio/video system	23	High	High
24	Restore after power fail	23	N/A	N/A
17	Controls HVAC	22	High	High
28	Voice activation	7	High	High
27	Web site–like user presentation	4	Med	Low

Table 18–7   Baseline for HOLIS v1.0 Features

ID	Feature	Votes	Effort	Risk	Marketing Comments
23	Custom lighting scenes	121	Med	Low	As flexible as possible
16	Automatic timing settings for lights and so on	107	Low	Low	As flexible as possible
4	Built-in security features: lights, alarms, and bells	105	Low	High	Marketing to do more research
6	100 percent reliability	90	High	High	Get as close to 100 percent as possible
8	Easy-to-program, non-PC control unit	88	High	Med	Provide dedicated controller
1	Easy-to-program control stations	77	Med	Med	As easy as feasible with measured effort
5	Vacation settings	77	Low	Med	
13	Any light can be dimmed	74	Low	Low	
9	Uses my own PC for programming	73	High	Med	Only one configuration supported in v1.0
25	**Internationalized CCU user interface**	24	Med	Med	Per agreement with European distributor
14	~~Entertain feature~~	~~66~~	~~Low~~	~~Low~~	(Not applicable, included in 23)
7	Instant lighting on/off	44	High	High	Make intelligent investments

v1.0 Mandatory Baseline: Everything above the line must be included or we will delay release.

ID	Feature	Votes	Effort	Risk	Marketing Comments
20	Close garage doors	66	Low	Low	May be little impact on software
2	Easy to install	50	Med	Med	Level of effort basis
11	Can drive drapes, shades, pumps, and motors	44	Low	Low	May be little impact on software
22	Gradual mode: slowly increase/decrease illumination	34	Med	Low	Nice if we can get it

v1.0 Optional: Do as many of the preceding as you can. (Alyssa)

Future Features: Below this line, no current development.

ID	Feature	Votes	Effort	Risk	Marketing Comments
29	**Internationalized PC Programmer interface**	N/A	**High**	Med	**Will become mandatory for version 2.0**
3	Interface to home security system	52	High	High	Can we at least provide a hardware interface? (Rick)
19	Automatically turn on closet lights when door opened	55	Low	High	

(continued on next page)

Table 18–7   *Continued*

ID	Feature	Votes	Effort	Risk	Marketing Comments
19	Automatically turn on closet lights when door opened	55	Low	High	
18	Turn on lights automatically when someone approaches a door	50	Med	Med	
15	Control lighting and so on via phone	44	High	High	
10	Interfaces to home automation system	43	High	High	
26	Master control stations	31	High	High	
12	Easily expanded when remodeling	25	Med	Med	
21	Interface to audio/video system	23	High	High	
24	Restore after power fail	23	N/A	N/A	
17	Controls HVAC	22	High	High	
28	Voice activation	7	High	High	
27	Web site–like user presentation	4	Med	Low	

SUMMARY

In this chapter, we've visited that endemic software development bugaboo—the problem of project scope. We've "discovered" (something that in reality we must admit we already knew) that overscoped projects are typical. Since adding resources may well be impractical, in order to have any hope of succeeding, it may be necessary to reduce the scope by as much as a factor of two. Doing so will not be easy, so we'll move on to addressing that challenge in the next chapter.

Chapter 19

MANAGING YOUR CUSTOMER

Key Points

- Managing your customers means engaging them in managing their requirements and their project scope.
- Customers who are part of the process will own the result.
- Getting the job done right means providing enough functionality at the right time to meet the customers' real needs.
- Negotiating skills are an invaluable aid to the scope management challenge.

ENGAGING CUSTOMERS TO MANAGE THEIR PROJECT SCOPE

Reducing project scope to within shouting distance of available time and resources has the potential to create an adversarial relationship between the project team and the customers, whose needs we must meet. Let's be honest. We've all been there. Fortunately, it does not have to be so. Instead, *we can actively engage our customers in managing **their** requirements and **their** project scope to ensure both the quality and the timeliness of the software outcomes.*

This conclusion is based on some important insights.

- It is in our customers' best financial interests to meet their external commitments to their marketplaces. Therefore, delivering a high-quality and, if necessary, scope-reduced application—on time and on budget—is the highest overall benefit the team can provide.
- The application, its key features, and the business needs it fulfills all belong to the customers, not to the application development team.

We need customers' input to make the key decisions, and only the customers can really determine how to manage scope and achieve a useful deliverable. We are their humble technological servants. It is their project.

COMMUNICATING THE RESULT

If the project scope must be reduced, make sure that the customer is a direct participant. A customer who is part of the process will own the result. A customer who is excluded from the process will be unhappy with the result and will naturally tend to blame the developers for not trying hard enough.

Engaging the customer in this dialogue helps lay the problems of scope management ever so gently on the customer's doorstep. With the philosophy we've described in the previous chapter, smart customers will make commitments to their external marketplaces only for the critical items included in the baseline. The embarrassment of missed schedules and missing features is avoided. Any extra features accomplished beyond the baseline will be perceived positively as exceeding expectations.

Sometimes, the discovery of the scope management problem occurs outside of the customer engagement process; then, in all likelihood, some bad news is about to be delivered. Delivering this message to our customers and/or management is a delicate process requiring both negotiation skills and a total commitment to the schedule and scope that results. After we deliver the bad news, we cannot afford to fail to deliver on the new promise lest *all* credibility be lost.

NEGOTIATING WITH THE CUSTOMER

Almost all business processes require negotiation. Consider negotiating with a customer for a delivery date for ball bearings, negotiating price on a large order, negotiating your annual increase with your manager, negotiating an achievable quota for your sales team, or negotiating additional resources for your project.

On behalf of both your project and your customer's business objective, you will need to negotiate the scope commitment for your team. The team should also keep in mind that, in many cases, the customer may have already developed the skills of negotiation and will naturally use them in their discussions with you and your team. Therefore, if you are a team leader, project manager, or project champion, you should *develop these skills* as well. Negotiation is a professional business activity. It is not a particularly difficult process, and it can be done with integrity, grace, and style. Take the opportunity to gain some training in this process; your human resources department can probably help, or you may want to take an external seminar. Failing that, you should at least familiarize yourself with some of the rules of the game. For example, a good overview of the negotiating process can be found in *Getting to Yes* [Fisher et al. 1983], which can be read in a few hours. They recommend a few helpful guidelines for every negotiating session.

- Start high but not unreasonable.
- Separate the people from the problem.
- Focus on interests, not positions.
- Understand your walk-away position.
- Invent options for mutual gain.
- Apply objective criteria.

> The guiding principle for scope management: underpromise and overdeliver.

As you negotiate with your customer, your guiding principle in establishing the baseline should be *underpromise and overdeliver*. Doing so ensures that the inevitable vagaries of software development, unanticipated technological risks, changing requirements, delays in the availability of purchased components, a key team member's unanticipated leave, and so on can be accommodated within your project schedule. If you should happen to run the one project in a thousand free of these unfortunate circumstances, it's OK: at worst, you will embarrass yourself only by delivering early! Even that would provide at least some entertainment value within your company!

MANAGING THE BASELINE

Successful development managers create margins for error in estimating effort and allow for time to incorporate legitimate changes during the development cycle. These managers also resist feature creep, which Weinberg [1995] notes can increase scope by as much as 50 percent to 100 percent after the start of a project. Focusing the development effort on the customer's critical priorities can mitigate even hostile political environments. With scope negotiated to an achievable level, and with development focused almost exclusively on the customer's "must haves," the team will establish credibility by meeting schedules with quality and, occasionally, with utility that could not have been predicted in advance.

However, your customers, be they internal or external, naturally want as much functionality as possible with each release of a software system. After all, it's the functionality that delivers the added value they need to meet their business objectives. Indeed, we must have a healthy respect for customers who are demanding, for they are the ones who will ultimately be the most successful in the marketplace. Demanding, competent customers are the only ones really worth having.

Left unchecked, however, the demand for more and more functionality can compromise the quality and the overall viability of the project. *More* becomes the enemy of *adequate. Better* becomes the enemy of *good enough.*

If we were operating in a business sector where the physics are better defined, where the industry had a few hundred years of experience in reliably delivering the goods, things would be different. But we operate in the software world; the physics are indeterminate, the processes are immature, and the technology changes with every application. Let's first focus on learning how to get the job done right: *enough functionality at the right time to meet the customer's real need.* We can tune our process later to see if we can exceed expectations, but for now, let's focus on just *meeting* them! In order to do so, we need to manage the baseline.

Once established, the baseline provides the center of focus for many project activities. The features baseline can be used to assess progress more realistically. Resources can be adjusted, based on progress relative to the baseline. The features within the baseline can be refined into further detail suited for code development. Requirements traceability can be applied from user needs to the features in the baseline. Traceability can be further extended from features into additional specifications and implementation.

Perhaps most important, the high-level baseline can be used as part of an effective change management process. Change is an integral part of every application development activity. Managing change is so critical that we have devoted Chapter 28 to this topic. For now, we'll look at how we can apply the features baseline to this important aspect of software management.

Official Changes

The features baseline provides an excellent mechanism for managing high-level change. For example, when the customer requests a new system capability (an official change) and that capability is not part of the features baseline, the impact of the change must be assessed before including the new feature in the baseline. If the project team has done a good job of defining the baseline to begin with, the assumption must be that *any change to the baseline must affect the resources, the schedule, or the features set* to be delivered in the release.

If the resources are fixed and the schedule cannot be changed, the project team must engage the customer in a decision-making process that prioritizes the new feature relative to the other features scheduled for the release. If the new feature is *critical*, it must, by definition, be included in the release, and the customer and the project team should jointly determine which features will be excluded from the release or at least lowered in priority, with accompanying lower expectations. If the feature is *important* but not *critical*, the project team can proceed with the implementation of the feature on a best-efforts basis, allowing progress to dictate whether the feature makes the release.

Unofficial Changes

Paradoxically, the problem of customer-initiated change may be the easiest scope management challenge to handle. It is externally focused, we can establish certain safeguards, and the impact of change can be assessed and made clear to this external stakeholder.

However, experience shows that another class of change threat is even more subversive to the development process. In Chapter 28, we will discuss the hidden dangers of various forms of change and gain additional ammunition with which to address the scope management challenge.

SUMMARY

Managing the scope of an application is one of the toughest challenges faced by every application development team. Doing so effectively requires reasonable estimating ability, negotiating skills, and some political savvy—three commodities that are often rare in technical communities such as our software project team. However, failing to manage the scope is at best unprofessional, and at worst will likely lead to a terrible fate: missed expectations, unhappy customers, angry management, and real career challenges. Take this challenge into your team's hands and manage scope early and often. You will be glad you did.

Team Skill 4 Summary

In Team Skill 4, Managing Scope, we learned that the problem of project scope is endemic. Projects typically are initiated with approximately twice the amount of functionality that the team can reasonably implement in a quality manner. This shouldn't surprise us since it is the nature of the beast: customers want more, marketing wants more, and we want more, too. We just need to put ourselves on a diet sufficient to make sure that we can deliver *something* on time.

We looked at various techniques for setting priorities, and we defined the notion of the baseline—an agreed-to understanding of what the system will do—as a key project work product, our touchstone and reference point for decisions and assessment. We learned that if scope and the concomitant expectations exceed reality, in all probability, some bad news is about to be delivered. We decided on a philosophy of approach that engages our customer in the hard decisions. After all, we are just the resources, not the decision makers; it's the customer's project. So the question is, "What exactly *must* be accomplished in the next release, given the resources available to the project?"

Even then, we expect to do some negotiating. All of life, and certainly all of business, is a negotiation in a sense, and we shouldn't be surprised by this either. We briefly mentioned a few negotiation skills and hinted that the team may need to use these skills on occasion.

We cannot expect that this process will make the scope challenge go away, any more than any other single process will solve the problems of the application development world. However, the steps we have outlined can be expected to have a material effect on the scope of the problem, allowing application developers to focus on critical subsets and to deliver high-quality systems incrementally that meet or exceed the expectations of the user. Further, engaging the customer in helping solve the scope management problem increases commitment on the part of both parties and fosters improved communication and trust between the customer and the application development teams. With a comprehensive definition of the product (the Vision document) in hand and scope managed to a reasonable level, although it's too early to start bragging, we at least have the *opportunity* to succeed in the next phases of the project.

Team Skill 5

REFINING THE SYSTEM DEFINITION

The previous team skills focused on the processes of analyzing the problem, eliciting user needs, and collecting, documenting, and managing the desired product features. Once the product features have been specified, the next task is to refine the specification to a level of detail suitable to drive the design, coding, and testing processes. We have now arrived at the bottom of the requirements pyramid, as shown in Figure 1.

In Team Skill 5, we examine an organized method for elaborating, organizing, and communicating the software requirements. Later in Team Skill 5, we'll look at one of the more perplexing issues: how to state the requirements in a clear and appropriately precise manner.

Regardless of the method you use to collect the requirements, *it is important that you adopt a rule that the collected requirements and only those requirements will drive the project.* If they are discovered to be insufficient or just wrong, they must be quickly and officially changed so that the rule remains true. In this way, the entire team has an unambiguous target, and its efforts can focus on discovering and implementing requirements, minimizing the time spent "in the weeds." We will start by taking a closer look at the nature of the requirements themselves.

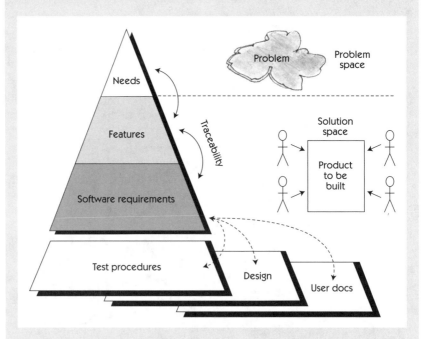

Figure 1 The requirements pyramid

Chapter 20

SOFTWARE REQUIREMENTS— A MORE RIGOROUS LOOK

Key Points

- A complete set of requirements can be determined by defining the inputs, outputs, functions, and attributes of the system plus the attributes of the system environment.

- Requirements should exclude project-related information, such as schedules, project plans, budgets, and tests, as well as design information.

- The requirements/design process is iterative; requirements lead to the selection of certain design options, which in turn may initiate new requirements.

- Design constraints are restrictions on the design of the system or on the process by which a system is developed.

In the prior team skills, the features we defined and the use-case model we developed for the system were purposely left at a high level of abstraction for the following reasons.

- We can better understand the main characteristics of the system by focusing on its features and key use cases and how they fulfill user needs.
- We can assess the system for its completeness, its consistency, and its fit within its environment.
- We can use this information to determine feasibility and to manage the scope of the system before making significant resource investments.

In addition, staying at a high level of abstraction kept us from making overly constraining requirements decisions too early, that is, before the people closest to the system implementation have their opportunity to add their perspective and value to the system definition. In Team Skill 5, Refining the System

Definition, our discussions transition to elaborating the system features in detail sufficient to ensure that the design and coding activities result in a system that fully conforms to the user needs. In so doing, we drive to the next level of specificity and detail, and we create a richer, deeper requirements model for the system to be built. Of course, we also create more information to be managed, and we will have to be better organized to handle this additional detail.

Looking Deeper into Software Requirements

In Chapter 2, quoting Dorfman and Thayer [1990], we provided the definition for a software requirement:

1. *A software capability needed by the user to solve a problem or to achieve an objective*
2. *A software capability that must be met or possessed by a system or a system component to satisfy a contract, standard, specification, or other formally imposed documentation*

Since that time, we've been speaking of these requirements things—features and use cases—at a fairly high level of abstraction. It was sufficient to understand the system at a macro-level view. However, as we get closer to implementation, additional specificity is required. To understand how and where the specificity is needed, and to make sure that we have discovered all the requirements to be imposed on the system at a given point in time, we'll need some additional guidance.

Davis [1999] suggests that we need five major classes of things in order to fully describe the behavior of a software system (Figure 20–1).

1. *Inputs to the system*—not only the *content* of the input but also, as necessary, the details of input devices and the form, look, and feel—protocol—of the input. As most developers are well aware, this area can involve significant detail and may be subject to volatility, especially for GUI, multimedia, or Internet environments.
2. *Outputs from the system*—a description of the output devices, such as voice-output or visual display, that must be supported, as well as the protocol and formats of the information generated by the system.
3. *Functions of the system*—the mapping of inputs to outputs, and their various combinations.

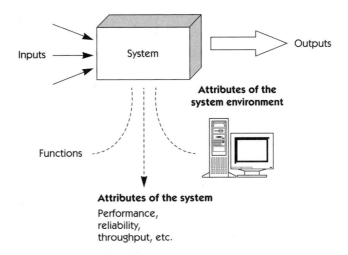

Figure 20–1   System elements

4. *Attributes of the system*—such typical non-behavioral requirements as reliability, maintainability, availability, and throughput, that the developers must taken into account.

5. *Attributes of the system environment*—such additional non-behavioral requirements as the ability of the system to operate with other applications, loads, and operating systems.

We have worked with this categorization for a number of years and have found that it works quite well; it helps people think about the requirements problem in a complete and more organized manner. Accordingly, we can determine a complete set of software requirements by defining all of the five system elements.

In addition, we'll be able to evaluate whether a "thing" is a software requirement by testing it against these guidelines.

The Relationship between Software Requirements and Use Cases

"But," you might say, "we haven't talked about these software requirements things much at all—we've been talking about use cases, haven't we?" Indeed we have, and that is because

Use cases are just one way to express software requirements.

Use cases are a convenient way for certain, but just one way nonetheless. In addition, we'll also discover that use cases can't conveniently express certain types of requirements ("the application must support up to 100 simultaneous users"), and there are better ways to express other types of requirements as well. We'll cover this issue in Chapter 22.

The Relationship between Features and Software Requirements

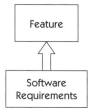

We also spent some time exploring the "features" of a system, simple descriptions of desired and useful behaviors. We can now see that there is a direct relationship between features and software requirements. Features are simple descriptions of systems services described in a shorthand manner. Software requirements, whether stated as use cases or in other forms, express those features in much more detailed terms. In other words, features help us understand and communicate at a high level of abstraction, but we probably can't fully describe the system and write code from those descriptions. They are too abstract for this purpose.

Software requirements, however, are specific. We can code from them, and they should be specific enough to be "testable"; that is, we should be able to test a system to validate that it really does implement the requirement. For example, suppose we are developing a defect-tracking system for an assembly-line manufacturing organization or for a software development organization. Table 20–1 shows the relationship between one of the features identified in the Vision document and its associated use cases. This mapping (and the ability to trace between the various features, use cases, and other requirements) will form the backbone of a requirements management concept known as "traceability," a topic we'll discuss later.

THE REQUIREMENTS DILEMMA: *WHAT* VERSUS *HOW*

As we have seen, requirements tell the developers what their system must do and therefore must cover the issues of the system inputs, outputs, functions, and attributes, along with the attributes of the system environment.

Table 20–1   Use Cases Associated with Particular Vision Document Features

Vision Document Feature	Use Cases
The defect-tracking system will provide trending information to help the user assess project status.	Configure Report Utility Compile History Trend

But there's a lot of other information that the requirements should *not* contain. In particular, they should avoid stipulating any unnecessary design or implementation details, information associated with project management, and information about how the system will be tested. In this way, the requirements focus on the *behavior* of the system, and they are volatile only to the extent that the behavior is volatile or subject to change. Davis [1993] calls this the "what versus how" paradigm, where *what* represents the requirements, or what the system is to do, and *how* represents the design or other project information that is to be implemented to achieve this objective.

Excluding Project Information

Project-related information (such as schedules, configuration management plans, verification and validation plans, budgets, and staffing schedules) is sometimes bundled into the set of requirements for the convenience of the project manager. In general, this must be avoided since changes in this information (for example, schedule changes) increase volatility and the tendency for the "requirements" to be out of date. When the requirements are dated, they become less trustworthy and more likely to be ignored. In addition, the inevitable debates about such things should be well separated from the discussion of *what the system is supposed to do.* There are different stakeholders involved, and they serve different purposes.

The budget could be construed as a requirement too; however, this is another type of information that doesn't fit our definition and therefore doesn't belong with the overall system or software requirements. The budget may turn out to be an important piece of information when the developers try to decide which implementation strategies they'll choose; some strategies may be too expensive or may take too long to carry out. Nevertheless, they are not system requirements.

In a similar fashion, information describing how we'll know that the requirements have actually been met—test procedures or acceptance procedures—also don't meet the definition and therefore don't belong in the requirements.

Excluding Design Information

The requirements should also exclude information about the system design or architecture. Otherwise, you may accidentally restrict your team from pursuing whatever design options make the most sense for your application. ("Hey, we have to design it that way; it's in the requirements.")

Whereas the elimination of project management and testing details from the list of requirements is fairly straightforward, the elimination of design/implementation details is usually much more difficult and much more subtle. Suppose, for example, that the requirement in Table 20–1 had been worded like this: "Trending information will be provided in a histogram report written in Visual Basic, showing major contributing causes on the x-axis and the number of defects found on the y-axis" (Figure 20–2).

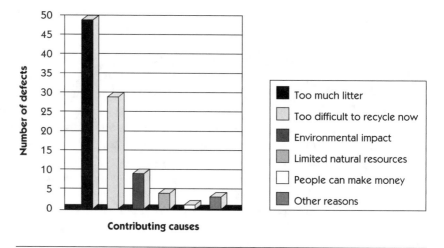

Figure 20–2   Example histogram report

Although the reference to Visual Basic appears to be a fairly blatant violation of the guidelines we've recommended (because it doesn't represent any input, output, function, or behavioral attribute), it's useful to ask, "Who decided to impose the requirement that the histogram be implemented in Visual Basic, and why was that decision made?" Possible answers to that question might include the following.

- One of the technically oriented members of the group defining the Vision document decided that Visual Basic should be specified because it is the "best" solution for the problem.
- The user may have specified it. Knowing just enough about technology to be dangerous, the user, worried that the technical people may adopt another technology that's more expensive or less readily avail-

able, knows that Visual Basic is readily available and relatively cheap, and the user wants that technology to be used.

- A process or political decision within the development organization may have mandated that all applications will be developed with Visual Basic. In an effort to ensure compliance and to prevent its policies from being ignored, management insists that references to Visual Basic be inserted whenever possible into requirements documents.

If a technical developer decides to insert a reference to Visual Basic because of an arbitrary preference for the language, it obviously has no legitimate place in the list of requirements. If the user provided the requirement, things get a little stickier. If the customer refuses to pay for a system unless it's written in Visual Basic, the best course of action is to treat it like a requirement, *although we will place it in a special class, called* design constraints, *so that it is separated from the normal requirements, which influence only the external behavior.* Nevertheless, it's an implementation constraint that has been imposed on the development team. (By the way, if you think this example is unrealistic, consider the common requirement imposed until the late 1990s by the U.S. Defense Department on its software contractors to build systems using Ada.)

Meanwhile, the discussion of Visual Basic in this example may have obscured a subtler and perhaps more important requirements analysis: Why does the trending information have to be shown in a histogram report? Why not a bar chart, a pie chart, or another representation of the information? Furthermore, does the word *report* imply a hard-copy printed document, or does it also imply that the information can be otherwise displayed? Is it necessary to capture the information so that it can be imported into other programs or exposed to the corporate extranet? The feature described in the Vision document can almost certainly be fulfilled in various ways, some of which have very definite implementation consequences.

In many cases, the description of a problem from which a requirement can be formulated is influenced by the user's perception of the potential solutions that are available to solve the problem. The same is true of the developers who participate with the user to formulate the features that make up the Vision document and the requirements. As the old adage reminds us, "If your only tool is a hammer, all your problems look like a nail." But we need to be vigilant about unnecessary and unconscious implementation constraints creeping into the requirements, and we need to remove such constraints whenever we can.

MORE ON REQUIREMENTS VERSUS DESIGN

So far, we have treated software requirements, design decisions, and design constraints as if they were distinct entities that can be clearly differentiated in both time and type. That is, we have stated or implied the following.

- Requirements (mostly) precede design.
- Users and customers, because they are closest to the need, make requirements decisions.
- Technologists make design decisions because they are best suited to pick, among the many design options, which option will best meet the need.

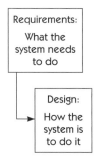

This is a good model, and it is the right starting point for a requirements management philosophy. We've presented the story in this fashion for a reason. It is best to understand requirements before design, and most design constraints ("use XYZ class library for database access") are important design decisions recorded in the requirements assets so that we can ensure that we achieve them for a contractual or legitimate technical reason.

If we couldn't make these classifications at all, the picture would be very muddled, and we couldn't differentiate requirements from design. Further, we would no longer know *who* is responsible for *what* in the development process. Even worse, our customers would dictate design, and our designers would dictate requirements.

But a subtle yet serious complication underlies this discussion and belies the simple paradigm we've presented. Returning to our case study, for example, if the team makes a design decision, such as selection of a PC technology to run in the HOLIS CCU subsystem, it's likely to have some external impact on the user. For example, a system prompt or log-on screen will show up somewhere in the user's world. Better yet, we will probably want to take advantage of some user input capabilities of the OS, and those functions will certainly exhibit external behaviors to the user. (Note to the techies among you: Yes, we could hide it, but that's beside the point.)

Given the definitions we've provided in this chapter, the question becomes: Once the impact of a design decision causes external behavior seen by the user, does that same decision, which now clearly affects "input or output from the system," now become a requirement? You could argue that the correct answer is "yes," or "no," or even "it doesn't really matter," based on your individual interpretation of the definitions and analysis we've provided so far. But that makes light of a very important matter, as an understanding of this issue is critical to an understanding of requirements design and indeed the nature of the iterative process itself. Let's take a closer look.

Iterating Requirements and Design

In reality, the requirements versus design activities must be iterative. Requirements *discovery*, definition, and *design decisions* are circular. The process is a continual give and take, in that

current requirements cause us to consider selecting certain design options,

and

selected design options may initiate new requirements.

Occasionally, inclusion of a new technology may cause us to throw out a host of assumptions about what the requirements were supposed to be. We may have discovered an entirely new approach that obviates the old strategy. ("Let's throw out the entire client/data access/GUI module and substitute a browser-based interface.") This is a prime and legitimate source of requirements change.

This process is as it should be; to attempt to do otherwise would be folly. On the other hand, there is grave danger in all of this, for if we do not truly understand the customer's needs *and* the customer is not engaged actively in the requirements process—and yes, in some cases, even understanding our *design-related decision*—the *wrong* decision might be made. When properly managed, this "continual reconsideration of requirements and design" is a truly fantastic process, as technology drives our continually improving ability to meet our customer's real needs. *That's the essence of what effective and iterative requirements management is all about.* But when improperly managed, we continually "chase our technology tail," and disaster results. We never said it would be easy.

A FURTHER CHARACTERIZATION OF REQUIREMENTS

The preceding discussions on requirements suggested that various "kinds" of requirements exist. Specifically, we have found it useful to think about three types of requirements, as shown in Figure 20–3:

- Functional software requirements
- Nonfunctional software requirements
- Design constraints

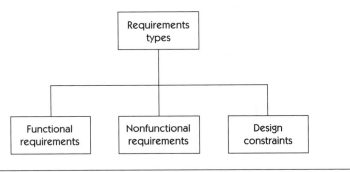

Figure 20–3   Types of requirements

Functional Software Requirements

As you might expect, functional requirements express how the system behaves—its inputs, its outputs, and the functions it provides to its users. These requirements are usually system action-oriented. These are the types of requirements we have been capturing in the use cases for HOLIS.

Nonfunctional Software Requirements

However, functional requirements alone are insufficient to describe the requirements of a system completely. We must also consider other types of requirements. Grady [1992] called these types of requirements *nonfunctional requirements* and suggested that they arise because it is necessary to specify other aspects of the system, such as:

- Usability
- Reliability
- Performance
- Supportability

These requirements are used to express some of the "attributes of the system" or "attributes of the system environment" elements of our elaborated guidelines [Davis 1999].

Design Constraints

This last class of requirements may be the trickiest of all. Design constraints typically impose limits on the design of the systems.

We'll define constraints as

> *restrictions on the design of a system, or the process by which a system is developed by which a system is developed, that do not affect the external behavior of the system but that must be fulfilled to meet technical, business, or contractual obligations.*

This convenient three-type classification helps us understand more about the system we are to build. We'll revisit each of these three types of requirements in Chapter 22, Developing the Supplementary Specification.

SUMMARY

In this chapter, we've started the move from the abstract world of features to the more specific world of software requirements. Accordingly, we've provided some more specific definitions and classification guidance for the work that lies ahead. We've described the three different types of requirements we'll be looking for: functional requirements, nonfunctional requirements, and design constraints. We've described the *"what* versus *how"* distinction and yet also noted that this must all be considered within the scope of an iterative requirements-influence-design-influences-requirements framework. These are not trivial concepts. Maybe that's why we love technology the way we do.

LOOKING AHEAD

Now that we understand the nature of requirements at this next level of detail, we'll turn to techniques for *capturing* and *organizing* them. Our next chapter will focus on refining our use-case technique for capturing requirements.

Chapter 21

REFINING THE USE CASES

Key Points

- To support development and testing activities, the use cases defined earlier in the project must be more fully elaborated.
- The use-case model is reviewed and will often be refactored as well.
- A well-elaborated use case also defines all alternative flows, pre- and post-conditions, and special requirements.
- The additional use-case relationships *extend* and *include* help the team structure and maintain the use-case model.

In the earlier team skills, we introduced use cases as a means of expressing requirements for a system. In this chapter, we'll build on what you learned earlier and show you how to describe your increasingly-detailed understanding of the necessary system behavior. If you've kept your thinking at the right level of specificity so far, the defined use cases are insufficiently detailed to drive design and implementation. Also, it's unlikely that you've defined all of the use cases that would be needed, and you probably haven't considered the exception conditions, state conditions, and other special conditions that are of less interest to the user but that may materially affect the design of the system. The time to add this level of specificity is now.

HOW USE CASES EVOLVE

In the early iterations of Team Skill 3, Defining the System, most of the major use cases are identified, but only a few—perhaps those considered architecturally significant or particularly descriptive of the system behavior—are well described. The refining stages complete the process by describing all the use cases needed to define the system. The test for "enough" use cases is that the complete collection of use cases describes all possible ways in which the system can be used, at a level of specificity suitable to drive design, implementation, and testing.

It's worth noting that use-case elaboration is *not* system decomposition. That is, we don't start with a high-level use case and decompose it into more and more use cases. Instead, we are searching for more and more detailed interactions of the actors with the system. Thus, use-case elaboration is more closely aligned with refining a series of actions rather than hierarchically dividing actions into subactions. However, your model may have use cases that are so simple that they do not need a detailed description of the flow of events; a simple outline is quite enough. The criteria for making this elaboration decision are that users don't disagree on what the use case means and that designers and testers are comfortable with the level of detail provided by the simple format. If all is well, you can then proceed straight to design and coding.

THE SCOPE OF A USE CASE

However, a use case usually requires a fair amount of additional elaboration, and more work lies ahead. One of these tasks is the decision about whether a set of user interactions is one or several use cases. Consider the use of a recycling machine. The customer inserts cans and bottles into the recycling machine, presses a button, and receives a printed receipt that can be exchanged for money.

Is it one use case to insert a deposit item, another use case to press the button, and yet another to acquire the receipt? Or is this all one use case? Three actions occur, but one without the others is of little value to the customer. The complete process is required to make sense to the customer. Thus, the complete dialogue—from inserting the first deposit item to pressing the button to getting the receipt—is a complete instance of use, a use case.

Additionally, you want to keep the three actions together, to be able to review them at the same time, modify them together, test them together, change them together when necessary, write user documentation that describes them, and in general manage them as a unit. This becomes particularly important in larger systems.

THE CASE STUDY: ANATOMY OF A SIMPLE USE CASE

As an example of the refinement process, let's look at a step-by-step proce-dure for refining a use case. Recall that in Chapter 14, we developed the pre-liminary use-case model for HOLIS. At that time, it was necessary only to decide on what the basic use cases would be. We took care in doing our sys-tems analysis work to try to identify all the significant use cases, but we didn't elaborate them. We just named them and provided a brief description. That was appropriate, and it reflected the level of abstraction at which we needed to understand the system at that time.

In later iterations, however, we need to revisit the use cases and refine them so they can be implemented and tested. Even then, we have to pick the right level of abstraction or else we may overspecify or underspecify system behavior. We'll use a simple HOLIS example: a resident activating a light in a house, us-ing the HOLIS home automation lighting system. While the use case is a sim-ple one, it has a few interesting facets that illustrate some of the complexities of the system and demonstrate how we can handle them with our techniques. Let's look at the use case we named Turn Light On/Off (Figure 21–1).

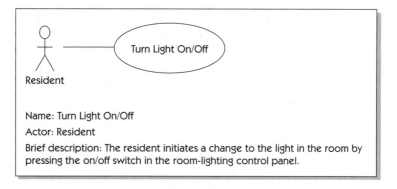

Figure 21–1 The HOLIS Turn Light On/Off use case

Reviewing the Actors

When we first identified the actors, we saw only one user that interacted with the light switch, so we named only one actor, the user (Resident) pressing the switch. However, from the perspective of HOLIS as a *system*, we also recog-nized that the system automatically controls the lighting and thus involves another actor, which we named Light Bank.

Reviewing the Name

As we described, each use case should have a name indicating what is achieved by its interaction with the actor(s). The name is important since, ideally, it describes in shorthand form what the actor accomplishes with the use case. We also noted that no two use cases can have the same name, and each should be unique and easily distinguishable among the use cases defined for the project. Further, use-case names often begin with an action verb to indicate the intent of the use case.

In our case study, we now discover that the HOLIS systems engineers have made some key design decisions that affect the software for the system. Suppose the team is now presented with a finalized control panel design that looks as shown on the left.

We note from this design that a single switch controls the on and off function as well as "dim." Perhaps we assumed there would be a separate slide switch or something for the dimming function, but in any case, the design is what it is. Now we have to look at our use case *in light of this new information* and decide what we want our use case to do. Let's make the decision to provide only one use case to control the lighting function since this would seem to simplify things. However, based on what we know now, it looks like we haven't named the use case very well. After all, the user can do more than turn the light on or off; with the same button on the control panel the resident can also brighten or dim the light. So, let's rename our use case to become Control Light since that seems more descriptive. Now the representation of our "simple and obvious" use case Turn Light On/Off has been refined as well (Figure 21–2).

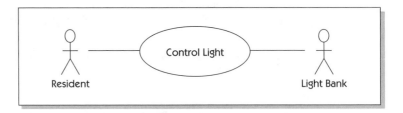

Figure 21–2   The HOLIS Control Light use case

You may want to use a formal method to structure the names of use cases so as to group similar use cases with similar names. Or you may want to incorporate a "serial number" or other unique identifier into the use-case name to facilitate managing a list of the use cases. For example, a designer might specify the name of this use case as "031 Control Light." Although the spirit of this approach is laudable, our experience has shown that proper use-case naming, and perhaps the application of tools that allow us to search, sort, and analyze use cases, are usually adequate to the task, so we'll just stick with "Control Light."

Refining the Description

Since the role and purpose of our use case has evolved, let's update its description as follows.

Use-Case Description for Control Light

This use case prescribes the way in which lights are turned on and off and also how they are dimmed and brightened in accordance with how long the user presses a light switch.

Defining and Refining the Flow of Events

The heart of the use case is the event flow, usually a textual description of the operations by the actor and the system's various responses. The event flow describes what the system does, based on the actor's behavior. By the way, it is not required that the flow be described textually. You can use UML interaction diagrams for this purpose, and many of the other methods discussed in Chapter 24 might apply equally well to your use-case documentation, so be sure to select an appropriate technique. Remember, the goal is to convey *understanding*, and there is no "one-size-fits-all" approach. However, in most cases, you'll find that natural language works just fine.

Whether we previously defined a brief event flow during the inception phase of our project or just created a short description, our *understanding of the system has changed*, and we need to adapt. First, let's look at the basic flow of events for our use case, keeping in mind that the flow of events does not specify *how* the system does any of those things. It specifies only *what* happens from the user's perspective.

We'll define the basic flow to cover the simple on/off case we started with earlier.

Basic Flow for the Control Light Use Case

Basic flow begins when the Resident presses the On/Off/Dim button on the Control Switch.

When the Resident removes pressure on the On/Off/Dim button within the timer period, the system "toggles" the state of the light as follows.

- If the light is On, the light is then turned Off, and there is no illumination.
- If the light is Off, the light is turned On to the last remembered brightness level.

End of basic flow.

As we've described, the use case may have different flows, depending on conditions present. In some cases, these flows deal with error conditions detected during processing, or they may record optional ways of handling certain conditions. Many times, these are errors and exception conditions, and discovering these is a key activity in the process of refining use cases. For example, a use case that prints a receipt for a credit card transaction may discover that the printer has run out of paper. This special case would be described within the use case as an alternative flow of events. When you record the alternative flows, don't forget to document the conditions giving rise to the flows.

There is no set limit on alternative flows, so be sure to document all alternative flows, including all possible error conditions. Indeed, one of the "dirty little secrets" of system development, and one that seems to come only with experience, is the following.

> *Defining and managing alternative flows and errors conditions may be as much work, and contribute as much or more to the ultimate success of the system, as developing the requirements, architecture, and implementation for the "happy day" flow.*

No wonder we have trouble estimating software projects!

So now is not the time to skimp on brainstorming and asking the hard "what if" questions. But it is an excellent time to involve the testers since, for reasons you can readily guess, they seem to have a real knack for the "non-happy day" problems.

Back to our example: an alternative flow of events will occur when the Resident holds a button on the Control Switch down for more than "the timer period," which we have since determined to be exactly one second. We need to add an alternative flow to the use case.

Alternative Flow of Events: Dimming

When the Resident holds down the On/Off/Dim button for more than 1 second, the system initiates a brightening/dimming activity for the room's Light Bank.

While the Resident continues to press the On/Off/Dim button:

1. The brightness of the controlled light is smoothly increased to a system-wide maximum value at a rate of 10 percent per second.

2. When the brightness reaches its maximum value, the brightness of the controlled light is then smoothly decreased to a system-wide minimum value at a rate of 10 percent per second.

3. When the brightness reaches its minimum value, the use case continues at subflow step 1.

When the Resident releases the On/Off/Dim button:

4. The use case terminates and the brightness stays at the current level.

Identifying the Pre- and Post-conditions

For most cases, you will need to identify pre-conditions that affect the behavior of the system described in the use case and to describe post-conditions, such as system state or persistent data that is left when the use case is complete. There can be significant work involved in fully defining pre- and post-conditions; however, you need to use pre- and post-conditions only when necessary to clarify the behavior expressed in the use case. Figure 21–3 may help you discover the pre- and post-conditions for your use case.

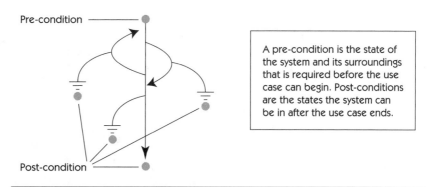

Pre-condition

A pre-condition is the state of the system and its surroundings that is required before the use case can begin. Post-conditions are the states the system can be in after the use case ends.

Post-condition

Figure 21–3   Pre- and post-conditions

You may also wish to consider the following guidelines [Rational Software Corporation 2002].

■ The states described by pre- or post-conditions should be states that the user can observe. "The user has logged on to the system" or "The user has opened the document" are examples of observable states.

- A pre-condition is a constraint on when a use case can start. It is not the event that starts the use case.
- Pre- and post-conditions for a use case are not for only one individual flow, although you can define them at the level of an individual flow.
- A post-condition for a use case should be true regardless of which alternative flows were executed; it should not be true only for the main flow. If something could fail, you would cover that in the post-condition by saying "The action is completed, or if something failed, the action is not performed," rather than just "The action is completed."
- Post-conditions can be an important tool for describing use cases. You first define what the use case is supposed to achieve, the post-condition. You can then describe how to reach this condition (the flow of events needed).

As we noted, it is important to distinguish between the events that start the use-case flows and the pre-conditions, which must be met before the use-case flow can be initiated. For example, a pre-condition to the Control Light use case is that the Homeowner/Programmer has enabled a specific bank of lights for the dimming action. Another pre-condition is that the selected Control Switch button must be preprogrammed to control the Light Bank. (Presumably, other use cases describe how these pre-conditions are accomplished.)

So we'll need to state the pre-conditions for our use case.

Pre-conditions for the Control Light Use Case
- The selected On/Off/Dim button must be Dim Enabled.
- The selected On/Off/Dim button must be preprogrammed to control a Light Bank.

Similarly, we need to identify post-conditions. In our use case, in order for the brightness to begin at the proper level when the Resident uses the switch the next time, the system must remember the previous brightness level that was set for a selected Control Switch button after a dimming action has occurred. So, this is a post-condition that we'll record in the use case.

Post-condition for the Control Light Use Case
- On leaving this use case, the system remembers the current brightness level for the selected On/Off/Dim button.

Identifying Special Requirements

There is another discovery process that we must complete before we are finished with the use case: we must understand any special requirements to be imposed. Typically, these are nonfunctional specifications of usability, reliability, performance, and so on that are defined in the supplementary specification or perhaps in a regulatory standard referred to in the Vision document. In any case, we must identify those conditions that are relevant to the implementation of a specific use case. With HOLIS, for example, the Vision document has stated that there must be no "visible, perceptible delays between a homeowner action and system response." This, in turn, has caused the creation of a number of performance standards, including the following requirement that the team found in the HOLIS system-level specification.

> Performance: For any action that is perceptible to the Resident, the response time from a control panel action to system response must be less than 50 milliseconds.

Now let's put it all together. Table 21–1 outlines what we have after filling in all the important pieces of our use case. (Although many other pieces can be defined for a use case, they are not important to our needs now.) This use case is documented in the narrative style and may be found in the HOLIS artifacts in Appendix A.

Summary of Our Refined Use Case

For most users, especially those who are just beginning to apply use cases, the refinement steps we described above are more than adequate. Properly identifying and elaborating alternative flows, pre- and post-conditions, and special requirements provides a sufficiently comprehensive description of the system behavior in most circumstances.

However, as the complexity of the application grows and evolves over time, there are some additional use-case constructs, supported by the UML, that benefit the use-case practitioner. These topics are more advanced than those we've described so far, and we'll introduce these in the next few sections. For a more detailed discussion of these constructs, we refer you to the treatment by Armour and Miller [2001].

EXTENDING USE CASES

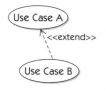

As the system evolves over time, additional features and functionality will be added to meet new or existing user needs. Indeed, if the scope of your project was originally two times what your team could accomplish, then you will have necessarily eliminated half of the functionality in the first release or you will not have released the project on time. In some cases, this means

Table 21–1   Defining a Use Case

Item	Value
Use-case name	Control Light
Actors	Resident and Light Bank
Brief description	This use case prescribes the way in which lights are turned on and off and also how they are dimmed and brightened in accordance with how long the user presses a button on the Control Switch.
Flow of events	Basic flow begins when the Resident presses the On/Off/Dim button on the Control Switch.
	When the Resident removes pressure on the On/Off/Dim button within the timer period, the system "toggles" the state of the light as follows.
	■ If the light is On, the light is then turned Off, and there is no illumination.
	■ If the light is Off, the light is then turned On to the last remembered brightness level.
Alternative flow of events	When the Resident holds down the On/Off/Dim button for more than 1 second, the system initiates a brightening/dimming activity for the room's Light Bank.
	While the Resident continues to press the On/Off/Dim button:
	1. The brightness of the controlled light is smoothly increased to a system-wide maximum value at a rate of 10 percent per second.
	2. When the brightness reaches its maximum value, the brightness of the controlled light is then smoothly decreased to a system-wide minimum value at a rate of 10 percent per second.
	3. When the brightness reaches its minimum value, the use case continues at subflow step 1.
	When the Resident releases the On/Off/Dim button:
	4. The use case terminates and the brightness stays at the current level.
Pre-conditions	The selected On/Off/Dim button must be Dim Enabled.
	The selected On/Off/Dim button must be preprogrammed to control a Light Bank.
Post-condition	On leaving this use case, the system remembers the current brightness level for the selected On/Off/Dim button.
Special requirements	Performance: For any action that is perceptible to the Resident, the response time from a control panel action to system response must be less than 50 milliseconds.

that you simply deferred use cases from that release to the next, and you can add them to the use-case model at the next iteration. However, it's even more likely that many of the use cases you've implemented didn't do everything you could envision doing for the user. In other words, you "scope managed" the use cases themselves by not implementing all that was envisioned.

In these cases, you may wish to *extend*[1] an existing use case at the later release. Of course, you might also ask, "Why not simply update the use case to include this functionality? Why use the extend concept at all?" There are three primary reasons for this construct.

1. The extend relationship can simplify maintenance of the use case and allow the team to focus and elaborate on the extended ("what's new or different") functionality, as an entity, without worrying about rereading or managing the base use case itself.
2. When an extension is envisioned as a use case is developed, extension points can be provided in the base use case as a map to "future features." This provides an indication of future intent to the design team and may aid development of a more robust architecture. It also provides a pointer to the area of the use case that needs further development in the next release.
3. The extended use case may represent optional behavior, as opposed to a new, basic, or alternative flow.

The last rationale is perhaps the most useful. For example, if some of the HOLIS systems included an optional "light bar" indicator on the Control Switch, then an extended use case could extend the behavior of the base Control Light use case as shown in Figure 21–4.

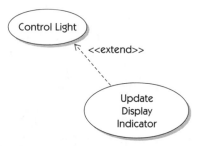

Figure 21–4   Extended Control Light use case

From the perspective of the flow of events, under certain defined circumstances a use case executes the extended flow of the use case as if it were an

1. [UML 1.3] An extend relationship defines that instances of a use case may be augmented by some additional behavior in an extended use case.

alternate flow, but upon completion, flow of the use case returns to the extension point in the base use case, as shown in Figure 21–5.

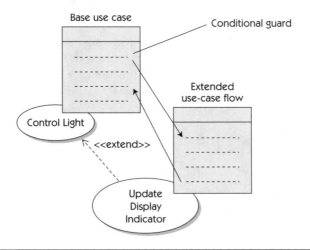

Figure 21–5   A base use case with extended flow

In order to apply this construct, all that is required is to indicate the extension points in the basic flow and the conditions (customer has purchased the light indicator option) under which the extended flow is to be executed. These conditions are expressed in what is called a *conditional guard*, which is the state that must be true for the extension to execute. In order to simplify maintenance, the conditional guard and extension points may be described in the extending use case, in which case the base use case will be entirely unaffected by the existence of the extension.

INCLUDING USE CASES IN OTHER USE CASES

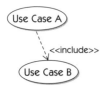

As the use cases are refined and elaborated, it is likely that the team will discover that certain patterns of user and system behavior reoccur in a variety of places. Indeed, it's possible that some significant percentage of the functionality of the system occurs in multiple use cases. Examples include entering a password for user validation, performing a system status check before proceeding with a transaction that commits a change to data, selecting separate items from a table in a user interface, and so on. As this develops, the team members will find that they are creating redundant documentation in multiple use cases.

Besides the volume problem, a worse problem happens when the common be-havior changes since the change must be reflected in every use case that uses the common behavior. Those locations may not be obvious, and the process of making all necessary changes may be tedious and error prone.

This problem is addressed by the *include*[2] relationship. While it may seem com-plicated on the surface, the relationship is quite easy for the development team to grasp since it is analogous to a subroutine or *include* function in software. When the basic flow of events reaches the point of inclusion of the included use case, control switches directly to the flow of events in the included use case. When that flow is included, flow returns directly to the included use case at the next logical step past the *include* indicator, as illustrated in Figure 21–6.

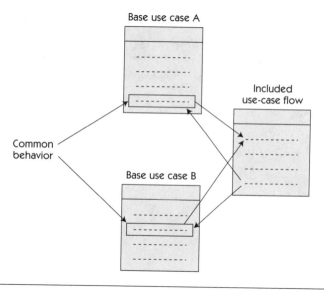

Figure 21–6   The flow of an included use case

When used properly, the *include* relationship can simplify the development and maintenance activities. Your team members should apply this construct as soon as they have mastered the basic use-case techniques.

---

2. [UML 1.3] An include relationship is a directed relationship between use cases, imply-ing that the behavior in the additional use case is inserted into the behavior of the base use case.

SUMMARY

Continuous refinement is a guiding principle of an iterative software development process. We continuously refine our understanding of the system behavior and codify that in the various artifacts we produce, eventually resulting in the most important artifact: the actual code that implements the application. As we've described in this chapter, this process applies specifically to the use-case technique. At this next level of specificity, the use case also provides a degree of structure and rigor that assists us in refining and recording our increasingly detailed understanding of system behavior. That is yet another benefit of this particular technique.

LOOKING AHEAD

When all use cases have been discovered and elaborated at this level of detail, the refining process is complete for those portions of the system that we decide to elaborate in use cases. But not everything is a use case. In the next chapter, we'll look at how to organize, define, and document these other requirements.

Chapter 22

DEVELOPING THE SUPPLEMENTARY SPECIFICATION

THE ROLE OF THE SUPPLEMENTARY SPECIFICATION

In Chapter 20 we took a more rigorous look at specificity in software requirements and noted that there are a significant number of requirements that are not a natural fit for the use-case "container." For example, a statement such as "The application must run on Windows XP" is fairly clear, so it seems silly to try to include such a requirement in a use-case format just because we like use cases.

In this chapter we introduce the concept of the supplementary specification. It's called "supplementary" because we assume the use-case format will contain most of the functional requirements for the system, and we'll supplement the use-case model with these additional requirements. This may be the 80/20 rule for software requirements, in that most of the expressed requirements for many systems may be best expressed in use-case form. However, effective requirements management requires that we focus as seriously on the 20 percent of the requirements not expressed as use cases as we do on the other 80 percent. Otherwise, our application may fail because it doesn't run on the platforms of choice for the user, doesn't meet some crucial quality or regulatory standard, or in some other way fails to meet the needs of our customers or the extended stakeholder community.

Sometimes, when requirements are being defined for systems that, although complex, do not exhibit a high degree of externally visible functional behavior, the supplementary specification may carry the bulk of the requirements while the use cases carry only those behaviors more directly visible to a user or external device.

EXPRESSING FUNCTIONAL REQUIREMENTS IN THE SUPPLEMENTARY SPECIFICATION

We've focused on the use-case method for capturing the majority of requirements for our system, and we've suggested that functional requirements are best expressed in use cases. In so doing, we may have overstated the case. In fact, there are many kinds of functional requirements that we cannot express so conveniently in the context of a use case, and for these cases we often recommend a traditional "declarative" requirements technique, simple text-based sentences, or other techniques that describe what the system needs to do without the structure of a use case.

Indeed, many complex systems tend to have minimal human interfaces or even other device interfaces, but that doesn't mean they don't do a lot of work on behalf of someone or something. For example, the following types of systems are not so easily described with the use-case technique.

- Systems that are primarily algorithmic and computational in nature (such as satellite-tracking, telecommunication-switching, or optimization systems) achieve their results by implementing a variety of scientific and other algorithms. In these cases you may choose to use mathematical expressions, statistical algorithms, and so on to represent the majority of the requirements.
- Many applications work behind the scenes, for example, in industrial automation and robotics. Since these embedded-controls systems primarily execute sophisticated logical and control algorithms, you may wish to augment the use-case model with state machines, sequential logic expressions, or other techniques.
- Applications that parse input strings, compile code, or translate from one language to another may have significant functional requirements that are better expressed in other ways.

In these cases, the supplementary specification will take on a more primary role in the requirements process. In the extreme, most of the requirements will be recorded in the supplementary specification and the use-case model will reflect a much smaller set of externally visible behaviors.

EXPLORING NONFUNCTIONAL REQUIREMENTS

In Chapter 20 we introduced the concept of nonfunctional requirements and implied that they can play a crucial role in defining a system. To assist with reasoning, discovery, and completeness, we suggested that these requirements be organized into four categories: usability, reliability, performance, and supportability. In the next sections we take a closer look at how each of these nonfunctional requirements provide you with some guidelines to help you discover and record them. Later, we'll briefly discuss one final requirements category, "other," which will be the "catchall" placeholder for everything else we need to identify and record but that did not fit conveniently anywhere else.

Usability

In today's software products, *ease of use* may rank as one of the top criteria for commercial success and/or successful user adoption. However, since usability tends to be in the eye of the beholder, specifying usability can present a formidable challenge for the requirements team. How do we specify such a fuzzy set of requirements? There is no simple solution to this problem, and the best we can do is to offer a set of guidelines (or at least things to think about) to help your team address the usability requirements challenge. Some suggestions follow.

- Specify the required training time for a user to become minimally productive (able to accomplish simple tasks) and operationally productive (able to accomplish normal day-to-day tasks). This may need to be further described in terms of novice users, who may have never seen a computer or an application of this type before, as well as normal users and "power" users.
- Specify measurable task times for typical tasks or transactions that the end user will be carrying out. If we're building a system for order entry, it's likely that the most common tasks carried out by end users will be entering, deleting, or modifying orders and checking on order status. Once the users have been trained to perform those tasks, how long should it take them to enter a typical order? Of course, this could be affected by performance issues in the technical implementation (such as network speed, network capacity, memory, and CPU power) that collectively determine the response time provided by the system, but task-performance times are also strongly affected by the usability of the system, and we should be able to specify that separately.
- Compare the usability of the new system with other state-of-the-art systems that the user community knows and likes. Thus, the requirement might state, "The new system shall be judged by 90 percent of the user community to be at least as usable as the existing XYZ system."

- Specify the existence and required features of online help systems, wizards, tool tips, context-sensitive help, user manuals, and other forms of documentation and assistance.
- Follow conventions and standards that have been developed for the human-to-machine interface. Having a system work "just like what I'm used to" can be accomplished by following consistent standards from application to application. For example, you can specify a requirement to conform to common usability standards, such as IBM's Common User Access (CUA) standards or the Windows applications standards published by Microsoft.

Several interesting attempts to strengthen the fuzzy notion of usability have been made. One of the more interesting efforts has resulted in the "User's Bill of Rights" [Karat 1998]. The bill contains ten key points.

1. The user is always right. If there is a problem with the use of the system, the system is the problem, not the user.
2. The user has the right to easily install and uninstall software and hardware systems without negative consequences.
3. The user has a right to a system that performs exactly as promised.
4. The user has a right to easy-to-use instructions (user guides, online or contextual help, and error messages) for understanding and utilizing a system to achieve desired goals and recover efficiently and gracefully from problem situations.
5. The user has a right to be in control of the system and to be able to get the system to respond to a request for attention.
6. The user has the right to a system that provides clear, understandable, and accurate information regarding the task it is performing and the progress toward completion.
7. The user has a right to be clearly informed about all system requirements for successfully using software or hardware.
8. The user has a right to know the limits of the system's capabilities.
9. The user has a right to communicate with the technology provider and receive a thoughtful and helpful response when raising concerns.
10. The user should be the master of software and hardware technology, not vice versa. Products should be natural and intuitive to use.

Note that some of the topics covered in the Bill of Rights are essentially unmeasurable and are probably not good candidates for requirements per se. On the other hand, the bill should be useful as a starting point in developing questions and defining requirements for the usability of the proposed product.

Reliability

Of course, nobody likes bugs, defects, system failures, or lost data, and in the absence of any reference to such phenomena in the requirements, the user will naturally assume that none will exist. But in today's computer-literate world, even the most optimistic user is aware that things do go wrong. Thus, the requirements should describe the degree to which the system *must* behave in a user-acceptable fashion. This typically includes the following issues:

- *Availability.* The system must be available for operational use during a specified percentage of the time. In the extreme case, the requirement(s) might specify "nonstop" availability, that is, 24 hours a day, 365 days a year. It's more common to see a stipulation of 99 percent availability or a stipulation of 99.9 percent availability between the hours of 8 A.M. and midnight. Note that the requirement(s) must define what "availability" means. Does 100 percent availability mean that all of the users must be able to use all of the system's services all of the time?
- *Mean time between failures (MTBF).* This is usually specified in hours, but it also could be specified in days, months, or years. Again, this requires precision: the requirement(s) must carefully define what is meant by a "failure."
- *Mean time to repair (MTTR).* How long is the system allowed to be out of operation after it has failed? A range of MTTR values may be appropriate; for example, the user might stipulate that 90 percent of all system failures must be repairable within 5 minutes and that 99.9 percent of all failures must be repairable within 1 hour. Again, precision is important: the requirement(s) must clarify whether "repair" means that all of the users will once again be able to access all of the services or whether a subset of full recovery is acceptable.
- *Accuracy.* What precision is required in systems that produce numerical outputs? Must the results in a financial system, for example, be accurate to the nearest penny or to the nearest dollar?
- *Maximum bugs, or defect rate.* This is usually expressed in terms of bugs/KLOC (thousands of lines of code) or bugs per function-point.
- *Bugs per type.* This is usually categorized in terms of minor, significant, and critical bugs. Definitions are important here, too: the requirement(s) must define what is meant by a "critical" bug, such as complete loss of data or complete inability to use certain parts of the system.

In some cases, the requirements may specify some "predictor" metrics for reliability. A typical example of this is the use of a *complexity metric*, such as the cyclomatic complexity metric, which can be used to assess the complexity—and therefore the potential "bugginess"—of a software program.

Performance

Performance requirements usually cover such categories as the following:

- Response time for a transaction: average, maximum
- Throughput: transactions per second
- Capacity: the number of customers or transactions the system can accommodate
- Degradation modes: the acceptable mode of operation when the system has been degraded

If the new system has to share hardware resources with other systems or applications, it may also be necessary to stipulate the degree to which the implementation will make "civilized" use of such scarce resources as the CPU, memory, channels, disk storage, and network bandwidth.

Supportability

Supportability is the ability of the software to be easily modified to accommodate enhancements and repairs. For some application domains, the likely nature of future enhancements can be anticipated in advance, and a requirement could stipulate the "response time" of the maintenance group for simple enhancements, moderate enhancements, and complex enhancements.

For example, suppose we are building a new payroll system. One of the many requirements of such a system is that it must compute the government withholding taxes for each employee. The user knows, of course, that the government changes the algorithm for this calculation each year. This change involves two numbers: instead of withholding X percent of an employee's gross salary up to a maximum of P, the new law requires the payroll system to withhold Y percent up to a maximum of Q. As a result, a requirement might say, "Modifications to the system for a new set of withholding tax rates shall be accomplished by the team within 1 day of notification by the tax regulatory authority."

But suppose that the tax authority also periodically introduced "exceptions" to this algorithm: "For left-handed people with blue eyes, the withholding tax rate shall be Z percent, up to a maximum of R." Modifications of this kind would be more difficult for the software people to anticipate. Although they might try to build their system in as flexible a manner as possible, they would still argue that the modification for left-handed employees falls into the category of "medium-level" changes, for which the requirement might stipulate a response time of 1 week. Assuming that such a "requirement" made any sense at all, it could probably be stated only in terms of goals and intentions; it would be difficult to measure and verify such a requirement.

However, what the requirement statement *can* do, in order to increase the chances that the system will be supportable in the manner just described, is stipulate the use of certain programming languages, database management system (DBMS) environments, programming tools, table-driven support utilities, maintenance routines, programming styles and standards, and so on. (In this case, these really become design constraints, as we'll see below.) Whether this produces a system that can be maintained more easily is a topic for debate and discussion, but perhaps we can get closer to the goal.

UNDERSTANDING DESIGN CONSTRAINTS

As we described in Chapter 20, design constraints typically impose limitations on the design of the system or the processes we use to build a system.

We provided the following definition

> *restrictions on the design of a system, or the process by which a system is developed, that do not affect the external behavior of the system but that must be fulfilled to meet technical, business, or contractual obligations.*

Sources of Design Constraints

While the sources are varied, design constraints typically originate from one of three sources: restriction of design options, conditions imposed on the development process, and regulations and imposed standards.

Restriction of Design Options Most requirements allow for more than one design option. Whenever possible, we want to leave that choice to the designers rather than specifying it in the requirements, for they will be in the best position to evaluate the technical and economic merits of each option. Whenever we do not allow a choice to be made ("Use Oracle DBMS"), the design has been constrained, and a degree of flexibility and development freedom has been lost.

Conditions Imposed on the Development Process Another type of design constraint occurs when a requirement is imposed on the process of building software. These types of design constraints can often be found when specifying the team's developmental infrastructure. Here are some examples.

- Compatibility with existing systems: "The application must run on both our new and old platforms."
- Application standards: "Use the class library from Developer's Library 99-724 on the corporate IT server."
- Corporate best practices and standards: "Compatibility with the legacy database must be maintained." "Use our C++ coding standards."

There may be many such sources and rationales, and the designers may have to accept them whether they like them or not. But it's important to distinguish them from the other types of requirements, for many of the constraints may be arbitrary, political, or subject to rapid technological change and might thus be subject to review or renegotiation at a later point.

Regulations and Imposed Standards Another important source of design constraints is the body of regulations and standards under which the project is being developed. For example, the development of a medical product in the United States is subject to a significant number of Food and Drug Administration standards and regulations, imposed not only on the product but also on the process by which the product is developed and documented. Typical regulatory design constraints might include regulations and standards from the following:

- Food and Drug Administration (FDA)
- Federal Communications Commission (FCC)
- Department of Defense (DOD)
- International Organization for Standardization (ISO)
- Underwriters Laboratory (UL)
- International standards such as the German Industrial Standard (DIN)

Typically, the body of regulation imposed by these types of design constraints is too lengthy to incorporate directly into your requirements. In most cases, it is sufficient to include the design constraints *by reference* into your package. Thus, your requirements might appear in the form "The software shall fail safely per the provisions of TüV Software Standard, Sections 3.1–3.4."

Incorporation by reference has its hazards, however. Where necessary, you should be careful to incorporate specific and relevant references instead of more general references. For example, a single reference of the form "The product must conform to ISO 601" effectively binds your product to *all* the standards in the entire document. As usual, you should strive for the "sweet spot" between too much specificity and not enough. (We'll explore this issue further in Chapter 23.)

Handling Design Constraints

Almost all projects have some design constraints. Generally, the best way to handle them is to follow these guidelines.

- Distinguish them from the other requirements. For example, if you identified other software requirements with a tag, such as "SR," you might consider using "DC" for design constraints.
- Include all design constraints in a special section of your requirements, or use a special attribute so they can be readily aggregated. That way, you can easily find them and review them when the factors that influenced them change.
- Identify the source of each design constraint. By doing so, you can use the reference later to question or revise the requirement. You may wish to supply a specific bibliographic reference in the case of regulatory standard references. That way, you can find the standard more easily when you need to refer to it later.
- Document the rationale for each design constraint. Write a sentence or two explaining why the design constraint was placed in the project. This will help remind you later of the motive for the design constraint.

Are Design Constraints True Requirements?

You could argue that design constraints are not true software requirements because they do not represent one of the five system elements in our elaborated definition. But when a design constraint is elevated to the level of legitimate business, political, or technical concern, it does meet our definition of a requirement as something necessary to satisfy a contract, standard, specification, or other formally imposed documentation.

In those cases, it's easiest to treat the design constraint just like any other requirement and to make certain that the system is designed and developed in compliance with that design constraint. However, we should strive to have as few design constraints as possible since their existence may often restrict our options for implementing the other requirements, those that directly fulfill a user need.

A Cautionary Tale

We were working with a Fortune 500 company well known in the industry for its adherence to process and procedure. Imagine our surprise when we found that the company was totally paralyzed in its current requirements collection activities because the team could not agree on whether certain requirements were functional requirements, nonfunctional requirements, or design constraints. In effect, the team's ability to move ahead with its project was stalled on semantic quibbles. We told the team that it didn't matter, just move on with something!

The value of the classification scheme is simply to spur your thinking, to assist you on your search for "Undiscovered Ruins," and to help you think about these things in different ways. But in a very real sense, the classification doesn't matter, so long as you understand that the requirement is something that you, or the system, will be measured against. Moving ahead with some sort of organized effort is superior to not moving ahead while preparing the perfect requirements categorization plan.

IDENTIFYING OTHER REQUIREMENTS

Even with this fairly exhaustive list, there may well be additional requirements that need to be known and communicated in order to develop a successful system. They may come from a variety of sources; they may be similar to some of the categories above or they may not. In any case, we hope that by now you will recognize them when you see them and will record them accordingly. Examples include

- Physical artifacts (CDs and so on) that are deliverables of the system
- Target system configuration and preparation requirements
- Support or training requirements
- Internationalization and localization requirements

With a little forethought, you should be able to determine the other types of requirements that will impact the development of your particular system. With a little practice and a little experience, you will be able to determine when you have "discovered enough."

LINKING THE SUPPLEMENTARY SPECIFICATION TO THE USE CASES

We've described the role that use cases play in defining the functional behavior of the system, and we've defined how the nonfunctional requirements are captured in the supplementary specification. Some questions naturally arise: How do these nonfunctional requirements apply to the use cases? Do specific use cases have associated nonfunctional requirements, and, if so, how could we indicate that?

One way to do so is to define certain classes of nonfunctional requirements. For example, we might define "Quality of Service" classes for response time as follows:

- Class 1: 0 to 250 milliseconds
- Class 2: 251 to 499 milliseconds
- Class 3: 0.5 to 2 seconds
- Class 4: 2.1 to 12 seconds
- Class 5: 12.1 seconds to 60 minutes

Then we could associate these classes with special requirements recorded in the use case itself. For example, Use Case A might record

- Response time: Class 2 for main flow of events
                  Class 4 for all exceptions

Use Case B might record

- Response time: Class 5

You can do the same for other classes of nonfunctional requirements (such as reliability, safety, and so on) and map these requirements to the specific use cases.

Alternately, if you have traceability tools, you can simply trace the nonfunctional requirements to those use cases to which they are applied. (We'll explore traceability in detail in Chapter 27.)

TEMPLATE FOR THE SUPPLEMENTARY SPECIFICATION

All these requirements—functional requirements that do not lend themselves to the use-case technique; nonfunctional requirements that define the usability, reliability, performance, and supportability of the system; design constraints and other requirements—find their home in the supplementary specification. Figure 22–1 provides a brief annotated outline of a supplementary specification. A more fully elaborated and annotated version of this document appears in Appendix D.

1. **Introduction**

   1.1. **Purpose**

   State the purpose of the document (to collect all functional requirements not expressed in the use-case model, as well as nonfunctional requirements and design constraints).

   1.2. **Scope**

   1.3. **Definitions, Acronyms, and Abbreviations**

   1.4. **References**

2. **Functional Requirements**

   Describe the functional requirements of the system for those requirements that are expressed in the natural language style or are otherwise not included in the use-case model.

3. **Usability**

   State the requirements that affect usability.

4. **Reliability**

   State the requirements for reliability.

5. **Performance**

   State the performance characteristics of the system, expressed quantitatively where possible and related to use cases where applicable.

6. **Supportability**

   State the requirements that enhance system supportability or maintainability.

7. **Design Constraints**

   State the design or development constraints imposed on the system or development process.

8. **Documentation Requirements**

   State the requirements for user and/or administrator documentation.

9. **Purchased Components**

   List the purchased components used with the system, licensing or usage restrictions, and compatibility/interoperability requirements.

10. **Interfaces**

    Define the interfaces that must be supported by the application.

    10.1. **User Interfaces**

    10.2. **Hardware Interfaces**

    10.3. **Software Interfaces**

    10.4. **Communications Interfaces**

11. **Licensing and Security Requirements**

    Describe the licensing and usage enforcement requirements or other restrictions for usage, security, and accessibility.

12. **Legal, Copyright, and Other Notices**

    State any required legal disclaimers, warranties, copyright notices, patent notices, trademarks, or logo compliance issues.

(continued on next page)

Figure 22–1   Template for the supplementary specification

13. **Applicable Standards**
    Reference any applicable standards and the specific sections of any such standards that apply.

14. **Internationalization and Localization**
    State any requirements for support and application of different user languages and dialects.

15. **Physical Deliverables**
    Define any specific deliverable artifacts required by the user or customer.

16. **Installation and Deployment**
    Describe any specific configuration or target system preparation required to support installation and deployment of the system.

Figure 22–1   *Continued*

SUMMARY

As ubiquitous as the use-case technique is, it doesn't capture all the requirements for a typical system and, for certain classes of systems, the technique might not be particularly helpful at all. In these cases, we have the supplementary specification to fall back on. At best, it's a standard document with well-articulated requirements organized as we've described in this chapter. At worst, it's a great repository for "all those other things we know the system has to do."

LOOKING AHEAD

In all this discussion about requirements, you might note that we've so far avoided a fairly vexing topic, the issue of just how detailed our refined use cases and specifications need to be. It's time to take a look at this matter in the next chapter.

Chapter 23

ON AMBIGUITY AND SPECIFICITY

> **Key Points**
> - The requirements "sweet spot" is the balance point of the greatest amount of understandability and the least amount of ambiguity.
> - A learned skill, finding the sweet spot will depend on the team members' abilities, the application context, and the level of certainty you must provide so that your system works as intended.
> - If the risk of misunderstanding is unacceptable, more formal requirements techniques may need to be applied.

FINDING THE "SWEET SPOT"

One of the most difficult challenges we face in the requirements process is making the requirements detailed enough to be well understood without overconstraining the system and predefining a whole host of things that may be better left to others downstream in the process. ("Do we really have to specify Pantone 287 as the background color in our GUI spec? No? How do you like the color they came up with last time?")

Time after time, our students pose the following question, which represents one of their biggest concerns: "*To what level of specificity must I state the requirements in order to avoid any chance of being misunderstood?*" Although many students are hoping for a simple answer, unfortunately, there isn't one. The only answer we can truthfully provide is, "It just depends." For example, as an exercise in requirements writing, we often use the light box exercise (Figure 23–1).

The goal of the exercise is to write clear and simple requirements using natural language or the use-case technique to describe the behavior of this device. In the exercise, the user is available for interviewing, so the requirements writer can refine the specification with clear user input. As an example of an

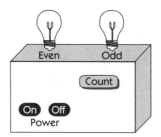

Features

- Microprocessor controlled
- Keeps track of whether count button has been pressed an even or odd number of times
- Burned-out-bulb detector flashes remaining bulb

Figure 23–1   Light box exercise

effort in the natural language style, let's look at the following requirements specification [Davis 1993].

> After On pushed but before Off pushed, system is termed "powered on."
>
> After Off pushed but before On pushed, system is termed "powered off," and no lights shall be lit.
>
> Since most recent On press, if Count has been pressed an odd number of times, Odd shall be lit.
>
> Since most recent On press, if Count has been pressed an even number of times, Even shall be lit.
>
> If either light burns out, the other light shall flash every 1 second.

This specification is fairly tight and would be quite adequate for most purposes. More important, it reflects the way the device user intended it to work!

However, a programmer who has the task of writing a program to simulate this behavior will discover at least one ambiguity in this exercise almost immediately: *What does it mean to flash the bulb every 1 second?* Still seem obvious? Let's take a look at the duty cycles in Figure 23–2.

If you were the programmer, would you pick duty cycle A or duty cycle B? Although most pick duty cycle B, it becomes clear that the requirement is ambiguous. A requirements-sensitized programmer will recognize this ambiguity and will attempt to resolve it by asking the customer, "Which duty cycle should I use?" But if the programmer is not so savvy, does not recognize the ambiguity, or thinks, "I know what you meant because I know how this thing should work," the behavior of the device when delivered may deviate perceptibly from the customer's stated requirements. Your project may be at risk.

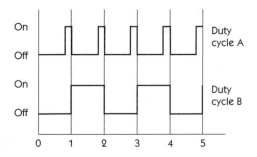

Figure 23–2 Possible lamp duty cycles

In most potential applications, it probably doesn't matter whether the bulb flashes on for 1 second or 0.25 second. But if this were an electrosurgical device, it would matter *a lot*. The power delivered to the electrode would be 100 percent higher in duty cycle B than in A, with perhaps unfortunate results.

So, the answer to "What level of specificity must I provide?" is "*It depends on the context of your application and on how well those doing the implementation can make the right decisions or at least ask questions when there is ambiguity.*"

In the case of the even and odd counting device, the specification as stated is probably adequate. In the case of the electrosurgical device, more investment in describing the requirement would be needed. A timing diagram would be needed, and the specification would probably also have to define such issues as the rise time on the upslope of the "on" current, the precision with which the "on" time must be controlled ($\pm x$ milliseconds), and other factors; otherwise, the power delivered will not be right, and the device will operate incorrectly. Figure 23–3 summarizes this dilemma.

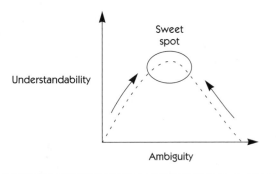

Figure 23–3 Ambiguity versus understandability

The goal is to find the sweet spot—the balance point where the investment in requirements provides "just the right amount of specificity" and leaves "just the right amount of ambiguity" for others to resolve further downstream.

As you move to the left from the sweet spot on the curve in Figure 23–3, you lower both ambiguity and understandability. For example, if we provided timing diagrams, complete with timing tolerances, to an unsophisticated user and if we maintained that level of specificity throughout, the user may well *not* be able to understand the specification at all or might even be unwilling to take the time to read it. Worse, due to your apparent thoroughness, the user might trust you too much and not take the time for a careful review. You are also at the risk of the customer's inability to see the forest for the trees. ("I didn't want a light bulb; I wanted you to turn on the emergency light at the end of the production line.")

As you move to the right of the sweet spot, ambiguity goes up, but understandability again goes down. For example, at the extreme limit, you might simply say, "Build me an even/odd counting device," and no one could possibly understand what you mean.

Finding the sweet spot is a learned skill. It will depend on the abilities of the team members, the context of the application, and the level of certainty you must provide so that your system works as intended.

Mary Had a Little Lamb

Let's have a little fun with the issue of ambiguity and also see whether we can find some more tips that will help us remove ambiguity whenever and wherever it's necessary to do so. (If you are a fairly formal sort, without much use for the "softer" side of this problem space, you may wish to skip this short section.)

For the rest of us, let's have a little fun, courtesy of Gause and Weinberg [1989], whose book leads us through an exercise that illustrates the ambiguity problem and also provides some serious insights about possible solutions.

Consider the familiar nursery rhyme "Mary Had a Little Lamb." Although it's unlikely that anyone will build an information system based on this sentence, it's nevertheless interesting to ask, "What does it mean?" In order to disambiguate this example, we can perhaps use the *keyword* or *dictionary technique*. In this technique, we focus on the keywords in the statement and look at the options, based on various meanings for each. Here we'll focus on the words "had" and "lamb." "Had" is the past tense of "have," so we'll use the definition of "have"; we can use "lamb" directly. Here's what we find for "have."

> ***have 1a:*** *to hold in possession as property . . .* ***4a:*** *to acquire or get possession of: to obtain (as in "the best to be had") . . .* ***4c:*** *ACCEPT; to have in marriage . . .* ***5a:*** *to be marked or characterized by (to have red hair) . . .* ***10a:*** *to hold in a position of disadvantage or certain defeat . . .* ***10b:*** *TRICK, FOOL (been had by a partner or friend) . . .* ***12:*** *BEGET, BEAR (have a baby) . . .* ***13:*** *to partake of (have dinner) . . .* ***14:*** *BRIBE, SUBORN (can be had for a price)[1]*

And here's what we have for "lamb."

> ***lamb 1a:*** *a young sheep esp. less than one year old or without permanent teeth . . .* ***1b:*** *the young of various other animals (e.g., smaller antelopes) . . .* ***2a:*** *a person as gentle or weak as a lamb . . .* ***2b:*** *DEAR, PET . . .* ***2c:*** *a person easily cheated or deceived, esp. in trading securities . . .* ***3a:*** *the flesh of lamb used as food[2]*

Accordingly, we could interpret the phrase "Mary had a little lamb" to mean any one of the entries in Table 23–1.

For people who grew up with this nursery rhyme and who read the rhyme to their children each night, this discussion might sound preposterous: "How could any reasonable person interpret such a familiar phrase in so many bizarre, outlandish ways?" But such a complaint is neither fair nor realistic if we expect someone from a different background, and perhaps even a different nationality and culture, to attempt an interpretation based strictly on the dictionary definition of the two keywords. If it can happen with nursery rhymes, surely it can happen with complex software systems the likes of which have never yet been created.

---

1. Adapted from *Webster's Seventh New Collegiate Dictionary* (Springfield, MA: Merriam Co., 1967).
2. Ibid.

Table 23–1 Lambic Interpretations

"Have"	"Lamb"	Interpretation
1a	1a	Mary held in possession a little sheep less than one year old or without permanent teeth.
4a	1a	Mary acquired a little sheep less than one year old or without permanent teeth.
5a	1a	Mary is the person who owned a little sheep less than one year old or without permanent teeth.
10a	1a	Mary held in a position of disadvantage a little sheep under one year old or without permanent teeth.
10b	1a	Mary tricked a little sheep under one year old or without permanent teeth.
12	1b	Mary gave birth to a little young antelope.
12	2a	Mary is (or was) the mother of a particular small, gentle person.
13	3a	Mary ate a little of the flesh of a lamb.
14	2c	Mary bribed a small person trading in securities who was easily cheated.

TECHNIQUES FOR DISAMBIGUATION

One way to cope with ambiguity is to not use natural language and to apply more "formal" requirements specification techniques, which we'll discuss in Chapter 24. For obvious reasons, the user and the stakeholders outside the development group typically prefer natural language, and even computer people manage to carry on most of their day-to-day communication in natural language. Even though both groups have some facility for communication in a natural language, they do come from very different cultures; they have a different focus, orientation, and set of assumptions.

Although it may be impossible to eliminate ambiguity entirely, we can attack it in a variety of different ways. Gause and Weinberg [1989] provide some techniques we can use when faced with this all-too-common situation.

- *Memorization heuristic.* Ask several individuals, both from the development group and from the user/stakeholder group, to try recalling, from memory the customer's real requirement. Parts that are not clear and cannot be easily remembered are likely to be the most ambiguous. Focus on them and try to restate them with more clarity so they can be remembered.
- *Keyword technique.* As illustrated with Mary's lamb, it often helps to identify the key operational words in a statement and to list all their

definitions, using an authoritative source that the various members of the project environment will accept. Then mix and match the definitions to determine different interpretations, as we did with Mary and her lamb. As a quick test of this technique, you may also note that interpretation 1(a) and 1(a) above, "Mary held in possession a little sheep less than one year old or without permanent teeth," is probably closest to the meaning in the nursery rhyme.

- *Emphasis technique.* Read the requirement aloud and emphasize individual words until as many different interpretations as possible have been discovered. If only one of the interpretations is correct, restate the requirement appropriately; if multiple interpretations are correct, additional requirements may need to be generated accordingly. We'll illustrate this point with another investigation of Mary and her lamb below.
- *Other techniques.* If appropriate, try using pictures, graphics, or formal methods to flush out the ambiguity and eliminate it.

Returning to our nursery rhyme example, we can use the emphasis technique to see if we understand what the user really means by including "Mary had a little lamb" in the requirements set. Saying the sentence aloud and emphasizing individual words might help us elicit any one of the following.

- *Mary* had a little lamb; if this is the case, perhaps the user is telling us that it was Mary's lamb, not Richard's or anyone else's.
- Mary *had* a little lamb; perhaps she no longer has it. Perhaps it's the tense of the statement that's significant.
- Mary had *a* little lamb; thus, the key point may be that Mary had only one lamb, not an entire flock.
- Mary had a *little* lamb; indeed, it was one of the littlest lambs you ever saw.
- Mary had a little *lamb*; the emphasis here reminds us that Mary didn't have a pig, a cow, or even a grown-up sheep. Nevertheless, we might still be misled into thinking she had a baby antelope.

SUMMARY

There is no right answer as to how much specificity is needed in a particular project context, and when it comes to providing adequate specificity, no one technique will work in every circumstance. Achieving the right balance of ambiguity and specificity will be a practiced skill your team will need to develop. The amount of specificity you need to provide may even vary over time, based on the changing skills of those downstream in the process and their understanding of the domain in which you operate.

Here are our recommendations to find the sweet spot in your project context.

- Use natural language whenever possible.
- Use pictures and diagrams to illustrate the intent further.
- When in doubt, ask! When you're not in doubt, consider asking anyway.
- Augment your specifications with more formal methods (Chapter 24) when you cannot afford to be misunderstood.

Train your people to recognize both the problem of ambiguity and the solutions that can be applied.

Chapter 24

TECHNICAL METHODS FOR SPECIFYING REQUIREMENTS

Key Points

- Technical methods for specifying requirements are appropriate when the requirement description is too complex for natural language or if you cannot afford to have the specification misunderstood.
- Technical methods include pseudocode, finite state machines, decision trees, activity diagrams, entity-relationship models, and many others.

Throughout this book, we have assumed that most requirements will be written in the team's natural language via the use-case method or in the context of a supplementary specification. We also suggested that requirements can readily be augmented with diagrams, tables, charts, or other techniques to help clarify the meaning. But as we described in the last chapter, there are cases in which the ambiguity of natural language is simply not tolerable, particularly when the requirements deal with life-and-death issues or when the erroneous behavior of a system could have extreme financial or legal consequences.

If the description of the requirement is too complex for natural language and if you cannot afford to have the specification misunderstood, you should consider writing or augmenting that portion of the requirements set with a "technical methods" approach.

You can choose from a variety of technical specification methods:

- Pseudocode
- Finite state machines
- Decision tables and decision trees

- Activity diagrams (flowcharts)
- Entity-relationship models

And there are many others.

We won't attempt to teach you any of these techniques in detail since each is worthy of a book of its own. But we can provide a brief introduction to each so that you'll have a sense of what to use and when. All of these techniques were considered by the HOLIS project team members as they prepared the HOLIS requirements set. The first incarnation of the set is shown in the HOLIS artifacts found in Appendix A.

Where possible, only one of these technical methods should be used to augment natural language requirements specification for a system. This simplifies the nontechnical reviewers' task of reading and understanding these special elements. If all the systems developed by an organization fall into one application domain, such as telephone switching systems, perhaps the same technical method can be used for all the systems. But in most organizations it's unrealistic to mandate a single technique for all requirements in all systems. The requirements writers need to pick the approach that best suits the situation and help the users and reviewers understand how the technique expresses system behavior.

Let's look briefly at a few of the choices.

PSEUDOCODE

As the term implies, pseudocode is a "quasi" programming language, an attempt to combine the informality of natural language with the strict syntax and control structures of a programming language. In the extreme form, pseudocode consists of combinations of:

- Imperative sentences with a single verb and a single object
- A limited set, typically not more than 40–50, of "action-oriented" verbs from which the sentences must be constructed
- Decisions represented with a formal IF-ELSE-ENDIF structure
- Iterative activities represented with DO-WHILE or FOR-NEXT structures

Figure 24–1 shows an example of a pseudocode specification of an algorithm for calculating deferred-service revenue earned within a given month in a business application. Note that the text of the pseudocode is indented, in an outline-style format, in order to show "blocks" of logic. The combination of the syntax restrictions and the format and layout of the text greatly reduces the ambiguity of what could otherwise be a very difficult and error-prone requirement. (It certainly was before we wrote the pseudocode.) At the same time, it should be possible for a nonprogramming person (for example, Rhonda the bookkeeper) to read and understand the requirement in the form shown in Figure 24–1.

```
The algorithm for calculating deferred-service revenue earned for any
month is:

Set  SUM(x)=0
FOR each customer X
    IF customer purchased paid support
       AND ((Current month) >= (2 months after ship date))
       AND ((Current month) <= (14 months after ship date))
    THEN Sum(X)=Sum(X) + (amount customer paid)/12
END
```

Figure 24–1   Example of pseudocode

FINITE STATE MACHINES

In some cases it's convenient to regard the system or a discrete subset of the system as a "hypothetical machine that can be in only one of a given number of 'states' at any specific time" [Davis 1993]. In response to an input, such as data entry from the user or an input from an external device, the machine changes its state and then generates an output or carries out an action. Both the output and the next state can be determined solely on the basis of understanding the current state and the event that caused the transition. In that way, a system's behavior can be said to be deterministic; we can mathematically determine every possible state and, therefore, the outputs of the system, based on any set of inputs provided.

Hardware designers have used finite state machines (FSMs) for decades, and a large body of literature describes the creation and analysis of such machines. Indeed, the mathematical nature of the FSM notation lends itself to formal and rigorous analysis, so that the problems of consistency, completeness, and ambiguity described earlier in Team Skill 5 can be largely mitigated using this technique.

A popular notation for FSMs is the state transition diagram (Figure 24–2). In this notation, the boxes represent the state the device is in, and the arrows represent actions that transition the device to alternative states. Figure 24–2 illustrates state transitions for the light box described in Chapter 23. In that example, the natural language expression "the other light shall flash every 1 second" was ambiguous. The state transition diagram in Figure 24–2 is not ambiguous since it illustrates that duty cycle B was indeed the right choice. If a bulb burns out, the device alternates between attempting to light the even light and attempting to light the odd light, each for a period of one second.

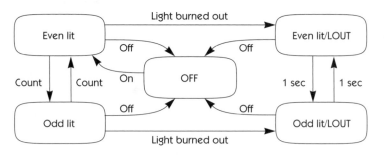

Figure 24–2   Example of a state transition diagram

Here's an interesting exercise to try. Consider using the FSM technique to restate the HOLIS Control Light use case. You may immediately notice that the Dim alternative flow in the use case lends itself nicely to the FSM style of representation.

An even more precise form of representing an FSM is the state transition matrix, which is represented as a table that shows every possible state the device can be in, the output of the system for each state, and the effect of every possible stimulus or event on every possible state. This ensures a higher degree of specificity because every state and the effect of every possible event must be represented in the table. For example, Table 24–1 defines the behavior of our light box in the form of a state transition matrix.

With this technique, we can resolve additional ambiguities that may have been present in our attempt to understand the behavior of the device.

- What happens if the user presses the On switch and the device is already on? Answer: Nothing.
- What happens if both bulbs are burned out? Answer: The device powers itself off.

Table 24–1 Example of a State Transition Matrix for an On/Off Counting Device

State	On Press	Off Press	Count Press	Bulb Burns Out	Every Second	Output
			Event			
Off	Even lit	—	—	—	—	Both off
Even lit	—	Off	Odd lit	LO/Even lit	—	Even lit
Odd lit	—	Off	Even lit	LO/Odd lit	—	Odd lit
Light out/Even lit	—	Off	—	Off	LO/Odd lit	Even lit
Light out/Odd lit	—	Off	—	Off	LO/Even lit	Odd lit

FSMs are very popular for certain categories of systems programming applications, such as message-switching systems, operating systems, and process control systems. FSMs also provide an elegant way to describe the interaction between an external human user and a system (consider, for example, the interaction between a bank customer and an automated teller machine when the customer wants to withdraw money). However, FSMs can become unwieldy, particularly if we need to represent the system's behavior as a function of *several* inputs. In such cases, the required system behavior is typically a function of all current conditions and stimuli rather than the current stimulus or a history of stimuli.

DECISION TABLES AND DECISION TREES

It's common to see a requirement that deals with a combination of inputs; different combinations of those inputs lead to different behaviors or outputs. Suppose, for example, that we have a system with five inputs—A, B, C, D, and E—and we see a requirement that starts with a pseudocode-like statement: "If A is true, then if B and C are also true, generate output X, unless E is true, in which case the required output is Y." The combination of IF-THEN-ELSE clauses quickly becomes tangled, especially if, as in this example, it involves *nested* IFs. Typically, nontechnical users are not sure that they understand any of it, and nobody is sure whether all the possible combinations and permutations of A, B, C, D, and E have been covered.

The solution in this case is to enumerate all the combinations of inputs and to describe each one explicitly in a *decision table*. In our example, if the only permissible values of the inputs are "true" and "false," we have 2^5, or 32, combinations. These can be represented in a table containing 5 rows—one for each input variable—and 32 columns.

Alternatively, a *decision tree* can be drawn to portray the same information. Figure 24–3 shows a decision tree used to describe the HOLIS emergency sequence.

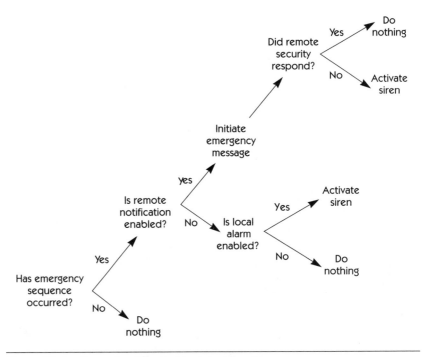

Figure 24–3   Example of a graphical decision tree

ACTIVITY DIAGRAMS

Flowcharts and their new incarnation, the UML activity diagram, have the advantage of reasonable familiarity: even people with no computer-related training or background know what a flowchart is. For example, a local newspaper recently published a flowchart that described an algorithm by which the brain processes the decisions involved in purchasing a Saab convertible. For reasons that are pretty clear, all paths through that particular flowchart ended up at the same activity: "Buy the Saab." There must have been a logic error in there somewhere, although we couldn't find it. But we sure are enjoying the car!

Figure 24–4 shows a typical activity diagram in UML notation. Although the same information could have been presented in pseudocode form, the UML notation provides a visual representation that may be easier to understand.

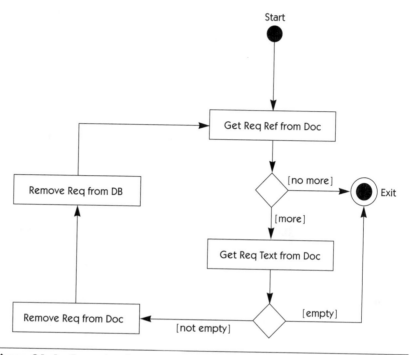

Figure 24–4 Example of an activity diagram

The problem with activity diagrams, as the technical computer community has learned over the past 30 years, is that they are a nuisance to keep up-to-date. Of course, it can be a nuisance to keep any visual representation of a requirement up-to-date without automated tools; nobody wants to redraw a state transition diagram or a decision tree, either.

ENTITY-RELATIONSHIP MODELS

If the requirements within a set involve a description of the structure and relationships among *data* within the system, it's often convenient to represent that information in an entity-relationship diagram (ERD). Figure 24–5 shows a typical ERD.

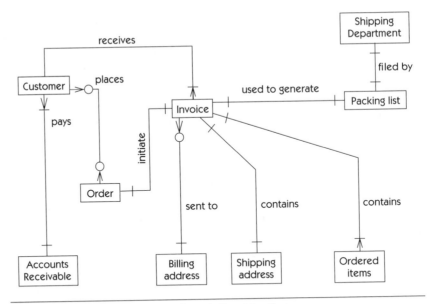

Figure 24–5   Example of an entity-relationship diagram

Note that the ERD provides a high-level "architectural" view of the data represented by customers, invoices, packing lists, and so on; it would be further augmented with appropriate details about the required information to describe a customer. The ERD does correctly focus on the external behaviors of the system and allows us to define such questions as "Can there be more than one billing address per invoice?" *Answer:* no.

Although an ERD is a capable modeling technique, it has the potential disadvantage of being difficult for a nontechnical reader to understand. As you can see in Figure 24–5, the lines connecting "Customer" to "Order" and "Order" to "Invoice" are annotated with circles and "crows-feet" indicators. The obvious question is: What does all of this mean? Attempting to answer such a question within this book would be a major digression which we will avoid, but avoiding the question in the review of a requirements set is likely to mean that some users simply won't understand what's going on. The alternatives are to send the appropriate users to a two-day training course in ERD notation, which they may or may not appreciate, or to use the notation as a "technical" form of documentation within the development group.

SUMMARY

When natural language isn't good enough, your team may apply technical methods to reduce the risk of misunderstanding and to thereby provide additional safety, security, and reliability for your system. In general, technical methods should be used sparingly, and common sense should guide the decision as to *which* formal technique will be used in a particular project. If you're building a nuclear reactor control system, perhaps *every* aspect of the system is critical; in most systems, however, it's unlikely that more than 10 percent of the requirements will require this degree of formality. Choose the method that suits your team best and apply it only where it is really needed.

Team Skill 5 Summary

In Team Skill 5, we learned how to refine requirements so as to completely and concisely capture the user's needs in such a way that the developer can build an application to meet those needs. In addition, requirements need to have sufficient specificity so that we can tell when they have been met. We needn't be alarmed by this. Often, it is our team—after all, we are closest to the project—that can provide this specificity; this is one of our opportunities to make sure that the right system gets defined.

Various ways of organizing and documenting these requirements exist. We focused on the use-case technique for functional requirements and the supplementary specification for nonfunctional requirements. Although we made some suggestions about how to organize this requirements set, we don't really care what form it takes, so long as it contains the right things.

All development should flow from the requirements specified in the requirements set, and all specifications in the set should be reflected in the development activities. Since these are the governing elements, it follows that all activities, such as regulatory constraints, should be reflected in the set and vice versa. The requirements set is a living entity that should be reviewed and updated throughout the lifetime of the project. The set should specify *what* functions are to be accomplished, not *how* they are to be accomplished. The set should be used to specify functional requirements, nonfunctional requirements, and design constraints.

The requirements set provides the detail you need to proceed to *implement*, or *build*, the right system. We'll discuss this part of the project next, in Team Skill 6, Building the Right System.

BUILDING THE RIGHT SYSTEM

Team Skill 5 led us through the activities of refining the system definition to better support the implementation and testing activities. In Team Skill 6, we focus on moving from the definition of a solution system to finally building a system that meets stakeholder needs. This next step, actually building the system, is the most difficult, and it will consume many times the resources that have been expended to date.

We've all been involved in projects that moved quickly from requirements into a flurry of development activities with lots of apparently favorable progress. However, at the end of the day, it turned out that the mighty dust cloud of development obscured the fact that the client did not get the desired system. To help you avoid this outcome, in this team skill we describe a logical and stepwise method of moving from an understanding of the requirements to designing and implementing the system that fulfills them. This method is a key factor in helping you assure that you are "building the right system right."

Of course, no development project is immune to changes as time passes. Accordingly, in this team skill we investigate the sources and impacts of requirements changes and discuss ways to embrace change and control it so that your project stays on the right track.

Chapter 25

FROM USE CASES TO IMPLEMENTATION

Key Points

- Some requirements map well from design to implementation in code.

- Other requirements have little correlation to design and implementation; the form of the requirement differs from the form of the design and implementation (the problem of orthogonality).

- Object orientation and use cases can help alleviate the problem of orthogonality.

- Use cases drive design by allowing all stakeholders to examine the proposed system implementation against a backdrop of system uses and requirements.

- Good system design is not necessarily optimized to make it easy to see how and where the requirements are implemented.

We have been building complex software systems for over 40 years. And yes, we have struggled and had our share of failures, but we have also achieved an extraordinary degree of success: online trading, the Internet, desktop productivity tools, lifesaving medical equipment, and safe power plants, to name a few.

It's clear that we have somehow managed to move from the world of requirements to the world of design and implementation. We have implemented many complex systems that conform to their requirements. However, when it comes to building complex systems that require a high degree of safety or reliability assurance, it hasn't always been a pretty (or at least a rigorously scientific) matter. The reason is that requirements do not lend themselves to being readily exposed for inspection within the implementation. Proving that any particular requirement is fulfilled in the code is a nontrivial matter. In this chapter, we explore this particular problem to see if we can gain some insights into a potential solution.

MAPPING REQUIREMENTS DIRECTLY TO DESIGN AND CODE

Fortunately, for some percentage of our requirements, we can design the software so that it is relatively easy to follow our requirements into design and then into code. This also means that we can test a significant portion of our code, using a requirement-to-module test, since there will be a reasonable degree of correlation between the statement of a requirement and the code that implements it. For example, it's probably fairly straightforward to find, inspect, and validate the code that fulfills the requirement "Support up to an eight-digit floating-point input parameter," or "Indicate compilation progress to the user," as we can see in Figure 25–1. Depending on the type of system we are building, this approach may work for a substantial portion of our code, so the requirements-to-design-to-implementation process is not so difficult in these cases.

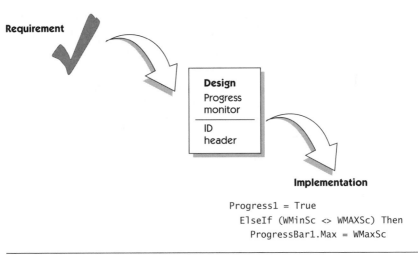

Requirement

Design
Progress
monitor

ID
header

Implementation

```
Progress1 = True
  ElseIf (WMinSc <> WMAXSc) Then
    ProgressBar1.Max = WMaxSc
```

Figure 25–1   From requirements to design to implementation—a direct mapping

The Orthogonality Problem

Requirement:
"100,000 trades
an hour"

Code

However, when it comes to such requirements as "The system shall handle up to 100,000 trades an hour" or a use-case step like "The user can edit each of the highlighted fields in accordance with user privileges that have been established by the system administrator," things get a little trickier. In these cases, there is little correlation between the requirement and the design and implementation; they are *orthogonal*, or nearly so. In other words, *the form of our requirements and the form of our design and implementation are different.* There is no one-to-one mapping to make implementation and validation easier. There are many reasons why this is true.

- Requirements speak of real-world items, such as engines and paychecks, but code speaks of stacks, queues, and computation algorithms. The two are different languages.
- Certain requirements, such as performance requirements, have little to do with the logical structure of code but lots to do with the process structure, or how various pieces of code interact, how fast a particular piece of code runs, how often we get interrupted while in module A, and so on. When you can't physically map to the logical structure, there is no place to "point" your requirement to within the implementation.
- Other functional requirements require that a number of system elements interact to achieve the functionality. Looking at a part is not the same as looking at the whole, and the implementation of the requirement may be distributed throughout the code.
- Perhaps most importantly, good system design is driven not by optimizing the ease with which we can prove that a requirement is met but by more important factors. For example, the designer may be optimizing the use of scarce resources, reusing an architectural pattern that has been proven in other applications but is not the exact paradigm of the current application, reusing code, or applying purchased components that bring their own overhead and functional behaviors.

In any case, the design of the solution does not follow the form of the requirements, and there is no easy way to definitively follow, or trace, from requirements to design and code. For those of us who have been building high-assurance systems and/or have been forced by political or contractual considerations into demonstrating on paper the direct correlation between requirements and code, we managed to get by. But, we admit, the formulation consisted of one part real-and-deadly-serious-requirements-traceability mechanisms and one part pixie dust.

Object Orientation

In many ways, this problem of orthogonality—a lack of direct relationship between requirements reflecting the problem space and the code we implemented—was substantially improved with the advent of object-oriented (OO) technology. In applying OO concepts, we tended to build code entities that were a better match to the problem domain, and we discovered that an improved degree of robustness resulted. This was due not only to the OO principles of abstraction, information hiding, inheritance, and so on but also to the fact that the real-world entities simply changed less often than the transactions and the data on which we formerly designed our system. Therefore, our code changed less often, too. (For example, people still get paychecks today, just as they did 40 years ago, but in many cases the form of delivery—electronic versus paper—has changed dramatically.)

With OO technology, we did start to find engine objects and paycheck objects in the code, and we used this to good advantage to decrease the degree of orthogonality in requirements verification. We could look at the requirements for "paycheck stub" and see whether the implied operations and attributes were supported in the design model.

However, we must be careful because a purposeful attempt to provide a one-to-one mapping from requirements to code can lead to a *very non-OO* architecture, one that is functionally organized. The basic principles of OO technology drive the designer to describe a small number of mechanisms that satisfy the key requirements of the system, resulting in a set of classes that collaborate and yield behavior that's bigger than the sum of its parts. This "bigger behavior" is intended to provide a more robust, more extensible design that can deliver the current and, ideally, future requirements in the *aggregate*, but it is not a one-to-one mapping from requirements. Therefore, even with OO technology, some degree of orthogonality with requirements will always, and should always, remain.

The Use Case as a Requirement

As we mentioned earlier, the "itemized" nature of the requirements can further compound the problem of orthogonality. Each requirement by itself may not present a huge problem, but it makes it difficult to look at system behavior in the aggregate to see whether it does all the right things and in the right sequence. How could we examine the system to determine whether requirement 3 ("Display progress bar") immediately followed requirement 7 ("During compilation, the algorithm is . . .")?

- Client inserts ATM card.
- System prompts for PIN.
- Client enters PIN.

The use case, which provides a sequence of actions between the system and the user instead of an itemized individual requirement, improves this problem significantly. Now the requirements themselves, in the form of the use cases, do a better job of providing the behavior of the system in sequential fashion, complete with alternatives and exceptions. As we said before, use cases simply tell a better story about how the system does what it is intended to do. In addition, as we will see, they also give us a head start on the design process.

Managing the Transition

Although, with OO methods and use cases, we haven't solved the problem of orthogonality, we do have a number of existing assets and a few new techniques that can help us deal with the problem. If we can use these assets to increase the parallels between requirements and code, it seems likely that we can use our understanding of the requirements to more logically drive the design of the system. In so doing, it should also be easier to translate between these dissimilar worlds, to improve the design of the system, and to improve the overall quality of the system that results. Before we do so, however, we need to make a small digression into the world of modeling and software architecture.

Modeling Software Systems

Nontrivial software systems today are extraordinarily complex undertakings. It is common to find systems and applications that are composed of *millions* of lines of code. These systems or applications may, in turn, be embedded in other systems that also have an extraordinary complexity in their own right, not to mention the complex interactions that may occur between the systems. We take it as a given that no one person or even group of persons can possibly understand the details of each of these systems and their planned interactions.

In the face of this complexity and to keep our wits about us, a useful technique is to abstract the system into a simplified *model*, removing the minutia of the system in order to view a more comprehensible version. The purpose of modeling is to simplify the details down to an understandable "essence" but not to oversimplify to the point that the model does not adequately represent the real system. In this way, we can think about the system without being buried in the details.

Selection of the model is an important issue. We want the model to help us understand the system in the proper way, but we don't want the model to mislead us because of errors or abstractions. You've undoubtedly seen pictures of drawings and machines that helped the early philosophers, astronomers, and mathematicians understand the workings of the solar system. Many of these models, based on a geocentric view of the solar system with Earth at the center of the universe, thus led to many blind alleys and incorrect theories. Only when sun-centered, or heliocentric, models were proposed did a better understanding of our solar system emerge.

Remember, the model is not the reality.

Models provide a powerful way to reason about a complex problem and to derive useful insights. However, we must be aware that *the model is not the reality*. We must continually check and assure ourselves that the model has not led us astray.

For example, the heliocentric (sun-centric) models of the universe opened up many new possibilities and ideas regarding the universe at large (very large). Early scientists were able to reason from the model and to propose refined mathematical theories relating motion, gravity, and so on. However, it's important to note that the model was *not* the reality. In some cases, the mechanical views of the universe, as exemplified by the model, did not exactly match the observed realities. For example, one of the early confirmations of Einstein's relativity theory was observed in some previously unexplained anomalies of the planet Mercury's orbit.

Many different aspects of a system can be modeled. If you are interested in application concurrency, you may model that. If you are interested in the system's logical structure, you may model that. In addition, these models need to interact in some way, and that aspect too can be modeled. Each of these mechanisms contributes to our understanding of the system in the aggregate, and taken together they allow us to consider the *system architecture* in the whole.

The Architecture of Software Systems

According to Shaw and Garlan [1996], software architecture involves the

> *description of elements from which systems are built, interactions amongst those elements, patterns that guide their composition, and constraints on those patterns.*

According to Kruchten [1999], we use architecture to help us:

- Understand what the system does
- Understand how the system works
- Think and work on pieces of the system
- Extend the system
- Reuse part(s) of the system to build another one

Architecture becomes the tool by which decisions are made about what and how the system will be built. In many projects, we know at the start how we are going to put the pieces together because we, or others, have developed such systems before. The easy starting decisions are reflected in the *dominant architecture* notion, which is just a fancy way to say that "everyone knows how to build a payroll system."

Dominant architecture helps us kick-start the decision process and minimizes risk through the reuse of pieces of a successful solution. If you're going to build a payroll system, it would be silly to start from scratch and invent the entire concept of FICA, check writing, medical deductions, and so on. Start by looking at models of existing systems, and use them to prompt your thinking.

Different groups of stakeholders need to consider your architectural models and will want to view the proposed architecture from different perspectives. The parallel to a "building a house" metaphor holds. You'd want to have views of the house that were suitable for the framers, the roofers, the electricians, the plumbers, and so on. It's all the same house, but our *view* of it may differ, depending on the need.

> Different stake-holders need different perspectives of the system.

The "4+1" View of Architecture   There is usually a small set of common needs for viewing the system architecture. The views that best illustrate these needs are discussed by Kruchten [1995] as the "4+1" view shown in Figure 25–2. The figure identifies a number of stakeholders (programmers, managers, users)

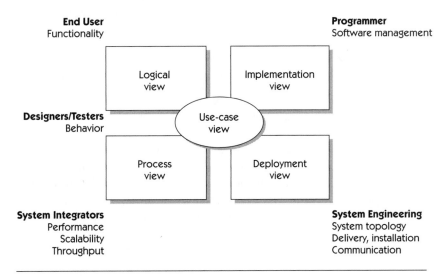

Figure 25–2   The 4+1 architectural view

and positions them near the types of views they would normally need to consider.

1. The *logical view* addresses the functionality of the system. This abstraction of the design model represents the logical structure of the system in terms of subsystems and classes, which in turn are the entities that deliver the functionality to the user.
2. The *implementation view* describes the bits and pieces that are relevant to the implementation of the system: source code, libraries, object classes, and so on. This view represents the static view of these pieces, not how they interact.
3. *Process views*, generally more useful to describe operations of the system, are extremely important for systems that have parallel tasks, interfaces with other systems, and other interactions that occur during execution. Since many modern systems exhibit high degrees of parallelism and multithreading, this view allows the reviewer to determine potential problems, such as race conditions or deadlocks. You should also use the process view to examine throughput issues and other performance issues that the user specified in the nonfunctional requirements.
4. Because the project modules rarely exist in a vacuum, the *deployment view* allocates the implementation elements to the supporting infrastructure, such as operating systems and computing platforms. This view is not especially concerned with what the interactions are but rather with the fact that there are interactions and constraints where the two systems meet.

The Role of the Use-Case Model in Architecture

Finally, we return to our problem of orthogonality. Within the architecture, the *use-case view*, as the holder of requirements, plays a special role in the architectural model. This view presents key use cases of the use-case model, drives the design, and ties all the various views of the architecture together. We favor this view because it allows all stakeholders to examine the proposed system implementation plans against a backdrop of actual use cases and requirements of the system. Therefore, the use-case view, which represents the functionality of the system, is the "tie that binds," that is, the one view that binds the other views together.

For example, the HOLIS use case Initiate Emergency Sequence would impact the design of the system in each of the four views as follows.

1. The *logical view* would describe the various classes and subsystems that implemented the behaviors called for by the emergency sequence functionality.
2. The *implementation view* would describe the various code artifacts for HOLIS, including source and executable files.
3. The *process view* would demonstrate how the multitasking capability of HOLIS was always available to initiate an emergency sequence, even when it was being programmed or was busy doing other tasks.
4. The *deployment view* would show that the functionality of HOLIS was distributed across the three HOLIS nodes, or subsystems: Control Switch, Central Control Unit, and Homeowner's PC.

REALIZING USE CASES IN THE DESIGN MODEL

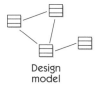

Design
model

This strategy of "use-case-driven design" is a key theme in a variety of software processes based on the UML and the associated book, *The Unified Software Development Process* [Jacobson, Booch, and Rumbaugh 1999]. The technique we describe here is the means by which the designers of the UML and the affiliated process help the design team transition from an understanding of the requirements to the design and implementation of the solution.

Further, the UML contains specific modeling constructs that support *realizing* the use case in the implementation. Specifically, use cases are realized via *collaborations*, which are societies of classes, interfaces, subsystems, or other elements that cooperate to achieve some behavior. A common UML stereotype, the *use-case realization*, is used for this purpose and is simply a special form of collaboration, one that shows how the functionality of a specific use case is achieved in the design model.

Collaborations, then, are key modeling constructs within our area of concern, for it is within the collaborations that you see the systematic and aggregate behavioral aspects of the system, or how the system achieves its overall goals. These key constructs deliver some of the "bigger-than-the-sum-of-its-parts behavior" through the activities of participating classes and other logical elements. The graphical symbol for a collaboration is a simple dotted-line ellipse with a name inside, as shown in Figure 25–3. (The UML authors have commented that the similarity to use-case notation is intentional.)

Collaborations have another useful aspect. Since the collaboration represents the way in which the use case is implemented in the design model, we now have a method we can use to trace from the requirements expressed in the use-case model into the design (Figure 25–4).

Figure 25–3   Symbolic representation of a collaboration

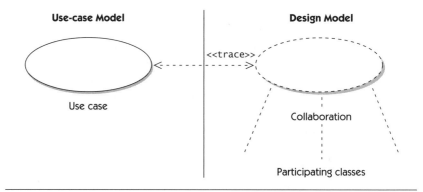

Figure 25–4   A use-case realization in the design model

Structural and Behavioral Aspects of Collaborations

Collaborations have two aspects: a structural part that specifies the static structure of the system (the classes, elements, interfaces, and subsystems on which the implementation is structured) and a behavioral part that specifies the dynamics of how the elements interact to accomplish the result. However, a collaboration is not a physical thing; it is just a description of how co-operating elements of the system work together. To know more about how the collaboration is affected, you must look inside.

Inside the collaboration, a class diagram can represent the structural aspects. Figure 25–5 shows a class diagram for the HOLIS Emergency Message Sequence collaboration. For behavioral aspects, you might choose to model its behavior by using an interaction diagram such as the one shown in Figure 25–6.

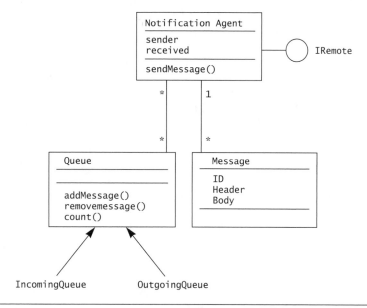

Figure 25–5   Class diagram for the HOLIS Emergency Message Sequence collaboration

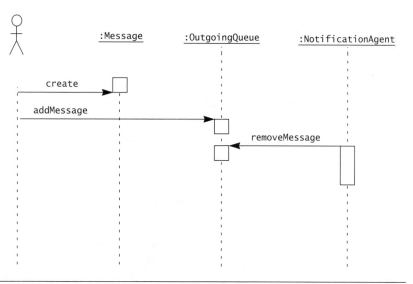

Figure 25–6   Behavioral aspects of the HOLIS Emergency Message Sequence collaboration

Using Collaborations to Realize Sets of Individual Requirements

We've used the mechanism of the use case and the use-case realization to help us cross a very difficult chasm—the gap between the statement of requirements and the design of a system that fulfills the requirements. We applied use cases to demonstrate this technique. Note that it is also true that we can model the implementation of any individual requirement, or any set of requirements, as a collaboration and apply that technique to achieve requirements-to-design traceability for those requirements as well (Figure 25–7). Although the use case does have some special properties, namely, the sequence of events, we can often group our itemized requirements to accomplish a similar objective. With this slight extension, we have a meaningful way to use requirements of all types to drive design and implementation.

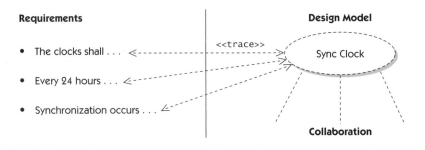

Figure 25–7   Model of requirements implementation as a collaboration

Design elements that support nonfunctional requirements such as safety, performance, and so on can be modeled this way as well. Indeed, we already knew that many nonfunctional requirements require a coordinated effort on the part of many classes, subsystems, or systems to achieve the desired result; now we have a way to express that directly.

FROM DESIGN TO IMPLEMENTATION

By modeling the system this way, we can ensure that the significant use cases and requirements of the system are properly realized in the design model. In turn, this helps ensure that the software design conforms to the requirements. Thus we can achieve a major step in the process of *design verification*.

The next step follows quite logically, although admittedly not easily. The classes and the objects defined in the design model are further refined in the iterative design process and eventually implemented in terms of the physical software components—source files, binaries, executables, and others—that will be used to create the executable software. Unfortunately, even this mapping has its complications. For example, the decisions that lead you to a certain componentization of the logical models will often be driven by such requirements as the need for resilience, constraints on the system's deployment, and so on. So, while the work is not easy and cannot be dictated directly by the form of requirements, it should now be clear that every view of a system's architecture is, or should be, influenced by the system's requirements. If we keep these factors in mind, we should be able to complete the transition from requirements to design to implementation in a more predictable and reliable manner.

SUMMARY

It would be nice if you could go directly from the requirements to the code with some simple push-button technology. Unfortunately, it simply doesn't work that way. The best that modern practice can offer is a series of constructs that will help you move closer to the direct translation goal.

One of these techniques, the use-case realization, takes advantage of the unique characteristics of the use case and the UML's modeling constructs and stereotypes to help drive design. This has many advantages in shortening the path from requirements to implementation.

Other modern practices offer us the clarity of viewing our efforts in the "4+1" architectural views construct. We have found that this helps provide a separation of concerns that increases resilience and improves out understanding of the system, while at the same time assuring that the system design conforms to all necessary requirements. This makes it much easier for the various stakeholders in the implementation process to develop and assess the design as it evolves.

LOOKING AHEAD

We admit it. We've only skimmed the top layer of implementation. The larger topic, in its own right, is the design and implementation of complex systems, and there are entire sections in the technical libraries devoted to this challenge. But hopefully, we've provided some techniques you can use to assist with that effort and, more specifically, techniques that can help you implement the *right* system to begin with. But since this is *not* a book on implementing software systems, this is as deep as we need to go on that topic. We'll now move on to the next large problem, *system testing*.

Chapter 26

FROM USE CASES TO TEST CASES

Key Points

- One of the greatest benefits of the use-case technique is that it builds a set of assets that can be used to drive the testing process.
- Use cases can directly drive, or seed, the development of test cases.
- The scenarios of a use case create templates for individual test cases.
- Adding data values completes the test cases.
- Testing nonfunctional requirements completes the testing process.

A TESTER'S PERSPECTIVE: MUSINGS ON THE BIG BLACK BOX

Let's consider for a moment the perspective of the testing team in a traditional, non-use-case-driven development process. In most situations, the test team enters the development process relatively late in the game. Perhaps the testers have been provided with at least a minimal set of specifications, perhaps not; but in either case they will most likely approach the system to be tested as an unknown, a "black box" that needs to be tested. While reasoning about the task, each tester may ask the following questions.

- "What, exactly, is this system supposed to do, and in what order is it supposed to do it?"
- "What are all the things that can go wrong with the system, and how is the system supposed to behave when this happens?"
- "How can I create and record a set of testing scenarios in which I can put this system through its paces?"

- "How will I know when I've tested the system completely and thoroughly?"
- "Is there anything else this system is supposed to do, or not do, that I need to know about?"

And perhaps the last, even more telling question:

- "Given that the system is coming out of development late, and given that the shipment date has not been moved, is there any way the testing team can start earlier on the next project and avoid this inefficient 'late discovery' process?"

Now let's consider the perspective of a testing team in an organization that has successfully adopted the use-case technique for expressing the majority of the functional requirements of the system. In this case, in addition to the black box itself, the team members will discover the following assets:

- A comprehensive set of use cases that documents an ordered sequence of events describing how the system interacts with the user and how it delivers its results to that user
- A use-case model that documents all the use cases for the system, as well as how they interact and what actors drive them
- Within each use case, both a basic flow of events (the main or "happy day" path through the system) and a series of alternate flows that defines what the system does in various "what if" scenarios
- Descriptions of pre-conditions (system states that must be true before the use cases executes) and post-conditions (system states that must persist after the use case has executed)
- A supplementary specification that defines the nonfunctional requirements of the system, including the usability, reliability, performance, and supportability of the system

In this case, the tester's question might well be different: "Have I died and gone to heaven?"

It seems clear from these two scenarios that one of the most significant benefits of the use-case technique has now come to light.

The use-case technique builds a set of assets that can directly drive the testing process.

From the standpoint of developmental efficiency *and* resultant product quality, it also seems clear that by employing use cases the team can achieve a *vastly improved development process* over whatever process existed before.

IS A USE CASE A TEST CASE?

Use case =
test case?
No.

Leaping to conclusions, you might assume that the use case is itself a test case and that the team can go right to work testing use cases immediately without much further thought to the process. Well, not exactly. In the following sections we show that a fair amount of test design work is still ahead of us and that, while the use cases do indeed *drive* this process, some serious analytical work has to be done to convert these assets into the proper stage for system testing. Before we do even that, however, we need to take a moment to define some of the terms we will be using.

COMMON TESTING TERMS

Testing is not a new process; we needn't reinvent the wheel of testing methodology, and we can leverage some of the standards work promulgated by the IEEE and other industry groups. So, for purposes of common understanding, we'll summarize some of these definitions here.

- A **test plan** contains information about the purpose and goals of testing within the project. Additionally, the test plan identifies the strategies to be used to implement and execute testing and the resources needed.
- A **test case** is a set of test inputs, execution conditions, and expected results developed for a particular objective, such as to exercise a particular program path or to verify compliance with a specific requirement.
- A **test procedure** is a set of detailed instructions for the setup, execution, and evaluation of results for a given test case.
- A **test script** is a software script that automates the execution of a test procedure (or a portion of a test procedure).
- **Test coverage** defines the degree to which a given test or set of tests addresses all specified test cases for a given system or component.
- A **test item** is a build that is an object of testing.
- **Test results** are a repository of data captured during the execution of a test used in calculating the different key measures of testing.

RELATIONSHIPS OF TEST ARTIFACTS

Given these definitions, you can see that it takes a fair number of test artifacts to define, implement, and manage a comprehensive testing process. Figure 26–1 illustrates the relationships among these artifacts.

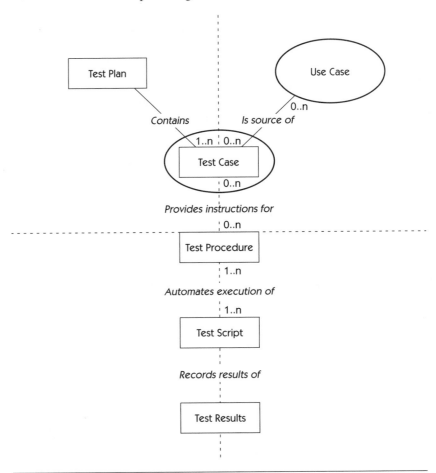

Figure 26–1   Relationships among test artifacts

The foundation for the testing process is the test plan, which contains the strategy for testing and refers to or contains the test cases themselves. The use cases are a source of potential test cases. For each test case, there are one or more test procedures that define how to execute the specific test case. The test cases are executed either manually or by running a test script. The results of the testing are recorded in the test results.

THE ROLE OF THE TEST CASES

Pivotal to all this testing activity are the test cases. The creation and execution of the test cases themselves constitute the bulk of the testing activity, and the quality and thoroughness with which they are designed and executed determine the quality of the final result.

- Test cases form the foundation on which to design and develop test procedures.
- The "depth" of the testing is proportional to the number of test cases.
- The scale of the test effort is proportional to the number of test cases.
- Test design and development, and the resources needed, are largely governed by the required test cases.

The use cases created during the inception, elaboration, and construction phases of the project serve directly as the input to this process, and since the bulk of the testing workload lies in defining and implementing the test cases, this is where we get the "bang for the buck" from our use-case approach.

USE-CASE SCENARIOS

Earlier in the book we described a use case as a sequence of events between an actor and a system. We also stated that a variety of alternate paths can be executed. In each case, we described this in the abstract, that is, things the system can do and things the user can do, but without specifics. As we move into test cases, we need to be more specific, and we need to think in terms of specific *scenarios* that occur for each use case.

> *A scenario, or an instance of a use case, is a use-case execution wherein a specific user executes the use case in a specific way.*

For example, let's look at Figure 26–2. You'll note that there are multiple possible scenarios. For example, a user might begin by following the basic flow, followed by alternate flow #1. Or, a user might execute part of the basic flow, followed by alternate flow #1, followed by alternate flow #2, resulting in a premature exit from the use case, perhaps due to an error condition. *Each of these paths is a scenario, or use-case instance, that can be both executed and tested.*

In understanding this, we also come to understand one of the most significant challenges with system testing: even with a limited number of use cases, a large number of specific scenarios must be tested to assure that the system behaves in accordance with its requirements.

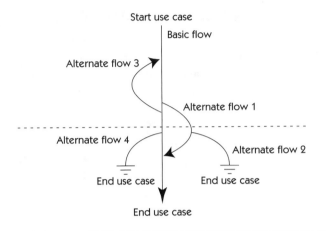

Figure 26–2   Scenarios for a use case

DERIVING TEST CASES FROM USE CASES: A FOUR-STEP PROCESS

Use cases and test cases come from different origins and serve different, albeit related, purposes. Moving from one to another is a nontrivial but reasonably stepwise process. Now that we've defined the concept of use-case scenarios, we can prescribe a four-step process to accomplish this objective.

1. Identify the use-case scenarios.
2. For each scenario, identify one or more test cases.
3. For each test case, identify the conditions that will cause it to execute.
4. Complete the test case by adding data values.

Step 1: Identify the Use-Case Scenarios

Since we have a one–to-many relationship between use cases and scenarios, we need some organizing technique to manage this potential information explosion. We'll use a simple matrix that can be implemented in a spreadsheet, database, or test management tool. In order to keep track of things, we also need to number each scenario and define exactly what combination of basic and alternate flows that particular scenario represents. Returning to Figure 26–2, we could construct a matrix similar to the one in Table 26–1.

In Table 26–1 we've identified eight possible scenarios for the sample use case. Note that the use case we've described is not an overly complex one, and

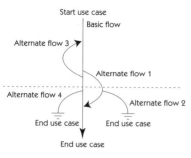

Table 26–1 Scenario Matrix for Figure 26–2

Scenario Number	Originating Flow	Alternate Flow	Next Alternate	Next Alternate
1	Basic flow			
2	Basic flow	Alternate flow 1		
3	Basic flow	Alternate flow 1	Alternate flow 2	
4	Basic flow	Alternate flow 3		
5	Basic flow	Alternate flow 3	Alternate flow 1	
6	Basic flow	Alternate flow 3	Alternate flow 1	Alternate flow 2
7	Basic flow	Alternate flow 4		
8	Basic flow	Alternate flow 3	Alternate flow 4	

yet a significant number of scenarios may result. As the use cases grow more complex, more and more scenarios will result. In many situations, the tester will need to devise a testing strategy that recognizes that it is impractical to test all possible scenarios but still assures that adequate testing is achieved. Even then, this technique can be used to identify all the possible scenarios that *could* be tested.

In addition, the tester should be aware that not all scenarios may be described in the original use case and that this scenario discovery process may well need to be conducted interactively with the development team. There are two reasons for this.

1. The use cases developed for implementation are not 100 percent exhaustive and are written at a level of detail that may be insufficient for testing.
2. The test team's review process will create new discoveries and additional scenarios that may result from executing the use case. Some of these may not even have been considered in the design and may thus require design modifications.

This is yet another reason we've adopted the iterative model in our lifecycle approach; it allows us to effectively plan for and manage this process. In any event, the process is a beneficial one, and a better system should result as the testing team reviews the use cases and finds holes and additional alternate scenarios.

Step 2: Identify the Test Cases

Testing processes vary from company to company and even from project to project, but in each situation a test case documents a number of common items. Whether in a spreadsheet, document, database, or testing tool, the test case should contain the parameters of the test to be conducted, including the conditions of the test and the expected results. One common format, illustrated in Table 26–2, is to use a matrix in which each row represents a specific test case and the columns represent scenarios, conditions, data values, and expected and actual results.

Table 26–2   Matrix for Testing Specific Scenarios

Test Case ID	Scenario/ Condition	Data Value 1	Data Value 2	Data Value N	Expected Result	Actual Result
1	Scenario 1					
2	Scenario 2					
3	Scenario 2					

Note in Table 26–2 that more than one test case can result from a specific scenario (see test case IDs 2 and 3, both for scenario 2). Typically, this arises because of various logical constructs identified in a single step in a use case. For example, consider the following step in a HOLIS use case.

> *The homeowner enters the desired lighting sequence for each day of the week up to a maximum of seven different daily settings. The system confirms acceptance of each daily entry with a beep.*

This single step in the use case will produce two test cases from this step (Table 26–3).

In addition, note that in this process we've discovered an ambiguity that will have to be resolved: "What does the system do if the user attempts to enter more than seven settings?" The test team will have to caucus with the development team on that one. Such is the nature of our iterative discovery process.

Table 26–3   Two Test Cases for One Scenario

Test Case ID	Scenario/ Condition	Description	Expected Result
1	Scenario 6	Less than seven sequences entered	Sequence saved System beeps
2	Scenario 6	Attempt to enter an eighth sequence	Error?

Step 3: Identify the Test Conditions

The next step is to identify the specific conditions in the test case that would cause it to execute. In other words, what conditions cause a user to execute a specific event or sequence of events within a use case? During this process, the tester searches the use-case steps for the various data conditions, branches, and so on that would cause a specific test case to occur. For each such condition identified, the tester enters a new column in the matrix, representing the specific condition identified. In this initial pass, it is adequate to simply identify that a condition exists, create the column entry, and then indicate which of the three states that could occur for that condition (valid, invalid, or not applicable) is appropriate.

1. Valid (V) indicates a condition that must be true for the basic flow to execute.
2. Invalid (I) indicates a condition that will invoke the alternate flow, causing a specific scenario to occur.
3. Not applicable (N/A) indicates that an identified condition is not applicable to that specific test case ID.

To illustrate, let's look at another HOLIS example. Consider the Control Light use case described in Table 26–4.

In this use case, we have three separate conditions to consider (button pressed for less than one second, button pressed for greater than one second, and button released after being pressed for more than one second) that trigger changes in the behavior of the system. Specifically, they trigger scenario 1, scenario 2, and scenario 3, which in this case translates to the basic flow and alternate flows plus a branch on the alternate flow.

We can now create a matrix of the test cases, Table 26–5, which identifies each of these conditions as valid or invalid, and we can document the expected result in each case.

Table 26–4   Sample HOLIS Use Case: Control Light

Item	Value
Use-case name	Control Light
Actors	Resident and Light Bank
Brief description	This use case prescribes the way in which lights are turned on and off and also how they are dimmed and brightened in accordance with how long the user presses a button on the Control Switch.
Flow of events	Basic flow begins when the Resident presses the On/Off/Dim button on the Control Switch. When the Resident removes pressure on the On/Off/Dim button within the timer period, the system "toggles" the state of the light as follows. ▪ If the light is On, the light is then turned Off, and there is no illumination. ▪ If the light is Off, the light is then turned On to the last remembered brightness level.
Alternative flow of events	When the Resident holds down the On/Off/Dim button for more than 1 second, the system initiates a brightening/dimming activity for the room's Light Bank. While the Resident continues to press the On/Off/Dim button: 1. The brightness of the controlled light is smoothly increased to a system-wide maximum value at a rate of 10 percent per second. 2. When the brightness reaches its maximum value, the brightness of the controlled light is then smoothly decreased to a system-wide minimum value at a rate of 10 percent per second. 3. When the brightness reaches its minimum value, the use case continues at subflow step 1. When the Resident releases the On/Off/Dim button: 4. The use case terminates and the brightness stays at the current level.
Pre-conditions	The selected On/Off/Dim button must be Dim Enabled. The selected On/Off/Dim button must be preprogrammed to control a Light Bank.
Post-condition	On leaving this use case, the system remembers the current brightness level for the selected On/Off/Dim button.
Special requirements	Performance: For any action that is perceptible to the Resident, the response time from a control panel action to system response must be less than 50 milliseconds.

Step 4: Add Data Values to Complete the Test Case

We've made good progress. We have now identified all the conditions that need to be tested to test a specific use case fully. We're not quite done, however—without real data, test cases are merely descriptions of conditions, scenarios,

Table 26–5   Control Light Test Cases with Identified Conditions

Test Case ID	Scenario	Description	Condition: Button Pressed < Timer Period	Condition: Button Pressed > Timer Period	Condition: Button Released After Being Held	Condition	Expected Result
1	1	Basic flow: Resident releases button before timer period ends	V	I	N/A	Light on	Light goes off
2	1	Basic flow: Resident releases button before timer period ends	V	I	N/A	Light off	Light goes on
3	2	Alternate flow: Resident continuously presses button for longer than timer period	I	V	N/A	N/A	Light level goes up and down continuously
4	3	Resident releases switch after continuously pressing button	I	I	V	N/A	Light stays at last brightness

and paths without concrete values to identify them succinctly. Without such data, it's not possible to execute the test case and determine the results. In many cases, the use cases themselves will not directly identify these data values, and you will have to look to supplementary specifications to find performance specs, valid data ranges for input forms and interface protocols, and so on. However, this is not a new problem to the tester; just use your normal techniques for finding the data ranges.

This is also the time to make sure that test cases address any special requirements defined for the use case. These include such things as minimum/maximum performance, sometimes combined with minimum/maximum loads, or data volumes expected during the execution of the use cases.

Once you have identified the data ranges, you can finalize the test matrix with those values. Then you are ready to execute the test cases. For our HOLIS Control Light test case, the result might look like Table 26–6.

Table 26–6 Control Light Test Cases with Data Values

Test Case ID	Scenario	Description	Condition: Button Pressed < Timer Period	Condition: Button Pressed > Timer Period	Condition: Button Released After Being Held	Condition	Expected Result
1	1	Basic flow: Resident releases button before timer period ends	< 1 sec. in .1-sec. intervals	I	N/A	Light on	Light goes off
2	1	Basic flow: Resident releases button before timer period ends	< 1 sec. in .1-sec. intervals	I	N/A	Light off	Light goes on
3	2	Alternate flow: Resident continuously presses button for longer than timer period	I	1–60 sec.	N/A	N/A	Light level goes up and down continuously
4	3	Resident releases switch after continuously pressing button	I	I	V	N/A	Light stays at last brightness

MANAGING TEST COVERAGE

It's clear that even simple use cases can drive a significant number of test cases. For many applications, testing all use cases at this level of thoroughness, at least for each successive release, may not be feasible. In higher assurance systems, however, it is likely that every specific test case not only will be identified but also must be rerun on every subsequent software release. Without tooling, this becomes a significant effort; with proper tooling, the effort is more manageable. Here are a few simple guidelines to help you think through this part of the testing challenge.

- Select the most appropriate or critical use cases for the most thorough testing. Often these use cases are primary user interfaces, are architecturally significant, or present a hazard or hardship of some kind to the user should a defect remain undiscovered.
- Choose each use case to test based on a balance between the cost, risk, and necessity of verifying the use case.
- Determine the relative importance of your use cases by using a priority algorithm specific to your context.

BLACK-BOX VERSUS WHITE-BOX TESTING WITH USE CASES

We began this chapter by considering the system as a black box. Our testing strategy was fundamentally based on the concept of testing "all the things that go into the box and all the things that come out." However, experience has shown that no amount of purely functional testing can assure that there are no defects in the system. In functional testing we see only the result of the implementation *against the limited test criteria we can establish*, and in systems of complexity there are a nearly infinite number of possible input sets, system conditions, environmental conditions, and so on. We cannot possibly test them all.

Therefore, in addition to testing the black-box behavior of the system, it may also be necessary to test the *white-box behavior* of the system. For white-box testing, we need to look inside the system and see how it does what it does. This process of internal inspection, often referred to as *design assurance*, looks at the architecture and implementation of the system to see whether or not it should perform correctly. Do use cases help us in white-box testing?

In a word, *yes*. We saw in Chapter 25 that the problem of orthogonality (the difference between the methods and representations we used to express the requirements imposed on the system and the methods and representations we used to implement the system) can be largely mitigated with use cases. With our method, for every use case, there is a *use-case realization* that represents how the system is designed to accomplish the use case. The use case itself lives in the problem or requirements domain and simply specifies necessary behavior. The use-case realization lives inside the solution domain and describes how the behavior is accomplished by the system (Figure 26–3).

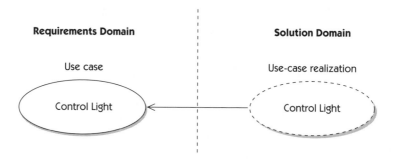

Figure 26–3 Use case and its associated use-case realization

Further, as we learned in Chapter 25, the use-case realization is composed of both a static and a dynamic part. The static part can be reviewed and analyzed for its fitness to the intended purpose. The dynamic part can be analyzed by inspection or viewed with runtime emulators, debug code stubs, and a variety of other execution testing techniques.

SUMMARY

We started this chapter by first considering the system as a black box. Before even starting the testing process, by applying use cases, the team could be reasonably confident that the requirements for the system were correct and that they had user buy-in and acceptance. In that sense, some of the testing had already begun.

Now, by using a comprehensive use-case-to-test-case strategy, we can fully test the behaviors of the black box, thereby assuring the team that *the system performs as specified in the use cases*.

We then described how we can look inside the box by analyzing the use-case realization design elements, both the static and dynamic behaviors, through inspection, emulation, and so on. This provides the team with assurance that *the system is designed right*, so that it should *behave right*.

Taken together, the team members can reach whatever degree of assurance is necessary for them to be confident that they have *defined, designed, and implemented a system that meets the needs of the users*. And that, after all, was the goal we established to begin with.

Chapter 27

TRACING REQUIREMENTS

Key Points

- Requirements traceability is a proven technique that can increase the quality and reliability of software.
- Traceability is mandated in certain high-assurance software development environments.
- Traceability extends from user needs to product features to use cases and supplementary requirements, and from there to implementation and testing.
- The value and cost of traceability varies with project context and available tooling.

Tracing requirements is an ongoing process used to ensure that each step in the development process is correct, conforms to the needs of the prior step, and is not superfluous to the needed activities. This chapter examines traceability techniques you can use to support tracing requirements from the time they are determined, to and through the use cases, and on to both implementation and testing.

THE ROLE OF TRACEABILITY IN SYSTEMS DEVELOPMENT

Experience has shown that the ability to trace requirements artifacts through the stages of specification, architecture, design, implementation, and testing is a significant factor in assuring a quality software implementation. The ability to track these relationships and to analyze the impacts of changes forms a key thread throughout many modern high-assurance software processes, particularly in life-critical medical products and business- or mission-critical activities.

Historical safety data has demonstrated that missing or unaddressed requirements and/or the impacts of changes are often missed and that small changes to a system can create significant safety and reliability problems. This has caused some regulatory agencies to mandate traceability as an integral part of the development process. For example, the latest U.S. Food and Drug Administration (FDA) guidance for traceability in medical software development activities is contained in the FDA Office of Device Evaluations (ODE) Guidance Document [FDA 1998]. In addition, the Design Controls section of the medical Current Good Manufacturing Practices (CGMP) document [FDA 1996], Subpart C of the CGMP, defines the obligations of the system designers to be able to trace relationships between various work products within the lifecycle of the product's development.

If traceability has been mandated for your project due to some regulatory or internal process standards, then your team won't have any choice. If it has not been mandated, then your team will need to decide whether to apply implicit and explicit requirements traceability or not, and if so, how much traceability is required to assure the outcome you need. We'll revisit this discussion again in just a bit, but first let's look at what traceability is and how to apply it.

For a starting point, IEEE [1994] provides the following compound definition of traceability.

- "The degree to which a relationship can be established between two or more products of the development process, especially products having a predecessor-successor or master-subordinate relationship to one another; for example, the degree to which the requirements and design of a given software component match." (IEEE 610.12-1990 §3)
- "The degree to which each element in a software development product establishes its reason for existing; for example, the degree to which each element in a bubble chart references the requirement it satisfies." (IEEE 610.12-1990 §3)

THE TRACEABILITY RELATIONSHIP

A traceability relationship is a relationship between two project elements.

The first definition above is a statement regarding the relationship of one element in the process to a successive element; the second is intended to assure that no superfluous elements (requirements, design, and so on) exist. In order to relate these elements, we need to introduce a third element, which is simply the element that relates the other two elements to each other. We call this element the *traceability relationship*. In other words, a traceability relationship is a relationship between two project elements.

There is no standard for exactly how a traceability relationship is constructed, how it is represented, what rules apply to it, and what attributes it exhibits. In highly complex, high-assurance systems developed under extreme software process rigor, this relationship can take on many facets. It may be navigable via tooling; it may contain a history of its existence; there may be many different types of such relationships (for example, "is fulfilled by," "is part of," "is derived from"); and there may be different types of relationships based on the types of related elements (for example, an explicit "tested by" relationship between A and B means that B exists to test A). If your team is operating in one of these environments, you will likely have process definitions, special tooling, and specific procedures you use to support traceability.

> A traceability relationship is a type of dependency relationship between elements.

However, for most project teams, this overcomplicates the matter. It is usually adequate to think of the relationship in terms of a simple "traced" model. In UML terms, we would simply be looking in one direction or the other (upstream or downstream) at a type of *dependency relationship*[1] (Figure 27–1).

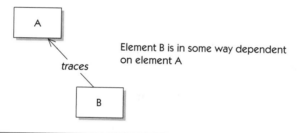

Figure 27–1 A trace dependency relationship

A dependency relationship states that a change in one element (for example, a use case) may affect another element (such as a test case), but the reverse is not necessarily true (a change to the test case would not necessarily imply that a use case needs to be changed). In other words, what happens upstream (a boat placed in the water) affects what happens downstream (the boat goes over the waterfall), but the opposite case is not true (no matter

---

1. In the UML, a dependency indicates a semantic relationship between two or more model elements.

how many boats we place in the water downstream, the upstream system behavior is unaffected).

As another example, we can envision how a specific requirement in the system is created in order to support a given feature specified in the Vision document. Thus, we can say that a software requirement (or use case) is *traced* from one or more features (see Figure 27-2). In this manner, the traceability relationship fulfills both halves of the definition since it both describes the predecessor-successor relationship and establishes the reason the second element exists (to implement the feature).

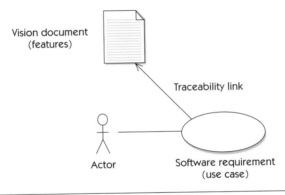

Vision document
(features)

Traceability link

Actor

Software requirement
(use case)

Figure 27–2   Traceability link from Vision document to software requirement

Without complicating matters much further, additional meaning can be inferred from the context of the types of requirements being related. For example, even without a specific "tested by" relationship type, a software requirement that is traced to a test case would suggest that the software requirement is "tested by" the test case that it is "traced to." A use-case realization that is traced from a use case would imply that the requirement is "implemented by" the referenced collaboration.

A Generalized Traceability Model

As we discussed in Chapter 15, different projects drive different types of requirements artifacts and different ways of organizing them. These decisions, in turn, drive differing needs for the number and nature of the artifacts to be traced. However, building on what you've learned, you can see that the static structure, or model, for your traceability strategy is common for most projects in that it follows a hierarchy from higher-level needs and features through more detailed requirements, and then on into implementation and testing. Therefore, no matter what type of project your team is executing, your traceability model will likely appear similar to Figure 27–3.

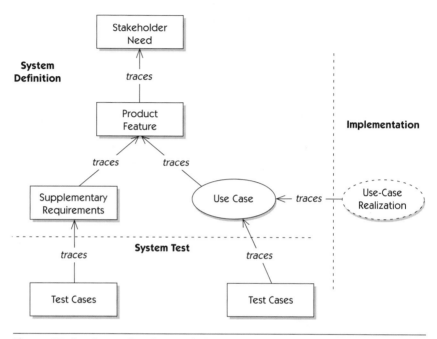

Figure 27–3 Generalized traceability hierarchy

The model shows that we are tracing requirements both within a domain, as in the system definition (or requirements) domain, and from there into the implementation and test domains. Although there are many additional "things" you could trace (requirements to glossary items and so on), experience has shown that these basic types of traces usually cover most needs. Of course, your conditions may differ, and it may be necessary to add or subtract from the core traceability list.

In the following sections, we show some examples of each of these major trace techniques and point out why you would want to do such tracing.

Tracing Requirements in the System Definition Domain

Let's look first at tracing requirements within the system, or product, definition domain. We'll call this *requirement-to-requirement traceability* because we'll be relating one type of requirement (for example, a feature) to another (for example, a use case).

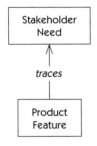

Tracing User Needs to Features By now, it's clear that the whole point of developing a system is *to satisfy user and other stakeholder needs.* Otherwise, you will likely have unhappy customers who tend to be irritable and are not inclined to pay their bills, or worse, you may have no customers at all.

As we described in Team Skill 2, the time spent understanding user needs is some of the most valuable time you can spend on the project. Defining the features of a system that meets those needs is the next step in the process, and it can be helpful to continually relate how the user needs are addressed by the features of your proposed solution. We can do so via a simple table, or *traceability matrix,* similar to the one shown in Table 27–1.

Table 27–1 Traceability Matrix: User Needs versus Features

	Feature 1	Feature 2	. . .	Feature n
Need 1	X			
Need 2		X		X
Need . . .		X	X	
Need m				X

In Table 27–1, we've listed all the user needs we identified down the left column. In the row across the top, we've listed all the application features we defined to satisfy the stated needs. Where did we get those features? We developed those features in the context of the Vision document described in Chapter 16. Team Skill 2 addresses the techniques your team can use to derive the user needs and features of the system.

Once the rows (needs) and columns (features defined to address those needs) are defined, we simply put an X in the appropriate cell(s) to record the fact that a specific feature has been defined for the sole purpose of supporting one or more user needs. Note that typically this is a one-to-many mapping since there are typically far fewer needs identified, and they are specified at higher levels of abstraction, than the number of features defined to implement those needs.

After you've recorded all known need–feature relationships, examining the traceability matrix for potential indications of error can be an instructive activity.

1. If inspection of a *row* fails to detect any Xs, a possibility exists that no feature is yet defined to respond to a user need. This may be acceptable if, for example, the feature is not fulfilled by software ("The case shall be of nonbreakable plastic"). Nevertheless, these potential red flags should be checked carefully. Modern requirements management tools have a facility to automate this type of inspection.

2. If inspection of a *column* fails to detect any Xs, a possibility exists that a feature has been included for which there is no defined product need. This may indicate a gratuitous feature, a misunderstanding of the role of the feature, or a dead feature (one that is still in the system but whose reason to exist has disappeared or at least is no longer clear). Again, modern requirements management tools should facilitate this type of review. In any case, you are not dealing with a great deal of data at this level.

In addition, because of the dependency relationship inherent in the traceability relationship, we can see what specific needs would need to be reconsidered if a user need should change during the implementation period. Hopefully, this *impact assessment process* will be supported by the automated change detection capabilities of your requirement tool.

Once you've mapped the need–feature relationships and have determined that the needs and features are correctly accounted for and understood, it's time to consider the next level of the hierarchy—relationships between the features and the use cases.

Tracing Features to Use Cases It is equally important to ensure that the features can be related to the use cases proposed for the system. After all, the use cases illuminate the proposed implementation of the system from a user's perspective, and our job is to ensure that we have a fully responsive design.

As before, you don't need much in the way of special tooling to perform this essential step. Again, we can consider a simple matrix similar to the one shown in Table 27–2.

In Table 27–2, we've listed all the features down the left column. In the row across the top, we've listed the use cases we derived to satisfy the stated features.

Table 27–2   Traceability Matrix: Features versus Use Cases

	Use Case 1	Use Case 2	. . .	Use Case k
Feature 1	X			X
Feature 2		X		X
Feature . . .			X	
Feature m		X		X

Team Skill 2 addresses the techniques your team can use to derive the features and use cases of the system. As in the previous section, mapping the features and use cases into a matrix as shown in Table 27–2 should be a straightforward process.

Once the rows (features) and columns (use cases) are defined, we indicate a traceability relationship with an X in the cell(s) that represents a use case that supports one or more features. Note that this is likely to be a set of many-to-many relationships because, although both features and use cases describe system behaviors, they do so in different means and at different levels of detail. A single feature may be supported or implemented by multiple use cases. In addition, it is not unusual that a single use case implements more than one feature.

After you've established all known feature–use case relationships, you should once again examine the traceability matrix for potential indications of error.

1. If inspection of a *row* fails to detect any Xs, a possibility exists that no use case is yet defined to respond to a feature. As before, these potential red flags should be checked carefully.
2. If inspection of a *column* fails to detect any Xs, a possibility exists that a use case has been included for which there is no known feature that requires it. This may indicate a gratuitous use case, a misunderstanding of the role of the use case, a use case that exists solely to support other use cases, or a dead or obsolete use case.

In any case, reviewing and analyzing the data will improve your understanding of the implementation, help you find the obvious errors, and increase the level of certainty in the design and implementation.

Once you've mapped the feature–use case relationships and have determined that the features and use cases are correctly accounted for, you need to apply similar thinking to the nonfunctional requirements and their specification.

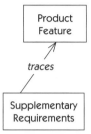

traces

Tracing Features to Supplementary Requirements While the use cases carry the majority of the functional behavior, keep in mind that the supplementary requirements also hold valuable system behavioral requirements. As we discussed in Chapter 22, these often include the nonfunctional requirements of the system such as usability, reliability, supportability, and so on. Regardless of the number of supplementary requirements, their criticality can be as great as or greater than (for example, "Results must be within an accuracy of ±1 percent") the use cases themselves. In addition, certain functional requirements (for example, those that are algorithmic or scientific in nature, such as a language parsing program) will likely not be expressed in use-case form.

Often we look to the Vision document for these special features, or additional high-level requirements, and trace them from there into the supplementary requirements that capture this important information. This can be captured in a matrix similar to Table 27–3. In other cases, these requirements may originate within the supplementary specification itself, and they would not have a further trace from their origin.

Table 27–3   Traceability Matrix: Features versus Supplementary Requirements

	Supplementary Requirement 1	Supplementary Requirement 2	...	Supplementary Requirement p
Feature or System Requirement 1	X			X
Feature or System Requirement 2		X		X
Feature or System Requirement ...		X	X	
Feature or System Requirement j				X

Tracing Requirements to Implementation

Having described the type of requirements tracing typical in the system definition domain (requirement-to-requirement traceability), we are now prepared to move from the requirements domain into the implementation and test domains. While the principles are the same—we use the dependency traceability relationship to navigate this chasm—the information content on the other side is remarkably different. Let's look first at crossing the chasm from requirements to implementation.

In Chapter 25, we discussed the problem of transitioning from requirements to code, which we called the *problem of orthogonality*, at some length. The context for the discussion was in developing an understanding of how the team makes this difficult transition and what role the requirements play in helping to do so. We also noted that tracing from requirements to implementation, and specifically from requirements to code, is extremely difficult, if not entirely impractical, and in general, we typically do not recommended it. For this reason, we suggested that the mapping of use case to use-case realization and from requirement to collaboration in the design model was perhaps the only pragmatic approach.

Tracing Use Cases to Use-Case Realizations As we described in Chapter 26, in making this transition, we move to relating one form of artifact, the use-case form, to another artifact, the *use-case realization*, in the design model. In so doing, we used these two specific elements to bridge the gap between requirements and design (Figure 27–4).

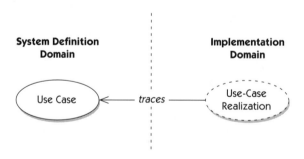

Figure 27–4 Tracing from use case to use-case realization

In this special case, the traceability problem is simplified immensely *because there is a one-to-one name space correspondence between a use case and its realization.* Therein we meet both traceability requirements: the relationship between the entities is expressed directly by their name sharing, and the reason for the existence of the subordinate or traced entity, the use-case realization, is implicit in its very nature. That is, the use-case realization exists for only one purpose: to implement the use case by the same name. Therefore, there is no matrix to analyze since the design practice we employed yielded inherent traceability by default!

Tracing from the Use-Case Realization into Implementation However, for those who require a higher degree of assurance or when traceability to code is mandated, it may not be adequate to stop at the design construct of the use-case realization. In this case, the traceability relationship must be followed from the use-case realization to its component parts, which are the classes (code) that implement the collaboration (Figure 27–5).

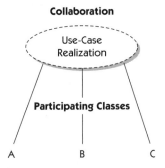

Figure 27–5   Tracing from use-case realization to implementation

How you will accomplish this mechanically depends on the types of tools you employ in your requirements, analysis, and design efforts. Without adequate tooling, the problem becomes quickly intractable since you will likely be dealing with dozens of use cases and hundreds of classes. Therefore, your choice of tooling will have a major impact on the practicality and efficacy of this level of traceability.

Tracing Supplementary Requirements into Implementation Of course, not everything is a use case, and for those who must drive to uncompromised degrees of quality and safety, it may also be necessary to trace from supplementary requirements into implementation as well. How does one do this? We use a technique similar to the one we described in Chapter 25. In this case, we trace individual requirements or groups of requirements (such as the HOLIS software clock requirements) to a collaboration in the implementation. After all, the use-case realization wasn't really so special; it was just a type of collaboration all along. In this case, we'll have to name the collaboration and keep track of the links via some special means because they don't come prenamed and conveniently collected in a use-case package. However, the principle is the same, as Figure 27–6 illustrates.

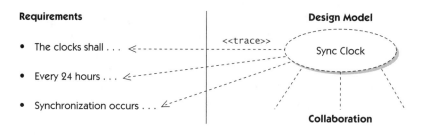

Figure 27–6   Tracing from supplementary requirements into implementation

From there, you can trace to the specific code contained in the classes that realize the collaboration. Again, the mechanics of this are determined by the types of tooling you choose to employ.

Tracing from Requirements to Testing

Tracing from Use Case to Test Case   Finally we approach the last system boundary we must bridge to implement a complete traceability strategy: *the bridge from the requirements domain to the testing domain.* As Heumann [2001] describes, and as we described in Chapter 26, one specific approach to comprehensive testing is to assure that every use case is "tested by" one or more test cases. This was already reflected in our generalized traceability model, as we now highlight in Figure 27–7.

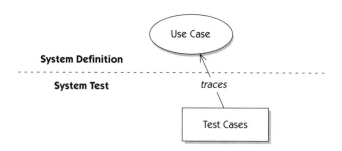

Figure 27–7   Tracing use cases to test cases

However, this simple diagram understates the complexity of the case somewhat, for it was not a trivial one-for-one transition that we described.

As you'll recall from Chapter 26, we first had to identify all the scenarios described in the use case itself. This is a one-to-many relationship since an elaborated use case will typically have a variety of possible scenarios that can be tested. From a traceability viewpoint, each use case traces to each scenario of the use case as shown in Figure 27–8.

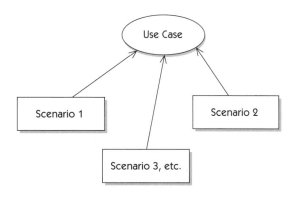

Figure 27–8   Tracing use cases to test case scenarios

This can be represented by listing the scenarios of a specific use case in the rows of a matrix (Table 27–4).

Table 27–4   Traceability Matrix for Use Cases to Scenarios

Use Case	Scenario Number	Originating Flow	Alternate Flow	Next Alternate	Next Alternate
Control Light	1	Basic flow			
	2	Basic flow	Alternate flow 1		
	3	Basic flow	Alternate flow 1	Alternate flow 2	
	4	Basic flow	Alternate flow 3		
	5	Basic flow	Alternate flow 3	Alternate flow 1	
	6	Basic flow	Alternate flow 3	Alternate flow 1	Alternate flow 2
	7	Basic flow	Alternate flow 4		
	8	Basic flow	Alternate flow 3	Alternate flow 4	
Run Vacation Profile	1	Basic flow			

However, we are still not done because each scenario can drive one or more specific test cases, as illustrated in Figure 27–9.

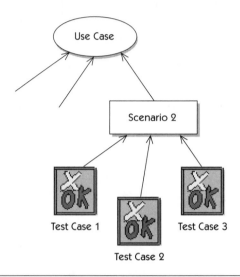

Figure 27–9   Tracing scenarios to test cases

However, in matrix form, this simply adds one more column to the matrix, as illustrated in Table 27–5.

In this way, a traceability matrix of one-to-many (use case to scenario) and an additional one-to-many (scenario to test case) relationship can fully describe the relationships among these elements. In a manner similar to the other matrices, automated tooling can help you build this matrix as well as perform certain inspections and quality tests. In addition, some tools provide immediate impact assessment by indicating which traced elements (for example, test cases) might be affected when a traced element (for example, a scenario) is changed.

Tracing from Supplementary Requirements to Test Cases   For those requirements that are not expressed in use-case form, the process is similar to the requirements-to-implementation process described above. More specifically, requirements are either traced individually to scenarios and test cases or grouped into "requirements packages" that operate in the same logical fashion as a use case. The matrices we describe above are unchanged, except that the column on the far left contains the specific requirement, or requirements package, that is being traced into implementation.

Table 27–5 Traceability Matrix for Use Cases to Test Cases

Use Case	Scenario Number	. . .	Test Case ID
Control Light	1		1.1
	2		2.1
	3		3.1
	4		4.1
	4		4.2
	4		4.3
	5		5.1
	6		6.1
	7		7.1
	7		7.2
	8		8.1
Run Vacation Profile	1		1.1

USING TRACEABILITY TOOLS

Powerful software development tools offer a simple user-guided procedure to "point and click" through the explicit relationships that may exist between two elements of the lifecycle.

Using these tools provides you with a more efficient way to take on larger projects than using the manual matrix methods discussed earlier. For example, after we have defined the relationships between the features and the software requirements on our HOLIS project, we can use a tool to display a matrix version of those relationships *automatically.*

These types of tools allow you to build the larger matrices required for more sophisticated projects and to examine the data automatically for many of the types of potential red flags we discussed earlier. This can be of significant value to your team in assuring the level of reliability and certainty that the system requires. In addition, these tools can also assist you in the aggravating task of *maintaining* the matrices as changes are made.

In addition, many of these tools provide support for some of the implicit forms of traceability (use case to use-case realization, collaboration to class), and provide navigational mechanisms and other methods to help assure that the implementation is correct as the application evolves.

PROCEEDING WITHOUT TRACEABILITY TOOLS

Of course, you may not have a tool specifically constructed to support the types of operations identified in the preceding sections. Without such a tool, how should you proceed?

As we've described, many of the matrix relationships could be easily handled with a spreadsheet. We've used spreadsheets extensively in the past and found them to be a useful aid in managing projects.

The problem with spreadsheets, however, is maintenance, especially in extensive hierarchies of relationships. Changing a single linkage could have far-flung impacts in the relationships at issue, as well as other relationships in other parts of the hierarchy. It could become a nightmare if extensive changes to the linkages had to be made.

Since it can be difficult to manually keep track of the changes and their "ripple effects," it is likely that the team would either:

1. Fall into a pattern of resisting any discussions to change the relationships, or
2. Abandon the matrices as the work becomes overwhelming

Of course, we *always* came to regret both of these behaviors, as they inevitably led to subsequent problems in the project.

The other alternative is to use a database. We used relational databases extensively and found it fairly easy to construct them and to input the data. Indeed, in the pre-tool days, we used relational databases to support traceability requirements for human-critical medical device development projects. Relational databases worked pretty well. Even though it was more difficult to expand the database application to include recursively tracking ripple effects from changes, it could be done. The problem, however, was that we ended up spending disproportionate amounts of time improving the tool's capability. Good for the ego, and downright fun at times, but bad for the project resources that should have been doing something else.

Therefore, although you *can* use spreadsheets or databases to maintain the traceability relationships, it won't be easy. If you have a small project, the pain and suffering will be minimal, and it *might* be worth considering simpler alternatives. On the other hand, we do *not* recommend tackling larger projects without the use of specialized requirements management tools.

SUMMARY

Tracing is an important technique your team can apply in the struggle to help ensure that you are designing and implementing the right system. The trick is to implement "just the right amount" of traceability in "just the right way" so that the risk-to-reward ratio benefit fits your project's circumstances. Otherwise, you may find that:

- Your project suffers from excessive overhead without commensurate quality improvement, or worse
- You fail to deliver the requisite quality and reliability demanded by your project circumstances

These are both in the class of "very bad things that can happen to your project," so it behooves the team to define and implement the right traceability strategy from the beginning.

Chapter 28

MANAGING CHANGE

Key Points

- A process to manage requirements can be useful only if it recognizes and addresses the issue of change.

- Internal change factors include failing to ask the right people the right questions at the right time and failing to create a practical process to help manage changes to requirements.

- In order to have a reasonable probability of success, requirements leakage must be stopped or at least reduced to a manageable level.

WHY DO REQUIREMENTS CHANGE?

A requirements management process can be useful only if it recognizes and addresses the issue of change.

If it were possible to create a definitive set of requirements for a system once and only once, life would be much simpler, and there would be no need for this chapter. We could simply create a perfect Vision document, use-case model, and supplementary specification; freeze them for the duration of the development effort; and then declare everything past that point to be the responsibility of the maintenance team. Alas, things don't work that way. They never did in the past, and even with a more systematic approach to requirements management in the context of an iterative process, they will not work that way in the future.

There are several reasons for the inevitability of changes to the requirements. Some of these reasons are internal factors and may be under our control, but many of them are external factors and are outside the control of the developers *and* the users. Let's talk about external factors first.

External Factors

External factors are those change agents over which the project team has little
or no control. No matter how we manage them, we must prepare ourselves
technically, emotionally, and managerially to be able to address these changes
as part of the normal course of software development activity. Changes occur
for the following reasons.

- There was a change to the problem that we were attempting to solve
  with the new system. Perhaps a change occurred in the economy, in
  government regulations, or in the marketplace and consumer preferences. Because of the fast pace of technology change, it is more and
  more likely that such changes will take place before we even finish
  solving the original problem the user described.

- The users changed their minds or their perceptions about what they
  wanted the system to do. This, too, can occur for a number of reasons:
  not only because users are fickle, particularly when specifying the
  details of the human interface for their system, but also because their
  perceptions are based on the marketplace, the economy, the state of
  government regulations, and so on. Moreover, the identity of the
  users themselves sometimes changes. For example, if the user who
  described the requirements for the system leaves the customer's team,
  the replacement is likely to be someone with an entirely different set
  of opinions and perceptions.

- The external environment has changed, which creates new constraints
  and/or new opportunities. One of the most obvious examples of environmental change is the ongoing improvements in computer hardware and software systems: If tomorrow's computers are 50 percent
  faster, cheaper, and smaller and run more advanced applications than
  do today's computers, they will likely trigger a change in the requirements for a system. Before 1995, hardly anyone anticipated the Internet and the World Wide Web. The requirements for a wide range of
  information systems—from word processors to customer information systems to banking systems—are clearly quite different today
  from what they were in the pre-Internet era.

- The new system comes into existence. As we discussed, one insidious
  external factor, and a prime one in the "Yes, But" syndrome, is that
  the very existence of a new system *causes the requirements for the system itself to change.* As the organizational behavior evolves around the
  new system, the old ways of doing things are no longer appropriate;
  the need for new types of information emerge, and new requirements
  for the system inevitably develop. Thus, the simple act of delivering a
  new system elicits additional new requirements for the new system!

As a practical matter, a process to manage requirements can be useful only if it recognizes and addresses the issue of change. We can't prevent change, but we can prepare ourselves for it and then manage it when it happens.

Internal Factors

Internal change agents will also contribute new requirements.

In addition to the external factors, a number of internal factors can contribute to the problem of change.

- We failed to ask the right people the right questions at the right time during the initial requirements gathering effort. If our process does not include all stakeholders or if we do not ask all the right questions of them, we contribute to the change problem by simply not understanding the true requirements for the system. In other words, there are far more "Undiscovered Ruins" than necessary, and we are making significant changes that could have been avoided had we developed a more comprehensive understanding up front.
- We failed to create a practical process to help manage changes to the requirements that would normally have happened on an incremental basis. We may have attempted to "freeze" the requirements; thus, the "latent," necessary changes piled up until they created such pressure that they inevitably exploded in the face of the developers and the users, causing rework and stress.
- Iterating from requirements to design begets new requirements. As we described in Chapter 20, even if we do everything right, the process of designing the system will expose new requirements and necessitate changes to requirements that have already been elaborated. To ignore this would deprive ourselves of innovative capabilities enabled by design decisions or changes in technology. Worse, we would be forced to pretend that every existing requirement was perfectly understood and elaborated earlier, that no negotiation, compromise, or alternate set of requirements discovered at this time could possibly achieve the user's need as well as (or perhaps better than) the original stated requirement. Either approach would constitute foolishness of the highest order.

Requirements
affect design
affect requirements
affect design

.
.
.

Therefore, if we are to prepare ourselves to properly manage change, we'll need to take each of the above factors into account. However, there is yet another, perhaps even more pernicious source of change that we have yet to explore. Let's look at a specific project and see what other factors we can discover.

"WE HAVE MET THE ENEMY, AND THEY IS US"

Weinberg [1995] notes that change can indeed be insidious. In attempting to understand and explore sources of requirements change, he compared the known requirements of the system at the end of one project to those known at the beginning of the project. In so doing, he discovered a variety of sources of requirements change. Some were "official" external change, representing customer requests made through the appropriate channels of communications, but many were surprisingly "unofficial," or what Weinberg calls "requirements leakage." These included

- Enhancements mentioned by distributors who had been overheard by programmers at a sales convention
- Direct customer requests to programmers
- Mistakes that had been made and shipped and had to be supported
- Hardware features that didn't get in or didn't work
- Knee-jerk change-of-scope reactions to competitors
- Functionality inserted by programmers with "careful consideration" of what's good for the customer
- Programmers' "Easter Eggs"

In one project, half of the total work product of the system was invested in requirements leakage!

Each of these sources may contribute only a small amount of change, but in accumulation, *unofficial sources contributed up to half of the total scope of one project!* In other words, half of the total work product of the system was invested in requirements leakage, or requirements that entered the system without visibility to the team members responsible for managing the schedule, budget, and quality criteria.

How can a project manager accommodate change of this type and still meet the schedule and quality criteria? *It can't be done!* In order to have a reasonable probability of success, requirements leakage *must* be stopped or at least reduced to manageable levels.

> **Programmers' Easter Eggs**
>
> Programmers' Easter Eggs are a particularly pathological form of requirements leakage. An Easter Egg is a hidden behavior built into the system for debugging purposes, for "the fun of it," or, occasionally, for worse motives. In our experience, Easter Eggs are extremely dangerous, and programmers must know that inserting them is completely unacceptable and that doing so will subject the offenders to dire consequences. Two painfully true cases follow.
>
> - A large military simulation system took a long time to execute, so the programmers built into the system a background game of Battleship to amuse themselves during the simulation. Unfortunately, they never took it out, nor did its existence appear on any of the verification and validation activities or reports. When it was discovered, the customer, having lost confidence in the subcontractor, canceled the entire program: a multimillion-dollar loss to the subcontractor and a serious detriment to future business opportunities.
>
> - A junior programmer contributing to the development of a shrink-wrapped software tool amused himself by building in derogatory user error messages in early stubs of error-recovery code. One such message was accidentally left in and discovered by a customer in a formal product training session. The software had to be repaired and re-released on an unplanned basis, causing the loss of critical team-weeks to the company.

A Process for Managing Change

Clearly, given the fact that change is a natural part of the process and that change will come from both external and internal sources, we need a process for managing change. Such a process puts the team in control so that it can effectively discover change, perform impact analysis, and incorporate those changes that are deemed both necessary and acceptable into the system in a systematic manner. Building on Weinberg's recommendations, a process for more effectively managing change must include the following steps.

1. Recognize that change is inevitable, and plan for it.
2. Baseline the requirements.
3. Establish a single channel to control change.
4. Use a change control system to capture changes.
5. Manage change hierarchically.

We'll look at each of these elements in more detail.

Step 1: Recognize That Change Is Inevitable, and Plan for It

The first step is a simple one. The team must recognize that changing requirements for the system is inevitable and even necessary. Some amount of change will occur, and the team should develop an awareness of this issue and a corresponding plan for managing change that should include some allowance for change in the initial baseline. (Fortunately, if you've accepted the iterative development guidelines espoused in this book, you are already well on your way to this understanding.)

As for the legitimacy of change, with the single exception of the Easter Egg, all requests for change can be considered legitimate in that they originate from a stakeholder who has both a real need and the potential to add value to the application.

For example, requests for changes from the development team are legitimate since that team knows more about the system than anyone else does. Some of the "best" requirements come from the implementers who are closest to the system; they best recognize what the system really can do. We should encourage their input to the process since the result will be a better system for our users.

Step 2: Baseline the Requirements

In each iteration, the team should baseline the requirements for the build. The baselining process may be as simple as putting version control on the pertinent artifacts—the Vision document, software requirements, and use-case models—and publishing the baseline for the development team. The collection of itemized requirements in these documents creates a baseline of information about the requirements and anticipated use cases for the system.

This simple step gives the team the ability to distinguish between known, or "old," requirements and new requirements (those being added, deleted, or modified and thus distinguishable from the "baseline" of known requirements). Once the baseline has been established, new requirements can be more easily identified and managed. A request for a new requirement can be compared against the existing baseline to see where it will fit in and whether it will create a conflict with any other requirements; this is often something that users overlook in their haste to respond to a change in their environment. If the change is accepted, we can manage the evolution of that change from the vision to the software requirements, from the software requirements to the appropriate technical design documents and models, and then to the code and the test procedures.

If this is done in an orderly, efficient, and responsive manner, the user community is likely to be much more cooperative. In the past, users in many organizations felt that they were being "stonewalled" by the technical development community when they asked for a change. Often, it was because the team had a chaotic, inefficient process for making the changes or because it was unable to describe the nature of that process to the users.

However, the fact that we can be responsive and efficient about making requirements changes doesn't mean that we want to invite vast numbers of frivolous changes. In the best of all worlds—from the perspectives of both the users *and* the developers—life would be a lot simpler if we could create a single set of stable, correct requirements. Even with a reasonably well-managed change control process, there's a limit to the number of such changes that the developers will be able to accommodate, especially during the design and implementation stages of the project. It's typical, for example, to see requirements change at the rate of 1 percent to 4 percent each month during the course of development. However, when the monthly change rate exceeds 2 percent, the phenomenon of "requirements churn" becomes a very serious risk to the customer's project.

> The fact that we can be responsive and efficient about making changes doesn't mean that we want to invite vast numbers of frivolous changes.

Step 3: Establish a Single Channel to Control Change

Ad hoc changes to a software system can easily cause significant and unintended consequences. Although it should be obvious that the existence of a new feature can cause significant impact to software requirements, system architecture, test plans, and so on, all of us have also experienced a worst case in which a "simple change" to code causes unanticipated consequences, occasionally even catastrophic ones. In addition, one proposed new feature might obviate, or make more difficult, an important future system feature that is not even being implemented in this release.

In addition, there is that thorny issue of the schedule and the budget for a project, which is typically the responsibility of the management team. The customer's wish for a change cannot be assumed to officially change the schedule and the budget, and a negotiation or budget reconciliation process must be initiated before a change can be approved.

> The customer's wish for a change cannot be assumed to officially change the schedule and the budget.

Therefore, it is crucial that every change *go through a single channel* to determine its impact on the system and to make the official decision as to whether the change is going to be made in the system at all. In a small project, this official channel can be the product manager or other "owner" of the Vision document and other requirements artifacts, someone who has an overall understanding of the system requirements and design.

In larger systems or ones that affect a variety of stakeholders, this official channel should consist of a few people (a change control board, or CCB) who share the responsibility and who, together, have the requisite authority and technical competence to decide when a change request is officially approved. (We briefly introduced this concept in Chapter 17.)

In any case, a change in the system should not be initiated until the change control mechanism makes the change "official."

Step 4: Use a Change Control System to Capture Changes

In a sense, it may be easiest to focus on the external, customer-requested changes because they are most readily identified and will tend to naturally find their way into the project via the project management or change control function. However, during development, there will be a tremendous number and variety of other types of potential changes to the system.

> We will have to make conscious decisions about which bugs will remain in the system.

Indeed, many of the proposed changes that occur during the design, coding, and testing of a system may appear to be unrelated to requirements, involving corrections to code- or design-level bugs. However, the impact must still be assessed. And yes, as the deadline approaches, we must even make conscious decisions about which bugs will be allowed to remain in the system—due to the potential for the fix to destabilize the entire system and thereby jeopardize the release date—and which ones will be removed. Also, many bugs may affect the requirements, require interpolation between the requirements, or require disambiguation of a known requirement.

In some cases, it won't even be obvious what kind of change is being requested. This is particularly common when end users discover problems after the system has been developed or when the members of the "help desk" team pass on their analysis of the user complaints to the technical developers. For example, suppose the end user calls the help desk and complains, "I'm trying to enter a new employee into my payroll system, but whenever I have an employee whose first name is more than 16 characters, the program crashes." The fact that the program crashes is presumably either a code-level bug or a design-level bug. (Perhaps the operating system or the DBMS package was being invoked in an illegal fashion.) Nevertheless, even if the program had produced a civilized error message for such names, there may be a bug in the requirements; they may need to be changed to allow employee names of up to 256 characters. In the extreme case, this may even involve a "feature" because the marketing department may decide that it wants to brag that its payroll system is the only one being marketed that can handle 256-character employee names.

The team should implement a system for capturing all change requests.

In any event, an analysis of the situation is required, along with a decision as to *where* the change will be implemented in the hierarchy of documents that we've discussed. Therefore, as Figure 28–1 illustrates, the team should implement a formal method for capturing *all* requested changes to the system. This could be accomplished through a change request and defect tracking system that provides a centralized repository of such requests, Web-based entry of items from any physical location, automatic status tracking and trending, automatic notification of affected parties, and a mechanism for promotion of change requests into the requirements management system when appropriate. (We use the "firewall" metaphor in Figure 28–1 to suggest that the process is controlled and attempts to prevent uncontrolled wildfires of change from sweeping through the system.)

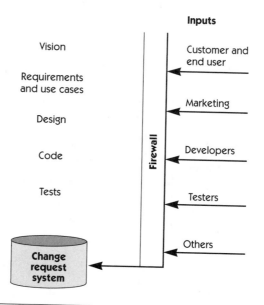

Figure 28–1   Capturing changes

The system should be used to capture *all* inputs and to transmit them to the authority of the CCB for resolution. The CCB plays a key role in helping the project achieve success and should consist of no more than three to five people who represent the key stakeholders for the project: customers, marketing, and program management.

When considering whether to approve a change request, the CCB must consider the following factors:

- The impact of the change on the cost and functionality of the system
- The impact of the change on customers and other external stakeholders not well represented on the CCB: other project contractors, component suppliers, and so on
- The potential for the change to destabilize the system

When the decision is made, the CCB also has the responsibility to ensure that all those affected by the change are notified, even if the decision is made *not* to approve the change.

Once a change has been determined, the next step is to decide *where* to insert the change. (For example, we need to determine whether to change a requirement or to change a test being proposed.) Subsequent changes will ripple through in the hierarchy, as shown in Figure 28–2.

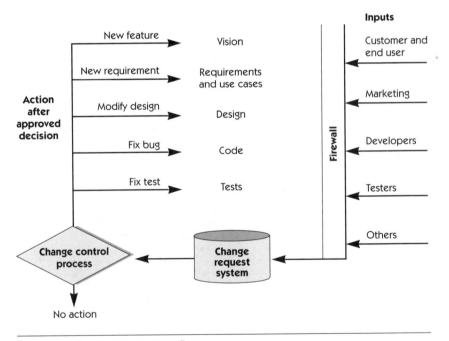

Figure 28–2   Change request flow

Step 5: Manage Change Hierarchically

The fact that all these people are interested in making changes to the system is not intrinsically bad; aside from the Easter Egg phenomenon, we could even imagine that all these changes are beneficial. However, the fact that the changes might not be documented or analyzed *is* a problem, and if they're not managed carefully, disaster can occur. A change to one requirement can have a ripple effect in other related requirements, the design, or other subsystems; further, this fact may not be obvious to the requester, who casually asks the programmer to make a "quick and easy" change to the system.

The problem is even worse without an explicit process. The changes typically occur in a "bottom-up" fashion. That is, if the change is envisioned while the code is being written for a new system, it's typically introduced directly into the code itself. If the developers are extremely disciplined, they *might* then ask themselves, "Hmmm, I wonder whether the changes we're making to the code will cause any changes in the design. Do the design-level changes have an impact on the requirements? And do the changes to the software requirements have any impact on the Vision document?" (Meanwhile, nobody remembers to tell *any* of this to the testing team, whose members thought they were supposed to be creating test plans for the original software requirements!)

A programmer doesn't have the authority to introduce new features and requirements directly into the code on the user's behalf.

In theory, it's possible to manage this "backward" ripple-effect phenomenon if all the respective documents are under the control of a sophisticated software tools environment. But even if all the documents are kept synchronized, the kind of bottom-up changes to the requirements that we've been discussing are still undesirable. To be blunt: *a programmer doesn't have the authority to introduce new features and requirements directly into the code on the user's behalf, no matter how well intentioned.* Similarly, the marketing representative who makes a casual request of the programmer for such a change, while they're both sipping a beer at the neighborhood brewpub, is not acting in an *official* capacity. *Every* new feature/requirement has an impact on the cost, schedule, reliability, and risk associated with the project.

In order to mitigate this ripple effect, changes to the requirements should be carried out in the top-down hierarchical fashion shown in Figure 28–3. As discussed earlier in this book, changes to a baseline Vision document can be documented in a separate Delta Vision document, which is normally a very small subset of the original document. However, since the Vision document changes may stipulate the *deletion* of features, we may need to regenerate a completely new baselined set of software requirements, and that can lead to appropriate changes in the design, the code, and the test plans.

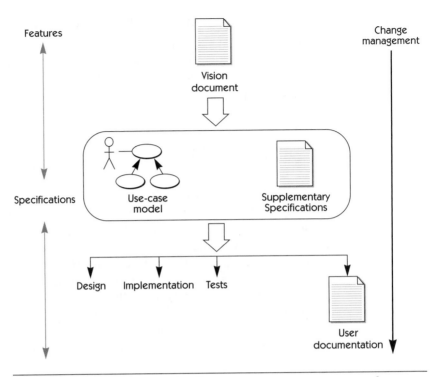

Figure 28–3   Hierarchical ripple effect

If we have followed the processes in this book and have reasonable support from our tool environment, the downward ripple effect will be highlighted by the traceability mechanism we used in building our requirements pyramid. This allows us to work downward through the pyramid, making further changes as necessary. Each subsequent change, in turn, highlights additional places lower in the pyramid where additional analysis needs to occur.

Thus, change is a controlled "brushfire," and we can proceed logically through the hierarchy. In addition, if we've done a good job of encapsulating the systems and subsystems and have used a well-structured requirements strategy, changes should be limited to the areas directly linked to the requirements that have changed.

Returning to our case study, for example, Figure 28–4 shows a traceability report for HOLIS that resulted when a change was made. Two features, FEA3 and FEA5, indicate traceability links that the automated tool has marked as suspect. These suspected impacts resulted from proposed changes to the two features. We need to review requirements SR3 and SR4 for possible interactions because of the changes proposed by FEA3 and FEA5. In turn, possible revisions to SR3 and SR4 may ripple down into the implementation, and so on. We will explore this issue again later in this chapter.

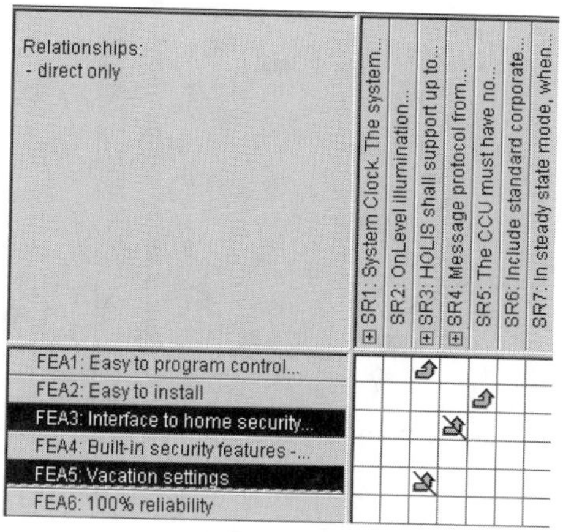

Figure 28–4 Impact analysis by traceability link

REQUIREMENTS CONFIGURATION MANAGEMENT

Some elements of the preceding change review and approval process are referred to as *change control*, *version control*, or *configuration management* in some organizations. Interestingly, most organizations have a reasonably rigorous process for configuration management of the source code produced during the implementation lifecycle phase of a project but no corresponding process for the project requirements. Even if the organization does have a formal process for generating the Vision document and software requirements, it often ignores the many requirements-oriented changes that creep into the project during the coding phase.

However, in today's modern tool environments, it's a reasonably straightforward matter to have all elements of the requirements hierarchy under configuration management (see Figure 28–5).

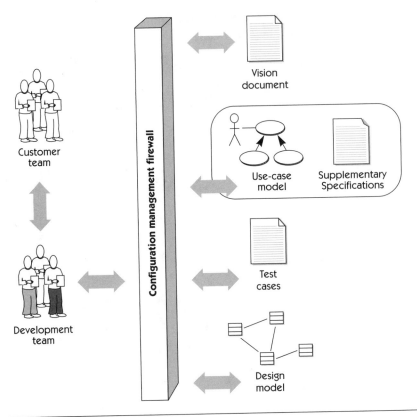

Figure 28–5   Requirements configuration management overview

The benefits of a requirements management process based on configuration management should be obvious by now, but let's review them briefly. Such a process:

- Prevents unauthorized and potentially destructive or frivolous changes to the requirements
- Preserves the revisions to requirements documents
- Facilitates the retrieval and/or reconstruction of previous versions of documents
- Supports a managed, organized baseline "release strategy" for incremental improvements or updates to a system
- Prevents simultaneous update of documents or conflicting and uncoordinated updates to different documents at the same time

Tool-Based Support for Change Management

In this recap of previous sections, we offer a practical approach for change management, *assuming that you have a set of tools to support this effort.* If you choose to use your own manual techniques, portions of this section may not be applicable, but the overall ideas are worth reviewing nonetheless.

Change management tooling helps you understand and manage the following important project development aspects.

- If a single product feature is proposed for a change, what are the work consequences of that change? In other words, change management helps you determine the amount of rework that may be required. The amount of work to effect a change may have significant impact on your project resource planning and workload planning.
- If an element is proposed for a change, what other elements of the system may be impacted by the change? This topic is of key concern both to your project planning and to your customer.
- Active projects inevitably take wrong turns. It is certain that your project will arrive at a point at which you would like to be able to "roll back" a requirement and to examine a previous revision of the requirement. In addition, it would be helpful to remember how and why the requirement was changed. In other words, an audit trail of each requirement is valuable and may even be mandated by regulatory agencies as part of the design process.

Elements Impacted by Change

After establishing the traceability relationships for your project, you should use the traceability linkages as a tool for change management. In the case of HOLIS, for example, suppose that we need to change the wording of FEA5 ("Vacation settings") in Figure 28–6 to reflect a revised statement of the product feature. Note the diagonal lines through the traceability arrows in the row for FEA5. These lines, the "suspect links," are intended to warn you that changing the feature may have an impact on SR1 and SR3 and that you should therefore review them.

As the project evolves, changes inevitably will be proposed for various aspects of the project, from the top-level Vision document through to specification, implementation, and testing. Whenever a change occurs, you should use the

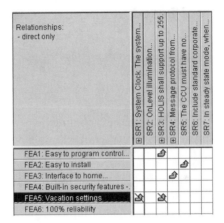

Figure 28–6   Abbreviated traceability matrix after FEA5 was altered

suspect links to warn you of possible relationships affected by the change. Your change management activities usually will involve one of two steps.

1. If the change to the feature does not impact a requirement, you need only clear the suspect link. Note that subsequent changes to the feature may again set the suspect link.
2. If the feature *does* impact a requirement, you may need to rework the affected element. For example, the proposed change to the feature may require a respecification of another requirement. After editing it, you will discover that additional suspect links now warn you of the potential interactions linked to changing it. Then you'll need to examine those interactions for changes, and so on.

Change management capability must exist throughout multiple levels of traceability relationships. That is, changing a feature entry in the Vision document may impact one or more use cases, which may in turn impact several use-case realizations (in the implementation model), as well as those test cases that were derived from the changed use case. If you have established a traceability strategy and you have proper tool support, these "suspect elements" (which are those elements that were "traced from" the changed element) should be brought to your attention automatically.

Audit Trail of Change History

You may also find it beneficial to maintain an audit trail of changes, especially changes made to individual use cases. With tool support, you should be able to manage each use case separately, regardless of the document or model it's in. Thus, changes you make to each use case will be captured automatically by your tool and can be recalled for later inspection and review.

The change history also allows you to view a chronological history of all prior changes to the requirement, including its attributes. The tool should automatically capture all changes to the text of the requirement, as well as changes to the values for the requirement's attributes.

Whenever the tool detects a change, the background for the change should be automatically captured. In addition, the tool should include an automatic capture of the name of the change's author as well as the date and time of the change. Then, at any future time, the chronology of the change and information on who created the change can be viewed as part of the history record.

The tool should also allow you to enter a change description to document the change. Typically, you might enter a sentence or two to explain why the change was made, to refer to project memos regarding the change, and so on. Documenting the change will provide a satisfactory rationale and cross-reference so that later inspection of the history can adequately recall the motivation for the change. This will be a key element in any regulatory or project review of those changes that affect the claims, efficacy, and safety of the device and its software.

Configuration Management and Change Management

A change history should exist at three levels within your project.

1. At the finest level of detail, the change history records all changes to each individual use case or requirement within the project.
2. At a middle level of detail, you should automatically maintain a similar change history for each project document. Document-level history is typically maintained by your source code control system or document control system.
3. At the most general level of detail, you should automatically maintain a similar change history for the entire project. Both the project and the archives can be fully integrated into a configuration management system.

In other words, you need a set of tools providing a fully automatic, comprehensive, and seamless integration to common applications that will assist you in the configuration management tasks involved in running a large software development project.

SUMMARY

Although requirements will change during project development, change itself need not destabilize the development process. With a comprehensive change control process in place and with requirements artifacts placed under the control of the development team's configuration management system, the team will be well prepared for the key requirements challenge of managing change.

It is important to realize that managing change in a large project is usually too big a job to handle with manual methods. While it can be fairly straightforward to implement a process to control the manner in which each change enters the project, it can still be a formidable task to attempt to understand the ramifications of the change without tools that help us find all the affected elements of the project. Current state-of-the-art tools for managing artifacts and managing code automate and facilitate much of the change management challenge. Use them.

LOOKING AHEAD

We're closing in on it. In the final chapter of Team Skill 6, we'll take a look at the vexing problem of software quality, and we'll use the requirements methods we've introduced so far to help the team members achieve quality in the products they create.

Chapter 29

ASSESSING REQUIREMENTS QUALITY IN ITERATIVE DEVELOPMENT

> **Key Points**
>
> - In iterative development, the primary quality check is the objective evidence provided by the availability and suitability of intermediate iterations.
>
> - Assessment of requirements process quality and requirements artifacts can also occur at these checkpoints.
>
> - Assessments must take into consideration the point in the lifecycle at which the assessment occurs.
>
> - Successive refinement, rather than absolute completeness or specificity, is the goal.

We've come a long way in this book. From early lifecycle methods designed to support early and effective interactions with potential users and stakeholders to later, more rigorous lifecycle methods designed to help assure that we've built what we said we would, we've provided a comprehensive process to help the software team produce a *quality system*.

In so doing, we've *implied* quality, *inferred* quality, and hopefully even *produced* quality, but we've never specifically *discussed* quality. While there is never a shortage of debates regarding the relative merits of methods, practices, and specific techniques for requirements, analysis, design, and coding activities, when taken together these debates imply a grander debate: the ongoing debate about *exactly how one goes about achieving quality in a software project*. After all, when the very nature of the thing we produce—this accumulation of source text, models and artifacts, and resultant millions of bits and bytes that we call software—is itself intangible, how can we possibly get a handle on that most intangible of all concepts, *quality*?

Well, get a handle on it we must, else we risk working in an empty intellectual forum where, in the end, all our labors are for naught because we did not produce the requisite quality in the product. So, in this chapter, we provide some background and context on the topic of software quality and show how this book, by its very nature, serves really only one purpose: *to help assure that the results you produce have the requisite quality to meet the needs of your users and extended stakeholders.* In so doing, we also provide some more specific guidelines to help the team assure that the requirements process employed is a quality process so that, in turn, a higher-quality result will be achieved.

SOFTWARE PROJECT QUALITY

A debate about software project quality would have to begin with attempting to define what software project quality *is*. There are many such definitions, each reflecting a particular quality philosophy and approach. For example, "quality is conformance to requirements," and "quality is achieved when the software is 'good enough.'" Perhaps Bach [1997] said it best when he noted that "quality is ultimately situational and objective." However, while all these definitions give us context for a quality debate, none of them give us a more objective approach we can readily apply to our context. So, we'll simply defer to a definition used in one significant segment of the software development community, one that also meets the requirements of this book. The Rational Unified Process [Rational Software Corporation 2002] defines software quality as:

> *the characteristic of having demonstrated the achievement of producing a product that meets or exceeds agreed-on requirements—as measured by agreed-on measures and criteria—and that is produced by an agreed-on process.*

According to this definition, quality is not simply "meeting requirements" or even producing a product or system that meets user needs and expectations. Rather, quality also includes identifying the measures and criteria to demonstrate the achievement of quality, and the implementation of a process and execution of a project to ensure the product created by the process has achieved the desired result. These additional aspects of quality include process and project measures such as time to market; overall budget adherence; and scope of team, project, and company investment. Quality is a multidimensional concept, and these two primary dimensions—the end result of the application itself and the business impact on the producer and consumer—must each get primary consideration.

Fortunately, the intent of this book addresses both. The techniques and methods we've been describing for effective requirements management are designed for the primary quality purpose: to help the team assure that the product or system developed meets or exceeds agreed-on requirements. And in so doing, we also provide a prescription for an agreed-on process that the team can use to help assure those results are achieved.

ASSESSING QUALITY IN ITERATIVE DEVELOPMENT

When we abandoned the waterfall development model earlier in the text, we also abandoned an apparent convenience, that is, the fixed mileposts in development where specific measures could be applied to "complete" artifacts. For example, at the end of the requirements "phase" we could hold a review to inspect requirements and assure that they were complete and unambiguous. At the end of the design phase, we could inspect the design, and so on. It looked so good on paper that we even believed it for a while, but we eventually came to recognize that it just doesn't work that way in real life. Oh well, methods, like time, march constantly forward, so let's look at how we apply quality measures in the context of iterative development. In Chapter 3 we described a process model that was iterative in nature, and we used the diagram shown in Figure 29–1 to convey the key concepts.

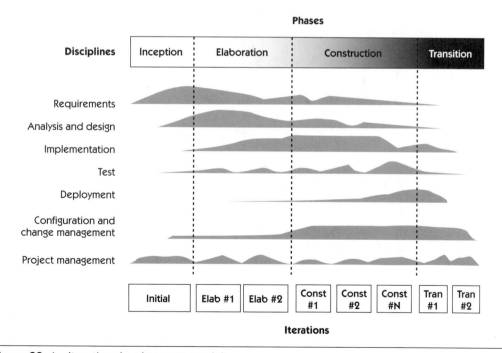

Figure 29–1   Iterative development model

As we described in Chapter 3, development progress is measured not by completion of artifacts but by incremental iterations, or a series of "builds" that more objectively demonstrate to ourselves and others the progress we've made in defining and building the system of interest. The *delivery of an iteration,* even a very early iteration that may not result in any executable or demonstrable code, *is by itself a primary quality measure.* For we can now ask and answer the following questions, basing our answers on the objective evidence exhibited by the iteration itself.

"Does it do what we said it would do?"

"Does it appear to meet the requirements as we know them at this time?", and

"Did we do it about when we said we would?"

Perhaps even more importantly, even if it does what we said it would do and performs as stated in the requirements:

"Now that you can see a bit of this thing, is this what you *really wanted? Is this what you really meant?*"

We can have some of that early feedback, thanks to iterative development, and alter the course of action *before* additional investment is made. When the team has the ability to ask and answer these questions early and often, the team can be assured that inherent quality processes and measures are built into the process itself.

However, since quality also requires adherence to agreed-upon processes, we can look at the artifacts of the process and inspect them for quality as well. In addition, in some early iterations, it's possible that preliminary artifacts are all that are available for assessment. These artifacts both demonstrate that the process is being followed and provide more tangible, system-oriented work products we can analyze and measure. This provides the assurances that the demonstrated iteration contains inherent quality, that there are no unexpected deviations from plan, and that follow-on activities are building on a solid foundation.

REQUIREMENTS ARTIFACTS SETS

Let's turn our attention to these various artifacts, or more broadly, these *sets of requirements artifacts we produce,* and see what we can learn about the quality of our process and both the measurable and the implied quality of the system under development. Using the organization of this book into six team skills as our method for organizing the requirements set, Table 29–1 summarizes the results of the analysis of what "requirements things" constitute each set.

Table 29–1   Requirements Artifacts

Team Skill	Requirements Set	Set Contents
1: Analyzing the Problem	Problem set	Problem statement Root cause analysis Systems model List of stakeholders and users List of design and development constraints List of actors Business use-case model
2: Understanding User and Stakeholder Needs	User needs set	Structured interview, process, and results Understanding of users and user needs Requirements workshop process and results Preliminary list of prioritized features Storyboards, example use cases, and other expository artifacts
3: Defining the System	Preliminary system definition set	Requirements organization Vision document Identification of initial use cases Empowerment of product manager/project champion Definitions of commercial factors
4: Managing Scope	Baseline set	Prioritization and estimation of features Requirements baseline Recognition and communication of achievable scope Agreed-on expectations
5: Refining the System Definition	Refined system definition set	Use-case model(s) Use-case specifications Supplementary specification(s) Ambiguity and specificity considerations Technical methods (if any)
6: Building the Right System	System under construction set	Transitioning method (from design to code) Test cases (derived and traceable from use cases) Requirements traceability Requirements change management process Requirements method

PERFORMING THE ASSESSMENT

The elements of the requirements sets in the rightmost column of Table 29–1 are tangible artifacts that can be reviewed, assessed, and reasoned about. However, since the process is iterative, the question naturally arises as to how to measure artifacts that are changing over time and are, technically speaking, never complete. In other words, can we actually measure something that is moving without stopping it first? Well, of course, we have to try. The answer to our dilemma is twofold.

1. We have already put in place an iterative process whereby the objective evidence of the iterations themselves are the primary quality measures. Everything else is secondary.
2. We can apply secondary measures by assessing each of the requirements artifacts at each iteration, or at any iteration we choose, by looking at the various aspects of quality that each artifact should contain *at that point* in the development process.

With respect to the latter, we'll see artifacts with varying breadths and depths of completeness over time. In order to assess them, we just have to know what to expect and when to expect it, and that depends on what iteration we are in. If we look to the iterative model for hints, you can envision that the state of these artifacts evolves over time, perhaps as Figure 29–2 illustrates. At each checkpoint we simply need to understand what level of completeness we should have achieved by that state and then assess accordingly.

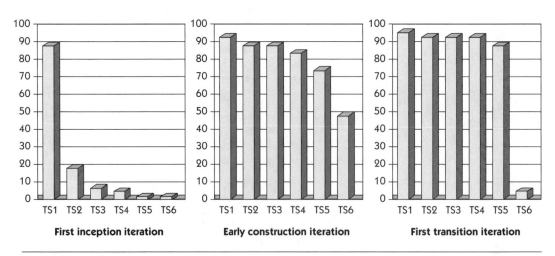

Figure 29–2   Completeness of requirements sets at various iterations

QUALITY ASSESSMENT CHECKLISTS FOR REQUIREMENTS

With the above framework in mind, we can move on to assessing the quality of each requirements set at its appropriate level of completeness. To assist your team in this endeavor, in this section we provide guidelines in the format of a quality assessment checklist for each team skill requirements artifacts set (Tables 29–2 through 29–7).

Many of the checklist items apply at any point of completion; others might apply only at some later and more final stage. In any case, those doing the assessment must keep in mind that the level of specificity and completeness must be appropriate for the particular iteration. There should be no "polishing of the artifact apple" in a contemporary and dynamic iterative software development process.

Table 29–2   Quality Assessment Checklist for Team Skill 1: Analyzing the Problem

Problem statement	Has a problem statement been drafted?	☐
	Is it written in an easy-to-understand way?	☐
	Does the team understand it?	☐
	Has it been circulated for agreement to the key stakeholders, including management?	☐
	Do the team members have agreement that this *is* the problem they are trying to solve (or the opportunity you are trying to address)?	☐
Root cause analysis	Was a root cause analysis performed?	☐
	Can the team members be sure they are addressing a real problem and not a symptom of a more basic problem?	☐
	Was sufficient effort invested in experimentation or other techniques to identify the root cause?	☐
Systems model	Is the solutions system boundary identified?	☐
	Have you identified all the things that interact with the system?	☐
	Has the system been partitioned into subsystems? If so, was the system decomposition driven by the right optimization criteria?	☐
	If so, have all the subsystems been identified?	☐
	Are the boundaries of each subsystem understood?	☐
	Is there a plan for identifying and addressing derived requirements?	☐

(continued on next page)

Table 29–2 *Continued*

List of stakeholders and users	Have you identified all the users of the system?	☐
	Have you identified all stakeholders who will be affected by the system?	☐
	Have you looked outside the sets of readily perceivable users and stakeholders and found the people dealing with administration, installation, and support or training?	☐
	How do the team members know they have identified them all?	☐
List of design and development constraints	Has the team identified all the constraints to be imposed on the system itself?	☐
	Has the team identified all the constraints to be imposed on the development process or project contracts?	☐
	Have all constraints sources (such as budget, product cost, political or contractual requirements, system requirements, environmental factors, regulations, staffing, software processes and tooling) been considered?	☐
List of actors	Have you found all the actors? That is, have you accounted for and modeled all the things (users, devices, other systems and applications) that interact with the system?	☐
	Is each actor involved with at least one use case?	☐
	Do any actors play similar roles in relation to the system? (If so, you should merge them into a single actor.)	☐
	Will a particular actor use the system in several completely different ways, or does the actor have several completely different purposes for using the use case? (If the actor uses the system in different ways, you should probably have more than one actor.)	☐
	Do the actors have intuitive and descriptive names? Can both users and customers understand the names?	☐
Business use-case model	Is a business use-case model required to understand the intended functions of the proposed system?	☐
	Is a business object model required to understand the entities involved in the business processes?	☐
	Does the team understand what specific functions will be allocated to the proposed system?	☐

Table 29–3 Quality Assessment Checklist for Team Skill 2: Understanding User and Stakeholder Needs

Structured interview, process, and results	Was a structured interview employed?	☐
	Did it cover all the major facets of product requirements, purpose, usage, reliability, performance, deployment, support, and so on?	☐
	Was it sufficiently free of interviewer biases so as to assure a quality result?	☐
	Were a sufficient number of users or stakeholders identified and interviewed?	☐
	Are there other key influencers whose needs must be understood?	☐
Understanding of users and user needs	Do you understand who the users are and what capabilities they possess to apply your application?	☐
	Did you discover any primary user or demographic differences that need to be addressed in the product?	☐
	Did the highest-priority needs converge after a reasonable number of interviews?	☐
	Are the user data, needs data, and any suggested features summarized somewhere for future reference?	☐
Requirements workshop process and results	Was a workshop conducted that included the requisite stakeholders?	☐
	Was it conducted in such a way as to encourage input by all stakeholders?	☐
	Did the results converge on a common understanding of the system to be built?	☐
	Was the development team engaged in such a way as to provide reasonable assurances of technical and project timeline feasibility?	☐
Preliminary list of prioritized features	Does a prioritized list of features exist?	☐
	Did the development team define rough estimates of effort for each?	☐
	Was the risk of each feature established?	☐
	Is this information captured somewhere for continuous reference?	☐
Storyboards, example use cases, and other expository artifacts	If the application is innovative, did you develop some means to demonstrate the application to the user?	☐
	Was their reaction taken into consideration and is it now reflected in your current understanding of the system?	☐
	Can you describe a few exemplary use cases that describe how the system is intended to be used?	☐

Table 29–4   Quality Assessment Checklist for Team Skill 3: Defining the System

Requirements organization	Have you established a plan for organizing requirements?	☐
	Do you understand what tooling you will apply to manage this process?	☐
	Does your organization system allow for capture of all types of requirements?	☐
	Are you on the lookout for design constraints?	☐
Vision document	Do you have a vision for the project?	☐
	Does it include input from relevant sources (authors/inventors, stakeholders, subject matter experts, development team) about key aspects of the project (system requirements, constraints, other systems and applications, competitive products)?	☐
	Is the vision captured in an established template (the Vision document) for this purpose?	☐
	Does it contain the requisite elements: user's profile, types, environments, product overview/perspective, product position statement, product features, applicable system requirements, and so on?	☐
	Have you established a Delta Vision document mechanism for future releases?	☐
Identification of initial use cases	Have you identified (named and described) the basic use cases that will be used to drive system development?	☐
Empowerment of product manager/ project champion	Is there a product manager or project champion empowered by the team?	☐
	Is he or she the official source of feature-level changes?	☐
	Have you identified a product road map that defines external releases and the features currently planned for each release?	☐
	Do you know how you will describe the product (messaging) to the outside world?	☐
Definitions of commercial factors	Have you defined and captured (whole product plan) requirements/policies for documentation; installation; pricing; configuration; support; licensing; end user training; and product naming, branding, and labeling?	☐

Table 29–5 Quality Assessment Checklist for Team Skill 4: Managing Scope

Prioritization and estimation of features	Have you estimated, prioritized, and assessed the risk for the various features that constitute the product vision?	☐
Requirements baseline	Have you established a requirements baseline for the release you are working on?	☐
	Do you understand what features are critical to this releases, as well as those that are important and useful?	☐
Recognition and communication of achievable scope	Does your project fit "in the scope box?" (Can it be executed with the available resources and within the available time line?)	☐
	Have you made the hard decisions for what can and can't be done during the known time line?	☐
	Have key managers and customer stakeholders agreed to this scope?	☐
Agreed-on expectations	Are expectations for the current release understood by the team?	☐
	Have the expectations been communicated and has agreement been reached with the key stakeholders outside the team, including the end user/customer?	☐

Table 29–6 Quality Assessment Checklist for Team Skill 5: Refining the System Definition

Use-case model(s)	If the system is composed of subsystems, does the use-case model appropriately reflect that?	☐
	Have you found all the use cases?	☐
	Do the use cases have unique, intuitive, and explanatory names so they cannot be mixed up at a later stage?	☐
	Are all required system behaviors identified in one or more use cases?	☐
	Do customers and users understand the names and descriptions of the use cases?	☐
	By looking at the use-case model, can you form a clear idea of the system's functions and how they are related?	☐

(continued on next page)

Table 29–6   *Continued*

Use-case model(s) *(continued)*	Do the elaborated use cases meet all the functional requirements?	☐
	Does the use-case model contain any superfluous behavior?	☐
	That is, does it present more functions than were called for in the requirements?	☐
	Does the model need the identified include and extend relationships?	☐
	Can the model be simplified with additional relationships?	☐
Use-case specifications	Is each use case involved with at least one actor?	☐
	Does the brief description give a true picture of the use case?	☐
	Is it clear who wishes to perform a use case? Is the purpose of the use case also clear?	☐
	Do the elaborated use cases contain the necessary sections and the appropriate content for name, actors, brief description, primary and alternate flow of events, pre- and post-conditions, and special requirements?	☐
	Is it clear how and when the use case's flow of events starts and ends?	☐
	Is each use case independent of the others?	☐
	Do any use cases have very similar behaviors or flows of events?	☐
	Has part of a use case's flow of events already been modeled as another use case?	☐
	Should the flow of events of one use case be inserted into the flow of events of another?	☐
	Does the use case meet all the requirements that obviously govern its performance? Are use-case-specific nonfunctional requirements referenced where necessary?	☐
	Does the communication sequence between actor and use case conform to the user's expectations?	☐
	Is there a description of what will happen if a given condition is not met?	☐
	Are any use cases overly complex?	☐
	Are the actor interactions and exchanged information clear?	☐

(continued on next page)

Table 29–6 *Continued*

Supplementary specification(s)	Have you established an appropriate template for your specific purposes?	☐
	Are almost all functional requirements included in the use-case model, and the balance, if any, reflected in the supplementary specification?	☐
	Have nonfunctional requirements such as usability, reliability, performance, and supportability all been identified and captured?	☐
	Have the appropriate design constraints been identified and captured?	☐
	Have supplementary requirements been linked to the use cases where appropriate?	☐
Ambiguity and specificity considerations	In general, has your team reached the appropriate level of specificity (the sweet spot) for your project context?	☐
	How do you know that this has been achieved?	☐
Technical methods (if any)	Have appropriate technical methods been employed to remove ambiguity in those cases where you cannot afford to be misunderstood?	☐
	If so, can these methods themselves be understood by the key stakeholders?	☐

Table 29–7 Quality Assessment Checklist for Team Skill 6: Building the Right System

Transitioning method (from design to code)	Do you understand the mechanism by which you'll be transitioning from requirements into design and implementation?	☐
	Is there a use-case realization (collaboration) for all use cases in the use-case model?	☐
	Are there realizations for other functional requirements as well?	☐
Test cases (derived and traceable from use cases)	Have the use cases been used to seed test case development?	☐
	Have you followed the four-step process (identify scenarios, identify test cases, identify test conditions, add data values)?	☐
	Are there one or more test cases for every use case?	☐

(continued on next page)

Table 29–7 *Continued*

Requirements traceability	Have you established a plan for requirements traceability?	☐
	Have you identified and implemented adequate tooling?	☐
	Have you identified and followed a specific traceability model for this project?	☐
	Have you exploited implicit traceability to the maximum extent possible?	☐
	Have you applied explicit traceability in all critical areas?	☐
Requirements change management process	Do you understand the change sources and change dynamics for this project?	☐
	Do you know a change when you see it?	☐
	Does the project champion/product manager have control of this process?	☐
	Is an appropriate change control board established and is it functional for your project?	☐
	Can you capture and manage change effectively with the tooling you've deployed?	☐
	Do you have a way to capture and track defects on the project?	☐
Requirements method*	Did you pick an appropriate requirements method?	☐
	Does it reflect the key priorities of criticality and safety on the project?	☐
	Does the method eliminate unnecessary documentation and overhead?	☐
	Does the tooling adequately support the method you've chosen?	☐

* We'll talk more about these issues in Chapter 30.

SUMMARY

In this chapter, we've taken a look at that most difficult topic, assessing quality in a software project, and created a framework for assessment in an iterative requirements process. We learned that the nature of iterative development adds a few quality assessment challenges, specifically, the lack of programmatic phases and complete artifacts that can be assessed. However, iterative development provides certain major advantages as well. The very existence of an iteration serves as objective evidence of both the product and the process used to create it. We just have to be clever enough to understand that we are operating in a mode of successive refinement, rather than in a search for absolute levels of completeness or conformance, at any particular time. In software development, at least, there are no such absolutes, and we must content ourselves with the fact that our iterative process provides us a way to get closer and closer to that ultimate quality goal.

Team Skill 6 Summary

Team Skill 6, Building the Right System, completes the transition from understanding the problem to implementing the solution system.

Designing and implementing the correct system is hard work. Transitioning from the world of requirements to the world of design requires changing paradigms from the world of natural language, text, and specifications to the world of software architecture and code. To assist the team with this challenge, we've described a specific technique that uses the requirements and use cases to directly drive the implementation architecture and design.

Testing systems of significant complexity is hard work, too. Once again, we've used the use-case workhorse to seed the testing activities, with each use case typically driving multiple test cases, thereby producing at least one test case for each scenario in the use case.

To assure that everything required for your project is present and accounted for, we've introduced traceability techniques that provide mechanisms for following from user needs to features and use cases, and from there into implementation and testing. In addition, these same techniques allow you to ferret out unnecessary or superfluous items that could change the behavior of the system in unanticipated ways.

A critical feature of building the right system is the matter of managing change. Change is a way of life; we can *plan* for change and *manage* it. Managing change helps us make sure that the system we built is the *right* system and, moreover, that it continues to *be* the right system over time.

And finally, we've confirmed that the purpose of an effective requirements process, *all along*, was simply to help assure a quality end result, and we've provided guidance and checklists to help your team assess requirements project quality within an iterative framework.

LOOKING AHEAD

With the completion of Team Skill 6, we are ready to move to two unique and final chapters. Chapter 30 addresses the issue of designing a requirements management process that meets the needs of your particular software process style and project context. Finally, Chapter 31 is designed to help you apply the skills you have learned and to help you get off to a good start on your next project.

GETTING STARTED

DEDICATION

Over the course of many years, we and others who have contributed to this book have taught, and have been taught by, thousands of students interested in improving project outcomes by doing a better job of managing their software requirements. In this second edition of the book, we've been more prescriptive, but we still recognize that there is no one right way to perform requirements management. No one single elicitation technique applies in every circumstance; no one single process fits all teams. Projects have varying degrees of scope and complexity. Application types vary tremendously and come from many different industries.

Yes, requirements management is a broad topic, and it is also very deep. A recurring theme from the classroom is that students feel the need to have a more prescriptive process—a recipe, if you will—for applying what they learned in class. "You've told us too much," our students might say. "Just give us a single generic process that we can start with," they continue. "We know it's not that simple, but we'll be happy to modify it as necessary for *our* project. We need a more prescriptive starting point, a step-by-step process so that we can better apply what we learned. *Just tell me how to get started!*"

OK, you've got it. These next two chapters are dedicated to these students and to those of you who share their point of view and this common "user need."

WHAT YOU'VE LEARNED SO FAR

Before we can kick-start your project requirements process, however, let's summarize what you've learned in the book so far.

Introduction

In the introductory chapters, we looked at why our industry often does a poor job of delivering quality applications on time and on budget. Some of the root causes of this problem are clear. *Lack of user input, incomplete requirements and specifications, and changing requirements and specifications* are commonly cited problems in projects that failed to meet their objectives.

Perhaps developers and customers alike have a common attitude that "since we can't determine everything we want in advance, it's better to get started with implementation now because we're behind schedule and in a hurry. We can pin down the requirements later." Since, even in this requirements text, we've agreed that it isn't possible to know everything in advance, that doesn't seem so inappropriate. But all too often, this well-intentioned approach degenerates into a chaotic, out-of-control development effort, with no one on the team quite sure what the user really wants or what the current system really does.

To address these issues, we've recommended an encompassing philosophy of requirements management, which we defined as

> *a systematic approach to eliciting, organizing, and documenting the requirements of the system, as well as a process that establishes and maintains agreement between the customer and the project team on the changing requirements of the system.*

Since the history of software development—and the future for at least as far as we can envision it—is one of ever-increasing complexity, we also understand that well-structured and well-trained software teams must address the software development problem. Every team member will eventually be involved in helping manage the requirements for the project. These teams must develop the requisite skills to understand the user needs, to manage the scope of the application, and to build systems that meet these user needs. The team must work *as a team* to address the requirements management challenge.

In addition, we discussed that we must take an "iterative and incremental" approach to the problem, an approach that recognizes that not all requirements can be determined in advance. By delivering increments to the users, we can further refine our understanding of their needs and better evolve the system to meet their real needs.

Team Skill 1: Analyzing the Problem

In Team Skill 1, we introduced a set of skills your team can apply to *understand the problem to be solved before too much is invested in the application.* We introduced a simple, five-step problem analysis technique that can help your team gain a better understanding of the problem to be solved.

1. Gain agreement on the problem definition.
2. Understand the root causes of the problem.
3. Identify the stakeholders and the users whose collective judgment will ultimately determine the success or failure of your system.
4. Determine where the boundaries of the solution are likely to be found.
5. Identify and understand the constraints that will be imposed on the team and on the solution.

All in all, following this process will improve your team's ability to address the challenge ahead, *providing a solution to the problem to be solved.*

We also noted that a variety of techniques could be used in problem analysis. Specifically, we looked at business modeling, a problem analysis technique that works quite well in complex information systems that support key business processes. The team members can use business modeling to both understand the way in which the business evolves and to define where within the system they can deploy applications most productively. We also recognized that the business model we defined will have parallels in the software application, and we use this commonality to seed the software design phases.

For embedded-system software applications, we applied systems engineering as a problem analysis technique to help decompose a complex system into more manageable subsystems. This process helps us understand where new software applications should come to exist and what purpose they serve. However, we complicate the requirements challenge somewhat by defining these new subsystems, for then we must determine the requirements to be imposed on them.

Team Skill 2: Understanding User and Stakeholder Needs

We started Team Skill 2 by introducing three "syndromes" that increase the challenge of understanding the real needs of users and other stakeholders. The "Yes, But," the "Undiscovered Ruins," and the "User and the Developer" syndromes are metaphors that helped us better understand the challenge ahead and provided a context for the elicitation techniques we developed in this team skill.

We also recognized that since we rarely have been given effective requirements specifications for the systems we are going to build, in order to do a better job of building these systems, we have to go out and *get* the information we need to be successful. *Requirements elicitation* is the term we used to describe this process, and we concluded that the team must play a more active role.

To help the team address these problems and better understand the real needs of users and other stakeholders, we then presented a variety of techniques:

- Interviewing
- Requirements workshops
- Brainstorming and idea reduction
- Storyboarding

Although no one technique is perfect in every circumstance, each represents a proactive way to push your knowledge of user needs forward and thereby convert "fuzzy" requirements into requirements that are "better known."

Team Skill 3: Defining the System

In Team Skill 3, we moved from understanding the needs of the user to defining the solution. In so doing, we took our first steps out of the problem domain, the land of the user, and into the solution domain, wherein our job is to define a system to solve the problem at hand.

We invested most of our time in developing the use-case technique since it can do most of the "heavy lifting." Use cases have a number of advantages over other techniques, including the way the use cases persist in the project to drive testing strategy and the development of the test cases themselves. We also discussed that complex systems require comprehensive strategies for managing requirements information, and we looked at a number of ways to organize requirements information. We recognized that we really have a hierarchy of information, starting with user needs, transitioning through features, then into the more detailed software requirements as expressed in use cases and supplementary specifications. Also, we noted that the hierarchy reflects the level of abstraction with which we view the problem space and the solution space.

We then "zoomed in" to look at the application definition process for a stand-alone software application and invested some time in defining a Vision document for such an application. We maintain that the Vision document, with modifications to the particular context of a company's software applications, is a crucial document and that *every* project should have one.

We also recognized that without someone to champion the requirements for our application and to support the needs of the customer and the development team, we would have no way to be certain that the hard decisions are made. Requirements drift, delays, and suboptimum decisions forced by project deadlines are likely to result. Therefore, we decided to appoint someone or to anoint someone to serve as *product manager*, someone to own the Vision document and the features it contains as well as to drive agreement on some of the commercial factors that convert an application into a *whole product solution*. In turn, the champion and the team empower a change control board to help with the really tough decisions and to ensure that requirements changes are reasoned about before being accepted.

Team Skill 4: Managing Scope

In Team Skill 4, we examined the endemic problem of project scope. It is not unusual to see projects initiated with *two to four times* the amount of functionality the team can reasonably implement in a quality manner. We shouldn't be surprised by this; it is the nature of the beast. Customers want more, marketing wants more, and the team wants more, too. Nevertheless, we have to manage this psychology aggressively if we intend to deliver *something* on time.

In order to manage scope, we looked at various techniques for setting priorities, and we defined the notion of the baseline, an agreed-to understanding of what the system will do, as a key project work product. We learned that if scope and the concomitant expectations exceed reality, in all probability, some bad news is about to be delivered. We decided on a philosophy of approach that engages our customer in the hard decisions. After all, we are just the implementers, not the decision makers; it's our customer's project. So, the question is, "What, exactly, *must* be accomplished in the next release, given the resources that are available to the project?"

Even then, we expect to do some negotiating. We briefly mentioned a few negotiation skills and hinted that the team may need to use them on occasion.

We cannot expect that the process described so far will make the scope challenge go away, any more than any other single process will solve the problems of the application development world. However, the steps outlined can be expected to have a material effect on the scope of the problem, allowing application developers to focus on critical subsets and to deliver high-quality systems incrementally that meet or exceed the expectations of the user. Further, engaging the customer in helping solve the scope management problem increases commitment on the part of both parties and fosters improved communication and trust between the customer and the application development team.

With a comprehensive project definition, or Vision document, in hand and scope managed to a reasonable level, we at least have the *opportunity* to succeed in the next phases of the project.

Team Skill 5: Refining the System Definition

In Team Skill 5, we first took a more rigorous look at requirements and commented on some of the issues that arise in transitioning from requirements to design. In addition, we refined the use cases to sufficient specificity so that we can both implement them and use them later to develop the test cases that will determine when the requirements have been met. We also discussed the importance of nonfunctional requirements, including the system's usability, reliability, performance, and supportability, as well as the design constraints that may be imposed on our process. We described how to organize them in a supplementary specification that, along with the use-case model, completes our information model of the system we are building.

Team Skill 6: Building the Right System

Designing and implementing the correct system is the biggest job of all. In Team Skill 6, we described how to use the developed use cases to drive implementation via the design construct of the *use-case realization*. We also described how to use the use cases to develop a comprehensive testing strategy by deriving the test cases directly from them.

We also developed the concepts and described the challenges associated with *requirements traceability* and demonstrated how that technique can improve the quality and reliability outcomes of a development effort.

In addition, building the right system right also depends on the team's ability to *manage change effectively.* Since change is just part of life we must plan for change and develop a process whereby we can manage it. Managing change helps us make sure that the system we built *is* the right system and, moreover, that it continues to *be* the right system over time.

Lastly, we looked at a framework for assessing requirements quality, as well as overall project quality, within an iterative development process, and we used this to create guidelines your team can use to help assure you will deliver a quality result.

With all that behind us, we're almost ready to look at that requirements prescription our students have been clamoring for. Before we do, however, we have one last meaty topic to cover: the topic of picking an overall requirements method you can apply in your specific project context.

Chapter 30

AGILE REQUIREMENTS METHODS

Key Points

- The purpose of the software development method is to mitigate the risks inherent in the project.

- The purpose of the requirements management method is to mitigate requirements-related risks on the project.

- No one method fits all projects, therefore the method must be tailored to the particular project.

- Three requirements methods (extreme, agile, and robust) are presented.

MITIGATING REQUIREMENTS RISK WITH EFFECTIVE REQUIREMENTS PRACTICES

So far in this book, we have described a comprehensive set of practices intended to help teams more effectively manage software requirements imposed on a system under development. Since the systems that teams are building today can be exceedingly complex, often comprising hundreds of thousands or even millions of lines of code and tens to hundreds of person-years in development time, it makes sense that requirements themselves are also likely to be exceedingly complex. Therefore, a significant variety of techniques and processes—collectively a complete *requirements discipline*—are required to manage requirements effectively.

However, lest we lose sight of the purpose of software development, which is to deliver working code that solves customer problems, we must constantly remind ourselves that the entire requirements discipline within the software lifecycle exists for only one reason: *to mitigate the risk that requirements-related issues will prevent a successful project outcome.* If there were no such risks, then it would be far more efficient to go straight to code and eliminate the overhead of requirements-related activities. Therefore, when your team chooses a requirements method, *it must reflect the types of risks inherent in your environment.*

Three Points to Remember about Method

1. The purpose of the software development method is to mitigate risks inherent in the project.

2. The purpose of the requirements management method is to mitigate requirements-related risks on the project.

3. No one method fits all projects; therefore, the requirements method must be tailored to the particular project.

Each of the requirements techniques we've discussed was developed solely to address one or more specific types of requirements-related risks. Table 30–1 summarizes these techniques, along with the nature and type of risks that each is intended to mitigate.

METHODOLOGY DESIGN GOALS

As we have said, the purpose of requirements methodology is to address requirements-related project risks. The purpose of the overall development methodology is to address collective project risks. In his book on agile development, Cockburn [2002] identifies four major principles to apply when designing and evaluating software methodologies.

1. Interactive, face-to-face communication is the cheapest and fastest channel for exchanging information.
2. Excess methodology weight is costly.
3. Larger teams need heavier methodologies.
4. Greater ceremony is appropriate for projects with greater criticality.

Let's examine these principles briefly to see what insight we can gain into selecting the correct requirements management methodology for a particular project context.

Table 30–1 Requirements Techniques and the Specific Project Risks They Address

Technique	Risk Addressed
Interviewing	■ The development team might not understand who the real stakeholders are. ■ The team might not understand the basic needs of one or more stakeholders.
Requirements workshops	■ The system might not appropriately address classes of specific user needs. ■ Lack of consensus among key stakeholders might prevent convergence on a set of requirements.
Brainstorming and idea reduction	■ The team might not discover key needs or prospective innovative features. ■ Priorities are not well established, and a plethora of features obscures the fundamental "must haves."
Storyboards	■ The prospective implementation misses the mark. ■ The approach is too hard to use or understand, or the operation's business purpose is lost in the planned implementation.
Use cases	■ Users might not feel they have a stake in the implementation process. ■ Implementation fails to fulfill basic users needs in some way because some features are missing or because of poor usability, poor error and exception handling, and so on.
Vision document	■ The development team members do not really understand what system they are trying to build, or what user needs or industry problem it addresses. ■ Lack of longer-term vision causes poor planning and poor architecture and design decisions.
Whole product plan	■ The solution might lack the commercial elements necessary for successful adoption.
Scoping activities	■ The project scope exceeds the time and resources available.
Supplementary specification	■ The development team might not understand nonfunctional requirements: platforms, reliability, standards, and so on.
Tracing use cases to implementation	■ Use cases might be described but not fully implemented in the system.
Tracing use cases to test cases	■ Some use cases might not be tested, or alternative and exception conditions might not be understood, implemented, and tested.
Requirements traceability	■ Critical requirements might be overlooked in the implementation. ■ The implementation might introduce requirements or features not called for in the original requirements. ■ A change in requirements might impact other parts of the system in unforeseen ways.
Change management	■ New system requirements might be introduced in an uncontrolled fashion. The team might underestimate the negative impact of a change.

Principle 1: Interactive, Face-to-Face Communication Is the Cheapest and Fastest Channel for Exchanging Information Whether eliciting requirements information from a customer or communicating that information to a team, face-to-face discussion is the best and most efficient way to communicate. If the customer is close to the team, if the customer is directly accessible, if requirements can be explained to the team directly, if the analyst can communicate directly with the customer and the team, then less documentation is needed.[1] However, due to the criticality of understanding requirements for the system, some requirements must be documented. Otherwise, the team bears the risk that implicit, tacit assumptions to the effect of "we all know what we are developing here" may again become a primary risk factor in the project. But certainly, fewer documents need be produced, and necessary documents—Vision documents, use cases, supplementary specifications, and the like—can be shorter and written with less specificity.

Principle 2: Excess Methodology Weight Is Costly This principle translates to "Do only what you have to do to be successful." Every unnecessary process or artifact slows the team down, adds weight to the project, and diverts time and energy from essential coding and testing activities. The team must balance the cost and weight of each requirements activity with the risks listed in Table 30–1. If a particular risk is not present or likely to occur, consider deleting the corresponding artifact or activity from your process. Alternatively, think of a way to "lighten" the artifact until it's a better fit for the risk in your particular project. Write abbreviated use cases, apply more implicit traceability, and hold fewer reviews of requirements artifacts.

Principle 3: Larger Teams Need Heavier Methodologies Clearly, an appropriate requirements methodology for a team of three developers who are subject matter experts and who have ready access to a customer may be entirely different than the right methodology for a team of 800 people at five different locations who are developing an integrated product line. What works for one will not work for the other. The requirements method must be scaled to the size of the team and the size of the project. However, you must not overshoot the mark either; an over-weighted method will result in lower efficiency for a team of any size.

---

1. It is important to take this notion with a grain of salt. As Philippe Kruchten pointed out to us recently, "I write to better understand what we said."

Principle 4: Greater Ceremony Is Appropriate for Projects with Greater Criticality The criticality of the project may be the greatest factor in determining methodology weight. For example, it may be quite feasible to develop software for a human pacemaker's external programming device with a two- or three-person coding team. Moreover, the work would likely be done by a development team with subject matter expertise as well as ready access to clinical experts who can describe exactly what algorithms must be implemented and why and how. However, on such a project, the cost of even a small error might be quite unacceptable since it could endanger human life. Therefore, all the intermediate artifacts that specify the use cases, algorithms, and reliability requirements must be documented in exceptional detail, and they must be reviewed and rationalized as necessary to ensure that only the "right" understanding appears in the final implementation. In such cases, a small team may need a heavyweight method. The opposite case may also be true. A noncritical project of scope sufficient to require a large team may be able to apply a lighter-weight method.

DOCUMENTATION IS A MEANS TO AN END

Most requirements artifacts, Vision documents, use cases, and so forth—and indeed software development artifacts in general, including the code—require documentation of some kind. Given that these documents divert time and attention from essential coding and testing activities, a reasonable question to ask with respect to each one is "Do we really need to write this document at all?"

You should answer "Yes" *only* if one or more of these four criteria apply.

1. The document communicates an important understanding or agreement for instances in which simpler verbal communication is either impractical (for example, a larger or more distributed team) or would create too great a project risk (for example, a pacemaker programmer device).
2. The documentation allows new team members to come up to speed more quickly and therefore renders both current and new team members more efficient.[2]

---

2. In our experience, this issue is often overrated, and the team may be better off focusing new members on the "live" documentation inside the requirements, analysis and design tools, and so forth.

3. Investment in the document has an obvious long-term payoff because it will evolve, be maintained, and persist as an ongoing part of the development, testing, or maintenance activity. Examples include use case and test case artifacts, which can be used repeatedly for regression testing of future releases.

4. Some company, customer, or regulatory standard imposes a requirement for the document.

Before including a specific artifact in your requirements method, your team should ask and answer the following two questions (and no, you needn't document the answers!).

1. Does this document meet one or more of the four criteria above? If not, then skip it.

2. What is the appropriate level of specificity that can be used to satisfy the need?

With this perspective in hand, let's move on to defining a few requirements approaches that can be effective in particular project contexts. We know, of course, that projects are not all the same style and that even individual projects are not homogenous throughout. A single project might have a set of extremely critical requirements or critical subsystems interspersed with a larger number of noncritical requirements or subsystems. Each element would require a different set of methods to manage the incumbent risk. Therefore, a bit of mixing and matching will be required in almost any case, but we can still provide guidelines for choosing among a few key approaches.

AN EXTREME REQUIREMENTS METHOD

In the last few years, the notion of *Extreme Programming* (XP) as originally espoused by Beck [2000] has achieved some popularity (along with a significant amount of notoriety and controversy). One can guess at what has motivated this trend. Perhaps it's a reaction to the inevitable and increasing time pressures of an increasingly efficient marketplace, or a reaction to the overzealous application of otherwise effective methodologies. Alternatively, perhaps it's a reaction to the wishes of software teams to be left alone to do what they think they do best: write code. In any case, there can be no doubt of the "buzz" that Extreme Programming has created in software circles and that the related Agile Methods movement is now creating as it attempts to add balance and practicality to the extreme approach.

Before examining how we might define an extreme requirements method, let's look at some of the key characteristics of XP.

- The scope of the application or component permits coding by a team of three to ten programmers working at one location.
- One or more customers are on site to provide constant requirements input.
- Development occurs in frequent builds or iterations, each of which is releasable and delivers incremental user functionality.
- The unit of requirements gathering is the *user story*, a chunk of functionality that provides value to the user. User stories are written by the customers on site.
- Programmers work in pairs and follow strict coding standards. They do their own unit testing and are supposed to routinely re-factor the code to keep the design simple.
- Since little attempt is made to understand or document future requirements, the code is constantly refactored (redesigned) to address changing user needs.

Let's assume you have a project scope that can be achieved by a small team working at one location. Further, let's assume that it's practical to have a customer on site during the majority of the development (an arrangement that is admittedly *not* very practical in most project contexts we've witnessed). Now, let's look at XP from the standpoint of requirements methods.

A key tenet of any effective requirements method is early and continuous user feedback. From this perspective, perhaps XP doesn't seem so extreme after all. Table 30–2 illustrates how some key tenets of XP can be used to mitigate requirements risks we've identified so far.

With this background, let's see if we can derive a simple, explicit requirements model that would reflect or support an XP process. Perhaps it would look like Figure 30–1 and have the characteristics described briefly below.

Concept. At the heart of any requirements process lives the product concept. In this case, the concept is communicated directly from the customer to the project team—verbally, frequently, and repeatedly as personnel come and go on the team.

Vision. The vision carries the product concept, both short-term and long-term. A Delta Vision document typically describes the new features and use

Table 30–2 Applying Extreme Programming Principles to Requirements Risk Mitigation

Extreme Programming Principle	Mitigated Requirements Risk
Application or component scope is such that three to ten programmers at one location can do the coding.	Constant informal communication can minimize or eliminate much requirements documentation.
One or more customers are on site to provide constant requirements input.	Constant customer input and feedback dramatically reduces requirements-related risk.
Development occurs in frequent builds or iterations, each of which is releasable and delivers incremental user functionality.	Customer value feedback is almost immediate; this ship can't go too far off course.
The unit of requirements gathering is the user story, a bite of functionality that provides value to the user. Customers on site write user stories.	A use case describes sequences of events that deliver value to a user, as written by the developer with user input. User stories are often short descriptions of a path or scenario of a use case. Each captures the same basic intent—how the user interacts with the system to get something done.

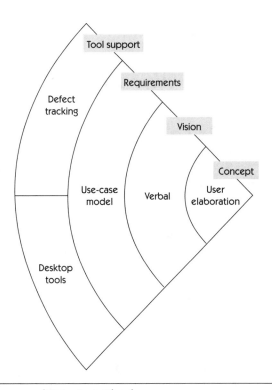

Figure 30–1 An extreme requirements method

cases to be implemented in a specific release. In XP, this document may not exist. We are dependent on the customer's ability to tell us what the product needs to do now and what it needs to do later, and we are dependent on the development team to make the right architectural decisions now—for both now and later. Whether or not this can be made to work in practice depends on a number of project factors and the relative risk the team is willing to take; you can't say for certain that it couldn't work, at least for some project scenarios.[3] Therefore, we'll leave this artifact out of our extreme requirements method.

Requirements. Another principal tenet of our text is that the use-case model carries the majority of functional requirements. It describes who uses the system and how they use it to accomplish their objectives. XP recommends the use of simple "stories" that are not unlike use cases but are typically shorter (they appear to be more like a use-case scenario) and at a higher level of abstraction. However, we recommend that there *always* be a use-case model, even if it's a simple, nongraphical summary of the key user stories that are implemented and what class of user implements them. We'd insist on this use-case model, even for our extreme requirements method.

Supplementary Specification/Nonfunctional Requirements. XP has no obvious placeholder for these items, perhaps because there are not very many, or perhaps the thinking is that they can be assumed or understood without mention. On the other hand, perhaps customers communicate these requirements directly to programmers whose work is affected by them. Seems a bit risky, but if that's not where the risk lies in your project, so be it; we'll leave this artifact out of our extreme requirements method.

Tooling. The tools of XP are whiteboards and desktop tools, such as spreadsheets with itemized user stories, priorities, and so forth. However, defects will naturally occur, and although XP is quiet on the tooling subject, let's assume we can add a tracking database of some kind to keep track of all these stories—perhaps their status as well as defects that will naturally occur and must be traded off with future enhancements.

---

3. As we said, the method is not without its critics. One reviewer noted the big drawback of the "one user story at a time" approach is the total lack of architectural work. If your initial assumption is wrong, you have to refactor the architecture one user story at a time. You build a whole system, and the nth story is, "OK, this is fine for one user. Now, let's make it work for 3,000."

With these simple documents, practices, and tools, we've defined an extreme requirements method that can work in appropriate, albeit somewhat extreme, circumstances.

AN AGILE REQUIREMENTS METHOD

But what if your customer can't be located on site? What if you are developing a new class of products for which no current customers exist? What if the concepts are so innovative that customers can't envision what stories they would fulfill? What if your system has to be integrated with either new systems or other existing systems? What if more than three to ten people are required? What if your system is so complex that it must be considered as a "system of systems"—with each system imposing requirements on others? What if some of your team members work from remote sites? What if a few potential failure modes are economically unacceptable? What then?

Then you will need a heavier method, one that can address the additional risks in your project context. You will need a method that looks more like the agile requirements method depicted in Figure 30–2. Its characteristics are described briefly below.

Concept. In the agile requirements method, the root of the project is still the concept, but that concept is tested and elaborated by a number of means, including requirements workshops or interviews with prospective customers.

Vision. The vision is no longer only verbal; it is defined incrementally in the Delta Vision document, which describes the new features to be implemented in a specific release. The whole product plan describes the other elements of your successful solution: the commercial and support factors, licensing requirements, and other factors that are keys to success.

Requirements. The use-case model diagram defines the use cases at the highest level of abstraction. In addition, in this more robust method, each use case has a specification that elaborates the sequence of events, the pre- and post-conditions, and the exceptions and alternative flows. The use-case specifications will likely be written at different levels of detail. Some areas are more critical than others are; other areas are more innovative and require further definition before coding begins. Still other areas are straightforward extensions to known or existing features and need little additional specification.

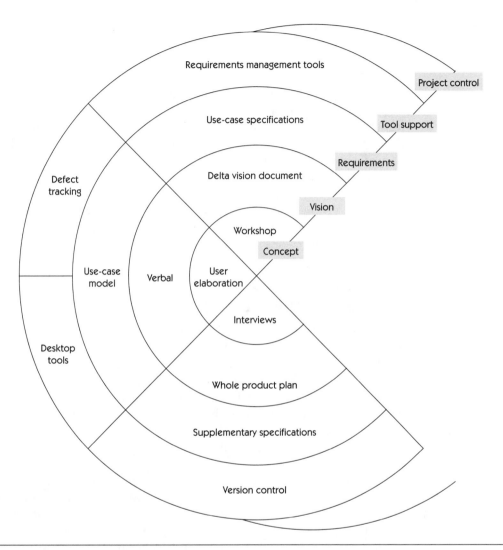

Figure 30–2 An agile requirements method

Supplementary Specification/Nonfunctional Requirements. Your application may run on multiple operating systems, support multiple databases, integrate with a customer application, or have specific requirements for security or user access. Perhaps external standards are imposed on it, or perhaps a host of performance requirements must be individually identified, discussed, agreed to, and tested. If so, the supplementary specification contains this information, and it is an integral artifact to an agile requirements management method.

Tooling. As the project complexity grows, so do the tooling requirements, and the team may find it beneficial to add a requirements tool for capturing and prioritizing the information or automatically creating a use-case summary from the developed use cases. The more people working on the project, and the more locations they work from, the more important version control becomes, both for the code itself and for the use cases and other requirements artifacts that define the system being built.

With some practical and modest extensions to our extreme requirements method, we've now defined a practical agile requirements method, one that is already well proven in a number of real-world projects.

A ROBUST REQUIREMENTS METHOD

But what if you are developing the pacemaker programmer we described above? What if your teams are developing six integrated products for a product family that is synchronized and released twice a year? You employ 800 developers in six locations worldwide, and yet your products must work together. Alternatively, what if you are a telecommunications company and the success of your company will be determined by the success of a third-generation digital switching system that will be based on the efforts of 1,000 programmers spanning a time measured in years? What then?

Then you will need a truly robust requirements method. One that scales to the challenge at hand. One that can be tailored to deliver extremely reliable products in critical areas. One that allows developers in other countries to understand the requirements imposed on the subsystem they are building. One that can help assure you that your system satisfies the hundreds of use cases and thousands of functional and nonfunctional requirements necessary for your application to work with other systems and applications—seamlessly, reliably, and flawlessly.

So now we come full circle to the robust requirements management method expressed in Figure 30–3. Its characteristics are briefly explored below.

Concept. Given the complexity of the application itself and the likelihood that few, if any, features can actually be implemented and released before a significant amount of architectural underpinnings are developed and implemented,

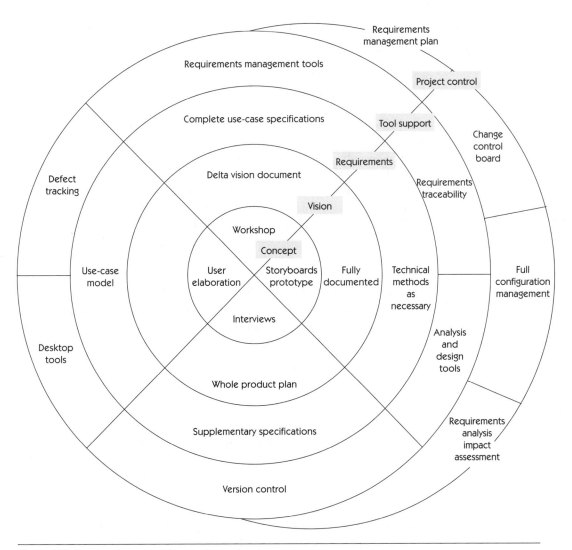

Figure 30–3 A robust requirements method

we add a range of concept validation techniques, storyboards, prototypes, architectural models, and the like. Each will bring us closer to our goal of understanding the intended behavior of the system we are about to build.

Vision. In order to assure understanding among a large number of stakeholders, developers, and testers, the vision, both short-term and long-term, must be documented. It must be sufficiently long-range for the architects and designers to design and implement the right architecture to support current and future features and use cases. The whole product plan should be extended to describe potential variations in purchase configurations and likely customer deployment options. The plan should also define supported revision levels of compatible applications.

Requirements. The use cases are elaborated as necessary so that prospective users can validate the implementation concepts. This ensures that all critical requirements will be implemented in a way that helps assure their utility and fitness. Because some elements of the application are critical, all alternative sequences of events are discussed and described. Pre- and post-conditions are specified as clearly and unambiguously as possible. Additional, technical specification methods (analysis models, activity diagrams, message sequence diagrams) are used to describe more clearly how the system does what it does and when it does it.

Supplementary Specification/Nonfunctional Requirements. The supplementary specification is as complete as possible. All platforms; application compatibility issues; applicable standards; branding and copyright requirements; and performance, usability, reliability, and supporting requirements are defined.

Tooling. Larger, more distributed teams require industrial-strength software tooling. Analysis and design tools further specific system behavior, both internal and external. Multisite configuration management systems are employed. Requirements tools both support requirements traceability from features through use cases and into test cases and track changes and change history. The defect tracking system extends to support users, including customers, from any location.

Project Control. Larger projects require higher levels of project support and control. Requirements dashboards are built so that teams can monitor and synchronize interdependent use-case implementations. A change control board is created to weigh and decide on possible requirements additions and defect fixes. Requirements analysis and impact assessment activities are performed to help understand the impact of proposed changes and additions.

Taken together, these techniques and activities in our robust requirements method help assure that this new system—in which many tens or hundreds of person-years have been invested and which will touch the lives of thousands of users across the globe—is accurate, reliable, safe, and well suited for its intended purpose.

SUMMARY

In this chapter, we reinforced the concept that the project methodology is designed solely to assure that we mitigate the risks present in our project environment. If in our projects we focus too much on methodology, we add overhead and burden the team with unnecessary activities. If we aren't careful, we'll become slow, expensive, and eventually uncompetitive. Some other team will get the next project, or some other company will get our next customer. If we focus too little on methodology, we assume too much risk on the part of our company or our customers, with perhaps even more severe consequences.

To manage this risk, we looked at three prototypical requirements methods: an *extreme requirements method*, an *agile requirements method*, and a *robust requirements method*, each of which is suitable for a particular project context. Yet we recognize that every project is unique, and every customer and every application is different; therefore, your optimal requirements method will likely be none of the above. Perhaps it will be some obvious hybrid, or perhaps a variant we did not explore. In any case, your team's job is to select the right requirements method for your next project while keeping the project as agile as possible.

Finally, with this understanding behind us, we can now move on to creating that specific requirements prescription you've all been asking for.

Chapter 31

YOUR PRESCRIPTION FOR REQUIREMENTS MANAGEMENT

Key Points

- Pick an overall requirements framework (extreme, agile, or robust) that applies to your general project type.
- Tailor that method to the details of your particular project context and to the skills of your project team.
- Develop a specific requirements management plan that documents your strategy.
- An example requirements management plan (prescription) is provided.

SELECTING YOUR REQUIREMENTS APPROACH

With an understanding of how to apply different requirements methods to different project contexts, we can now proceed to provide a prescription. However, if we are going to simplify the prescription, as is necessary to manage our level of abstraction—and to help us manage the scope of the prescription—we must first make some simplifying assumptions.

The Simplifying Assumptions

The following assumptions help us communicate more clearly what type of system the prescription can be applied to and also help manage your expectations for what the prescription can deliver.

- The followers of the prescription have read and understood this book and/or received some training reasonably consistent with its methodology and practices.
- The application being developed is a stand-alone application, not a complex system of subsystems or a project with a much larger scope. In addition, there are no contractual requirements for processes or documents in a specific format.

- The team size is small to moderate, perhaps 10–30 members.
- The software is being designed for use by others: an external customer who is reasonably available to the team.
- It's a new application, so the team can "start from scratch" when building the project.
- The team members will use modern software methods and are familiar with the basic concepts of use cases and iterative development.
- The team members have reasonable tool support, including requirements management tools, modeling tools, a change request system, and change management tools.

In other words, this looks like the right project context in which to deploy the agile requirements method we described in Chapter 30.

The Prescription

So finally, with this context in hand, here is a step-by-step prescription for a requirements method in the agile style.

Step 1: Get Organized

a. Meet with your team and agree on the basic software processes you will employ.

b. Decide how you will manage requirements on the project and document this process in a short one- to two-page requirements management plan.

c. Decide what types of software tooling you will apply to the project.

d. Determine a configuration management plan for your code and requirements artifacts.

e. Establish an iteration plan and determine the basic project metrics and reporting disciplines.

Step 2: Understand the Problem Being Solved

a. Execute the five-step problem analysis process.

1. Gain agreement on the problem being solved. Write it down.
2. Understand the root cause of the problem (if applicable to your situation).
3. Identify the stakeholders and users, or actors, in your system.
4. Define the system boundary. Document the boundary and the identified stakeholders and actors in a system context diagram or preliminary use-case model.
5. Identify constraints imposed on the solution. Write them down.

b. Circulate the problem statement to external stakeholders and insist that you gain agreement on the problem statement before moving forward.

Step 3: Understand User and Stakeholder Needs

a. Create a structured interview, using the generic template from Chapter 10, pertinent to your application.

b. Interview 5–15 users/stakeholders identified in step 2.

c. Summarize the interviews by aggregating the top 10–15 user needs, or use the "pithy quote approach"; that is, document 10 or 15 particularly memorable stakeholder's quotes that reflect their needs in their own words.

d. Use the quotes or the restated needs to start your requirements pyramid.

e. Facilitate a requirements workshop for your project. Use "out-of-the-box" and "in-the-box" warm-up papers (use "in-the-box" data from step 3c).

    1. Run a brainstorming session to identify/refine features.

    2. Perform idea reduction and feature prioritization.

    3. Use the *critical, important,* and *useful* classification.

f. Rerun the workshop once or twice during the project to provide a format for ongoing customer input.

g. Create storyboards for all innovative concepts. Present them, propose an initial set of use cases to your users, and get user feedback.

h. Ensure that your process yields early iterations that the users can test in *their* environment.

Step 4: Define the System

a. Adopt the Vision document concept and create a template to suit your project's needs.

b. Create a product position statement. Circulate it widely and make sure your customer agrees with it. If you don't have agreement, stop and get it.

c. Enter in the Vision document all features identified in step 3 and through other inputs, such as development, help desk, and marketing. Trace these features back to user needs. Use attributes of priority (critical, important, useful), risk (high, medium, low), effort (team-months), stability (high, medium, low), and release (v1.0 and so on). Define the commercial requirements (licensing, documentation, legal, regulatory, and so on) in the whole product plan.

d. Make the Vision document be *the* living document for your project. Publish it for easy access and review. Make the project champion, by default, the official channel for changing features. Use a Delta Vision document as you move forward.

e. Develop the use-case model for your project so that all stakeholders can see what actors the system supports and how it supports them.

Step 5: Continuously Manage Scope and Manage Change

a. Based on effort estimates from the team, determine the baseline for each release in the Vision document, using an attribute of "version number."

b. Get customer agreement on scope. Help the team make the hard scope decisions and *get the decisions behind you.*

c. Preach and teach iterative development. Build iterations monthly or weekly. Communicate and manage expectations everywhere.

d. Manage change by using the baseline. Use the Delta Vision document to capture all new features that arise through the normal course of events. Make sure that all suggested features are recorded so that none are lost. Empower a change control board to make the hard decisions.

e. Install a change request management system to capture all requests for change, and ensure that all requests go through that system to the change control board.

Step 6: Refine the System Definition

a. Refine the use-case model, use-case specifications, and supplementary specifications to whatever level of detail is necessary to assure that your team members are all developing the same system.

b. Have the development team and test team adopt and manage this workload. Assist them with training and find them help if they need it. Use formal analysis methods only when you cannot afford to be misunderstood.

c. Trace nonfunctional requirements to and from use cases and features.

d. Ensure that you have discovered all the nonfunctional requirements for your system, including design constraints. The template you use should prompt you to make sure that you have asked the right questions.

Step 7: Build the Right System

a. Engage the test department in the requirements management challenge now. Have testers involved in test planning from the beginning. Have the test team review the use cases as they are developed, and look for additional alternative flows and events. Brainstorm potential exception conditions. Develop scenarios and test cases directly from the use cases. Determine a strategy for testing nonfunctional requirements.

b. Rely on the use cases and use-case realizations in the design model to integrate design elements with the requirements. Use implicit traceability through the use-case realizations for impact assessment as change occurs.

c. Develop regression testing processes that are as automated and efficient as possible, with the goal being the ability to fully regression test the system at every new iteration.

Step 8: Manage the Requirements Process

a. The product manager or project champion should maintain responsibility for the Vision document, attend weekly reviews with the team to assess status, and set up default reports and queries to assist this effort.

b. Monitor the software requirements management process to assure that the vision is fulfilled in the use-case model and in the implementation.

c. Engage the quality assurance team to help monitor the requirements maintenance, change management, and test processes.

d. Participate or drive the change control process, assuring that impact is assessed *before* significant changes are allowed into the system.

Step 9: Congratulations! You've Shipped a Product!

ON TO THE NEXT RELEASE!

Congratulations! You and your team have shipped a quality, albeit scope-managed, first release of your new system. You did it with quality and perhaps even a little style, and you got to spend the year-end holidays at home with your family. And your customers are *happy*. OK, perhaps they are not ecstatic; many of them were hoping for more. But they are *still your customers*, and they *eagerly await the next release.*

Now, go back to (about) step 3e and build the next significant release of your new product or system.

By the way, don't forget to have some fun! Building great products and systems is a blast! We love this business!

APPENDIXES

- **Appendix A**   HOLIS Artifacts
- **Appendix B**   Vision Document Template
- **Appendix C**   Use-Case Specification Template
- **Appendix D**   Supplementary Specification Template
- **Appendix E**   Requirements Management in the Rational Unified Process
- **Appendix F**   Requirements Management in the SEI-CMM and within ISO 9000:2000

HOLIS ARTIFACTS

Note: This case study, including the names of the company, the participants, and the invented product, is entirely fictional.

BACKGROUND FOR THE CASE STUDY

Lumenations, Ltd.

Lumenations, Ltd. has been a worldwide supplier of commercial lighting systems for use in professional theater and amateur stage productions for more than 40 years. In 2002, its annual revenues peaked at approximately $120 million, and sales are flat. Lumenations is a public company, and the lack of growth in sales—no, worse, the lack of any reasonable prospect for improving growth in sales—is taking its toll on the company and its shareholders. The last annual meeting was quite uncomfortable since there was little new to report regarding the company's prospects for growth. The stock climbed briefly to $25 per share last spring on a spate of new orders but has since crept back down to around $15 per share.

The theater equipment industry as a whole is flat, and there is little new development. The industry is mature and already well consolidated, and since Lumenations' stock is in the tank and its capitalization is only modest, acquisition is not an option for the company.

What's needed is a *new* marketplace, not too remote from what the company does best, but one in which there is substantial opportunity for growth in revenue and profits. After conducting a thorough market research project and spending many dollars on marketing consultants, the company has decided to enter a new market, that of *lighting automation for high-end residential systems.* This market is apparently growing at 25 percent to 35 percent each year. Even better, the market is immature, and none of the established players has a dominant market position. Lumenations' strong worldwide distribution channel will be a real asset in the marketplace, and the distributors are hungry for new products. Looks like a great opportunity.

The HOLIS Software Development Team

The project for the case study is the development of HOLIS, our code name for an innovative new HOme LIghting automation System to be marketed by Lumenations. The HOLIS team is typical in terms of its size and scope. For the purposes of our case study, we've made it a fairly small team, only 15 team members, but it's large enough that all of the necessary skills can be fairly represented by individuals with some degree of specialization in their roles. It's the structure of the team that's most important, and by adding more developers and testers, the structure of the HOLIS team scales well to a size of 30–50 people and commensurately larger software applications than HOLIS will require.

To address the new marketplace, Lumenations has set up a new division, the Home Lighting Automation Division. Since the division and the technology are mostly new to Lumenations, the HOLIS team has been assembled mostly from new hires, although a few team members have been transferred from the Commercial Lighting Division. Figure A–1 is an organization chart showing the development team and the relationships among the team members.

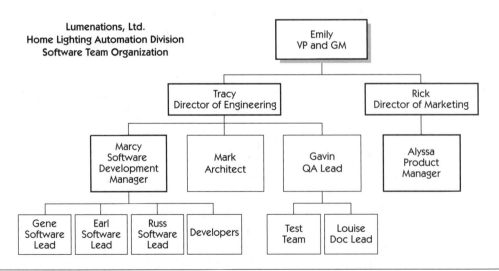

Figure A–1   The HOLIS software development team

Team Skill 1: Analyzing the Problem
Lumenations Problem Statement

In analyzing the problem, the team discovered that there are actually three different groups of stakeholders, each of whom sees the problem differently. Thus the team decided to develop three problem statements, the first of which seemed to state the obvious problem from the company's perspective (Table A–1).

Table A–1   Problem Statement for Lumenations

Element	Description
The problem of . . .	Slowing growth in the company's core professional theater marketplaces.
Affects . . .	The company, its employees, and its shareholders.
And results in . . .	Unacceptable business performance and lack of substantive opportunities for growth in revenue and profitability.
Benefits of a solution . . .	Involving new products and a potential new marketplace for the company's products and services include ▪ Revitalization of the company and its employees ▪ Increased loyalty and retention of the company's distributors ▪ Higher revenue growth and profitability ▪ Upturn in the company's stock price

Next, the team also decided to see whether it could understand the "problem" from the perspectives of a future customer (end user) and potential distributors/builders (Lumenations' customers). The team developed the problem statements shown in Tables A–2 and A–3, respectively.

Table A–2   Problem Statement for the Homeowner

Element	Description
The problem of . . .	The lack of product choices, limited functionality, and the high cost of existing home lighting automation systems.
Affects . . .	The homeowners of high-end residential systems.
And results in . . .	Unacceptable performance of the purchased systems or, more often than not, a decision not to automate.
Benefits of a solution . . .	That comprised the "right" lighting automation solution could include ▪ Higher homeowner satisfaction and pride of ownership ▪ Increased flexibility and usability of the residence ▪ Improved safety, comfort, and convenience

Table A–3   Problem Statement for the Distributor

Element	Description
The problem of . . .	The lack of product choices, limited functionality, and the high cost of existing home lighting automation systems.
Affects . . .	The distributors and builders of high-end residential systems.
And results in . . .	Few opportunities for marketplace differentiation and no new opportunities for higher-margin products.
Benefits of a solution . . .	That comprised the "right" lighting automation solution could include ■ Differentiation ■ Higher revenues and higher profitability ■ Increased market share

System Block Diagram with Actors Identified

Figure A–2 identifies the actors in this case study. Figures A–3, A–4, and A–5 show the subsystem block diagrams.

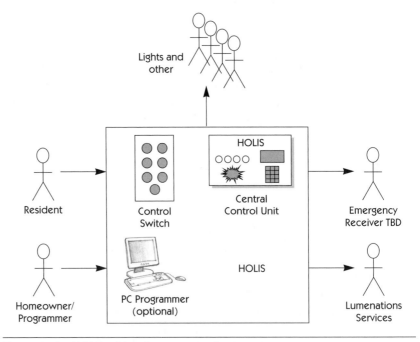

Figure A–2   HOLIS with subsystems and actors

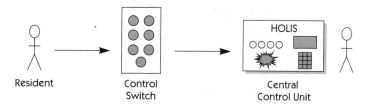

Figure A–3   Control Switch subsystem with actors

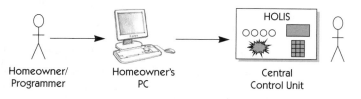

Figure A–4   PC Programmer subsystem with actors

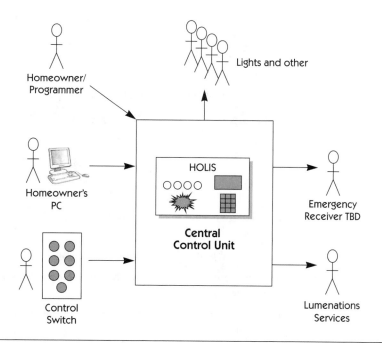

Figure A–5   Central Control Unit subsystem with actors

Actor Survey

A number of actors will interact with HOLIS (Table A–4).

Table A–4   Actors for HOLIS

Actor	Comments
Lights and other	Output devices, lights and dimmer controls, others to be determined
Homeowner/ Programmer	Homeowner programs direct to Central Control Unit or through programmer PC
Emergency Receiver	Unknown; under investigation
Resident	Homeowner using Control Switch to change lighting
Lumenations Services	Lumenations employees supporting remote programming and maintenance activities

Stakeholder Survey

HOLIS has a number of nonactor stakeholders, both external and internal (Table A–5).

Table A–5   Nonactor Stakeholders for HOLIS

Stakeholder	Comments
External	
Distributors	Lumenations' direct customer
Builders	Lumenations' customer's customer: the general contractor responsible to the homeowner for the end result
Electrical contractors	Responsible for installation and support
Internal	
Development team	Lumenations' team
Marketing/product management	Will be represented by Alyssa, product manager
Lumenations' general management	Funding and outcome accountability

Constraints Imposed on the Solution

Over a period of 45 days at the beginning of the product development effort, the HOLIS development team and Lumenations management identified, discussed, and agreed on the constraints listed in Table A–6.

Table A–6 Constraints for the HOLIS project

ID #	Description	Rationale
1	Version 1.0 will be released to manufacturing by January 5.	This is the only product launch opportunity this year.
2	The team will adopt UML modeling, OO-based methodologies, and the Unified Software Development Process.	We believe these technologies will provide increased productivity and more robust systems.
3	The software for the Central Control Unit and PC Programmer will be written in Java. Assembly language will be used for the Control Switch.	These choices provide consistency and maintainability; also, the team knows these languages.
4	A prototype system *must* be displayed at the December Home Automation trade show.	We want to take distributors' orders for the first quarter of the fiscal year.
5	The microprocessor subsystem for the Central Control Unit will be copied from the professional division's advanced lighting system project (ALSP).	We can use an existing design and an inventoried part.
6	The only PC Programmer configuration supported will be compatible with Windows 2000 and Windows XP.	This way we can better manage the scope for release 1.0.
7	The team will be allowed to hire two new full-time employees, after a successful inception phase, with whatever skill set is determined to be necessary.	The maximum allowable budget expansion limits us to two new hires.
8	The KCH5444 single-chip microprocessor will be used in the Control Switch.	The company already uses this microprocessor.
9	Purchased software components will be permitted as long as there is no continuing royalty obligation to the company.	We want to avoid any long-term cost of goods sold impact for software.

TEAM SKILL 2: UNDERSTANDING USER AND STAKEHOLDER NEEDS

Summary of User Needs as Collected from Interviews

A number of homeowners, two distributors, and one electrical contractor were interviewed.

From the homeowner's perspective:

- Flexible and modifiable lighting control for entire house
- "Futureproof" ("As technology changes, I'd like compatibility with new technologies that might emerge.")
- Attractive, unobtrusive, ergonomic
- Fully independent and programmable or (reconfigurable) switches for each room in the house
- Additional security and peace of mind
- Intuitive operation ("I'd like to be able to explain it to my 'techno-phobic' mother.")
- A reasonable system cost, with low switch costs
- Easy and inexpensive to fix
- Flexible switch configurations (from one to seven "buttons" per switch)
- Out of sight, out of mind
- 100 percent reliability
- Vacation security settings
- Ability to create scenes, such as special housewide lighting settings for a party
- No increase in electrical or fire hazards in the home
- Ability, after a power failure, to restore the lights the way they were
- Programmable by the homeowner, using an existing PC
- Dimmers wherever the homeowner wants them
- Programmable by the homeowner, without using a PC
- Programmable by somebody else, so the homeowner doesn't have to do it
- Ability to turn on some lights manually if the system fails
- Interfaces to the home security system
- Interfaces to other home automation (HVAC, audio/video, and so on)

From the distributor's perspective:

- A competitive product offering
- Some strong product differentiation
- An easy way to train salespeople

- Ability to demonstrate the system in the shop
- High gross margins

The Requirements Workshop

While the interviewing process was under way, the development team met with marketing and decided to hold a requirements workshop for the HOLIS project. They invited the attendees listed in Table A–7.

Table A–7 Attendees of the HOLIS Requirements Workshop

Name	Role	Title	Comments
Rick	Facilitator	Director of marketing	
Alyssa	Participant	HOLIS product manager	Project champion
Marcy	Participant	Software development manager	Development responsibility for HOLIS
Lucy	Participant		Prospective homeowner
Elmer	Participant		Prospective homeowner
E.C.	Participant	CEO, Automation Equip	Lumenations' largest distributor
Raquel	Participant	GM, EuroControls	Lumenations' European distributor
Betty	Participant	President, Krystel Electric	Local electrical contractor
Rusty	Participant	President, Rosewind Construction	Custom homebuilder
Emily	Observer	VP and GM, Lumenations	
Various members	Observer	Development team	All team members who were available

The Workshop Prior to the workshop, the team put together a warm-up package consisting of:

- A few recent magazines articles highlighting the trends in home automation
- Copies of selective interviews that had been conducted
- A summarized list of the needs that had been identified to date

Rick brushed up on his facilitation skills, and Alyssa handled the logistics for the workshop.

The Session   The session was held at a hotel near the airport and began promptly at 8 A.M. Rick introduced the agenda for the day and the rules for the workshop, including the workshop tickets. Figure A–6 provides a perspective on the workshop.

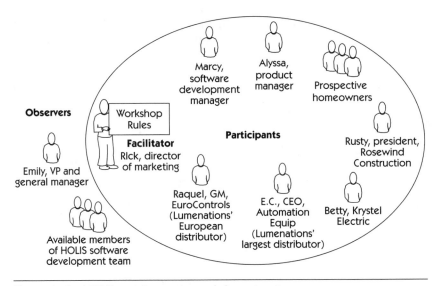

Figure A–6   HOLIS requirements workshop structure

In general, the workshop went very well, and all participants were able to have their input heard. Rick did a fine job of facilitating, but one awkward period occurred when Rick got into an argument with Alyssa about priorities for a couple of features. (The team members decided that for any future workshop, they would bring in an outside facilitator.) Rick led a brainstorming session on potential features for HOLIS, and the team used cumulative voting to decide on relative priorities. Table A–8 shows the results.

The Analysis of Results   The results of the process turned out as expected, except for two significant items.

1. "Built-in security" appeared very high on the priority list. This feature had been mentioned in previous interviews but had not made it to the top of anyone's priority list. After a quick offline review, Alyssa noted that built-in security, such as the ability to flash lights, an optional horn, and optional emergency call-out system, was apparently not

Table A–8   Features from the HOLIS Workshop, Sorted by Priority

ID	Features	Votes
23	Custom lighting scenes	121
16	Automatic timing settings for lights and so on	107
4	Built-in security features: lights, alarms, and bells	105
6	100 percent reliability	90
8	Easy-to-program, non-PC control unit	88
1	Easy-to-program control stations	77
5	Vacation settings	77
13	Any light can be dimmed	74
9	Uses my own PC for programming	73
14	Entertain feature	66
20	Close garage doors	66
19	Automatically turn on closet lights when door opened	55
3	Interface to home security system	52
2	Easy to install	50
18	Turn on lights automatically when someone approaches a door	50
7	Instant lighting on/off	44
11	Can drive drapes, shades, pumps, and motors	44
15	Control lighting and so on via phone	44
10	Interfaces to home automation system	43
22	Gradual mode: slowly increase/decrease illumination	34
26	Master control stations	31
12	Easily expanded when remodeling	25
25	Internationalized user interface	24
21	Interface to audio/video system	23
24	Restore after power fail	23
17	Controls HVAC	22
28	Voice activation	7
27	Web site–like user presentation	4

offered by any competitive system. The distributors commented that although they were surprised by this input, they felt that it *would* be a competitive differentiation and agreed that this should be a high-priority feature. Betty and Rusty agreed. Based on this conclusion, marketing decided to include this functionality and to position it as a unique, competitive differentiator in the marketplace. This became one of the *defining features* for HOLIS.

2. In addition, feature 25, "Internationalized user interface," did not get a lot of votes. (This seemed to make sense to the team because the U.S.-based homeowners could not have cared less about how well the product sold in Europe!) The distributor, however, stated flatly that if the product was not internationalized at version 1.0, it would *not* be introduced in Europe. The team noted this position and agreed to explore the level of effort necessary to achieve internationalization in the 1.0 release.

HOLIS System-Level Use-Case Model Survey

Table A–9 lists some of the use cases for the HOLIS project. Note that the remainder of the use cases are deleted for brevity; a total of 20 system-level use cases are defined for v1.0 release.

Table A–9   HOLIS Use Cases

Name	Description	Actor(s)
Create Custom Lighting Scene	Resident creates a custom lighting scene.	Resident, Lights
Initiate Emergency Receiver	Resident initiates emergency action.	Resident
Control Light	Resident turns light(s) on or off or sets desired dim effect.	Resident, Lights
Program Switch	Homeowner/Programmer changes or sets the actions for a particular button/switch.	Homeowner/Programmer
Remote Programming	Lumenations service provider does remote programming based on request from Resident.	Lumenations Services
On Vacation	Homeowner/Programmer sets vacation setting for extended away period.	Homeowner/Programmer
Set Timing Sequence	Homeowner/Programmer sets time-based automated lighting sequence.	Homeowner/Programmer

TEAM SKILL 3: DEFINING THE SYSTEM

HOLIS Requirements Organization

Figure A–7 shows the HOLIS requirements organization.

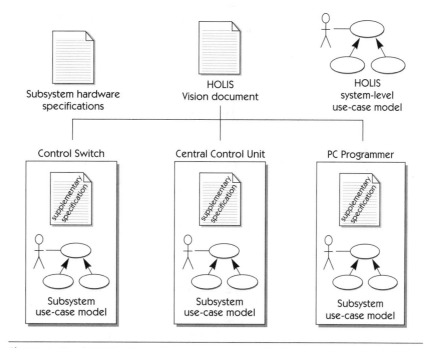

Figure A–7   Organization of HOLIS requirements information

HOLIS Vision Document

We present an abbreviated form of the HOLIS Vision document here, with many sections omitted. A full, generic Vision document template, which you might wish to adapt for your purposes, appears in Appendix B.

Lumenations, Ltd.

HOLIS
Vision Document

© 2002 Lumenations, Ltd.
102872 Cambridge Ave.
Marcy, NJ 12345

REVISION HISTORY			
Date	**Revision**	**Description**	**Author**
1/21/03	1.0	Initial version	Alyssa
2/11/03	1.1	Updated after requirements workshop	E. Green

TABLE OF CONTENTS

2.4.1   From the Homeowner's Perspective

- Flexible and modifiable lighting control for entire house
- "Futureproof" ("As technology changes, I'd like compatibility with new technologies that might emerge.")
- Attractive, unobtrusive, ergonomic
- Fully independent and programmable or (reconfigurable) switches for each room in the house
- Additional security and peace of mind
- Intuitive operation ("I'd like to be able to explain it to my 'technophobic' mother.")
- A reasonable system cost, with low switch costs
- Easy and inexpensive to fix
- Flexible switch configurations (from one to seven "buttons" per switch)
- Out of sight, out of mind
- 100 percent reliability
- Vacation security settings
- Ability to create scenes, such as special housewide lighting settings for a party
- No increase in electrical or fire hazards in the home
- Ability, after a power failure, to restore the lights the way they were
- Programmable by the homeowner, using an existing PC
- Dimmers wherever the homeowner wants them
- Programmable by the homeowner, without using a PC
- Programmable by somebody else, so the homeowner doesn't have to do it
- Ability to turn on some lights manually if the system fails
- Interfaces to the home security system
- Interfaces to other home automation (HVAC, audio/video, and so on)

2.4.2   From the Distributor's Perspective

- A competitive product offering
- Some strong product differentiation
- An easy way to train salespeople
- Ability to demonstrate the system in the shop
- High gross margins

2.5   Alternatives and Competition

3   Product Overview

3.1   Product Perspective

3.2   HOLIS Product Position Statement

For	homeowners building new, high-end homes
Who	would like to enhance their residence and their convenience, comfort, and safety
HOLIS	is a home lighting automation system
That	brings unprecedented, state-of-the-art lighting automation functionality, with ease of use and a reasonable price.
Unlike	the Lightomation Systems series from Skowron's Industrial Controls
Our product	combines the very latest in home automation functionality with built-in security features, and costs less to install and to maintain.

3.3   Summary of Capabilities

3.4   Assumptions and Dependencies

3.5   Cost and Pricing

4   Feature Attributes

4.1   Status

4.2   Priority
Apply a *critical*, *important*, *useful* prioritization scheme.

4.3   Effort
Low, *medium*, and *high* as set by the development team.

4.4   Risk
Set by development team.

4.5   Stability

4.6   Target Release

4.7   Assigned to

4.8   Reason

5   Product Features

5.1   Critical Features for v1.0

- Fea23: Custom lighting scenes. The system gives the homeowner the ability to create up to TBD custom lighting scenes. Each scene provides a preset level of illumination for each lighting bank throughout the residence. Scenes may be activated from either the Control Switch or the Central Control Unit.
- Fea16: Automatic lighting settings. The homeowner can create preset, time-based schedules for certain lighting events to happen.
- Fea4: Security sequence. The system has a built-in security feature that provides a one-button, panic alarm emergency sequence activation from any control switch in the house. The security sequence sets the lights to a predetermined scene setting and will also (optionally for each) flash the lights, activate an alarm, make a dial-up call to a predetermined number, and deliver a voice-based preprogrammed message. The system also closes a relay contact, which homeowners can use to control devices of their choice.
- Fea6: Reliability. Our homeowners have repeatedly stressed that the system be as close to 100 percent reliable as possible. This is a particular concern with the security sequence.

(Remainder of features deleted for brevity.)

5.2   Important Features for v1.0

- Fea20: Garage door control. The system supports the garage door as one of the controlled output devices. The software must manage the control of the output accordingly and will need to provide a garage door metaphor/icon and support for programming the feature.
- Fea2: Smart install. Ease of installation has been a key concern of our distributor/customers and will be a key differentiator for us with our channels organization. The software should support this need by whatever means are determined to be reasonable and viable. This could include online help for an installer's guide and instruction manual, a troubleshooting guide, in-process status assessment indication, automated fault detection, and so on.

(Remainder of optional features deleted for brevity.)

5.3   Future Features

Appendix A in the Vision document lists features that have been identified for possible future versions of the system. Although we agree that no significant investment is to be made in these in v1.0, we do ask that the marketing and engineering teams review this list and, wherever possible, keep these needs in mind as the design and development of the v1.0 system proceeds.

7   Other Product Requirements

7.1   Applicable Standards

7.2   System Requirements

7.3   Licensing, Security, and Installation

7.4   Performance Requirements

8   Documentation Requirements

8.1   User Manual

8.2   Online Help

8.3   Installation Guides, Configuration, Read Me File

8.4   Labeling and Packaging

9   Glossary

Appendix A   Future Features Identified in Requirements Workshop

Appendix B   Storyboard as Presented to Workshop Attendees

Appendix C   Exemplary Use Cases

TEAM SKILL 4: MANAGING SCOPE

After the requirements workshop, the team was chartered with the responsibility to assess the level of effort for each feature and to come up with a first draft of the v1.0 baseline. It was necessary to apply rigorous scope management because of the constraints on the team, including the "drop dead" date of having a prototype available at the trade show in December and the (even tougher) date of a release to manufacturing in January. The team used the high-medium-low heuristic to estimate the level of effort for each feature and then added the risk assessment for each feature. The team went on to perform the suggested scope management activities, with the results shown in Tables A–10 and A–11.

Table A–10   Prioritized HOLIS Features List with Effort and Risk Estimates

ID	Feature	Votes	Effort	Risk
23	Custom lighting scenes	121	Med	Low
16	Automatic timing settings for lights and so on	107	Low	Low
4	Built-in security features: lights, alarms, and bells	105	Low	High
6	100 percent reliability	90	High	High
8	Easy-to-program, non-PC control unit	88	High	Med
1	Easy-to-program control stations	77	Med	Med
5	Vacation settings	77	Low	Med
13	Any light can be dimmed	74	Low	Low
9	Uses my own PC for programming	73	High	Med
14	Entertain feature	66	Low	Low
20	Close garage doors	66	Low	Low
19	Automatically turn on closet lights when door opened	55	Low	High
3	Interface to home security system	52	High	High
2	Easy to install	50	Med	Med
18	Turn on lights automatically when someone approaches a door	50	Med	Med
7	Instant lighting on/off	44	High	High
11	Can drive drapes, shades, pumps, and motors	44	Low	Low
15	Control lighting and so on via phone	44	High	High
10	Interfaces to home automation system	43	High	High
22	Gradual mode: slowly increase/decrease illumination	34	Med	Low
26	Master control stations	31	High	High
12	Easily expanded when remodeling	25	Med	Med
25	Internationalized user interface	24	Med	High
21	Interface to audio/video system	23	High	High
24	Restore after power fail	23	N/A	N/A
17	Controls HVAC	22	High	High
28	Voice activation	7	High	High
27	Web site–like user presentation	4	Med	Low

Table A–11   Baseline for HOLIS v1.0 Features

ID	Feature	Votes	Effort	Risk	Marketing Comments
23	Custom lighting scenes	121	Med	Low	As flexible as possible
16	Automatic timing settings for lights and so on	107	Low	Low	As flexible as possible
4	Built-in security features: lights, alarms, and bells	105	Low	High	Marketing to do more research
6	100 percent reliability	90	High	High	Get as close to 100 percent as possible
8	Easy-to-program, non-PC control unit	88	High	Med	Provide dedicated controller
1	Easy-to-program control stations	77	Med	Med	As easy as feasible with measured effort
5	Vacation settings	77	Low	Med	
13	Any light can be dimmed	74	Low	Low	
9	Uses my own PC for programming	73	High	Med	Only one configuration supported in v1.0
25	**Internationalized CCU user interface**	24	Med	Med	Per agreement with European distributor
14	~~Entertain feature~~	~~66~~	~~Low~~	~~Low~~	(Not applicable, included in 23)
7	Instant lighting on/off	44	High	High	Make intelligent investments

v1.0 Mandatory Baseline: Everything above the line must be included or we will delay release.

ID	Feature	Votes	Effort	Risk	Marketing Comments
20	Close garage doors	66	Low	Low	May be little impact on software
2	Easy to install	50	Med	Med	Level of effort basis
11	Can drive drapes, shades, pumps, and motors	44	Low	Low	May be little impact on software
22	Gradual mode: slowly increase/decrease illumination	34	Med	Low	Nice if we can get it

v1.0 Optional: Do as many of the preceding as you can. (Alyssa)

Future Features: Below this line, no current development.

ID	Feature	Votes	Effort	Risk	Marketing Comments
29	**Internationalized PC Programmer interface**	N/A	**High**	**Med**	**Will become mandatory for version 2.0**
3	Interface to home security system	52	High	High	Can we at least provide a hardware interface? (Rick)
19	Automatically turn on closet lights when door opened	55	Low	High	

(continued on next page)

Table A–11 *Continued*

ID	Feature	Votes	Effort	Risk	Marketing Comments
19	Automatically turn on closet lights when door opened	55	Low	High	
18	Turn on lights automatically when someone approaches a door	50	Med	Med	
15	Control lighting and so on via phone	44	High	High	
10	Interfaces to home automation system	43	High	High	
26	Master control stations	31	High	High	
12	Easily expanded when remodeling	25	Med	Med	
21	Interface to audio/video system	23	High	High	
24	Restore after power fail	23	N/A	N/A	
17	Controls HVAC	22	High	High	
28	Voice activation	7	High	High	
27	Web site–like user presentation	4	Med	Low	

TEAM SKILL 5: REFINING THE SYSTEM DEFINITION
HOLIS Sample Use Case: Control Light

REVISION HISTORY			
Date	**Issue**	**Description**	**Author**
4/14/03	1.0	Initial creation of Control Light use case	Mark
4/15/03	1.1	Added second pre-condition to clarify operation	Gavin, QA lead

Brief Description This use case prescribes the way in which lights are turned on and off and also how they are dimmed and brightened in accordance with how long the user presses a button on the Control Switch.

Basic Flow   Basic flow begins when the Resident presses the On/Off/Dim button on the Control Switch. When the Resident removes pressure on the On/Off/Dim button within the timer period, the system "toggles" the state of the light as follows.

- If the light is On, the light is then turned Off, and there is no illumination.
- If the light is Off, the light is then turned On to the last remembered brightness level.

End of basic flow.

Alternative Flow of Events   When the Resident holds down the On/Off/Dim button for more than 1 second, the system initiates a brightening/dimming activity for the room's Light Bank.

While the Resident continues to press the On/Off/Dim button:

1. The brightness of the controlled light is smoothly increased to a system-wide maximum value at a rate of 10 percent per second.
2. When the brightness reaches its maximum value, the brightness of the controlled light is then smoothly decreased to a system-wide minimum value at a rate of 10 percent per second.
3. When the brightness reaches its minimum value, the use case continues at subflow step 1.

When the Resident releases the On/Off/Dim button:

4. The use case terminates and the brightness stays at the current level.

Pre-conditions for Control Light Use Case
- The selected On/Off/Dim button must be Dim Enabled.
- The selected On/Off/Dim button must be preprogrammed to control a Light Bank.

Post-condition for Control Light Use Case   On leaving this use case, the system remembers the current brightness level for the selected On/Off/Dim button.

Extension Points   None.

Special Requirements   Performance: For any action that is perceptible to the Resident, the response time from a control panel action to system response must be less than 50 milliseconds.

HOLIS Central Control Unit Supplementary Specification

For brevity, we present excerpts from the HOLIS supplementary specification here. Appendix D in this book contains a generic, annotated supplementary specification template you might wish to adopt.

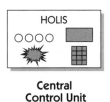

**Central
Control Unit**

Copyright © 2003 Lumenations, Ltd.

1 Introduction

1.1 Purpose

This is the supplementary specification for the v1.0 release of the HOLIS Central Control Unit (CCU) subsystem.

1.2 Scope

This specification is for the CCU only.

1.3 References

- HOLIS Vision Document
- HOLIS System Level Hardware Specification
- HOLIS System-Level Use-Case Model
- HOLIS Control Switch Use-Case Model and Supplementary Specification
- HOLIS PC Programmer Use-Case Model and Supplementary Specification

1.4 Assumptions and Dependencies

2 Functionality

SR1. OnLevel illumination parameter. Each controlled lighting bank that is Dim Enabled is controlled by the parameter OnLevel, which controls the percent of illumination to the light. The nine possible OnLevel settings are 10%, 20%, 30%, 40%, 50%, 60%, 70%, 80%, and 90%.

SR2. The system supports up to 255 event-time schedules. The allowable programming precision of an event-time schedule shall be 1 minute.

SR3. Event-time schedules can be programmed on either a 12-hour or a 24-hour clock. The user shall enter the data in the following format:

```
Event number (1-256), Time of day (in 24-hour HH:MM format)
```

SR4. Message protocol from Control Switch. Each button press on the control initiates a single 4-byte message to the CCU. The message protocol is as follows.

Address of sending device	Message number	Data	Checksum

The data fields in the message are mapped as follows.

SR4.1. **Address** 0–254, the logical address of the specific control switch sending the message

SR4.2. **Message Number** 0–255. Message numbers supported are

1. Normal key press
2. Emergency
3. Held down for the last 0.5 second

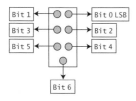

SR4.3. **Data**, each bit corresponding to a specific button on the key switch.

SR4.4. Message Acknowledgment. In reply to the message from the Control Switch, the CCU shall respond with the following message.

[55]	[FF]	Received data	Checksum

where 55 (hex) is the dedicated address of the CCU, FF (hex) is the Acknowledge Message code, Received data returns the data byte received from the CCU, and Checksum is the calculated checksum for the returned message.

3   Usability

4   Reliability

SR9. System availability must be greater than or equal to 99.99%.

SR10. The CCU shall have no defects that can interfere with normal operation of the homeowner's residence.

5   Performance

SR11. HOLIS shall execute event-time schedules with an accuracy of 1 minute ±5 seconds as measured by the system clock.

6   Supportability

7   Design Constraints

DC1. Control subsystem design is based on the controller module from the ALSP product line. BIOS should not be modified unless absolutely necessary.

DC2. The use case and supporting infrastructure for the emergency sequence must be validated to the highest reasonable commercial reliability standards.

8   Documentation Requirements

SR27. HOLIS ships with a Product Guide. The Product Guide contains all application guides, process guides, installation guides, tutorials, and glossary. The Product Guide is created as an HTML online guide. All applications needing to reference help link to the Product Guide. Microsoft Word copies of each of the guide sections are also shipped with the product.

SR29. The Installation Guide found in the Product Guide is also printed and shipped with the CD-ROM.

9   Purchased Components

10   Interfaces

10.1   User Interfaces

10.2   Hardware Interfaces

10.3   Software Interfaces

10.4   Communications Interfaces

11   Licensing, Security, and Installation Requirements

11.1   CCU Licensing Requirements

SR53. CCU software is factory installed and there are no user licensing or installation requirements.

11.2 Sublicensing Requirements

SR54. The Datamatch Java Library from the Oxford Foundation is incorporated in the application. The end user documentation included with the redistribution must include the following acknowledgment.

> *This product includes software developed by the Oxford Software Foundation (http://www.Oxfordxfound.org/).*

Alternately, this acknowledgment may appear in the software itself, if and wherever such third-party acknowledgments normally appear.

12 Legal, Copyright, and Other Notices

SR72. All code, product documents, online help, user interfaces, and About dialogs must contain the following copyright message.

> *Copyright © 2003-2004 Lumenations, Ltd. All rights reserved.*

SR75. Flash the standard corporate copyright notice, corporate logo, and HOLIS product logo for a minimum of 5 seconds during startup mode.

SR76. In idle mode, (when no programming is active), the display shall show the HOLIS logo.

13 Applicable Standards

14 Internationalization and Localization

SR89. All data processing components support UTF-8 character encoding.

SR90. All output text files must be ISO-8859-1 and –2 encoded. This supports all Latin-1 and Cyrillic languages.

SR97. The following are acceptable input content text file encodings: ASCII, Latin-1&2 (ISO-8859-1&2), UTF-8.

15 Physical Deliverables

16 Installation and Deployment

Appendix A   Glossary

TEAM SKILL 6: BUILDING THE RIGHT SYSTEM

HOLIS Sample Test Case 01: Test Control Light

REVISION HISTORY			
Date	**Revision**	**Description**	**Author**
4/14/03	1.0	First draft	Luis R.
4/15/03	1.1	Correction to increase/decrease rate	Bob S.

Description This test case, used to test instances of the use case Control Light, is used only to test dim-enabled Control Switch buttons that have been preassigned to a light bank.

Note: Run the test case multiple times and with different lengths of hold-button time to verify that the system is restoring OnLevel properly.

Test Case ID	Scenario	Description	Condition: Button Pressed < Timer Period	Condition: Button Pressed > Timer Period	Condition: Button Released After Being Held	Condition	Expected Result
1	1	Basic flow: Resident releases button before timer period ends	< 1 sec. in .1-sec. intervals	I	N/A	Light on	Light goes off
2	1	Basic flow: Resident releases button before timer period ends	< 1 sec. in .1-sec. intervals	I	N/A	Light off	Light goes on
3	2	Alternate flow: Resident continuously presses button for longer than timer period	I	1–60 sec.	N/A	N/A	Light level goes up and down continuously
4	3	Resident releases switch after continuously pressing button	I	I	V	N/A	Light stays at last brightness

HOLIS Sample Test Case 02:
Test Round-Trip Message Protocol

REVISION HISTORY			
Date	**Revision**	**Description**	**Author**
4/14/03	1.0	First draft	Adrienne

Description This test case tests the round-trip message protocol between the CCU and the Control Switch according to the requirements defined in the CCU Supplementary Specification. This test case tests the following requirements from the CCU and Control Switch Supplementary Specifications.

CCU Supplementary Specs	Control Switch Supplementary Specs
SR4, SR4.1, SR4.2, SR4.3, SR4.4	CSSR88, CSSR91–97, CSSR100–107*

* Note to file: The table above can be deleted after the traceability matrix is established. To minimize maintenance, the trace matrix is the only place we will maintain these links.

Events

Test Case ID	Event Description	Input 1	Input 2	Expected Result
5300	Press switch button 0 on Control Switch 1 and initiate message from CS to CCU.	Button only		CCU message-received indicator is lit, and CS message-received indicator is lit.
5301	Examine received message in diagnostic line of CCU display.			[01][01][01][5A]
5302	Examine sent message in CCU display.			[55][FF][01][F7]

(continued on next page)

Test Case ID	Event Description	Input 1	Input 2	Expected Result
5303	Press Control Switch buttons 0–5 simultaneously and hold for 3 seconds.	All buttons depressed 3+ seconds		CCU message-received indicator is lit. Three messages should be in the message display buffer.
	Examine message 1.			[01][01][3F][3C]
	(Remainder of test case deleted for brevity.)			

VISION DOCUMENT TEMPLATE

Fundamental to the success of a project is a Vision document that identifies and organizes the high-level user needs and features of an application. This document is updated as needed and shared among team members and other involved personnel. The document template in this appendix is intended to be used as a starting point and may be customized according to your organization's needs.

Company Name

Project Name
Vision Document

© 200X Company Name

REVISION HISTORY			
Date	**Revision**	**Description**	**Author**
mm/dd/yy	1.0	Initial version	Author name

TABLE OF CONTENTS

This section should provide an overview of the document and should contain the following subsections.

This document collects, analyzes, and defines high-level user needs and product features. Focus on capabilities needed by the target users and why these needs exist. The specific requirements of how the application fulfills these needs should be provided elsewhere in the use-case model and supplementary specification.

State the purpose of the product, its version, and intended use. This subsection should

- Identify the product or application to be created or enhanced
- Provide a general description of what the product will and, if necessary, will not do
- Describe the intended use of the product, including its relevant benefits, goals, and objectives

This subsection should

- Provide a list of all documents referenced elsewhere in the Vision document
- Identify each document by title, report number (if applicable), date, and publishing organization
- Specify the sources from which the references can be obtained
- This information may be provided by reference to an appendix or to another document.

To effectively provide products and services that meet your customers' needs, it is necessary to understand the challenges they confront when performing their jobs. This section should profile the intended users of the application and the key problems that limit the user's productivity. *This section should not be used to state specific requirements.* Instead, provide the background and the justification for why the features specified in Section 5 are needed.

2.1 User/Market Demographics

Summarize the key market demographics that motivate your product decisions. Describe and position target-market segments. Estimate the market's size and growth by using the number of potential users or the amount of money your customers spend trying to meet needs that your product/enhancement would fulfill. Review major industry trends and technologies. Answer these strategic questions.

- What is your organization's position in these markets?
- What would you like it to be?
- How does this product or service support your goals?

2.2 User Profiles

Describe each unique user of the system. User types can be as divergent as gurus and novices. For example, a guru might need a sophisticated, flexible tool with cross-platform support, whereas a novice might need an easy-to-use and user-friendly tool. A thorough profile should cover the following topics for each type of user:

- Technical background and degree of sophistication
- Key responsibilities
- Deliverables the user produces and for whom
- Trends that make the user's job easier or more difficult
- Problems that interfere with success
- The target user's definition of success and how the user is rewarded

2.3 User Environment

Detail the working environment of the target user. Here are some suggestions.

- How many people are involved in completing the task? Is this changing?
- How long is a task cycle? How much time is spent in each activity? Is this changing?
- Are there any unique environmental constraints: mobile, outdoors, in-flight, and so on?
- Which system platforms are in use today? Future platforms?
- What other applications are in use? Does your application need to integrate with them?

2.4   Key User Needs

List the key problems or needs as perceived by the user. Clarify the following issues for each problem.

- What are the reasons for this problem?
- How is it solved now?
- What solutions does the user envision?

It is important to understand the relative importance the user places on solving each problem. Ranking and cumulative-voting techniques indicate problems that *must* be solved versus issues the user would like addressed.

2.5   Alternatives and Competition

Identify alternatives the user perceives as available. These can include buying a competitor's product, building a homegrown solution, or simply maintaining the status quo. List any known competitive choices that exist or that may become available. Include the major strengths and weaknesses of each competitor as perceived by the end user.

2.5.1   Competitor 1

2.5.2   Competitor 2

3   Product Overview

This section provides a high-level view of the product capabilities, interfaces to other applications, and systems configurations. This section usually consists of three subsections, as follows.

3.1   Product Perspective

This subsection should put the product in perspective to other related products and the user's environment. If the product is independent and totally self-contained, state so here. If the product is a component of a larger system, this subsection should relate how these systems interact and should identify the relevant interfaces among the systems. One easy way to display the major components of the larger system, interconnections, and external interfaces is via a block diagram.

3.2   Product Position Statement

Provide an overall statement summarizing, at the highest level, the unique position the product intends to fill in the marketplace. Moore [1991] calls this the product position statement and recommends the following format.

For	*(target customer)*
Who	*(statement of the need or opportunity)*
The *(product name)*	is a *(product category)*
That	*(statement of key benefit, that is, compelling reason to buy)*
Unlike	*(primary competitive alternative)*
Our product	*(statement of primary differentiation)*

A product position statement communicates the intent of the application and the importance of the project to all concerned personnel.

3.3   Summary of Capabilities

Summarize the major benefits and features the product will provide. For example, a Vision document for a customer support system may use this subsection to address problem documentation, routing, and status reporting—without mentioning the amount of detail each of these functions requires.

Organize the features so that the list is understandable to the customer or to anyone else reading the document for the first time. A simple table listing the key benefits and their supporting features might suffice.

Customer Support System

Customer Benefit	Supporting Features
Benefit 1	Feature 1

3.4   Assumptions and Dependencies

List assumptions that, if changed, will alter the vision for the product. For example, an assumption may state that a specific operating system will be available for the hardware designated for the software product. If the operating system is not available, the vision will need to change.

3.5   Cost and Pricing

For products sold to external customers and for many in-house applications, cost and pricing issues can directly impact the application's definition and implementation. In this section, record any relevant cost and pricing constraints. For example, distribution costs (CD-ROMs, CD mastering) or other cost-of-goods-sold constraints (manuals, packaging) may be material to the project's success or irrelevant, depending on the nature of the application.

4   Feature Attributes

Features have attributes that provide additional project information that can be used to evaluate, track, prioritize, and manage the product items proposed for implementation. This section provides suggested attributes for use in your Vision document. This section need describe only the attributes you've chosen and their meaning, so all parties can better understand the context of each feature.

4.1   Status

The status is set after negotiation and review by the project management team. Status information tracks progress during definition of the project baseline.

- **Proposed:** Used to describe features that are under discussion but have not yet been reviewed and accepted by the "official channel," such as a working group consisting of representatives from the project team, product management, and user or customer community
- **Approved:** Capabilities that are deemed useful and feasible and have been approved by the official channel for implementation
- **Incorporated:** Features incorporated into the product baseline at a specific time

4.2   Priority

Product priorities (benefits) are set by the marketing team, the product manager, or the business analyst. Ranking features by their relative priority to the end user opens a dialogue with customers, analysts, and members of the development team. Priorities are used in managing scope and determining development priority. One possible prioritization scheme follows.

- **Critical:** Essential features. Failure to implement means that the system will not meet customer needs. All critical features must be implemented in the release, or the schedule will slip.
- **Important:** Features important to the effectiveness and efficiency of the system for most applications. The functionality cannot be easily provided in another way. Lack of inclusion of an important feature may affect customer or user satisfaction or even revenue, but release will not be delayed due to lack of any important feature.
- **Useful:** Features that are useful in less typical applications, will be used less frequently, or for which reasonably efficient workarounds can be achieved. No significant revenue loss or customer satisfaction impact can be expected if such an item is not included in a release.

4.3   Effort

The level of effort is set by the development team and used in managing scope and determining development priority. Because some features require more time and resources than others, estimating the number of team- or person-weeks, lines of code required, or function points, for example, is the best way to gauge complexity and to set expectations of what can and cannot be accomplished in a given time frame.

4.4   Risk

The development team sets the level of risk, based on the probability that the project will experience undesirable events, such as cost overruns, schedule delays, or even cancellation. Most project managers find categorizing risks as **High**, **Medium**, and **Low** sufficient, although finer gradations are possible. Risk can often be assessed indirectly by measuring the uncertainty (range) of the project team's schedule estimate.

4.5   Stability

The analyst and development team sets the stability attribute, based on the probability that the feature will change or the team's understanding of the feature will change. This information is used to help establish development priorities and to determine those items for which additional elicitation is the appropriate next action.

4.6   Target Release

The target release attribute records the intended product version in which the feature will first appear. This field can be used to allocate features into a particular baseline release. When the target release is combined with the status field, your team can propose, record, and discuss various features of the release without committing them to development. Only features whose status is set to Incorporated and whose target release is defined will be implemented. When scope management occurs, the target release version number can be increased so the item will remain in the Vision document but will be scheduled for a later release.

4.7   Assigned To

In many projects, features will be assigned to "feature teams" responsible for further elicitation, writing the software requirements, and implementation. This simple list will help everyone on the project team better understand responsibilities.

4.8   Reason

This text field is used to track the source of the requested feature. Features exist for specific reasons. This field records an explanation or a reference to an explanation. For example, the reference might be to a page and line number of a product requirement specification, or to a minute marker on a video of an important customer interview.

5   Product Features

This section documents the product features. Features provide the system capabilities that are necessary to deliver benefits to the users. Each feature provides a service that fulfills a user need. For example, a feature of a problem-tracking system might be the ability to "provide trending reports." Trending reports might, in turn, support a user need to "better understand the status of my project."

Because the Vision document is reviewed by a wide variety of involved personnel and serves as the basis of agreement, features should be expressed in the user's natural language. Features descriptions should be short and pithy, typically one or two sentences.

To effectively manage application complexity, we recommend that for any new system or increment to an existing system the capabilities be abstracted to a high enough level to result in 25–50 features. These features provide the fundamental basis for product definition, scope management, and project management. Each feature will be expanded in greater detail in the follow-on specifications.

Throughout this section, each feature should be perceivable by users, operators, or other external systems.

5.1   Feature 1

5.2   Feature 2

6   Exemplary Use Cases

[Optional] You may wish to describe a few exemplary use cases, perhaps those that are architecturally significant or those that will most readily help the reader understand how the system is intended to be used. In any event, all use cases will be found in the use-case model.

Note: The following sections contain some of the identified primary nonfunctional requirements for the system. These will typically be elaborated in the supplementary specification (template provided in Appendix D) later in the development cycle. Once the supplementary specification has been developed, you may wish to delete these sections from the Vision document so that these items are not maintained in two places.

However, new nonfunctional requirements may often be recorded here in the Delta Vision document format.

---

7   Other Product Requirements

7.1   Applicable Standards

List all standards the product must comply with, such as legal and regulatory (FDA, FCC), communications standards (TCP/IP, ISDN), platform compliance standards (Windows, UNIX), and quality and safety standards (UL, ISO, CMM).

7.2   System Requirements

Define any system requirements necessary to support the application. These may include the supported host operating systems and network platforms, configurations, memory, peripherals, and companion software.

7.3   Licensing, Security, and Installation

Licensing, security, and installation issues can also directly impact the development effort. For example, the need to support restrictions on use, trial or evaluation usage, copy protection, right to create a backup, and provisions for individual or concurrent user licensing will create additional system requirements that must be considered in the development effort. Installation requirements may also affect coding or create the need for separate installation software.

7.4   Performance Requirements

Performance issues can include such items as user load factors, bandwidth or communication capacity, throughput, accuracy, reliability, or response times under a variety of loading conditions.

8   Documentation Requirements

This section describes the documentation that must be developed to support successful application deployment.

8.1   User Manual

Describe the purpose and contents of the user manual. Discuss its desired length, level of detail, need for index and glossary, tutorial versus reference manual strategy, and so on. Formatting and printing constraints should also be identified.

8.2   Online Help

Many applications provide an online help system to assist the user. The nature of these systems is unique to application development since they combine aspects of programming, such as hyperlinks, with aspects of technical writing, such as organization and presentation. Many people have found that the development of an online help system is a project within a project that benefits from up-front scope management and planning activity.

8.3   Installation Guides, Configuration, Read Me File

A document that includes installation instructions and configuration guidelines is important to a full solution. Also, a read me file is typically included as a standard component. The read me file may include a "What's New with This Release" section and a discussion of compatibility issues with earlier releases. Most users also appreciate documentation in the read me file defining any known bugs and workarounds.

8.4   Labeling and Packaging

Today's state-of-the-art applications provide a consistent look and feel that begins with product packaging and manifests itself through installation menus, splash screens, help systems, GUI dialogs, and so on. This section defines the needs and types of labeling to be incorporated into the code. Examples include copyright and patent notices, corporate logos, standardized icons and other graphic elements, and so on.

9   Glossary

The glossary defines all terms that are unique to the project. Include any acronyms or abbreviations that may not be understood by users or other readers of this document.

Use-Case Specification Template

The following template is provided for a use-case specification, which contains the textual properties of the use case. This document may be created with a word processing system, requirements management tool, or other documentation tool. The use-case diagrams can be developed in a visual modeling or graphical drawing tool.

REVISION HISTORY			
Date	**Issue**	**Description**	**Author**
mm/dd/yy	x.x	Details	Author name

Note: The revision history may be provided by a requirements management or configuration management tool.

TABLE OF CONTENTS

Normally, a use-case specification will not be long enough to warrant a table of contents for the use case. But this element may be required if the use case presents unusual problems in finding portions of the specification.

USE-CASE NAME
Brief Description

State the role and purpose of the use case. A single paragraph should suffice for this description.

System or SubSystem

Give the name of the system or subsystem to which the use case applies.

Flow of Events

Basic Flow

This use case starts when the actor does something. An actor always initiates use cases. The use case should describe what the actor does and what the system does in response. The use case should be phrased in the form of a dialogue between the actor and the system.

The use case should describe what happens inside the system but not how or why. If information is exchanged, be specific about what is passed back and forth. For example, it is not very illuminating to say that the actor enters customer information—it is better to say that the actor enters the customer's name and address. A glossary is often useful to keep the complexity of the use case manageable; you may want to define customer information there, to keep the use case from drowning in details.

Simple alternatives may be presented within the text of the use case. If it takes only a few sentences to describe what happens when there is an alternative, do it directly within the flow-of-events section. If the alternative flows are more complex, use a separate section. For example, an alternative flow describes how to describe more complex alternatives.

A picture is sometimes worth a thousand words, although there is no substitute for clean, clear prose. If doing so improves clarity, feel free to include graphical depictions of user interfaces, process flows, or other figures in the use case. If a technical method, such as an activity diagram, is useful to present a complex decision process, by all means use it. Similarly for state-dependent behavior, a state transition diagram often clarifies the behavior of a system better than do pages upon pages of text. Use the right presentation medium for your problem, but be wary of using terminology, notation, or figures that your audience may not understand. Remember that your purpose is to clarify, not to obscure.

Alternative Flows

1. **First alternative flow:** More complex alternatives should be described in a separate section, which is referred to in the Basic Flow section. Think of the Alternative Flows sections as *alternative behavior*; each

alternative flow represents alternative behavior (many times because of exceptions that occur in the main flow). They may be as long as necessary to describe the events associated with the alternative behavior. When an alternative flow ends, the events of the main flow of events are resumed unless otherwise stated.

Alternative flows may, in turn, be broken down into subsections.

2. **Second alternative flow:** There may be, and most likely will be, a number of alternative flows in a use case. Keep each alternative separate, to improve clarity. Using alternative flows improves the readability of the use case and prevents use cases from being decomposed into hierarchies of use cases. Keep in mind that use cases are just textual descriptions and that their main purpose is to document the behavior of a system in a clear, concise, and understandable way.

Special Requirements

These are typically nonfunctional requirements that are specific to a use case but are not easily or naturally specified in the text of the use case's event flow. Examples of special requirements include legal and regulatory requirements, application standards, and quality attributes of the system to be built, including usability, reliability, performance, and supportability requirements. Other requirements, such as operating systems and environments, compatibility requirements, and design constraints, should also be captured in this section.

1. First special requirement
2. Second special requirement

Pre-conditions

A pre-condition of a use case is the state of the system that must be present prior to a use case being performed.

1. Pre-condition 1
2. Pre-condition 2

Post-conditions

A post-condition of a use case is a list of possible states the system can be in immediately after a use case has finished.

1. Post-condition 1
2. Post-condition 2

Extension Points

Extension points are named markers that reference a location or set of locations within the flow of events of the use case, at which additional behavior can be inserted.

1. Extension point 1
2. Extension point 2

SUPPLEMENTARY
SPECIFICATION TEMPLATE

The supplementary specification contains three major classes of software requirements. First, it contains those *functional requirements* that are not expressed in the use cases. Second, it contains *nonfunctional requirements,* those requirements that describe attributes of the system and of the systems environment, including items such as usability, reliability, and performance requirements, as well as legal, regulatory, and documentation requirements. Finally, the supplementary specification contains any *design constraints* imposed on the system or the development process used to develop the system. This document is updated as needed and is shared among team members and other involved personnel. The document template in this appendix is intended to be used as a starting point and may be customized according to your organization's needs.

Company Name

Project Name
Supplementary Specification

© 200X Company Name

REVISION HISTORY			
Date	**Revision**	**Description**	**Author**
mm/dd/yy	1.0	Initial version	Author name

TABLE OF CONTENTS

1   Introduction

This section should provide an overview of the supplementary specification and should contain the following subsections.

1.1   Purpose of the Supplementary Specification

The document collects and organizes all the requirements of the system that are not contained within the use-case model. These include functional requirements, nonfunctional requirements, and design constraints.

1.2   Scope

State the scope of the document and any systems or subsystems to which it applies.

1.3   Definitions, Acronyms, and Abbreviations

Provide the definitions of all terms, acronyms, and abbreviations required to properly interpret the supplementary specification. This information may be provided by reference to a project glossary.

1.4   References

This subsection should

- Provide a list of all documents referenced elsewhere in the supplementary specification
- Identify each document by title, report number (if applicable), date, and publishing organization
- Specify the sources from which the references can be obtained

This information may be provided by reference to an appendix or to another document.

2   Functionality

This section describes the functional requirements of the system for those requirements that are expressed in declarative, natural language style or via other, more formal methods. For some applications, this may constitute the bulk of the requirements, and thought should be given to the organization of this section. This section may be organized by feature, by subsystem, or by other strategies as appropriate.

3   Usability

This section includes those requirements that affect usability. Examples follow. (See Chapter 22 for additional guidance on usability requirements.)

- Specify the required training time for normal users and power users to become productive at particular operations.
- Specify measurable task times for typical tasks.
- Specify requirements to conform to common usability standards, for example, IBM's CUA standards or Microsoft's GUI standards.

4 Reliability

This section includes those requirements that affect reliability and availability of the system. Examples follow below.

- Availability: Specify the percentage of time the system is expected to be available, hours of use, maintenance access, degraded mode operations, and so on.
- Mean time between failures (MTBF): This is usually specified in hours but could also be specified in terms of days, months, or years.
- Mean time to repair (MTTR): How long is the system allowed to be out of operation after it has failed?
- Maximum bugs or defect rate: This is usually expressed in terms of bugs/KLOC (thousands of lines of code) or bugs/function-point.
- Bugs or defect rate: This is categorized in terms of minor, significant, and critical bugs. The requirement(s) must define what is meant by a critical bug (for example, complete loss of data or complete inability to use certain parts of the functionality of the system).

5 Performance

The performance characteristics of the system are outlined in this section, including specific quantitative parameters. Where applicable, reference the related use cases by name. Examples of performance requirements include the following:

- Response time for a transaction (average, maximum)
- Precision (resolution) and accuracy (by some known standard) required in the systems output
- Throughput (for example, transactions per second)
- Capacity (for example, the number of customers or transactions the system can accommodate)
- Degradation modes (the acceptable mode of operation when the system has been degraded in some manner)
- Resource utilization for memory, disk, communications, and so on

6 Supportability

This section includes any requirements that will enhance the support-ability or maintainability of the system being built, including coding standards, naming conventions, class libraries, maintenance access, maintenance utilities, and so on.

7 Design Constraints

This section includes any design constraints on the system being built. Design constraints represent design decisions that have been mandated and must be adhered to. Examples include software languages, software process requirements, prescribed use of developmental tools, specific architectural constraints, mandated use of purchased components, class libraries, and so on.

8 User Documentation and Help System Requirements

This section describes the requirements for documentation for the system. Examples include the following:

- Getting started guides
- User guides
- Online help
- Administration guide
- User glossary
- Read Me files and release notes
- Labeling and packing requirements

9 Purchased Components

This section describes any purchased components to be used with the system, any applicable licensing or usage restrictions, and any associated compatibility/interoperability or interface standards.

10 Interfaces

This section defines the interfaces that must be supported by the application. It should contain adequate specificity, protocols, ports and logical addresses, and so on to enable development and verification of the software against the interface requirements.

10.1 User Interfaces

Describe the user interfaces to be implemented by the software.

10.2 Hardware Interfaces

Define any hardware interfaces to be supported by the software, including logical structure, physical addresses, expected behavior, and so on.

10.3 Software Interfaces

Define software interfaces to other components of the software system such as operating systems, databases, and so on. These may be purchased components, components reused from another application, or components being developed for subsystems outside of the scope of this specification but with which this software application must interact.

10.4 Communications Interfaces

Describe any communications interfaces to other systems or devices such as local area networks, local or remote devices, and so on.

11 Licensing and Security Requirements

This section includes any licensing requirements or usage enforcement restrictions to be implemented in the software, as well as any sublicensing requirements for any OEM components or other licensed applications required for system operation.

This section may also define requirements for security and accessibility, encryption of source code or user data, and so on.

12 Legal, Copyright, and Other Notices

This section includes any necessary legal disclaimers, including warranties, copyright notices, patent notices, trademark, or logo compliance requirements.

13 Applicable Standards

This section includes by reference any applicable standards and the specific sections of any such standards that apply to the system being built. For example, this could include legal, quality, and regulatory standards or industry standards for usability or interoperability.

14 Internationalization and Localization

This section describes any applicable requirements for internationalization (the ability to support multiple user language environments) and localization (requirements to provide or support GUI dialogs, displays and report formats, entry of user data, and so on) in the user's native language or local dialect.

15 Physical Deliverables

This section defines any specific physical deliverables (CDs, manuals, and so on) produced to support deployment and operation of the system.

16 Installation and Deployment

This section describes any special requirements for system configuration or preparation, third-party components, installation or conversion utilities, and any other requirements for successful implementation and deployment.

REQUIREMENTS MANAGEMENT IN THE RATIONAL UNIFIED PROCESS

With Philippe Kruchten and Leslee Probasco

This book provides an overview of a software requirements management best practice. The team skills described in the book, along with the requirements prescription provided in Chapter 31, will help your team start down the right path on your next project. However, to better ensure success, you need some way to reinforce and support the application of these best practices throughout the course of development. This must be accomplished in a way that integrates requirements management smoothly with other software development activities, including design, implementation, testing, and deployment. Ideally, this information would be provided online, in the team's desktop environment. Further, it would be prescriptive in describing which team members performed which activities and when they needed to produce the outputs of these activities for other team members to use. This is the role of a *software development process*. In this appendix, we look at an example of an industrial software development process, the Rational Unified Process, and see how the skills we have presented map into it.

The Rational Unified Process, a software engineering process developed and commercialized by the Rational Software Corporation [2002], captures some of the best practices of the industry for software development. It is use case driven and takes an iterative approach to the software development lifecycle. It embraces object-oriented techniques, and many of its activities focus on the development of *models*, all described using the UML. The Rational Unified Process is a descendant of Objectory [Jacobson et al. 1992] and of the Rational Approach. It has benefited over the years from the contributions of many industry experts, including the authors of this book and the teams from Requisite, Inc., SQA, Inc., and many others.

As a product, the Rational Unified Process is a Web-enabled guidebook that brings process guidance directly onto the desktops of software developers. It is composed of approximately 2,800 files presenting an HTML-based interactive desktop coach, which can be tailored to suit the needs of a wide range of software development organizations.

Although it uses slightly different terminology from that presented in this book, the Rational Unified Process provides an effective implementation of the requirements management best practices we offered, in a form that can be readily applied by software development teams.

THE STRUCTURE OF THE RATIONAL UNIFIED PROCESS[1]

A process describes *who* is doing *what, how,* and *when.* The Rational Unified Process is described using four key modeling elements (Figure E–1):

- Role, the *who*
- Activities, the *how*
- Artifacts, the *what*
- Disciplines, the *when*

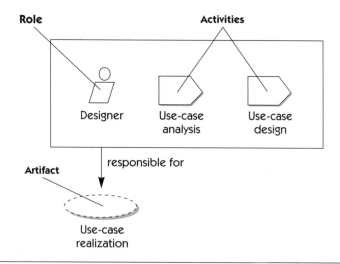

Figure E–1   Roles, activities, and artifacts

---

1. This section is extracted from Philippe Kruchten, *The Rational Unified Process: An Introduction* (Reading, MA: Addison-Wesley, 1999), pp. 35–48, and reproduced with permission from the publisher.

A *role* defines the behavior and responsibilities of an individual or a group of individuals working together as a team. The behavior is expressed in terms of *activities* the worker performs, and each worker is associated with a set of cohesive activities. The responsibilities of each worker are expressed in relation to certain *artifacts*, or work products, that the worker creates, modifies, or controls.

Disciplines allow the grouping of activities into meaningful sets that provide some result for the development organization and show how various workers interact. Beyond these four main concepts, the Rational Unified Process introduces specific techniques in the form of *guidelines* mapped to activities, *templates* for major artifacts, and *tool mentors*, that is, guidance on how to proceed using software development tools.

REQUIREMENTS MANAGEMENT IN THE RATIONAL UNIFIED PROCESS

The best practice of requirements management is captured in the Rational Unified Process in the requirements *discipline*, one of nine core disciplines described in the process. This requirements discipline produces and updates the *artifacts* shown in Figure E–2.

Many of these artifacts are consistent with those described in this book, including the following:

- Stakeholder requests and the collection of any type of requests (including formal change requests, needs, or other input from any stakeholders) during the lifecycle of the project that might affect the product requirements
- The Vision document, which summarizes the overall vision of the system under consideration: main characteristics, major features, key stakeholder needs, and key services provided
- The use-case model, the organized set of use cases that constitute the bulk of the requirements
- The supplementary specification, which captures any requirements that cannot be tied directly to any specific use case, in particular, many of the nonfunctional requirements and design constraints

Other artifacts are also developed as a result of this discipline, including

- Requirements attributes, a repository of information containing requirements-related information that is used to track requirements status and to maintain traceability to other project elements

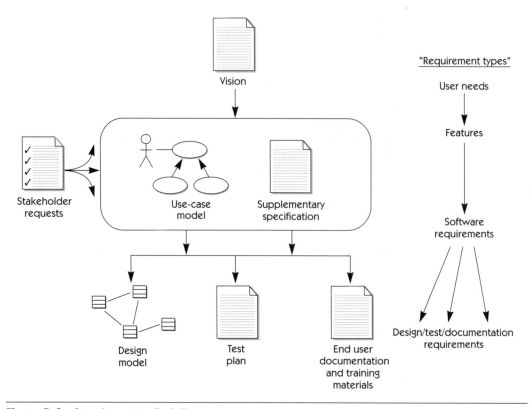

Figure E–2   Requirements discipline

- Use-case storyboards, systematically derived from the essential use cases involving human actors to model the user interface and to elaborate some of the usability requirements
- User interface prototypes, developed to get feedback from the various stakeholders
- A project glossary, which captures and defines the terms used in the project domain

Workers involved in this discipline include

- Stakeholder, customer, end user, or whoever within the development organization represents the role of anyone providing input to the requirements process (the marketing manager in some companies)

- System analyst, who leads and coordinates requirements elicitation and use-case modeling by outlining the system's functionality and delimiting the system: for example, establishing what actors and use cases exist and how they interact, along with nonfunctional requirements and design constraints
- Use-case specifier, who details the specification of a part of the system's functionality by describing the requirements aspect of one or several use cases
- User interface designer, who develops use-case storyboards and user interface prototypes and involves other stakeholders in their evaluation
- Requirements reviewer (a role usually played by several team members), who plans and conducts the formal review of the use-case model and other requirements specified in the supplementary specification

The description of the requirements discipline activities and steps is organized in the Rational Unified Process into six smaller disciplines (called *discipline details*), which parallels many of the team skills described in this book.

Analyzing the Problem

As shown in Figure E–3, the purpose of this discipline detail is to

- Produce a Vision document for the project
- Agree on system features and goals

This discipline detail may be revisited several times during inception and early elaboration. As requests from stakeholders are more clearly understood, both business process solutions and technical solutions will evolve.

The primary activity in this discipline is to develop the Vision document, which identifies the high-level user or customer view of the system to be built. In the Vision document, initial requirements are expressed as key features the system must possess in order to solve the most critical problems. The features should be assigned attributes, such as rationale, relative value or priority, source of request, and so on, so that dependencies can begin to be managed. As the vision develops, the system analyst identifies users and system interfaces—the *actors* of the system.

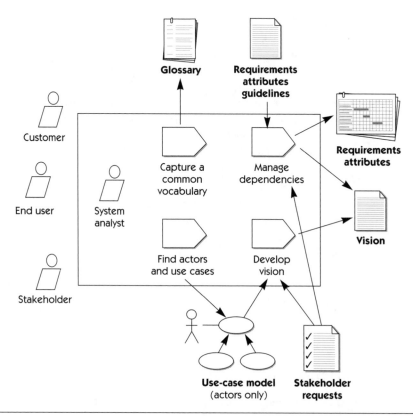

Figure E–3   Analyzing the problem

Understanding User and Stakeholder Needs

The purpose of this discipline detail is to elicit and collect information from stakeholders of the project (Figure E–4). The collected stakeholder requests can be regarded as a "wish list" that will be used as primary input to defining the *use-case model, use cases,* and *supplementary specification.* Typically, this is performed only during iterations in the inception and elaboration phases.

The key activity is to *elicit stakeholder requests.* The primary outputs are collection(s) of prioritized stakeholder requests, which enable refinement of the Vision document, as well as a better understanding of the requirements attributes. Also, during this discipline, you may start discussing the system in terms of its use cases and actors. Another important output is an updated glossary of terms to facilitate a common vocabulary among team members.

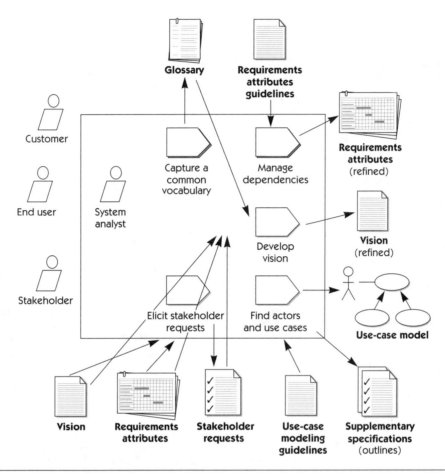

Figure E–4 Understanding user and stakeholder needs

Defining the System

The purpose of this discipline detail (Figure E–5) is to

- Align the project team in its understanding of the system
- Perform a high-level analysis of the results of collecting stakeholder requests
- More formally document the results in models and documents

Typically, this is performed only in iterations during the inception and elaboration phases.

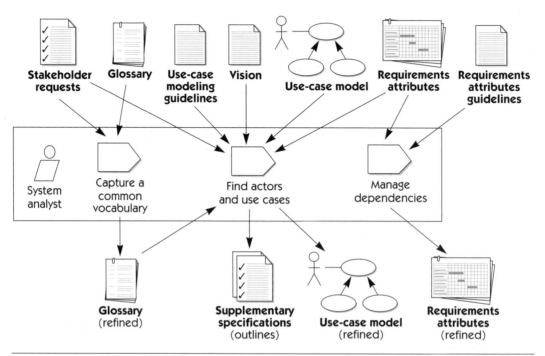

Figure E–5   Defining the system

Problem analysis and *understanding stakeholder needs* create early iterations of key system definitions, including the Vision document, a first outline to the use-case model, and the requirements attributes. In defining the system, you focus on identifying actors and use cases more completely and adding supplementary specifications.

Managing Scope

The purpose of this discipline detail (Figure E–6) is to

- Define input to the selection of requirements to be included in the current iteration
- Define the set of features and use cases (or scenarios) that represent some significant, central functionality
- Define which requirement attributes and traceabilities to maintain

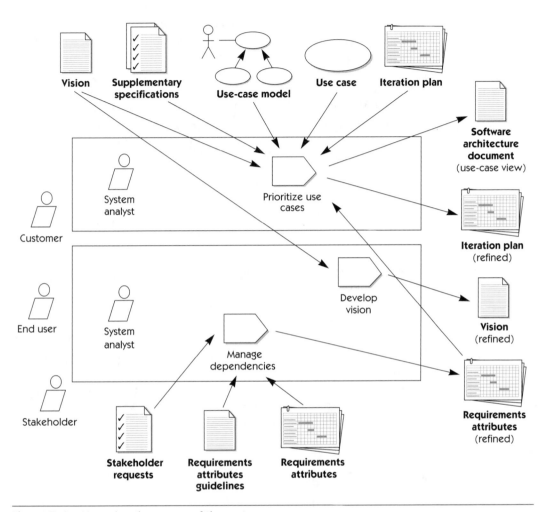

Figure E–6 Managing the scope of the system

Although project scope should be managed continuously, the better understanding of system functionality obtained from identifying most actors, use cases, and supplementary specifications will allow the system analyst to apply priority, effort, cost, risk values, and so on to requirements attributes more accurately and will enable the architect to identify the architecturally significant use cases. An input to managing scope not seen in other discipline details of the requirements discipline is the *iteration plan*, developed in parallel by project and development management. The iteration plan defines the number and frequency of iterations planned for the release. The scope of the project defined in managing scope will have a significant impact on the iteration plan since the highest-risk elements within scope will be planned for early iterations. Other important outputs from managing scope include the initial iteration of the software architecture document and a revised Vision document that reflects the system analyst's and key stakeholders' better understanding of system functionality and project resources.

Refining the System Definition

The purpose of this discipline detail (Figure E–7) is to further refine the requirements in order to

- Describe the use case's flow of events in detail
- Detail supplementary specifications
- Model and prototype the user interfaces

Refining the system begins with use cases outlined, actors described at least briefly, and a revised understanding of project scope reflected in reprioritized features in the vision and believed to be achievable by fairly firm budgets and dates. The output of this discipline is more in-depth understanding of system functionality expressed in detailed use cases, revised and detailed supplementary specifications, and user interface elements.

Managing Changing Requirements

The purpose of this discipline detail (Figure E–8) is to

- Structure the use-case model
- Set up appropriate requirements attributes and traceabilities
- Formally verify that the results of the requirements discipline conform to the customer's view of the system

Changes to requirements naturally impact the models produced in the analysis and design discipline, as well as the test model created as part of the test discipline. Traceability relationships between requirements identified in the manage dependency activity of this discipline and others are the key to understanding these impacts.

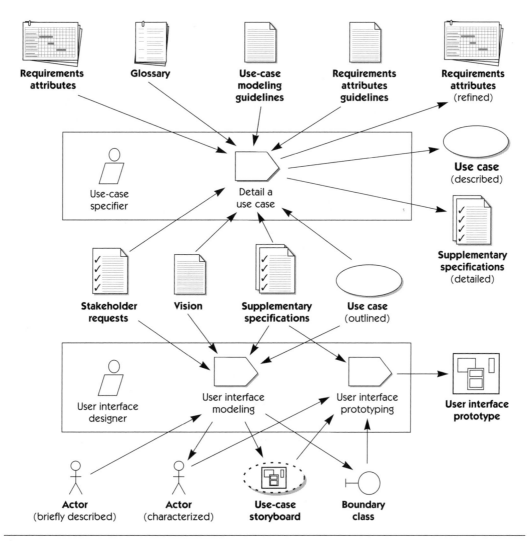

Figure E–7 Refining the system definition

Another important concept is the tracking of requirements history. By capturing the nature and rationale of requirements changes, reviewers (in this case, the role is played by anyone on the software project team whose work is affected by the change) receive the information needed to respond to the change properly.

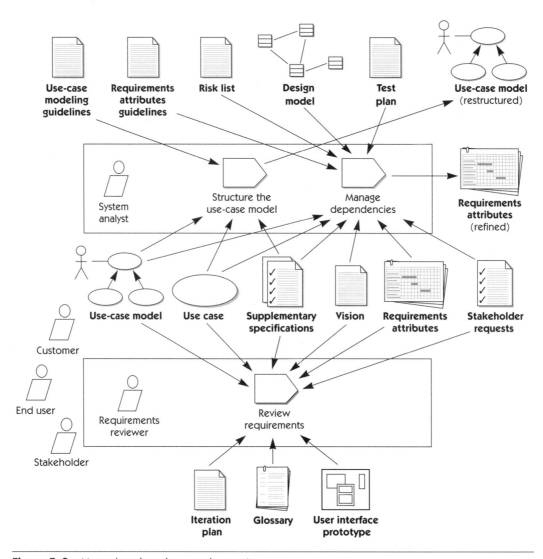

Figure E–8   Managing changing requirements

PROCESS INTEGRATION

The Rational Unified Process defines flows of information, transformations, guidelines, heuristics, and formal traceability links that tie these artifacts to other software development activities and artifacts. For example, the requirements artifact may be tied upstream in the process to a business model, constructed also using object-oriented technology and business use cases, and downstream to such artifacts as an analysis model or a design model, as well as to test cases and user documentation (see Figure E–2).

Software engineering tools support many of the best practices presented in the Rational Unified Process—from requirements management and visual modeling to report generation, configuration management, and automated testing. Tool mentors are also included, which provide detailed descriptions on how Rational's software tools can be used to support particular steps and activities within the process.

REQUIREMENTS MANAGEMENT IN THE SEI-CMM AND WITHIN ISO 9000:2000

REQUIREMENTS MANAGEMENT IN THE SEI-CMM

In November 1986, the Software Engineering Institute (SEI) at Carnegie-Mellon University began developing a process maturity framework to help developers improve their software process. In September 1987, the SEI released a brief description of the process maturity framework, later amplified in Humphrey's *Managing the Software Process* [1989]. By 1991, this framework had evolved into what has become known as version 1.0 of the Capability Maturity Model (CMM). In 1993, version 1.1 of the CMM was released [SEI 1993]. Version 1.1 defines five levels of software maturity for an organization and provides a framework for moving from one level to the next, as illustrated in Figure F–1. The CMM guides developers through activities designed to help an organization improve its software process, with the goal of achieving repeatability, controllability, and measurability.

Despite the ongoing debate and controversy about the advantages and disadvantages of the CMM, an accumulating body of data shows that adherence to the CMM and corresponding improvements in software quality have significantly lowered the cost of application development within many companies. By now, the CMM has been in use by many organizations long enough that meaningful and positive return-on-investment statistics are appearing. These payoffs should, ideally, provide results in productivity and significant reduction in time to market. In an era of increasingly competitive environments, any improvements to software productivity cannot be ignored.

The CMM provides a framework for process improvement that consists of "key process areas," or organizational activities that have been found, through experience, to be influential in various aspects of the development

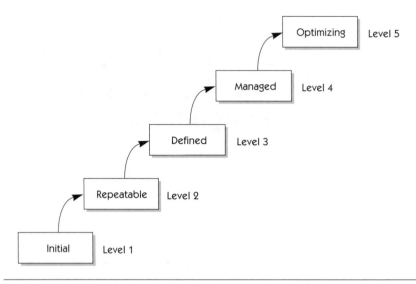

Figure F–1 CMM maturity levels

process and resultant software quality. Table F–1 identifies the key process areas of each of the five levels of the CMM. (The reason we're discussing all of this at length in this book is that Table F–1 shows that the *first* key process area that must be addressed to move from level 1 to level 2 is requirements management.)

The CMM summarizes the process area of requirements management as follows: *The purpose of requirements management is to establish a common understanding between the customer and the software team of the customer's requirements.*

This common understanding serves as the basis of agreement between the customer and the development team and, as such, is the central document that defines and controls the activity to follow. Requirements are controlled to establish a *baseline* for software engineering management use. Throughout the CMM, guidelines specify that all activities, plans, schedules, and software work products are to be developed and modified as necessary to be consistent with the requirements allocated to software. In this manner, the CMM moves the organization toward an integrated view wherein technical requirements must be kept consistent with project plans and activities. To support this process, software requirements must be documented and reviewed by software managers and affected groups, including representatives of the customer and user community.

Table F–1   Levels of the CMM with Key Process Areas

Level	Key Process Areas
1. Initial: Ad hoc, even chaotic; success depends solely on individual heroics and efforts.	Not applicable
2. Repeatable: Basic project management to track application functionality, cost, and schedule.	Requirements management Software project planning Software project tracking and oversight Software subcontract management Software quality assurance Software configuration management
3. Defined: The process for management and engineering is documented, standardized, and integrated. All projects use an approved, tailored version of the process.	Organization process focus Organization process definition Training program Integrated software management Software product engineering Intergroup coordination Peer reviews
4. Managed: Detailed measures of the software process and software quality metrics are collected. Both process and software products are understood and controlled.	Quantitative process management Software quality management
5. Optimizing: Continuous process improvement is enabled by use of metrics and from piloting innovative ideas and technologies.	Defect prevention Technology change management Process change management

The software requirements specification serves as a central project document, a defining element with relationships to other elements of the project plan. The requirements include both technical (the behavior of the application) and nontechnical (for example, schedule and budget) requirements.[1] In addition, acceptance criteria, which are the tests and measures that will be used to validate that the software meets its requirements, must be established and documented.

In order to accomplish these objectives and to demonstrate compliance with the CMM process area of requirements management, adequate resources

---

1. Note that the recommendation in this book excludes these project parameters from the application's requirements set.

and funding must be provided for managing requirements. Members of the software engineering group and other affected groups should be trained to perform their requirements management activities. Training should cover methods and standards, as well as training activities designed to create an understanding on the part of the engineering team as to the unique nature and problems of the application domain.

The CMM further specifies that requirements should be managed and controlled and should serve as the basis for software plans, work products, and activities. Changes to the requirements should be reviewed and incorporated into the project plans, and the impact of change must be assessed and negotiated with the affected groups. In order to provide feedback on the results of these activities and in order to verify compliance, the CMM provides guidelines for measurements and analysis, as well as activities for verifying implementation. Suggested measures include

- Status of each of the allocated requirements
- Change activity of the requirements, cumulative number of changes
- Total number of changes that are open, proposed, approved, and incorporated into the baseline

One of the most enlightened aspects of the CMM is its understanding that requirements management is not simply a "document-it-up-front-and-go" process of the sort often prescribed in the waterfall methodologies of the 1970s (Chapter 3). With the CMM, requirements are living entities at the center of the application development process. Not surprisingly, the process of effective requirements management appears at virtually all levels of the process model and within many key process areas. As an organization moves to level 3 on the CMM scale, the focus is on managing software activities based on defined and documented standard practices. Key process areas for level 3 include organization process focus, organization process definition, training program, integrated software management, software product engineering, intergroup coordination, and peer reviews. The software product engineering key practice is designed to cause an organization to integrate all software engineering activities to produce high-quality software products effectively and efficiently. The software engineering key practice states that the "*software requirements are developed, maintained, documented, and verified by systematically analyzing the requirements according to the project's defined software process*" [SEI 1993].

The analysis process is necessary to ensure that the requirements make sense and are clearly stated, complete and unambiguous, consistent with one another, and testable. Various analysis techniques are suggested, including simulations, modeling, scenario generation, and functional and object-oriented decomposition. The results of this process will be a better understanding of the requirements of the application, which are then reflected in revised requirements documentation. In addition, the group responsible for system and acceptance testing also analyzes the requirements to ensure testability.

The resulting software requirements document is reviewed and approved by the affected parties to make sure that the points of view represented by these parties are included in the requirements. Reviewers include customers and end users, project management, and software test personnel. In order to manage change in a controlled way, the CMM also calls for placing the software requirements document under configuration management control.

Another important concept in the CMM is *traceability*. Under the CMM, all worthwhile software work products are documented, and the documentation must be maintained and readily available. The software requirements, design, code, and test cases are traced to the source from which they were derived and to the products of the subsequent engineering activity. Requirements traceability provides a means of analyzing impact before a change is made, as well as a way to determine what components are affected when processing a change. Traceability also provides the mechanism for determining the adequacy of test coverage.

All approved changes are tracked to completion. The documentation that traces the allocated requirements is also managed and controlled. Measurements are made to determine the functionality and the quality of the software products and to determine the status of the software activity. Example measurements include

- Status of each allocated requirement throughout the lifecycle
- Change activity of the allocated requirements
- Allocated requirements summarized by category

Finally, the CMM recognizes that change is an integral part of software activity in any development project. In place of frozen specifications, we instead strive for a stable baseline of requirements that are well elicited, documented, and placed into systems that provide support for managing change. Specifically, the CMM requires the following.

- As understanding of the software improves, changes to the software work products and activities are proposed, analyzed, and incorporated as appropriate. Where changes to the requirements are needed, they are approved and incorporated before any work products or activities are changed.

- The project determines the impact of change before the change is made.
- Changes are negotiated and communicated to the affected groups.
- All changes are tracked to completion.

In summary, the CMM provides a comprehensive view of the activities that must be applied to improve software quality and to increase productivity. Requirements management is an integral part of this process, wherein requirements serve as living entities that are at the center of development activity. Once elicited, requirements are documented and managed with the same degree of care that we provide to our code work products. This process puts the team in control of its project and helps team members manage both the project and its scope. Lastly, actively managing changing requirements keeps the project under control and helps ensure the reliable, repeatable production of high-quality software products.

Although all of this provides an important "validation" of the concept of requirements management, along with some high-level advice for inserting requirements-oriented processes into the development lifecycle, it doesn't tell us how to *do* requirements management. The detailed activities of eliciting, organizing, documenting, and managing requirements are the subject of this book, and these activities have been influenced by the CMM framework.

REQUIREMENTS MANAGEMENT IN ISO 9000:2000

For the past two decades or so, a number of organizations around the world have been applying a series of comprehensive quality management standards known as ISO 9000 to improve operating efficiency and productivity and to reduce costs. In December 2000, these documents were revised to conform more closely to the lessons learned in the previous five years, and the resulting update to the standards became known as ISO 9000:2000. As opposed to the CMM, which addresses software development exclusively, the ISO standards are a much broader set of standards intended to cover virtually all business process activities in all businesses that engage in domestic and international trade of any sort. As such, ISO standards apply equally well to a small import company that simply resells products manufactured by others and to the largest global manufacturers of goods and services. In so doing, ISO has tremendous breadth and must be "all things to all people," but it cannot possibly contain the depth of coverage for any specific area as does a standard, such as the CMM, which is designed for a specific business process.

The standards apply to all facets of operations, from sales order activity to customer support, as well as product development activity and the role of software suppliers (developers) in the process of producing goods and services that depend on software. In this respect, the ISO 9000:2000 revisions are particularly significant to this book because the changes had the effect of shifting ISO 9000 into much more of a *process* orientation and away from its *audit* orientation. Figure F–2 illustrates how the focus has shifted to the implementation of a process that has continual feedback loops and therefore provides a built-in mechanism for *continual* quality improvement. And when the process being analyzed is product development, the input is based on requirements derived from the "interested parties," that is, stakeholders, to help ensure that the resultant solution meets their needs. So yes, an effective requirements management process stands at the very front of this business process, and in that way the philosophy of ISO is consistent with the philosophy of this book.

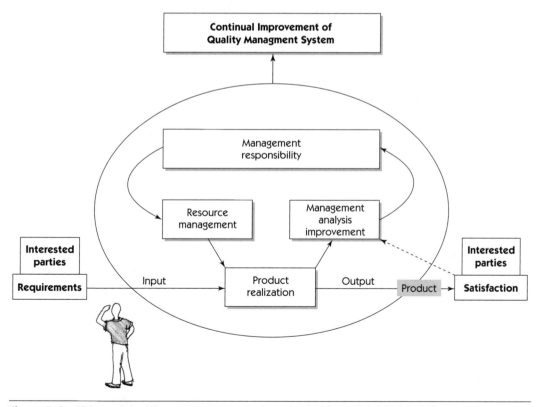

Figure F–2   ISO model of the process approach (adapted from ISO 9000:2000)

Today, ISO 9000 has been adopted by the European Community as EN29000 and has become an important factor for international trade; organizations wishing to do business in Europe, for example, often have to demonstrate ISO 9000 certification. Thus, in today's global economy, many American businesses have adopted ISO 9000 to ensure their credibility in the world marketplace. Certification to ISO standards requires an on-site assessment by an independent, ISO-approved assessor, so adopting such a set of standards represents a significant commitment. Companies are reassessed periodically to maintain their certification. ISO 9000 consists of four primary quality standards:

1. ISO 9000:2000 Quality management systems: Fundamentals and vocabulary (supersedes ISO 8402 and ISO 9000-1)
2. ISO 9001:2000 Quality management systems: Requirements (supersedes ISO 9001:1994, ISO 9002, and ISO 9003)
3. ISO 9004:2000 Quality management systems: Guidelines for performance improvement (supersedes ISO 9004-1)
4. ISO 19011: Guidelines on auditing quality and environmental management systems (supersedes parts 1–3 of ISO 10011, ISO 14010, ISO 14011, and ISO 14012)

Within these documents, ISO 9001 contains a number of specifications that focus on using an effective requirements management process to control and improve the quality of a product or service. In addition, the document now makes a distinction between *product-oriented* requirements and *process-oriented* requirements. Again, this philosophy is consistent with the definitions we provided for quality in Chapter 29, wherein we described software project quality as the characteristic of having demonstrated the achievement of producing a product that meets or exceeds agreed-on requirements (as measured by agreed-on measures and criteria) and that is produced by an agreed-on process.

The same document also stipulates that the information thus provided to the supplier (which we've described as the "developer" throughout this book) should include all performance, safety, reliability, security, and privacy requirements (a subset of the nonfunctional requirements described in this book) that collectively determine whether the delivered system is acceptable.

Like the CMM, ISO 9000 standards have been the subject of considerable debate, particularly in U.S. organizations that worry about the possibility of the standards degenerating into a bureaucratic demand for excessive documentation. Our purpose here is not to endorse or attack ISO 9000; like all such commonsense concepts, it can be used or misused. But to the extent that many organizations are adopting ISO 9000 because they think it's a good idea or because it's a necessary prerequisite for doing business in Europe and other parts of the world, it's interesting to note the emphasis that the standard puts on requirements management. For example, ISO 9000 emphasizes the need for *mutual cooperation* between the customer and the developer for software systems. Specifically, it calls for:

- Assignment of people from both groups to be responsible for establishing requirements
- Establishment of methods and procedures for agreement and approval of changes to the requirements
- Efforts to prevent misunderstandings of the requirements
- Establishment of procedures for recording and reviewing the results of discussions about the requirements

Although it's easy to dismiss all of this as obvious and commonsense, remember what happens during the assessment required to achieve certification. An assessor will visit the organization and ask, "Where are your methods and procedures for approving changes to the requirements? Show them to me in writing. Let me visit some project teams and make some spot-checks to ensure that the procedures are actually being followed."

ISO 9000 also stipulates that the input to the development phase of a project— the lifecycle activity in which technical design and programming usually take place—should be defined and documented. These "inputs" are, of course, *requirements*, and ISO 9000 also states that the requirements should be defined so that their achievement can be verified. The *use-case-to-test-case approach* we have described could be of real value here. ISO 9000 also calls for processes to ensure that incomplete, ambiguous, or conflicting requirements will be resolved in an orderly fashion. Your team may wish to apply an *iterative* and *incremental* process for successive refinement of requirements as we have described.

In summary, the ISO 9000 emphasis on requirements at the beginning of a development effort is intended to help ensure that, if the technical design and development efforts are carried out in a disciplined fashion, the organization is more likely to produce a system that meets specifications, or requirements, rather than relying on frantic testing and validation activities at the end of the lifecycle to assure quality. With respect to software development at least, that also nicely summarizes the purpose of this book!

Like the SEI-CMM, ISO 9000 doesn't tell you specifically *how* to actually do requirements management. Rather, your team members will be obligated to define, implement, and adhere to an effective requirements management process that they themselves declare to be sufficient for the intended purpose. But armed with the procedures and techniques described in this book, and with Chapters 30 and 31 as a comprehensive summary and process guide, your team will be able to create a comprehensive requirements management approach that should satisfy the most demanding ISO 9000 or CMM assessors.

BIBLIOGRAPHY

Armour, Frank, and Granville Miller. 2001. *Advanced Use Case Modeling.* Boston, MA: Addison-Wesley.

Bach, James. 1997. "Good Enough Quality: Beyond the Buzzword." *IEEE Computer Society,* August, p. 97.

Beck, Kent. 2000. *Extreme Programming Explained: Embrace Change.* Boston, MA: Addison-Wesley.

Boehm, Barry W. 1981. *Software Engineering Economics.* Englewood Cliffs, NJ: Prentice-Hall.

———. 1988. "A Spiral Model of Software Development and Enhancement." *IEEE Computer* 21(5), pp. 61–72.

Boehm, Barry W., and Philip N. Papaccio. 1988. "Understanding and Controlling Software Costs." *IEEE Transactions on Software Engineering* 14(10), pp. 1462–1473.

Booch, Grady, James Rumbaugh, and Ivar Jacobson. 1999. *The Unified Modeling Language User Guide.* Reading, MA: Addison-Wesley.

Brooks, Frederick P., Jr. 1975. *The Mythical Man Month: Essays on Software Engineering.* Reading, MA: Addison-Wesley.

Cockburn, Alistair. 2002. *Agile Software Development.* Boston, MA: Addison-Wesley.

Davis, Alan M. 1993. *Software Requirements: Objects, Functions, and States.* Englewood Cliffs, NJ: Prentice-Hall.

———. 1995. *201 Principles of Software Development.* New York: McGraw-Hill.

———. 1999. "Achieving Quality in Software Requirements." *Software Quality Professional* 1(3), pp. 37–44.

Dorfman, Merlin, and Richard H. Thayer. 1990. *Standards, Guidelines, and Examples of System and Software Requirements Engineering.* Los Alamitos, CA: IEEE Computer Society Press.

European Software Process Improvement Training Initiative. 1995. *User Survey Report.*

FDA (Food and Drug Administration). 1996. "Medical Devices; Current Good Manufacturing Practice (CGMP) Final Rule; Quality System Regulation." *Federal Register* 61(195) (7 October), Subpart C, pp. 52657–52658.

———. 1998. "Guidance for the Content of Premarket Submissions for Software Contained in Medical Devices." Final version (May 29).

Fisher, Roger, William Ury, and Bruce Patton. 1983. *Getting to Yes: Negotiating Agreement without Giving In*, 2nd ed. New York: Penguin Books.

Gause, Donald, and Gerald Weinberg. 1989. *Exploring Requirements: Quality Before Design.* New York: Dorset House Publishing.

Grady, Robert B. 1992. *Practical Software Metrics for Project Management and Process Improvement.* Englewood Cliffs, NJ: Prentice-Hall.

Heumann, James. 2001. "Generating Test Cases from Use Cases." Cupertino, CA: Rational Software Corporation. Available online (February 2003) at http://www.therationaledge.com/content/jun_01/m_cases_jh.html.

Humphrey, Watts S. 1989. *Managing the Software Process.* Reading, MA: Addison-Wesley.

IEEE. 1994. *IEEE Standards Collection, Software Engineering.* New York: IEEE.

INCOSE (International Council on Systems Engineering). 1993. "An Identification of Pragmatic Principles—Final Report." INCOSE WMA Chapter. Available online (February 2003) at http:// http://www.incose.org/ workgrps/practice/pragprin.html.

————. 2003. "What Is Systems Engineering?" Available online (February 2003) at http://www.incose.org/whatis.html.

Jacobson, Ivar, Grady Booch, and James Rumbaugh. 1999. *The Unified Software Development Process*. Reading, MA: Addison-Wesley.

Jacobson, Ivar, Magnus Christerson, Patrik Jonsson, and Gunnar Övergaard. 1992. *Object-Oriented Software Engineering: A Use Case Driven Approach*. Harlow, U.K.: Addison-Wesley.

Jacobson, Ivar, Maria Ericsson, and Agneta Jacobson. 1995. *The Object Advantage: Business Process Reengineering with Object Technology*. Wokingham, U.K.: Addison-Wesley.

Jones, Capers. 1994. "Revitalizing Software Project Management." *American Programmer* 6(7), pp. 3–12.

Karat, Claire-Marie. 1998. "Guaranteeing Rights for the User." *Communications of the ACM* 41(12), p. 29.

Kruchten, Philippe. 1995. "The 4+1 View of Architecture." *IEEE Software* 12(6), pp. 45–50.

————. 1999. *The Rational Unified Process: An Introduction*. Reading, MA: Addison-Wesley.

Moore, Geoffrey A. 1991. *Crossing the Chasm: Marketing and Selling Technology Products to Mainstream Customers*. New York: HarperCollins.

Rational Software Corporation. 2002. "Rational Unified Process 2002." Cupertino, CA: Rational Software Corporation.

Rechtin, Eberhardt, and Mark W. Maier. 1997. *The Art of Systems Architecting*. Boca Raton, FL: CRC Press.

Royce, Walker. 1998. *Software Project Management: A Unified Approach*. Reading MA: Addison-Wesley.

Royce, Winston W. 1970. "Managing the Development of Large Software Systems: Concepts and Techniques." In *WESCON Technical Papers,* Vol. 14. Los Angeles: WESCON. Reprinted in *Proceedings of the Ninth International Conference on Software Engineering*, 1987, pp. 328–338.

Rumbaugh, James, Ivar Jacobson, and Grady Booch. 1998. *The Unified Modeling Language Reference Manual.* Reading, MA: Addison-Wesley.

Scharer, Laura. 1981. "Pinpointing Requirements." Originally published as an article in *Datamation.* Reprinted in Merlin Dorfman and Richard H. Thayer (eds), *Software Requirements Engineering.* Los Alamitos, CA: IEEE Computer Society Press, 1990.

Schneider, Geri, and Jason P. Winters. 1998. *Applying Use Cases: A Practical Guide.* Reading, MA: Addison-Wesley.

SEI (Software Engineering Institute). 1993. *Capability Maturity Model for Software.* Version 1.1, Document No. CMU/SEI-93-TR-25, ESC-TR-93-178. Pittsburgh, PA: Carnegie-Mellon University Software Engineering Institute.

Shaw, Mary, and David Garlan. 1996. *Software Architecture: Perspective on an Emerging Discipline.* Upper Saddle River, NJ: Prentice-Hall.

Snyder, Terry, and Ken Shumate. 1992. "Kaizen Project Management." *American Programmer* 5(10), pp. 12–22.

The Standish Group. 1994. "Charting the Seas of Information Technology—Chaos." West Yarmouth, MA: The Standish Group International.

Weinberg, Gerald. 1971. *The Psychology of Computer Programming.* New York: Van Nostrand Reinhold.

———. 1995. "Just Say No! Improving the Requirements Process." *American Programmer* 8(10), pp. 19–23.

Wood, Bill J., and Julia W. Ermes. 1993a. "Applying Hazard Analysis to Medical Devices" (Part I). *Medical Device & Diagnostic Industry Magazine* 15(1), pp. 79–83.

———. 1993b. "Applying Hazard Analysis to Medical Devices" (Part II). *Medical Device & Diagnostic Industry Magazine* 15(3), pp. 58–64.

Index

"4 + 1" view of architecture, 297–298

A

abstraction levels, 96–99
acceptance tests. *See* testing.
accuracy, requirements for, 261
active storyboards, 134
activity diagrams, 284–285
actors
  business modeling, 62–63
  case study, 80–81, 245, 412
  definition, 53
  problem analysis
    case study, 80–81
    definition, 53
    identifying, 54
  use cases
    case study, 161–163
    definition, 150
    identifying and describing, 153
    use-case relationships, 155
agendas, requirements workshops, 114
agile requirements methods, 392–394,
    400–403. *See also* risk mitigation
    methods.
Allie, as product champion, 199
alternative flow. *See* flow of events.
Alyssa
  HOLIS team role, 38, 408
  interviewing, 106–107
  as product manager, 186, 412
  requirements workshops, 126–130, 415–418

scope management, 221, 426
vision document, 420
ambiguity
  disambiguation, 274–277
  versus specificity, 271–277
Analyst's Summary, 106
architecture, software, 296–299
artifact sets, 358–359
artifacts, definition, 29
assessing development effort. *See* scope
    management.
attributes, system, 232
attributes of features, 99–100
audit trails, 352–353
availability, requirements for, 261

B

baseline for requirements
  case study, 426–427
  change management, 342–343
  CMM (Capability Maturity Model),
    474–475
  establishing, 211–212
Betty, requirements workshops, 127–130,
    415–418
Bill, partitioning subsystems, 77
black-box testing, 305–307, 317–318
brainstorming
  benefits of, 119–120
  cumulative voting, 124–125
  defining features, 123–124
  grouping ideas, 123

Register
Your Book

at www.awprofessional.com/register

You may be eligible to receive:

- Advance notice of forthcoming editions of the book
- Related book recommendations
- Chapter excerpts and supplements of forthcoming titles
- Information about special contests and promotions throughout the year
- Notices and reminders about author appearances, tradeshows, and online chats with special guests

Contact us

If you are interested in writing a book or reviewing manuscripts prior to publication, please write to us at:

Editorial Department
Addison-Wesley Professional
75 Arlington Street, Suite 300
Boston, MA 02116 USA
Email: AWPro@aw.com

Addison-Wesley

Visit us on the Web: http://www.awprofessional.com